S0-AXZ-576

SUNSHINE AND DUST

By ANNE BOSWORTH GREENE

DIPPER HILL
GREYLIGHT
LAMBS IN MARCH: AND OTHER ESSAYS
LIGHTHEARTED JOURNEY
THE LONE WINTER
THE WHITE PONY IN THE HILLS
SUNSHINE AND DUST

A STREET IN SUNNY ASSISI

SUNSHINE AND DUST

A Journey through Italy and the Alps

by

ANNE BOSWORTH GREENE

With photographs by
Lorna Greene and the Author

D. APPLETON-CENTURY COMPANY
INCORPORATED
NEW YORK 1936 LONDON

PRINTED IN THE UNITED STATES OF AMERICA

To my daughter, Lorna:
the Babs of this story

FOREWORD

This book has no intention of being a guide-book, or even a travel book, per se; just a personal story, with every one of its experiences filtered through some feeling of the moment —our wearinesses, our amazed thrills, our moments of coruscating rage, our happiness and peace. . . . Indeed (since it could not be the second volume of the *Lighthearted Journey* —second volumes are not "done"!), I very much wanted to name it *Ourselves and Italy,* but did not. Also I had hours of wild and hopeful inclination to call the book *Italy Will Be Like This Again!* and once more desisted.

Who can tell? We caught her, it seems to me, at a precious moment; yet one lives in the hope that Italy will swiftly be herself again—her sweet, ingenuous, and happy self; never willingly, I know—we all know, who love her—has she been anything else. . . .

So here are the days of our beloved wanderings—unforgettable, to me, every one—in rain or twilight, sunset or bright noon.

A. B. G.

Star Hill

CONTENTS

ILLUSTRATIONS

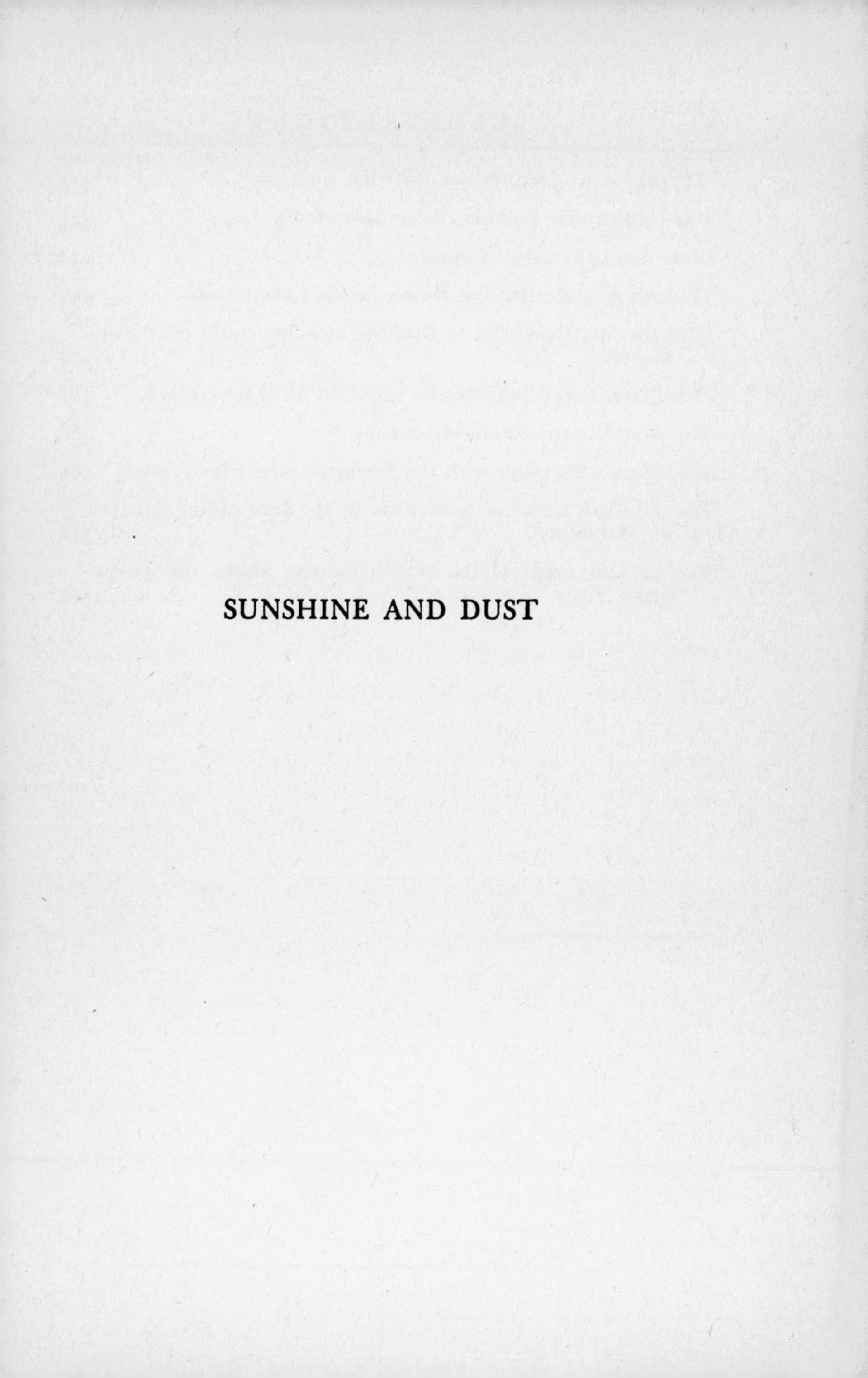

SUNSHINE AND DUST

SUNSHINE AND DUST

CHAPTER I

FINDING LAIGUEGLIA

LOOKS as if this might do," said Babs; swinging Nicolette in toward a palm in a green tub.

"This" was a glass-fronted *ristorante* in Ventimiglia, with rubber-plants peering through its windows; and we were famished. We had left Sospel early that morning after a night in a hotel we didn't like, roared back across the wall of mountains to Mentone and shopped and dallied in that pleasant town till, catching sight of a bit of blue down a sea-going lane—Italian blue—we made a dash for customs just as lunch-hour was coming on.

Somehow one does not lunch during that rather agonizing process, though a restaurant stood by giving out most savory smells; besides we were the last car in their noonday batch and feared the Italian officers would be cross.

Little we knew of the resources of that vital nation. They smiled merrily at us, and we drove off blessing them; but it seemed very long to Ventimiglia. Orange and lemon trees and dust; olives and dust; villas whose rather straggling flowers needed water: yes, this was Italy, though it didn't look much like it. We met a river with a dry and thirsty-looking bed, then the old part of town; the road swung encouragingly seaward—and here at last were rubber-plants, and a bored waiter watering the road.

Rubber-plants abroad always mean meals; we dismounted. The boulevard was empty at this hour—a nice boulevard with great trees, and a peep of sea at its end; we stood a moment shaking down our coats, smiling little weary smiles at each other and giving a half-worried pat to our possessions in the rear seat; for how about leaving Nicolette? We had grown hardened by now to leaving her in all sorts of places in France, but after all this *was* Italy. Would it be good to a little Citroën with a dusty nose? (Her top was down, she was very near the earth and accessible. . . .)

"Oh well," I said, "we can see her through the glass front!" So we settled ourselves close beside it, picking up a menu and feeling highly experimental.

Hooray! omelet is omelet in almost any tongue. Ours may have had an Italian tinge, but we always seem to have wonderful ones just after we get through customs. No one else was lunching this late so we had the rubber-plants to ourselves, also the attentions of a tall, somewhat weary, but surprisingly sympathetic waiter. He poured and served and superintended, asked if the omelet was *"buono,"* said *"si, signora"* a hundred unnecessary times, and altogether made us feel beautifully taken care of.

Nice place, Ventimiglia! said we; and her population, what we saw of it, singularly harmless. Nicolette reposed in peace under the great trees: two Italian boys strolled idly up, bent their young heads, and with amused squealings made what they could of her name and lineage, then strolled away again, pushing each other innocently off the curbstone; while the bored waiter, coiling up his hose, burst unexpectedly into most loud song and galloped like a greyhound in at a near-by door.

Babs and I looked at each other; with melted eyes. Ah, this *was* our Italy—and her loved enthusiasms . . . over nothing.

Ever since we had caught sight of her the day before from a high point on the Corniche—"That's Italy! We're seeing Italy!"—memories of her had come thick and fast. Her blue sea, her silvery olive-slopes, were in our souls; and now as we drove off, the mountains rearing behind the river had new color. Ventimiglia seemed to be at its siesta still, and Nicolette had some water from an old stone fountain in the middle of what would otherwise have been a busy piazza; feeling sleepy ourselves, we joggled benevolently along.

Speed was necessary no longer, we told each other; was not this our Riviera di Ponente that we had been longing to reach? Yet we kept up, out of mere habit, a certain pace. . . .

Benefits forgot! For France had been very sweet to us, and here we were bobbing heartlessly along as fast as potholes would let us (potholes in Italy, too!) with a great sense of marvels about to happen; driving and driving in our little dark-red Citroën to get as far as possible into real Italy that night. When you are just over the border, a country takes some time to be itself. Bits of the other country stick to it—roadsides, stucco, the general shape of things; and though it was nice to have bits of France left (we had been driving down through her for eighteen days, and were fond of her), still we were anxious to have Italy set in in earnest—and Nicolette's bonnet, as I have intimated, was in lively action.

"Bow!" said she crossly; "potholes *ought* to be softer, in this stupid country"—Nicolette, you perceive, was a French car—"and they're not. *Wump!*"

We hoped our little friend was going to like Italy. She had already pulled us with great cheer over rocky and reconstructed roads in the Basses Alps—but that was France; her next stiff job would be Apennines, the hill-villages, and after that the real, Swiss Alps on our way back to London. . . . Some undertaking, we knew, for a little five-horse-power—she was rated as a seven in England, but a sporting five in France, and we preferred to call her that—loaded, too, as the agent in Piccadilly had told us we ought not to load her.

"Alps?" he said. "With suit-cases? No, madam. Without suit-cases!"

But other and larger Cits had made records in the African deserts; and what are mountains to sand?

"Right across *there,* too!" said Nicolette, with a proud jiggle toward the sea; for a strip of it was now visible.

We were glad it was. When it became more visible, we could perhaps begin looking for a place to stop in, our first night in Italy—a little, paradaisical place it must be, all flowers and peasants, fishing-boats and lapping water.

So far we had not come near enough to the sea to have it lap. We had trifled with railway crossings, passed villas of every degree, and marveled at the ever-thickening flowers; commercial flowers, alas, but with nice, brown-skinned peasants picking them—unmistakable Italian peasants who smiled at us with merry flashings of white teeth. Fields and fields of yellow marguerites there were—that incessant flower of the Riviera; as for the white ones, donkeys are fed on them. (We saw a peasant dismounting from his wagon, pulling up a great plant that grew by the roadside and handing it to his donkey, who consumed it with gluttonous relish.) Beyond this, tier upon tier of carnations grew on terraces, their moonlight-colored foliage set off by stretches of pink, white, or crimson blossoms; and along the edge of almost anybody's land, hedges and hedges of stock, flowering madly.

One should have expected commerce, with all this acreage of color; somehow we did not expect it at all, along the Italian Riviera. But the peasants had to live off something, Babs and I told each other, trying hard to be broadminded; one may inhabit a water color land and still have a need or two, and the marguerites were sweet, even if they were being picked in wheelbarrows.

An old peasant met us, pushing one of them right into our wreath of dust; bushels of pale-yellow heads, prostrate and mortified in that barrow, bobbing and shaking along on their way to market. They'd look lovely, we agreed, in gray Paris, or beside a little bridge in Venice; but we were sorry about the dust.

Ours was not the only cloud of it drifting off across the fields or among the olives; traffic was waking up. Donkey-carts were frequent, limousines flew hectically by; one Rolls charged at us round a sharp corner, keeping, and filling, the entire middle of the narrow road, and for a moment it looked like Farewell to Mudguards. But Babs, muttering uncompli-

THE FISHERMEN'S BEACH AT LAIGUEGLIA

mentary things, did one of her double-quick dives into the ditch, and as it wasn't a bad ditch we got by.

English cars didn't often drive like that, we told each other, with surprised eyebrows; maybe they had an Italian chauffeur . . . maybe that Rolls was owned by an Italian! (We wished to give it every chance.)

But above us was a sky of faultless blue; our road made soothing twists at the sea or sudden climbs into old villages . . . short, concentrated old towns, rather; once stately, now a little haggard; arcaded and cool in shadow, but with a hot strip of sunshine down the middle of their pavements. We began to wonder when we should find our perfect place to stay in; it had to be little, and we shouldn't mind an Alp or two looking down. We had heard there *were* such places, along this Riviera . . . For these were water color villages, not places to stay in . . . and small, unsavory streams ran beside their cobbles, yet the violet shadows of their down-dipping lanes, the colors of a belfry against the sky, were such that I was incessantly skewing in my seat to look back. San Lorenzo del Mare, San Stefano del Mare; someday when we had plenty of time, we would go back and revel in them. . . . Nobody mentions them, they had almost the deserted air of ruins; I think travelers must fly by them in their Nicolettes, as we were doing, and never stop.

The coast grew delightfully wooded, and deep little bays led into it: marvelous, deep-blue bays—if we could have seen them better. Towns got in the way. There should not have been towns, we agreed! We hooted and threaded our way through Bordighera, with its shops and its twistings and its trams, also through Ospadeletti, "famous for its carnations"—what place here but was?—then, much more lengthily, through the Via Garibaldi in San Remo, and its subsequent clean rustlings.

"I don't want to stop *here!*" said Babs, surveying with amused hostility its succession of large, cream-yellow hotels with just so many palms in each garden, iron chairs and iris in rows, and a tram-line conclusively passing every one of them.

Very obviously an English colony, San Remo, with English shop windows, frequent tea-shops, and Englishwomen patroling the streets; but not for this had we been hasty with the map of France. . . . "Several fine palms," says Baedeker, "rise in the principal street." They did. We saw them. They waved down at us over yellow gate-posts, or by boastful entrances; they even rattled their leaves at us.

Surviving them, we motored on.

This first part of the Riviera indeed had astonished us by not being ravishingly attractive. Italy here saws stone, tears up the earth—and with the greatest ferocity; builds queer-looking huts, and in spite of peach orchards and the sea—which should be enough for her—is quite mistakenly industrious . . . But we were now about sixty kilometers beyond Mentone. Things were growing seductive. It really began to seem like the Italian Riviera; it had spots like one's visions. Our road was not any better, but it clung to the sea—whose deep blue, aided by patches of brilliant green or vivid purple, and a nice splashing edge, was of course the great thing. Also the villages began to be smothered in olive groves.

Olives and the Mediterranean go so perfectly together. A sea of such hectic color with so many bright flowers about needs these silver-dusky trees—which in spite of assiduous pruning, will hang out a crooked arm here and there; though these were not the towering ones we remembered in southern Italy.

Occasionally a kind town, like Oneglia, sat out on a point; and then—its colors against the sea! Dust was subsiding; the limousines that meant to reach Grenoble by nightfall had mostly gone by, so Nicolette sometimes had the road to herself. Good little thing, so dusty and busy—she took us steadfastly along; Babs could relax a little, and look at the view.

For the Riviera is not easy driving. For all you are following a shore it is surprisingly hilly, and carts and other things take their time getting out of your way. That is why it takes so long; especially if you are rendered speechless by flowers and roofs and little donkeys, by a peasant-woman in an orange kerchief. . . . Yes, said we, ambling contentedly along, it is no country for haste; which is perhaps why Italians drive as if their last moment had come.

We continued to amble; Nicolette, who is a great absorber of atmosphere, had her prophetic air of serenity.

"Surely," said she, "this begins to look like a good place—any minute!" and round a rocky corner we found ourselves by the transparent sea. Here was Diano Marina; a little fringe of a place, with fishing-boats; quite seashorey. But Nicolette kept on creeping.

"Not quite, somehow," I said.

"Not *quite,*" said Babs, with her smile at me.

"Too bad . . . I think Diano Marina wanted us to stop—" for indeed everybody had stared most hopefully at us."

More shore, more olive groves; wooded mountains swinging down closer and closer to the sea; late sunlight glorious on everything, especially on some thick old towers we were passing: Saracen towers, built to defend the coast against Barbary pirates. . . . It is worth defending. Squat and a trifly crumbly, the towers, with walls about eight feet thick; but the crumbliness just enhanced their atmosphere. One was being lived in; had been freshened up a bit and showed flowers and curtains in its small window.

A nice thick capable house, a ninth-century tower makes; it suited the shore wonderfully . . . and the little pine-clad capes.

This was lovely driving now. After Capo Male (another wooded promontory) we saw a stretch of duney shore with something pink at its end; as we approached it grew very pink indeed, with vines drizzling over a high rose-colored wall above which a flowering tree stuck up; but here the road seemed to end. How did one get in? *Through* the pink wall? No; the road gave an agile twist and had us at once in the intricacies of the little town; a street just wide enough for Nicolette—and perhaps half a pedestrian, if he economized himself.

And this was the main motor road along the Riviera. Enchanting. . . .

Dusky pink walls reared overhead, little open-mouthed shops gaped at us; cats darted in shadows, fisher-people smiled at us as they flattened themselves into doorways, and a little white dog got safely by, wagging his tail as he did so. We stole along, praying we should kill no one; under rose-colored arches, past bird-cages and plants on window-sills, then beside a sunny square with a *trattoria.* We passed fishermen with baskets, old women carrying bread and onions, and through an arch, came suddenly to the sound of the sea; a cobbled piazza with the statue of a sailor, and a rose-red building flanked with orange trees in tubs. "Albergo Laigueglia," it said.

Did this angelic place really have a hotel? Was that an actual Englishwoman sitting by one of the orange trees?

It had; and it was. It was Laigueglia; and the sails of fishing-boats showed through a gap in its houses. . . . We had never heard of Laigueglia; but what did that matter, when on its old stone steps the Mediterranean was splashing? High in sunlight above the town a white belfry reared itself against olive-clad mountains; in the square fisher-people lounged and basked; and the bronze sailor, gazing upward, was gaily hauling at the rope of a small bronze sail.

"*Do* stop," I cried—for Nicolette was doing her usual unbelieving creep by; "do let me inquire! Do you suppose it would poison us?"

For the little *albergo* was such a fearfully bright rose-color; the village seemed so entirely for the fisher-people.

Nicolette stopped; even backed a little, in an access of cordiality. There *was* the Englishwoman! The piazza was very clean, I saw as I hurried across its small cobbles. . . . Clean dark floors confronted me; insets of bright brass in the doors, a strip of spotless dining-room with the sea through its long windows; on my right, a counter with registry-book, blotters, pens—everything normal and usual—and behind it a tall young Italian padrone, brown-faced, smiling, but business-like.

"Signora?" said he invitingly.

I began my little recitative about a *camera,* absurd but beloved word: *"una camera col due letti?"*

"Do you speak English, signora?" he interrupted briskly; and on that basis, though still unbelievingly on my part, we climbed the mattinged stairs. A door was thrown open; I hastened across the floor. Here it was—our paradise. A wide window full of the sea, little golden waves splashing on a stone terrace below; fishing-boats, the sky, the sea; no sound but the sea, the gentle, lulling swash of it. . . . Behind me was a neat, almost stately room with two snowy beds, a red tile floor and nice old dark furniture, but that scarcely seemed to matter.

Running downstairs, I waved, and Nicolette wheeled swiftly over. Pleased dark eyes met mine; a nod, and out came the luggage, and was whisked away upstairs. Now, where was the garage? (Again, to my enraptured mind, a small consideration. Nicolette might lodge in the moon, I thought, if only we two could stay here.)

But an enormous key was brought; a medieval key. Did we know the other square, the *piazza piccola? Bene!* at the end of that . . . intricate and voluble directions, in Italian this time.

Blinking rather fast, I climbed into Nicolette.

"I'll go with you, darling. Goodness knows if we'll find it!"

But we did; tucked in around a multiplicity of corners, where brown brooms stood and a donkey looked over a half-door; hens and children scattering before us, the belfry right over our heads—and there in a sort of cliff it was; a cave with doors. It had a well-swept stone floor though—Laigueglia is very neat; and Nicolette just fitted. Taking out our maps and a forgotten Tauchnitz or two, we locked her, dust and all, securely in.

"We'll have her washed, poor woman!" said Babs, putting an arm through mine; and in a fellowship of happy weariness we tottered down the stony ways—past the *trattoria* again, under the arch and into our bright pink square. I felt quite at home already; though Laigueglia was still almost too much to believe.

"Is it *really* all right, do you think?" said Babs, as we climbed the stairs.

"Absolutely!" I replied with faith.

Babs crossed the floor quickly, as I had done; leaned her arms on the sill and looked at that sea. We both looked. An arm came into mine, and still we gazed. . . . That is what the Mediterranean does to you.

On shallow old steps below, it lapped and lapped; and its lappings were not as those of any other sea. Tideless, gentle, golden-clear . . . with a crystal breaking of ripples on whose backs rode now lavender, now silver, or satin-blue; but mostly one looked into transparent gold. To the west were pale gold sands leading away, their long ripples going and going to a point of yellow rock and the rich darkness of woods where a mountain closed round. Over the tip of it had come our road; a small globe of dust, white against the dark woods, was even now moving along it.

"Somebody else traveling," said Babs comfortably.

For it was good to be leaning here, *not* to be traveling; she took a long breath of that Riviera air, so mild, so sunset-cool and fresh, so scented with pines and wild orchids and the sea. Today had been from its first moments, I felt, a gritty and a testing day; my child deserved the Mediterranean. She should have it . . . after her winter of work in the University, our long journey down; this was what I most wanted for her, rest and the sea . . . and then a thought struck me.

"Babs!" I said; "I believe that Englishwoman was having tea out there!"

We dashed for the hot-water-jug, then downstairs. Yes, the sun was declining, the mountain was going purple, the sea silvery, with boats floating here and there—and people were sitting on the terrace beside trays. Think of tea, in a fishing-village, in Italy. . . .

"Si signora! Due tè—e tost?"

Two teas, and *tossed?* It took a second for that to penetrate, though the little, dark-eyed boy-waiter said it with all the energy of pride; indeed, with an air of what has this world to offer more? I dashed a look at Babs.

"Toast?" I said faintly. *"Si, per piacere!"*

And such is the childishness to which long deprivation, long absence from home, brings one (there had been no "tost" in France), that at this homelike touch, here in a bright pink *albergo* in a town we never heard of, with sunshine on the orange trees—we felt like falling on each other's necks with sobs of joy.

Instead we blinked a moment—Laigueglia seemed to induce blinks—then made a bee-line for the *terazzo.* Tables were set about on its stone floor; an English couple, slim, gray-haired, and composed (evidently old residents) had the best corner in the sun. . . . They would. We took the next best. Tide was going out, the foot or so the Mediterranean ever goes; one wet step showed; east of us, where the fishing-boats were drawn up, was the bit of beach where evidently the life of the town went on. We could see just an edge of it. Children played; mothers, working or sewing, leaned against the boats. Ropes lay upon the sand, nets and other fishing gear hung against the balconies; for this bit of beach was backed by pink or orange houses, huddled, bayed, indented, with deep sand coves running up among them, and a fat old Saracen tower, a bit crumbly like the others, sitting at the upper edge of the sands.

Pirates had tried to land here too, then; for Laigueglia, gathered in the green-purple arm of the mountain, was a spot to allure any one. One would have liked to see the lean, dark-armed wretches landing, and dashing around with their white robes flying; only we hoped the tower drove them off afterwards. Rather a long bit of shore for one old tower to handle, we thought—but, with all the frightened mothers and children huddling, there was doubtless desperate energy inside it—ancestor of that energy now hauling heavy boats across the sands; possibly the mothers and children, to this day, feel better protected with their backs against that tower.

But now came the agreeable clatter of our tea. Hot water; a strainer, everything Britishly complete; and in a reverently-covered heap, the "tost." A little pale, some of it, soot black, other pieces, but all achieved with labor and thought, with international strivings; doubtless with the patient holding of bread over a charcoal flame . . . a great strain for temperamental Italy.

"Somebody was breathing hard over this!" said Babs; and took a bite.

Ah, that crunch. The legitimate, five o'clock London sound; or four o'clock, if you can't wait till five . . . Cake was absent, and *biscotti* there to take its place—the weariful *biscuits secs* of our French journeyings; but *biscotti,* with the Mediterranean to look at, were not bad. In fact, we had had so many rich teas on the French Riviera that it was nice to see a plain biscuit again.

And how at home it all made one feel. Laigueglia—why, we lived in Laigueglia; what was there surprising about Laigueglia?

Out on the water a small sail or two was up, though the wind, what there was of it, was sinking.

Such peace settled over us. Here we were, and here we could stay: breathe this air, loiter on these sands, see the belfry against the mountains, the boats coming back over the water. We rose, and strolled idly along the beach. The sand was moist and firm, cool underfoot; the ripples had grown opalescent. The little white dog was with us, the same one we had seen in the street; a kind town, Laigueglia, and good to its little dogs. He had come upon the terrace just in time for tea, and lain beside our table, a charming, spaniel-like little dog with wavy coat and sweet though rather shallow eyes. . . . Babs, very fond of little dogs, had given him a *biscotto,* and he now pattered along, showing us the beach, and looking up at us confidingly. Was anything more needed to make us feel completely at home?

"Sunset time," say my notes. "Capo di Croce in the last light, gashes of dusty-blue shadow on dusty olive-gray. Colors of an old village at the foot of it. I picked up a yellow pebble, like a ginger-snap in texture, size, and thickness, watched my moment and skipped it at the incoming ripples. Bland, ceaseless ripples. . . . It hit a hollow, hopped a low wave, and made one leap into the next hollow before burying itself. Triumph! One felt one had accomplished great things. And so tangible a triumph."

These moist things one does on the sands are so delightful. We invariably do them, and they amuse us just as much as if we had never done them before. They amused the little dog too; as dogs will, out of the generosity of their hearts, he contributed his share of the fun. He feinted at ripples as if they were rabbits, then ran back when they pursued him and barked at them insultedly. We pretended to rush at the ripples too, and fled, shrieking, from their sleek approach; the little dog thought this was wonderful and joined in nobly, rushing after us again and again and saving us from the perils of the deep.

We walked back. Saltness was now our world; dark mountains and a clear soft splashing. Far out, there were silver gleams where boats were pulling home. . . . We thought we should be very late for dinner—not realizing how indefinitely Italian meals keep on; so we slipped into hasty silk blouses and went down, to confront a dining-room quite giddy with lights and costume. It was a clean, bare strip of a room opening on the terrazo, and with the padrone very much in charge; carving at a side table, motioning his young waiters about. On our table was just one velvet purple iris, supported by two spears of its foliage and a sprig of white-blossomed shrub; other tables had exactly the same arrangement, very impartial and fresh.

In a bay window the gray-haired couple were seated—a table by the view, of course. Marcelled locks the lady had;

pale-gray evening frock, diamond necklace, a supercilious expression. Diamonds in Laigueglia? Livingston dressing every evening in the wilds of Africa? But the diamonds did not quite strike that note.

"Swank," murmured my child.

The lady, with an air of mingled sweetness and temper—sweetness for the room, temper quite ready to flash forth at a harmless husband opposite—was silent at first; glancing guardedly about, moving her mouth as if eating were a pain to her. Then a tall man came in and dropped modestly into a seat at a table near by; phenomenally tall and thin he was, with gorilla-like arms and great emaciated hands with knobby joints. Embarrassed, he folded his long legs under the table and began his soup. He was still in tennis flannels, and his hands red with recent scrubbing; the lady sparkled at him.

"Saw you playing this afternoon, Mr. Grey. You were in *great* form!"

Mr. Grey mumbled something indistinguishable, glancing, however, with deprecating amiability in her direction.

"That was a splendid set, the last doubles you played," she went on. "You and your partner—was that Mr. Robbins, with you?—simply had it all your own way!"

"Plays a ripping game," murmured Mr. Grey. "Awf'lly nice chap to play with, too."

"And did you go in for a bathe afterwards?" she sweetly inquired. "They said the water was so lovely today."

Mr. Grey, to my surprise, said nothing; but ate his soup.

"How is your dear wife this evening?" she persevered; still sweetly, though in slightly higher tones. ("*Will* you pass me that newspaper, Henry?")

Mr. Grey, sending a glance at the vacant chair opposite him—a glance into which real life came for the first time—said briefly but gratefully, "She's better, thanks."

Something, a feeling of some sort, seemed to rise in him; he glowed slightly, but said nothing more. Not a loquacious man; yet one liked Mr. Grey. A safe neighborhood his, breathing that unspecifiable something with almost a fragrance about it, as from fresh grasses or some honest outdoor flower like clover; the aroma, clean as air, that comes from a chivalrous and modest nature. Tall, thin men so often have it. It may be their only beauty, but it is very real, and Babs and I, for no reason at all except that we were feeling the same thing, and knew we were, smiled at each other.

The entrée, a rather meager little Mediterranean fish, benefited by our warmed feeling. It was a good, fresh little fish, what there was of it, and Babs told me something learned and interesting about Mediterranean fish, only I forgot it at once, as I do anything accurate: something lovely that the ancients did, or didn't do, because they were such skinny little things (the fish); and how the Roman soldiers dried them and took them on marches for their chief food.

Apparently there isn't such a thing as a luscious, well-nourished *pesce* in all these angelic waters. Are they never allowed to grow up? And Babs, leaving her ground of historic security, joined me in wondering. Like dandelions in France, any poor creature with fins must have a hunted life along this inhabited coast; every bit of it that isn't rocks, every little stretch of beach, straight or half-moon, has its quota of fishing-boats, its swarms of active, bare-legged ones to push them off.

Cauliflower arrived at our elbows; cauliflower with cheese, very good; chicken to follow, well-roasted and brown, and browned potatoes with it. Well well, this padrone certainly had been in England. . . .

More and more amazing you grow, Laigueglia, though we had to run into your pink wall to find you; and we laughed again. The lady in gray turned her eyes appraisingly upon us—who were these two new arrivals, thus audibly enjoying themselves? They hadn't dressed for dinner—that was obvious; and she turned away to glow, though condescendingly, at a couple near her; a round, rosy little middle-aged couple blamelessly eating *arrosto* and not wishing to be glowed at.

But the diamonds insistently flashed, as did her narrow-lipped smile; the little couple, emerging from their contented duet and wielding of forks, had to respond. "*How* that woman does simper!" murmured Babs distressfully; aware of every one of these small complications, and taking them rather to heart.

"But her husband looks nice . . ." I tentatively said; and was met with a gleeful grin.

"Simps doesn't think so!" retorted my child.

CHAPTER II

ON ALONG THE RIVIERA

HOT water in a great copper jug burst brilliantly in upon us next morning. I had been awake a few minutes listening to the Mediterranean, beaming at the sunshine and thinking of writing notes; the satin of our quilts gleamed in the light, the flowers on the ceiling were pleasantly faded, and Babs, her dark head barely visible, was fast asleep. . . . She *should* sleep; and then came the brilliant rap.

"Entri!" I said, rather vexed.

The jug came swiftly in, with Gemma behind it. Gemma, evidently a north Italian; tall, with a fine bearing, great gray eyes and brown hair—inspired eyes, indeed, a remarkable brow. If Gemma had been a Russian peasant, she would have been a poet. She moved inspiredly to the wash-stand, then, turning, asked in a strangely soft and timid voice about *colazione. Caffè latte,* I told her; *pane e burro* . . . and what was the word for jam? The dictionary was far across the room, on the bureau. I stared deeply at the understanding sea. . . . Ah, *marmalatta!* which might mean anything.

Well anything, in this place, would do.

So a cordial Laigueglia breakfast soon came charging in, with golden honey as well as jam; what with the sunlight on the water and its reflection gleaming from our golden quilts, everything looked golden to us, eating and staring at the sea.

Breakfast in bed, for once, seemed just right. Sails of fishing-boats went by; voices distant, but full of vigor and sun, came in to us, and such was the call of things that I got up. Babs, weary with potholes, had settled down again to instant sleep; poor lamb, she hadn't rested at all in France. We meant to in Antibes, and drove all over the mountains instead. We would. Warning off the energetic Gemma, I tiptoed away.

Sunshine was blazing splendidly in at the foot of the stairs. Sun was on the cobbles, on our pink walls, on the rickety omnibus with its wobbly old horse that took the mail, or passengers, to Alassio. (No station in Laigueglia; I hoped there never would be.) Women and girls strode along the street, or gossiped in doorways; our little dog greeted me, but soon went his wagging way. Other little dogs, much like him, were distributed at intervals along the street, sitting on door-steps or basking in that April sun; evidently Laigueglia's own sort of little dog, her *spécialité,* like cheese or little cakes in other places.

Proceeding, I climbed a steep cobbled lane that very soon came to olive terraces and wild flowers. The white belfry was below me already, and Laigueglia's rosy jumble of roofs. One got high quickly, here. . . . And that blue, everywhere; blue, blue! One seemed to swim in it, things had thrice their value against it; it *was* the view. White was transfigured, pink things were pinker; yellow shone golden, mauve and purple shouted and exulted. Oh, why wasn't Babs here?

"She'll love it," I thought; "how glad I am we stopped in Laigueglia."

And here was Laigueglia's washing-place, a most advanced spot, with concrete troughs under an open-sided shed looking out on all the gorgeousness. Not bad, to wash to that blue; the sting and stimulus of it . . . with the flickering shade of olive trees outside, and wild orchids looking at you. Orchids always seem to be the right color for their surroundings; these Mediterranean ones under the silvery trees were rosy-mauve, and the water in the troughs bright blue.

No wonder Laigueglia's women looked cheerful; I had met one of them going down the lane, carrying a basket of clothes—a wholesome brown creature with such a smile, and a fine healthy-looking child beside her bearing a smaller basket. . . . But did everybody use that same soapy water, I wondered; or was she coming back to let it out?

A cheerful gentleman-cat had followed me up the path, and now came with me as I climbed among the terraces. He was black, fat, and amiable, with round white toes and a dainty, lady-like head; evidently resembled his mother, who must have been a nice cat. I picked flowers—thymey-smelling, purple ones I didn't know; while the cat went with me, in dashes across my feet. Sometimes he stiffened, staring at the view; then relaxed and played violently again. At length he rolled, leaped up, wiped the dust off on me with one last cordial rub, lashed his tail and left—at a mad cat-gallop; probably remembered a mouse-hole he was neglecting.

Wild flowers were thicker than ever about me, and olives scattered their light shade:

> Spring afternoons, when delicate shadows fall
> Pencilled upon the grass. . . .

only this was morning. . . .

I started, in a very hot sun on white rocks, down a path near by, and met three donkeys laboring up, with a graceful young driver who bowed and smiled. Each donkey had a sort of rough pillow-case thrown across his back, its ends filled with cement. . . . Somebody building, on the mountain? A shrine, perhaps. A very pretty, sleek, gray donkey was in the lead; she clambered steadily from rock to rock, while the two smaller ones painstakingly followed. Such tiny hoofs they had; and a beautiful youth their driver was, with the romantic eyes and tossed locks of another day. . . . Italy's day of high romance; a model for Donatello, not Angelo. Lithe as a leopard; brown-faced, oval-chinned, superb in the sculpturings of his cement-dusted shirt; he seemed to know he was beautiful, and stepped up those rocks with conscious grace.

"Gia!" he called in a melodious tenor, to the resting line of donkeys, and they all went winding away among the olive trees. A picture; and the sea was even a deeper blue now. I must hurry down.

Babs—up, and glad to see me—was tying an orange tie of rough silk under the collar of her *café-au-lait* shirt. I liked the colors, and told her so; told her about the donkeys; and we went downstairs arm in arm, beaming at the world. (Grand, to be going down Laigueglia stairs together.)

Nicolette must be looked at, of course, so we acquired the enormous key. . . . She had been washed, yes—but a rear tire was flat. Dash! It had been all right when we drove in; a circumstance we always find enraging.

"Though of course," said Babs, "it might have been a slow one, A.B.—something we picked up as we came along, you know." And when we had the spare on, there was still the invalid on our minds.

"Like to drive to Alassio, take our films along, and have this thing mended?" suggested Babs, putting her weight on the last nut. (A nut, by the way, is a *madrevite;* and I had just got so used to its being an *écrou.*)

"How about you, darling. Aren't you too tired?"

"Not to drive to Alassio," said she. "It's only four miles."

It seemed nice to be gliding along in Nicolette again, avoiding little dogs and seeing the sunlight on a pot of white carnations high over our heads on the pink wall; we went through a long, dusky-pink arch and came out, perfectly dazzled, to Riviera light and a palm tree against the sea; the very last of Laigueglia. The brilliance of it all was extraordinary. ". . . High summer morns," I thought, "When white light rains upon the quiet sea—" only George Eliot and I were once more in collision, for the sea was far from quiet. It was beating splashily on the rocks. Our road had potholes, and frequent hoardings, but across a beautiful little azure-blue bay and beneath dark, rough, pine-clad mountains was a yellow town: Alassio, no doubt.

Even so. Very sunny and clean; with low yellow buildings, amber water along a beach fringed with palm trees, and tennis-clad English striding purposefully about.

"Not a bad town," I said pulling my hat-brim down.

"But *what* a glare!" said Babs; and stopped in a patch of shade.

Everything in Alassio was under a deep awning and very

hard to find; the *farmacia* we wanted simply did not exist. We tooled around and around, gasped in the heat and yellowness; found a nice dusky film-shop to wait in, collected our spare at last, and tooled gladly back again to little shadowy Laigueglia. . . . We began to see why Italian towns are mostly pink. It is cooler so. They heat them up for the English—who come here sun-starved. San Remo had been yellow, too.

"Yais! Streets are var' tweested," said the padrone, smiling genially when we explained about the lack of chemists in his neighboring town; though we later discovered on his hall table a Czechoslovakian magazine with an "ad" of the very shop we had been looking for: "FARMACIE INTERNATIONELLE, ALASSIO."

Well, well; did Czechoslovakia know all about Alassio then? We didn't.

But peace again enveloped us. We and the sea had tea together, and sunset came on; we more or less dressed for dinner (to Simps's astonishment—we hadn't seen her all day, up to then) and later strolled on the beach, watching the evening star grow larger and larger, sinking toward the mountains till it twinkled on the very top of a dark ridge. . . . Then we went in. Other stars were twinkling hard, from our window; the sea far out was very smooth, but did its faithful swashing on the steps for us . . . the last sound one heard at night, the first in the morning.

Babs walked with me next day. "Getting rested," says the three-line diary. We picked flowers on the terraces, white unknown flowers, and tall purple ones, and lay about on the warm grass, never tiring of the colors of the view; the donkeys obligingly came by, their young Hermes of a driver very conscious when Babs' eyes fell on him—and his on her. . . . They were not a little alike, it interested me to see; both lithe, brown and oval-chinned, with the clear profile that delights one among the Latins—my child's professor of Italian literature (a short-sighted person) had once taken her dark head for that of an Italian youth; but the difference in their expressions—in the ancestry of their expressions, one might say—was striking. Babs' so composed, meditative, humorous-ironic, yet with that something open and Saxon about it so different from anything Latin, above all with the indefinable look that thought and cultivation give; the Hermes with his charming, transient, unthinking glance—aware of his own beauty, proud of his grace and strength; earnest about his job, yet defiant, just a hint, because of the cement-dusted shirt.

That is young working Italy, today.

"Gi-a!" he called, with special melodiousness, as he leaped upon a high rock; and the donkeys again clambered out of sight among the olives . . . little gray or brown backs, moving through that sunny, leafy fluttering.

Babs was charmed with it all. Even the cat arrived to show off for her benefit; capering madly down the lane, then dashing in, very pleased with himself, to show us which was his particular bit of garden behind a tiny fence . . . where he immediately sat on the doorstone, very sweetly tossing his nose at us—a complete demonstration of cat methods. We left him sitting there with his tail around his white toes, and went to lean over the wall across the lane.

Such a drop-down. In the labyrinths of Laigueglia far below was a deep-walled garden with fig trees, its plots of vegetables bordered with flowers, and in its pleasant paths a young fisherman was helping his child to walk; bending over the toddling baby, showing it the best way around beds and arbors, murmuring encouragement; at last lifting it in his arms with a cry of love and joy. That is young Italy, too.

Prowling on, we came upon a little *vicolo* named for a war hero. It is quite at the top of the town; it has (while it stays there) a most marvelous view, and though about six feet wide is the Via Capitano Vincenzo Maglione. It had an old yellow wall with fig trees looking over it, a precise grape-vine trained along its top and flowers peeping carelessly below; then all at once the little via dashed downhill and into a low-headed pink tunnel.

Going down it faster than we meant to, we ducked under

dark little arches and around corners with tiny gardens bursting at us through fence-palings, only to be completely lost in solid-walled little lanes where vines and flowers, from window-boxes, fell innocently about our heads. There was only the sky to appeal to—blue, with great white clouds; but we soon found ourselves in an extra-long dusky-pink tunnel (under most of Laigueglia, it seemed) and coming out, when we had no idea we were anywhere near it, upon the beach and the Saracen tower.

Good, to breathe that salt again. Great life was going on in the bit of beach; great shouts, great straining at ropes. Barelegged fishermen, women with their skirts tucked up, were hauling at a boat that had to be dragged a long way; everybody splashed in, took new hold, sang and heaved. . . . Such a business to go through with every night and morning—for these fishermen, like the men of Clovelly, go out at dawn.

But it seemed to be the frolic of the day. Even the old grandmothers rose from their baby-tending or their pans of vegetables, took hold of the upper end (where waves did not reach), and the great haul went on; with such giggling and cackling and rich contralto urging, broken into by bursts of tenor song. Up came the boat, little by little, out of the last shallow sliding of water; then everybody relaxed. Laughing, chattering, they did a few things with baskets and gear; then hastened over to help with another boat. Long sands that grow no shorter, long thin ripples, that do no lifting; even so, they make play of them. For these fisher-people of Laigueglia seemed extraordinarily happy, and included us in that joy; they smiled generously at us, dramatized their work, even their own rollicking (as dramatic folk do), and loved to have us watching it.

And they were beautiful while doing it. The women wore bright skirts and kerchiefs, the men bright shirts; the whole beach, as we sat on a piece of timber to look at it, was unforgettable, a life-work of painting right there. Women and children seem to spend all day on that beach; it is their life, this Mediterranean with its colors and its waves. They help the boats out into the water—out to their fate; they watch for them to come back, pulling lustily, or sailing lazily (who is rowing? they try to see; who is managing to make the dying wind fill his sail?) and then comes the grand moment when everybody flocks to help them in—twelve, often, bent over one rope, singing. What fun. . . .

Everything they do, they do together. Their shops are open to the street; the women market bareheaded, carrying long loaves in baskets, a child on their hips; they are brown, vigorous, glorious to look at. Their dusky, low-ceilinged homes—mere holes in the pink walls—are yet so swept and homelike; flowers on the window-ledges, flowers in the scrap of garden, pets in the sun. Black old furniture sits about—chests, a table—not much, but enough; home-made linen, copper pots along the wall, a bit of fire on a stone hearth . . . even their *osteria* in the little square, with its sanded stone floor, its orange trees, awnings and home-made, reed-bottomed chairs outside in the sun, seemed decorous and well-kept.

Then up against the mountain is their church: grim outside, gay with saints inside and a pretty, blond Virgin in blue, with gold stars . . . a nice kind saint for every day and ill . . . something to do for one's sorrows, which is what, in sorrow, there usually is not. Kneel on a stone floor, move your beads along—and rise, feeling much has been accomplished. No wonder that the women smile, and the men shout to each other with loud, happy unabashed voices; their lives are open as the sea.

We walked a bit by those waves, then took to the street.

Under an archway came a vivid-colored young woman, a strong bandit-looking creature in a short black frock half off one brown shoulder, carrying on her arm a fat child in a brilliant fuchsia dress; in the other hand she had a great jar of bright yet dark blue; she swung by, smiling broadly, shouting to friends in doorways. Past her came a slender girl in an orange jersey, strands of dark hair blown about her face, bearing a little fair boy in bright green; beyond, a mother, tidy and trim, with a most beautiful clean apron, was calling her young son from the beach. She came toward us smiling, with a spotless baby in pink on her arm; short pink cotton dress, fresh as a flower, little knitted jacket and a round pink-and-white cap—and such touching bits of short dark hair sticking out under the cap. . . . The baby, needless to say, was grinning from ear to ear.

Other children came dancing round making love to it, and when the nice, twelve-year-old son arrived from the boats, he walked straight and smiling to his mother, bent to cluck joyfully at baby sister and give her a hearty kiss. One doesn't as a rule see boys of twelve doing that, but evidently it was his habit; the baby fixed her eyes on him in delight.

Babies are the great thing in Laigueglia. Everybody has them, everybody adores them; what with the sunshine and the clean homes and that beach, it is a perfect place for them.

With our eyes full of bright walls and happy people, we turned in to lunch.

Hominyish substances with a cheese flavor, a leaf or two of salad, a rather sour orange; was our padrone, then, encouraging his guests to lunch in Alassio—as many of them did? And today there were four Italians at the center table who had ordered a special meal; a thick beefsteak, piles of oily, garlicky spaghetti, baskets of bread, large bottles of red wine. The Italians themselves were brown and thick, their dark faces shone and their little black eyes sparkled as they gobbled and swashed down wine, and yet more wine; yet the padrone, for all his select British proclivities, seemed to like them; he was perplexingly attentive. Oh well, he had to be, of course—or perhaps they were visiting relations; though they looked more like the Italian counterpart of a particularly horrid sort of *voyageurs de commerce* we had met in Carcassonne. They piled into a dirty car, hiccoughing, half-spilling out of it, and drove noisily away.

That evening, feeling very rested indeed, we dressed for dinner; the lady in gray stared. They could, then; how very amazing. After dinner she went so far as to smile at us from her sofa in the drawing-room; and the next morning, from her chair by the orange-tubs, smiled sweetly, almost appealingly at us.

"She'll be getting desperate and speaking to us, soon," laughed Babs, as we turned the corner of the square; for we had been there nearly three days now, and three days is usually the time it takes an English person to digest you.

But we were just going. Mediterranean-lulled sleep had restored us, all Italy was awaiting us; all *we* were waiting for was the wash . . . after the time I had had, too, trying to be helpful and make out the list in Italian. It had been promised for early that morning, and Gemma, her starry eyes perplexed, her brown hair flying, a line of care on her fine brow, was racing back and forth for us with messages.

At two o'clock the wash arrived. Beautifully done, not an article missing; *la lavandaia,* a thin, charming, self-contained creature in a brightly-striped petticoat, laying it out composedly on the bed. There was this, and that, and that; *"Si, signora; grazie, signora!"* And she withdrew her long, intelligent face through the doorway. There was history, on that face; had she lost sons in the war? possibly a husband? She had the look of one refined by sorrow; living in the calmness of bitter pain.

Nicolette stood ready for us at the steps; had been ready, for hours; though hating to leave Laigueglia, we piled in coats and books, the padrone tucked us in, and we moved off.

"A rivederci!" cried every one, beaming and waving.

How pink were Laigueglia's walls as we looked back; the belfry stood white against the hills; but the sea was blue before us. What a day! The Mediterranean had its most amazing colors, and cloud-shadows flew upon the mountains. Along the rocks of the causeway the clear water splashed, but here again were the billboards: "Lampo," "Mobiloil."

"Hate 'em!" said I, looking daggers at Lampo.

For that was the worst sinner of all, defacing landscape oftener than any of them; and Nicolette refused to run on it. We were delighted she did. She coughed and sputtered and took a day or two to get the stuff out of her system. Today, though not because of Lampo, she seemed to feel ill; she ground sadly up the hills. Was it the caves she had been living in of late? A cave at Sospel, an icy tunnel at Gap, and now this cavern at Laigueglia. Were they getting into her system?

"She's a sick woman," said Babs, peering worriedly at her.

But on the level she was normal, downhill she was sublime, so we slid happily along, following the coast in openness and sunshine. Our neighbor, the railway, was having a terrible time obliterating itself in tunnels—seventy-nine of them, Baddy said—while here we were out in the smiling blue view. We felt *so* superior; even if we did have to wait for the afternoon train at almost every crossing.

A chain would be down across the track and there we would sit; sometimes with a view, oftener looking at rock-walls, or the road. There was no arguing with that chain, once down. An American family in a big car slid up beside us at one of these waits—and three of them were red-haired; father, daughter, and small son; charming, vibrant and impatient, all three. For a minute or two they sat, fidgeting; then Father leaped out, strode to the little guard-house and came fuming back.

"Never *knew* such a dam' country as this! No matter how late the train is, they won't take down that chain and let you through . . . no sir—not if you wait half an hour!"

And the three red-heads paced furiously up and down. Twenty more minutes we waited, expecting that train every second; I thought those three would explode. As the chain fell their car shot by us like a catapult; later, however, we were amused to see them in a small village, Mother and all her red-heads, diving into one souvenir-shop after another, acquiring treasures, laughing and pleased.

"They've time for *that,* anyway," smiled Babs; and squeezed with difficulty past their big car, parked in an especially narrow turn by a bead-shop.

Bits of sea followed, and more villages—Loana with a

street where the mother of Garibaldi was born; there were country bits too, with hills and rocks and blossoming gorse —perilous goat-pastures which scaled mountainsides above us, or plunged violently toward the sea. Sheep and goats in this region seemed terrified of cars; "not motorbroken," say my notes, "or else too much so." Three large sheep went leaping away from us up the most inconvenient rocks; and we overtook two lady-goats with long hair and stiff, red-looking bags, their leading-strings trailing behind them in the dust, going downhill to be milked. They were chaperoned by a peasant-woman—a dirty, careless-looking creature, walking at a thoughtless distance from her charges; the poor things tried hard to be composed, but one of them turned and came hastily back to her woman, with such troubled eyes.

"Please take care of me. This is a very dangerous road!"

The peasant-woman picked up the string, Babs slowed down, and the goat, with a relieved glance at us out of her shrewd yellow eyes, let us by without a tremor.

We loved these pastoral bits; the dusty smell of the grazing creatures, or just wild flowers and rocks and the sea. It was a wonderful coast, now; we went through a rocky hole in the tip of a great yellow cliff, the Capo di Noli—and then what a view. Noli; a thousand gay fishing-boats on a white semi-circle of beach, with the blue water dancing; then the huddled old town, pink and yellow, with a gray medieval wall jogging up the wooded mountainside behind it to a half-ruined *castello* on its top. Noli's nice little Albergo Italia gave us tea; and just one old English spinster, also having hers in the *albergo's* glassed-in porch, gave the place atmosphere and a sort of security.

We sat long over ours, loving the curve of Noli's little white road, its flower-beds and clipped trees, the azure of the Mediterranean beyond . . . nay, the topaz and emerald, violet and cerulean, rose and silver and cobalt of that Mediterranean; laid upon it in streaks and belts, twinkles and patches, in gleams and rips and scuddings—or in wide, simple stretches.

There are no words for its colors, that day; its air of jaunti-

MOTOR-ROAD ALONG THE ITALIAN RIVIERA

Laigueglia

ness as it ceaselessly wriggled the anchored boats and slapped at rocks and jetties.

"I'm running this bay," said it; "just give me a chance!"

And somewhere along its town-dotted coast line, well-hidden by promontories, was Genoa. How far should we get along that sparkling shore tonight? A pamphlet we had picked up, entitled *From Alpine Snows to Volcano Fires,* had an optimistic opinion of our route: "A long winding road . . . runs the entire length of the Western Riviera, by which Genoa the Queen of the Seas can be reached. This road is described by Dickens in the *Pickwick Club*. . . . The last bend reveals Genoa which over-reaches the most ardent expectations."

Well, we would see.

Meanwhile Nicolette was being thoroughly inspected. A young man with a baby in his arms was stopping beside her, and the baby was being shown everything; a bright little soul who looked at everything with precocious black eyes. The young father gazed at the card on the dashboard; that small metal card which had my child's name and address on it. Babs absolutely blushed; then laughed at my surprised face.

"Bad as having your photo taken!" she explained.

"Expect he can't read it," I said consolingly, feeling in my pocket for a tip for the nice waitress.

"On through commerce and quarries," say the notes; "awful Savona, all chimneys and smoke, trying its best to be a decent town, however. Thick, interesting harbor"; and Nicolette here developed a soft tire. I remember drawing up by a low wall overlooking that harbor, and Babs lengthily pumping. (The pump leaked.) The tire did stiffen up, but we went rather gingerly along, and now that our attention was drawn to her, could not but perceive—what we were always reluctant to admit—that Nicolette was liking the hills less and less.

It was evident we should stop this side of Genoa for the night; and the sooner the better.

The shore was becoming more maritime: "Varazze. Boat-building village," say the notes; "long street with little gardens, a noisy river brawling down from the mountains, and an old schooner up on lofty ways, pointing her bowsprit at the sky."

A tumbling mass of wisteria, yellow tables beneath; a waiter with a napkin on his arm, smiling at us—ah, here by the river was Varazze's hotel. Two little hotels side by side, in fact, with the same wisteria and a waiter with identical smiles, at each. . . . This might do very well. We didn't feel nearly so particular tonight; besides, we liked Varazze. That nubbed old bowsprit, poking at the twilight, allured us very much; also the sound of the river.

We chose the first one, its wisteria was much nicer. A large and luscious signora, fairly blazing with Italian vitality, leaped to greet me, her big brown eyes and heaving, silk-clad bosom alike expanding with excitement and cordiality; while behind her palpitated her stocky little husband, the waiter, and a maid; the whole establishment. Two *Inglesi,* in a *macchina! Si si si si!*

Had the Albergo Torretti ever before had Anglo-Saxon guests? I think not.

The little peasant maid, charmed but frightened, ran before me up the twisting stairs and frankly hid herself behind the door she opened; but—the best, front, corner room? Well, rather.

A view of the sea, of old Varazze across the rushing river; voluminous lace curtains, yellow satin quilts on the two big beds. . . . Indeed this would do. Nicolette was soon bestowed in a stone-floored cavern across the road—where she looked around with composure, as if saying "Ah, I expected this"; and we joyfully possessed our room. . . . Wasn't this jolly? Nothing but Italian, here. Sweet place; and this view!

Downstairs, with immense ceremony and bowings, we were ushered into green-and-silver *sala à pranzo*—finding it to our surprise very large, ballroom-floored, and decorated with tubs of orange trees; then with more bows, with wreathing smiles, with unimaginable cordiality and chair pushings, the padrone and the excited waiter brought the menu and hovered over us.

Purely Italian hoverings, of course. My vocabulary chattered with fright. Minestrone—everybody knows that; *vitello* (veal)—how inflated I was because I remembered it. . . .

"Gli asparagi, signora?" hinted the waiter, almost dancing with excitement.

"Bene!" said I; and a salad I absolutely couldn't fathom, but was sure he knew what was good. We assented to everything, and he danced jubilantly off.

"This is fun," said Babs, looking after him with twinkling eyes.

"Some work, too," I replied; quite gasping after the exertion of ordering a whole meal in the Italian tongue. Two years before I had had two months' lessons, and one month of them that winter in London . . . but so noisy, in a small room looking out on Oxford Street and the stream of buses, that I gave up in despair. Now I wished I hadn't, and remarked as much.

"But you did marvelously, A.B.," said my generous child. "You haven't forgotten a thing!"

"Oh yes, I have," I groaned.

Yet tray after tray came hastening in, borne like banners high and gallantly above the head of the exuberant waiter. His hors d'œuvres were absolute bouquets: such red radishes, with great green Riviera leaves left on just to be beautiful; an enormous Mediterranean sardine or two, gleaming silver, and crisp little mountainside olives. In fact it was all so "just out of the garden," one had a feeling that the jubilant waiter had dashed out that minute and picked it, sardine and all.

"Isn't this fun?" we said again, and devoured everything.

The minestrone was hotter and more composed of everything-on-earth than any we had ever had, the salad turned out to be of the tenderest little interiors of fresh green artichokes and simply melting, when we had expected it to be hard and scaly; the drip coffee dripped indeed, very black and hair-raising; we rose from this meal feeling indulged and pampered . . . above all, amused by the almost lip-licking satisfactions of our waiter when he inquired, of every dish, *"È buono?"* and we replied without shame, *"Molto buono!"*

Later however a slight reaction set in, as we stood in our window. "Seems funny, doesn't it," I said, a trifle discontentedly, "making such a fuss about your meals!"

"I know it!" said Babs, turning to me as if struck by the thought; "I wonder why we do?"

"Well, I suppose you really can't help it, over here," I said; and promptly cheered up. "It's such a business to think up enough language, you know—and you feel so thrilled when the waiter understands you, and all!"

Babs laughed; full of beatitude, we looked out into the night.

Below us the river brawled, a bit of yellow light twisting here and there in its dark current; the roof lines of Varazze were cut black upon the stars, and the old hulk, opposite, was barely visible against a toneless sea, which was nevertheless swashing its interminable soft swash upon an invisible shore.

"Do love it so," I sighed; and as we leaned there, the fragrance of the wisteria came up to us, delicate, inevitable, as much a part of Varazze's night as the strange blue of the sky.

"Seems as if I could smell the mountains, too," said Babs, leaning out and looking toward their black mass, so near us. Indeed a trace of earth and rocks and olive-bark, of pine-needled paths and little mountain flowers, seemed to drift to us on the whiffs of cooler air that, following the stony bed of the river, went on—and out to sea.

CHAPTER III

A PLACE FOR THE WEEK-END

IN the morning we found our fine weather had broken. We were ready, indeed anxious to go on, but a storm was rolling up. We stood at our windows and watched it; our first Mediterranean storm.

It seemed to be coming over the mountains though; dark and rolling; a furious-looking sky. The wisteria was blowing toward the sea, and in the thickest part of it a large white tom-cat was curled up asleep; a snowy-clean, seashore cat who looked charming in his lavender bed, with golden sprays of foliage about him.

The rich clusters of blossom were fluttering sadly in the wind; dropping on the tables below. They had been lovely in the sunshine earlier, and were now superb against stormy grayness: a mass of shaken color under the ruthless activity of the winds.

Across the river everybody was scuttling. At an iron-monger's shop a row of dish-pans was being taken down and carried indoors, also brooms, pails and crockery; from the drapery-shop, next door, clothes were being hastily gathered in. An Italian maid conveying two select little boys home from school was wrestling frantically with their umbrellas; old women were running, children racing, drivers coming down from the hills with their long heavy wagons loaded with tile, were trotting beside their horses; "Heu! Eu-heu!" One team, a chestnut and a blue-roan, did not pull at all evenly, and their driver, cracking his whip, had to run and shout at them with special vehemence; while some single ox-loads of wood followed him—all hurrying.

"Heu! Eu-heu!"

It was enough to make anybody hurry. The wind was now howling steadily, the Mediterranean transformed into an ugly-colored thing with great waves smashing masses of dirty-brown foam on the shore. A terrific sky still rolled overhead, though only a few heavy drops were falling; what did the fishermen do in this sort of thing?

An old woman leaned out from a garret window opposite —wonderful old brown-purple tiles, the roof had—and felt anxiously of her drying clothes. Could she take them in? With sudden resolution she did; jerking wildly at them, her lean old brown arms flying out angularly, like windmills. Gorgeous lightning played above the mountains; it tore and jabbed, and in a wild rush came the rain. . . . We loved seeing it. It wouldn't last long; but swallows on a wire were having the best bath for weeks. They fluttered their wings, flicked at their breasts, and were delighted.

Hail came; first in small particles, then a shower of great white hailstones. Three swallows were hit and flew away, others sat on, in their same formation on the wires; like a contented swallow-school. They seemed to enjoy the battering; tough little Italian swallows.

But it was too much for the white tom-cat. He got up from his wisteria-bed, obviously cursing; crept down through its mazes, half-climbed, half-fell down the posts and stalked off swashing his tail.

The storm slackened; pedestrians ceased to scurry quite so madly, the wisteria to drop so many bits of lavender on the yellow tables, so we went across to Nicolette's cave and had a lovely time tinkering with her. At least Babs had a lovely time; I stood about, handed things, and tried not to be bored, but if one doesn't love grease and iron and cog-wheels one simply doesn't. Babs is amazing; she can not only take things apart but put them together again so that they work, and work better; which to me is a marvel. Admiration, indeed, helps greatly with these periods of looking-on, for if with a certain warmness around the heart one can say "Marvelous, darling!" or "When, I should like to know, did you find out how to do *that?*" boredom departs as by magic.

Besides Varrazze was charming to watch, out of our cave. Palm trees waved, the sea splashed, the river bustled, and carts went by; and I did hope Nicolette would go better today.

She did. We were seen enthusiastically off by our expansive signora; leaving the waiter leaning against the wisteria smiling at us, just as on the day before, we headed gaily for Genoa—and beyond.

Where? As usual we didn't know; some nice place for over Sunday. . . . A bit of lovely coast, then horridness began. We had expected it; all that smoke in the air: towns! A tram-track was the first symptom—an unutterable great track writhing back and forth across the road; and the road was muddy and slimy. Nicolette's tail twisted this way and that; Babs had to clutch her vehemently.

Near Genoa it grew worse. The road widened, but there were paving stones a foot square, with black mudholes between; and strings of four-horse teams, heavily loaded, were filling the wide road, their drivers tramping beside them. One's respect for the commerce of Italy grew. We went worming along at two m.p.h., barely finding room among the great struggling teams, whose horses were strung out in a line; splendid horses, but dreadfully in our way. We drove beside factories, coal-yards, and harbors with grimy shipping; high above it all was the head of a great lighthouse.

Coming onto cleaner pavement at last, we motored thankfully up toward that lighthouse. A nice, tall, hazel-eyed man sold us *benzina* for a very low price—lower than it had been anywhere on the Riviera; he had trouble with his pump but worked at it patiently, got it going, and wished us farewell with such a pleasant, somehow selfless smile. *"Buon' viaggio, signore!"*

Sweet of him, we thought; and sailed up into the mess that is Genoa. The mess of traffic, that is; of old *palazzi* with striped fronts. Our enthusiastic though weirdly spelled Türistiche pamphlet said that in the eighteenth century, "some Genoese noblemen had had each five or six palaces all splendidly furnished," and that the architect, Galeazzo Alessi, "understood the art of armonizing lines with the nature of the landscape and often drew inspiration from the same to the advantage of the design." Excellent thought.

But we were not going to stop in Genoa—oh, no; we would "do" it some other time (I vaguely remembered, in my childhood, not liking it very well). So we turned by a sort of instinct into a narrow via, lined with the black-and-white palaces, which led us just where we ought to have gone, only we didn't know it—up a steep hill into the busy piazza de Ferrari, with the *teatro* staring at us, and the *accademia,* and the Doges' Palace; and Garibaldi on a high pedestal. Streets branched from this piazza and we halted to decide where to go next—missing Michelin's *plan de ville* dreadfully.

But this was the first time we had driven into a large Italian city, and we were thrilled. Here we were, with the little dark-eyed Genoese populace raging at our elbows, little Genoese trams frantically hammering their gongs, and Genoese architecture confronting us. Our impression here was mostly of square cornices and solidity, though the crowds seemed actually our main concern—and, now that we had got ourselves into Genoa la Superba, how to get out of her. My wits absolutely left me, the noise was so fearful; Babs took the perplexing map, and bent over it.

"I think I see how," she muttered with knit brow; and swung the wheel.

"Awnk, Awnk!" Furious work with the horn, it took, to get us out of that corner; we slid down the Via Venti Settembre, past the yellow-and-black cathedral (poor thing, so crowded into commerce), then on through the smothering crowd.

For it was tea-time; and whether Genoa was out for tea or not—which of course she wasn't—she was all on her streets, babbling vivaciously. We held our breaths, and wished we were out of it; whirled to the right, on some inspiration of Babs', sailed across a viaduct and up a long hill, finding ourselves at last in a high, tree-shaded and altogether blessed boulevard where for some reason the crowds didn't come. There was a pleasant *pasticcheria,* too, with its green tables set in a sort of park and a waiter guarding them; we drew Nicolette by its friendly edge. The waiter drove away, with fury, some half-dozen laughing, dashing, little Italian boys that wanted to swarm over her—poor muddy little dear, who had done so well in all that mix-up—then came with the sweetest possible smile for our order.

Hot toasted muffins, we had, and little Genoese tarts, much like the Parisian ones, and more hot water for the tea; while it was coming I arranged my hat and hair, and Babs wiped the mud off Nicolette's doors. Altogether we had a most friendly and trampish time by that green park . . . and Genoa, being used to housekeeping in the street, didn't even stare. We liked Genoa.

If it had been England, we should have gone inside and prinked solemnly in dressing-rooms and been conventional and stately, but this was indulgent Italy. If we wanted to make ourselves at home in the middle of a boulevard, we somehow felt quite free to; besides, there was nowhere to go, inside that *pasticcheria.*

We even read up a little on Genoa's tumultuous history. Amazing, how these cities have been handed about through the centuries. Destroyed by the Carthaginians in the seventh century, rebuilt by the Romans, invaded by the Lombards, and sacked (of course) by the Saracens, she drove them all out and set off to conquer a few worlds for herself; secured Corsica and Sardinia, engaged in a 200-year war with her neighbor, Pisa, and went on and on, developing an empire which included the Crimea, Syria, and North Africa. . . . Embarrassingly distant, that seemed; and one was always sorry for Pisa. As I remarked to Babs, "There are so many plays, it seems to me, where somebody is sitting in a huge tent in a dim light—a general or somebody, and worrying about her. We saw one in Paris, you know. And then you worry too; and orderlies keep rushing in with bad news."

Babs laughed; and we tried without success, to remember the play I was thinking of—it had a most romantic hero, one of Paris's favorites.

But Genoa: hurled between kings of France and dukes of Italy; Spain nearly ruined her; back to France, then Austria. Napoleon entered her in 1796, the year he entered almost everything; it was not till after Waterloo that she was joined to Piedmont again, and although "a center of revolution and tumult" has succeeded in staying Italian ever since.

Well, well. As we climbed into Nicolette again, Genoa took on a glamour from the ages. Like Rome, she didn't *look* old, we told each other—except in spots; but she was. Pieces of her were Roman and had heard the clash of barbaric shields; and out of her harbor (that blue, down below us) had sailed fleets of galleys with slaves rowing . . . all the way to Africa.

At the end of our boulevard was sky and openness. "A view, I expect," said Babs.

It was; a marvelous panorama of Genoa, her *molo* and her coasts. Great blue places showed in the sky, the sun was breaking through; and what that does to such a prospect is beyond words. Colors flew, light and shadow darted about; the Mediterranean was just showing off. Genova la Superba, pearly in light, dark blue in shadow, her lighthouse silvery above the water, merited her title. Surrounding mountains were vivid green, and thunderheads reared above them; far-off mountains were violet and blue, and little golden towns lay at their feet. The whole sublime prospect was amusingly domestic with villages.

We went schooning down a fine long hill right into the view, but neither lasted very long. Nicolette soon had us in tram-tracks and buildings again; on we went, through mud and suburbs. Agreeable suburbs on this side, mostly villas with tall shrubbery over gates and walls; now and then, between them, a glimpse of blue. The Mediterranean was there beside us; we knew it was, because Garibaldi and his intrepid

Thousand had embarked near here on their dash to Naples; but walls and shrubs continued, in the most exasperating way, to intervene.

In a narrow swing of the road a syringa leaned over a wall, almost brushing our heads; it was in full bloom, and its fragrance smote down at us.

"Oh!" we said—and looked at each other; with a quite dreadful pang.

Our terrace, at the farm . . . the syringa bush! For one bleak minute the mud seemed very muddy, the villas impossible; even our Nicolette an inconsequent little creature bumping us, for no particular reason, over long and tiresome miles. . . . Then I laughed, uncertainly; Babs laughed a little too, and something flashed right-side-round, within us; a spark flew, a bell rang; it was Italy again, and the romance of it struck us in the breast-bone—as Italian romance does. The sea shone at us, Nicolette was once more our enchanted conveyance, with a halo of achievement around her little bonnet . . . but I never had before, and never expect to again, such a blow from a syringa bush.

"Well, we *are* rather far away," said my child, a little pensively.

I was surprised at the pensiveness, because Babs is usually so keen on foreign things and doings; but then this was *home* we were thinking of. Entirely different, that.

"It *is* about four thousand miles, you know," she said, still pensively, as she wrenched Nicolette out of a muddy rut.

"Dear me!" I said, dismayed; and then felt a sudden unconcern. . . . It might as well be four thousand as four hundred, I reflected—or four! If we weren't there, we weren't, that was all. . . . Absence was the point, not miles.

And this was all interesting; even the tram-tracks of Nervi, which we were now dodging. The steepness of Nervi, its bowered plunging to the sea, were attractive, as were its palms and camellias; but resorts are not for us. Even small ones. We saw a sign, "FLAT TO SUB-LET," hung from the window of a pink, gaunt-fronted Italian house; and agreed that its English occupants had evidently tired of Nervi and wanted to be somewhere else for a while.

"Don't blame 'em," said Babs, looking temperately about. "Sweet place—but limited. Catch *me* spending a winter here!"

"Exactly," I murmured. "This guide-book says it has '5400 inhab. surrounded by lemon groves' "; and we burst into shouts.

"But where, do you suppose is that fishing-town Russ told us about?" I said, when we had quieted down a little. "She said there was a wonderful one, you know. Out on rocks; a place we couldn't take Nicolette to. Wish we could find that!"

"Let's see that map," and Babs drew up beside a blue view. (Blue was becoming more frequent now.) The coast wriggled in and out and looked wonderful; Boliasco, Recco, Camogli—all little, all probably fascinating. Camogli was in the jog of a large cape that jutted out. Was it a mountainous cape, we wondered? It was hard to tell, on this black-and-white map; we were so used to our grand big one of France, with colors that gave you altitude.

"Might be Camogli," said Babs.

"But a road goes there."

"Perhaps there *is* a road now!"

Filled with visions of a little colorful town with its feet in the water, we started along our hilly route; increasingly lovely, but hard driving. Sharp turns were frequent, donkeys and peasant-carts uncommonly thick; there must have been a market somewhere. (We were always running into Saturday markets, in France.) Many large and shining G.B.'s * were also going swiftly along in search of a stopping place for Sunday—or rather, they doubtless knew just where they were going and were in haste to get there. Your British traveler engages rooms formally in advance; no such lightheartedness over living, for him.

Our little towns all had their charms, but seemed to be the kind you mostly motor through; they gave us transitory feelings. Camogli was unhygienically in a hole at the foot of

* The license plate on an English car, abroad; Great Britain.

a long hill; it was adorably pink and yellow and indigenous, with a little cliff-bound harbor, and boats, and many bewitchments, and I was about to enter the orange-colored *albergo,* in whose doorway a black-eyed Italian girl was artfully draped; but I somehow didn't like the girl's level-eyed expression. . . . After all there were a good many drains in Camogli's streets, and its people stared and seemed a bit ribald; concluding they had been spoiled by what Forster calls "the indefinable corruption which is produced by the passage of a large number of people"—in other words, that it was too near Genoa—we set Nicolette at the hill.

It climbed suddenly, turned hairpin-fashion within its wall and gave us a marvelous view of Camogli below; its bay, blue and violet, dotted with boats, and edged with cliffs; the rugged coast, all the way to Genoa and beyond; dark-wooded hills, pale hills, hills that were lavender and gold and green; rearing clouds that meant a fabulous sunset. . . . We *must* stop on this side of the cape, whose slope we were climbing. Mountainous? It was nothing but mountains. The Punta della Chiappa, it was, and if we once got round the other side of it, that view with the snowy Cottian Alps would be forever behind us.

But would there be a place to stop?

A priest was walking down the hill, a tall old man with an intelligent face; I would ask him. Desperately burnishing up some Italian, I alighted and hastened across the road; he halted gravely, looking down at me with a face not exactly hostile, but utterly impassive. Yes, there was a village farther up; yes, there was an *albergo. Prego,* how far was it? I besought, as he was turning away.

"Three miles more," he said, coldly averting his eyes.

Not impressed or cordial, not a bit Italian, he went on; leaning on his stick.

He hadn't smiled once, I ruefully thought. I did think he would smile. . . . But perhaps priests didn't; perhaps he didn't like having people ask questions of him. Perhaps his flock gossiped. I had never asked directions of a priest before, and I felt as if I never should again. Probably I looked too Protestant; that must have been it. But what would one have to do to look Catholic? It would be convenient sometimes to be able to.

"*You* could!" I said, looking enviously at my child's brown cheek. "You might be Spanish, or anything!"

But Nicolette was getting hot, and roaring. Wondrous glimpses we had, looking back; toward the wooded summit villas began. Only a few; with steep gardens behind them, and cypresses against the sea—there was room, on this beautiful declivity, for only a few; and one had a sign out, and some one standing by its gate.

"Capture by an old white-bearded man," my notes say.

He stood bareheaded in the little garden, looking sharply at everything that passed; the Spider! His head was large and silvery, with great arched brown eyes, his stained beard reached to his waist; somewhere in it, a mouth opened. He was addressing us. Not liking his looks, in fact disliking them extremely, we began driving slowly by . . . but there was a glassed-in dining-room at the end of the villa; we could see through it to the cypresses and the sea. And this seemed the last chance on this side of the Punta.

"Perhaps it would do," I said, very dubiously.

"It's exactly what we want, for view," said Babs, glancing over her shoulder and backing swiftly downhill—a specialty of hers. After an English training of getting into lanes that lead nowhere and have a nice deep ditch on each side, one backs gladly, for miles.

The white beard was hastening to greet us. Had he a room with *due letti?* Assuredly, signora! A thousand beds; or gestures to that effect. Dismount, dismount!

Just not clutching me by the arm he ushered me to the door, where stood a plump signorina; his daughter, evidently; the same great arched eyes and air of greed. She took me up one flight and showed me a room looking on the road. No? "*Allora*"—and I was led up another flight.

Ah, charming! Bright and fresh; white muslin, yellow satin; a long window opening on a balcony. I stepped out. Ye gods! Gardens and gardens dropped away to the sea . . . an old village sat on a point; across infinite bays and coast lines the dim snow of the Cottian Alps rose against a sunset sky. I went swiftly downstairs, but stopped, in flight to the door. Must ask the price! Daughter babbled in an undertone, the white beard moved swiftly; then they turned to me. It would be so much. . . . And meals? Again the consultation.

"È troppo," I said mildly, and moved toward the door. Good heavens, what thieving prices. I remembered what Laigueglia and Varazze had done for us, in that line.

But this time my arm was clutched; daughter, by main force, detained me. Both of them, peering into my face, began making offers, while from outside Babs looked on, surprised. . . . They proclaimed, they chattered, they fairly danced; it should be so much less—so *very* much less!

"Colazione," screamed the daughter, holding up both hands, *"tre lire!"*

They had come down nearly half, and I began to calculate. I had an odd feeling as if wolves were after us; but even in Italy three lire for breakfast is doing pretty well. Yes, that would come within our resources until Monday morning, and then we could go right to a bank.

For we had been forgetting about money. In Varazze we had been too enthralled by the storm to remember it, in Genoa the tumult was such that we had also forgotten it, and all along the coast—who would think of money on the Riviera di Levante?

So here we were on a Saturday afternoon, a bit short. But then our present funds ought to do us for a week-end in Italy; why should the Riviera di Levante be so much dearer than the Riviera di Ponente? Baedeker, gravely balancing, says that the former has "less luxuriant vegetation, although more striking scenery." Which, I wondered, should be the more valuable?

I went out to Babs with the situation.

"Well of course it's a frightful place, or they wouldn't come down that way; but was it really a nice room?"

"Awfully," I said, going round to my side of Nicolette; the signorina meanwhile darting after me, fairly wringing her hands.

"Let's chance it then!" said Babs, placidly ignoring her; and turned in her seat to fish out luggage. A glad tumult at once began; everybody leaped into action. Father seized some of our belongings, daughter helped, a tall, nice-looking *cameriera* did all the lugging up the long stairs; while a thin, ferret-like mother, who spoke French, preceded us to the room, opened our windows for us and with a coolly complaisant *"Voilà, mesdames!"* left us to the ministrations of hot water.

We were glad of them. Genoa seemed to take a deal of washing-off; and when at last we could get out on our balcony, it seemed difficult to leave that lovely scene and go down to a mere dinner. . . .

"But we can see it from down there!" said my child, putting a compelling arm in mine. So down we went into a sort of sub-kitchen, up some steps by a huge rubber-tree, and there we were in the glass box by a seaward window, looking out over gardens at the spectacle of that magnificent coast—and what was above it. The Alps were lilac-tinted with sunset now; it was a purple and gold sunset too . . . a towering sunset, yet everything beneath it melted and chimed; the sea was silver-turquoise, drifting into lilac.

It grew lovelier every moment. The snow peaks dimmed, but the sea kept its light; we did little but stare, or murmur under our breaths about it . . . though we did take time to notice that, beside ourselves, there were only three other guests.

"No wonder they were so bound to get us," and Babs lifted an amused eyebrow. "Not a bad dinner, either, A.B.!"

For the Riviera di Levante, like its western neighbor, had

greeted our arrival with *pollo arrosto;* an odd word, we agreed, for chicken.

"And yet—*pollo; poulet,* you know . . . and *we* have 'pullet.' After all, darling, it might be pollo!"

Strange, one's instinct that everything one meets, clothes, customs, even words, must be like one's own; racial egotism, this, of the finest—and Babs and I didn't think we had any. Graciously allowing the Italian language to retain its own vocabulary, we rose at last, almost pleased with the old Spider and his doings. So far, so good; and we climbed to our balcony.

With immeasurable content we leaned on its railing and watched the stars come out. Golden lights shone in the dark foliage below, a dimmer sparkling of them along the coast; dimmest ones across the bay. Bays and bays, as far as one could see along that shore upon which a purple gauze was falling; bays receding into lilac mistiness, and misty pearls. . . .

"Would that be Varazze, do you think?" said Babs, dropping her face an instant against my shoulder—as was her habit when asking a question more affectionately reminiscent than actual; and I nodded. It was nice to think it might be Varazze, looking across at us. "Cute hotel that was"—she added, with a smile; for we used that word "cute" with fell intent.

"Yes—the best bit of indigenousness we've had. . . . *This* isn't anything in particular—but it's not bad."

"Oh no," said Babs indulgently. "Glad we stayed, aren't you?"

"Heavens, yes!" I said, looking along the coast; "Babs! I can still see the Alps, all gone a sort of lavender. Can you?"

"Uh huh," said she dreamily. . . . Not a poetic response exactly, but one that went with our feeling of effortlessness and rest. "And there must be a fête going on, down in that village—" for bell-ringing had come to us.

The old belfry on the edge of the cliff was indeed doing wonderful things. It had long strings of red-and-yellow lights depending from its top, as well as the little flags we had seen by daylight—like a ship "dressed" for celebration; torches flared under the heavy foliage of trees beside it, and its bells were doing carillons; steady, soft, mad carillons, over and over, flinging and flinging down through the soft dark air like a golden spray. Coming over the mysterious palm-rustlings of the garden below, it was very sweet, and very festive; now and then there came a sound of cheering.

"Great day there tomorrow, probably," said Babs, as we watched the hot glow of torchlight on the old church wall and the thick trees; a strange and beautiful spot of edge-shadowed light, warm and yet greenish, on the vast darkness of the *punta* as it loomed off to sea.

"Well, if it *is* a fête, we shan't have to drive through it, that's one comfort!" I observed.

And we listened, in great ease of heart, to the bells, the rustling garden, and the tide below us faintly splashing; to music, distant voices, a far-away dog barking—night sounds of the Riviera, infinitely soothing.

CHAPTER IV

WALK TO FIND PORTOFINO

MORE bells were ringing, the same diddle-daddle bells, as we dressed, after a breakfast brought us by the watchful-eyed mother.

"Fête a l'église, là," she said, with a brief glance out of the window; then faded silently away.

"Lovely day, rose late," says Babs' diary. We intended to be leisurely; took a short walk before lunch, up a path of cobbled steps past a huge wall covered with ivy, and by a pink church with a white belfry; on up by little gardens and pink-and-white houses, their cats, flowers, and pieces of pottery basking in Sunday-morning sun: then along a sort of summit. A most conversational and dear little path this was, such as one finds over the hills of Sorrento; one of the hill-roads of the peasants, going on and on into the country-side like a little Appian Way. It turned gently downhill among olive trees and bits of vineyards.

Could anything go so divinely with dark-blue shadows and pink villages? We picked little purple flowers we didn't know —and yellow ones, and blue, and white; made arrangements of them, and held them up, and said, "*Do* look!"

Beyond us was the great dip and lift of the back-country, with our path disappearing into it; through the olive-foliage we saw something moving, and up the path came two old peasants in their Sunday best; coats and trousers of golden-brown corduroy, wide black hats. They were tall; their faces were carved and thin. At their unchanged slow pace, which by that time in the morning had doubtless climbed miles of hill-path, they approached us; courteously and in silence. . . . Not a faggot would they carry that day, not a mattock would they lift above their old heads; Sunday, in Italy, is inviolate. They were washed till they shone—such a nice brown shine; even their wooden shoes shone. They were going to the *festa*. From the pocket of one protruded a bottle of wine; from the other's a gay handkerchief.

"Buon' giorno!" I murmured, liking them enormously . . . the dignity, the gravity of them.

" 'Giorno!" they said, their eyes fixed before them.

Tramp, tramp—on and on; the backs of their coats rose among the olives; against the sky. . . . Magnificent! One felt, as one sat there picking flowers, as if a procession of the ages had gone by; all the primal laborings, the splendid simplicities, of earth and time itself.

But the little flowers waved frivolously at us. They quite tittered, in the tiny whiffs of mountain breeze; and round a corner we came upon a little green hut under tall old olives—the smallest *dazio* imaginable. . . . One would have loved to live in that hut. It had a weighing-machine outside; a hat, coat, chair and desk inside; it basked in sunny peace. Could it be that this innocent bit of grass, flowers, and flickering olive-shade was a fateful border-line between villages? And did a remote *dazio* like this one need to be open on Sunday?

The peasants, on their *Domenica,* would scarcely be bringing in anything except a bottle of wine, or their dinners; but the hut was sagely on duty. Italian villages must keep up a valiant protectiveness against each other.

Just then the official strolled into sight; a nice hatless youth in shirt-sleeves, with his hands behind his back. Obviously, in this Sunday idleness, he was extremely bored; still more obviously he wished he had his coat on, but was very glad to see us . . . something to look at beside that view he knew so well; and I could see how hard he tried not to stare. I said *buon' giorno* to him; if I had had a little more Italian, or more energy, that languorous Sunday morning, I should have liked to say more, for judging by his amiable glances the youth would have loved conversation. Contenting ourselves with amiable glances in return, Babs and I took a last look at the sage-green misty mountains (oh, beautiful!) and turned back.

Here was the road, and our garden. The Spider was at the gate as usual, luring in an English party of motorists; indoors, he hovered over them with suggestions for a large meal. Being hungry, they assented and did not ask prices. (Did our familiar-looking tweeds disarm them?) We felt like shouting a warning. . . . He was an efficient old Spider.

An Italian couple at the table next us were having a splendid time ordering all sorts of wine; then they had a splendid time just smiling at each other. She had tea-roses at her breast, a brilliant color, and flashing beautiful dark eyes; he had a camellia in his buttonhole and gestured at the view. (Italians don't often do that.) But the Mediterranean was at its most intense that day; as if giving it a chance, for a time the carillon was quiet.

The windows in our glass box were clean, the sunny world as clear as air; the Italian couple looked down into the garden—at the white iris, and the roses, and talked ecstatically about the *fiori.* (Italians always do that; and do it beautifully.) This couple discoursed for minutes, and with the greatest drama and expression, about a single yellow rose-bush below us and then had plenty more to say about it; *" 'i fioretti!"* I heard them murmur, caressingly. Flowers just went with their feeling that day, their voices were musical and full of *timbre;* it all sounded like Italian poems. . . . We were glad to have them for neighbors; their presence greatly adorned our meager lunch.

For it was; absurdly meager.

"Never again—table d'hôte meals at *that* cheating sort of place!" I said indignantly, as we set out to find Portofino—somewhere along the edge of this unexplored and mountainous *punta.* "You're at their mercy, you see. We'll have to find tea today, Babs, or expire!"

"Yes," said she with feeling. "And *did* you see those English people, when they got their bill? Their faces fell about six inches. Poor things— imagine what it must have been."

"Yes; I saw the Spider's gloating old face when he showed them out!"

But we were approaching the *festa,* down in the village by the cliff, a very aged, brown village this time, with the oldest of tiles; gay with flags and its decorated belfry. Madder and madder grew the clamor of bells, the roaring of voices; for the short, solidly-built street, curving to the piazza and the church, was lined with push-carts, color, and crowds. Behind every cart sat a stout and sunburnt peasant-woman with a bright kerchief on her head, and her best gown and apron on, shouting, and offering her wares—nuts, cakes, or strange brown substances; laughing, and showing her white teeth . . . so white in those dark faces. But one or two of the women sat stodgy and quiet, hands folded on their bulging aprons, their big black eyes turning, almost glowering, this way and that; their goods were not so popular?

For the most part it was a happy and endlessly-vociferating crowd; young peasants were dancing, and old ones gossiping. Peasants banked solidly around the booths, or under the old trees, and somewhere in the mobs was music—a braying band. The bells were deafeningly loud.

Noise must be necessary to one of these holidays, the peasants seemed to bask in it; for them it wouldn't be a *festa,* without this fearful clamor going on. . . . Wincing, edging ourselves along, often forced apart by hurtling dancers, or (once) by a file of serious old peasants who knew where they were going and intended to get there—in a straight line, too, no matter what foreign obstacle was in the way (needless to say, the foreign obstacle melted before them)—we nevertheless kept track of each other out of the tail of an eye, making our way toward the low wall beyond Ruta's church on the cliff's edge and leaning over it with amazement; for here at last was what we were seeking—intimacy with that marvelous coast.

Deep water, far below, was surging quietly yet tremendously about; emerald, violet and sapphire, with sun deeply mixed in it. Cypresses stood against the sea and sky, mountains rose from bays; just under us were rocky chasms and cliffs . . . and everywhere, dropping below us, the bright charm of Ligurian vegetation.

Never had we known a Mediterranean to equal this. Off Capri it is all a blueing blue—wonderful, intoxicating, but just blue; here it was ever-changing. Dark and light, one tint and another, sapphire flashing into silver; colors that scintillated, tide-rips that divided gentian blue from sunlit, ferocious green; shifting shapes of rosy-purple where a rock nearly came through. . . . For all its depth, you could *feel* the bottom of the sea—the surge and strength of the water, and jelly-fish helpless in it; crabs crawling or tilting across it, and above them, with all their heads pointed one way, the wandering, hovering, rock-evading schools of little Mediterranean fish, whose shadows we could see, a true shadow-color, on the sandy bottom of those pellucid depths.

Like two children, holding on to each other, we leaned as far over the edge as we dared. Gazing into the sea, anywhere, gives one many sorts of hair-lifting sensations . . . a good look into another element is inevitably an awesome thing; and here, the very heart of it seemed lying open. A wonderful gurgle and slop it was making down there, in and out of caves and chasms; soft and ominous-sounding, though not enough to put a Medusa to sleep, unless she had her ear right by it; but there is something immensely satisfying in hearing a wave plunge at a cliff. The wave has to do it; the cliff doesn't mind. Thud! says it serenely.

The yelps of the *festa* were rather loud, even here; we escaped by a paved path round the corner of an old house with two astonished hens on its door-step. Babs was sure we were trespassing, going straight into somebody's farmyard; we were, but we came out again. Italian paths do not end in farmyards; and after a bit of vineyard and a goat or two tethered in a sightly spot under olives, this one set us reassuringly in the open.

Goats like views, but these lucky animals had both situation and provender; plenty of cliffs to please the goatish eye, and tall grass with flowers in it. One brown creature with great topaz eyes took a step toward us and stopped, chewing, her head high in air. "I *think* I like you; but would you mind not coming any nearer?"

We said "Hello goat," and passed on, single file.

It *was* a narrow, up-and-down little path, and we hoped it would lead us to Portofino; for that is the region of *The Enchanted April.*

It led us to the cliff again; led us into a charming dell like a small Vale of Tempe, with a little stream, and flowers, and more grass—we had seen so little in southern France that we were thrilled by it; led us to old solitary pines, then out again into sunshine with the sea beautifully glinting at us—and into frequent domesticity. At last we came plump against what seemed the end of everything; the mossy wall of a cottage, and its rain-barrel.

Round this into deeper duskiness, however, twisted the intrepid path. Where could it go? except into more back-yards. . . . Even my faith in it wavered; and Babs, who was growing more and more annoyed with its impertinencies, halted—in a sort of rage. She would *not* go on!

I ran up some damp steps and took a peep beyond that rain-barrel—it jutted out at the top of them in a most forbidding way. Did our thoroughfare go on?

My goodness, it did. It must be a road; and this was one of its villages. Its damp and much-worn pavement twisted between a few old houses with stone door-steps, and bits of flowers behind little fences; round the corner of one of them bright sunshine fell on the stones . . . and there was a young peasant woman sitting flat down on them, her bare brown feet stretched in front of her. She stared a moment in astonishment, then smiled sweetly at me: a lovely creature in dark blue, with a red shawl about her shoulders. Her head was bare. On her lap was a bowl of greens.

" 'Permess!" I murmured as I stepped across her feet; then fled guiltily on.

A house or two, and more bursts of flowers; a gate where

two women were talking—nice, bareheaded creatures who smiled at me as the other one had done . . . and then the path switched upward into the safe shadows of a wood. Shadowy, damp, ancient; girdled with beauty. Like a dream, all of it . . . but I felt storm behind me. Babs, when she caught up with me, was positively panting—with her indignant dislike of "poking around into everything, the way tourists do!" but I pleaded—our necessity of finding Portofino—and persuaded, and was forgiven; and after this the path behaved in a most exemplary manner. It took us into one or two wood-shaded villages, only not so backyardy as the others, and we looked for tea and there wasn't any, and we felt thinner and thinner, but so pleased with life we didn't care; and at last we were out, climbing to the top of the promontory.

Real, Swiss climbing, this was; you leaned over and scrabbled, clutched at heather bushes, and sat down often to rest. But every time you rested the view had grown wider; a pink house here or there, broom against the sea's blue, the heads of the great pines below you, and the air wonderful; and a party of athletic English people, we were glad to see, didn't make any better time than we did, and panted just as much . . . till by and by there was the seeming top of things—and still the path went on.

But it was good striding now; we soon reached the *semaforo,* with cliffs and the sea and breeze and inspiration—a look at the two Rivieras, and a world of mountains besides. Alps and Alps; hordes of green foot-hills, dim snowy peaks . . . and the sea beating far below.

> The world is great: the wind comes rushing by,
> I wonder where it comes from; sea-birds cry. . . .

For in its sweep and color, with the crying of sea-birds, this height was magnificent. Worth ten times the climb. Besides, we had wanted to climb; to have our noses in a cliff and clutch bushes so as not to fall over backward. In France we had had no time for scrabbling about, "wasting" days on foot, and this was just the chance we had been longing for.

You couldn't save time by motoring, out here. Today's path, darksomeness and hayricks and all, had been the quintessence of romance; we had had all the enchanted April feelings and a million more; we looked about us, breathed the rushing winds, and marveled at the turmoil of the sky. We wondered if that bright-colored village in a nook of the cliffs could be Portofino; decided it could not, and swung off down the other side of the ridge.

It was a fine trail we were on, pine-needled and good going; feeling exhilarated, we flew.

After a bit the path changed to yellow clay, became wider, and plunged into woods. We plunged too, but not for long; this mountainside was too lovely for speed.

The wood itself was a marvel, and delayed us . . . a wood one might find at home on some steep mountainside radiant with spring. Only our woods do not have five-foot paths hair-pinning down through them; and many of the flowers were English. White may adorned the greenery; there were primroses, enormous wood-anemones, and in a clear grassy space, one immense cowslip. Almost tauntingly immense. I gave a covetous reach in its direction, then did not pick it. It was too much a solo in those Italian woods.

There was English ivy running up the trees, but brighter, paler green—a lighthearted, Riviera tint very much its own; there were multitudes of purely Riviera flowers; altogether, florally speaking, we did not know quite where we were, but concluded we were walking in a wood, so it didn't matter. The path grew steeper and more slippery; at last flung us out upon a bit of rocky level—and the mountains.

Merely the whole tops of the Apuan and Cottian Alps—under swift-moving storm-clouds. They wiped themselves into that sweeping gray and yellow; they might have been as high as Himalayas. Light and shadow flew, danced, drifted about; there were yellow-green patches, purple drivings, dark-blue valleys; a snowy bit peeping—now in brilliance, now submerged. . . . And to westward was the sea, and to eastward was the sea, now blown into wild waves; for we had come out on a sort of divide, and here were the two Rivieras again, and what that means only those who have stood on that height on such a day, can know.

Below us, though plainly visible, were flower-beds and parked motors— Italy simply can't be wild or natural very long; and though we could have lived a lifetime on those Himalaya driftings, the very gorgeousness of them sent us along down.

As we reached our door, down came the hurricane. The swashings of the garden were really notable, with the fat shiny palm trees turned into raving maniacs; no mountains were to be seen, or anything but storm, and through all the tumult one heard the pounding of the sea.

* *

Not another guest was dining tonight, and in the sub-cave where the family ate I detected an atmosphere of *laissez-faire*. Daughter, loudly haranguing, was serving the Spider and herself to food; a single maid trod unambitiously over the stone-paved floor; the thin mother did something at a side-table. A strange scent was on the air; some beetroot-colored sausages presently arrived. We abruptly returned them, and after a long pause, Maman again approached.

"Voilà, mesdames!" she said uninterestedly, and a finger of thin leather steak was on our plates, with some attenuated leaves of lettuce—the early-spring kind that grows in one's garden, and is really too small to pick. . . . After that, an equally attenuated orange. Coffee was extra, in this place, but we had it; then we stalked over to the garage, rifled Nicolette of some chocolate she had in her door pocket and climbed upstairs, too furious to articulate. But we got out our maps, and promptly cheered up; we even discovered a Wodehouse we hadn't read, and what with *Sam the Sudden*, and the gorgeous storm pelting at the windows, had a delightful evening.

For we really like vicissitudes.

CHAPTER V

THE HIGH DRIVE TO SPEZIA

THE nice chambermaid brought us our breakfast next morning; we were glad of that. She had no French, but we had struck up in a wordless way a sort of friendship, and this morning she looked at us, I thought, almost pityingly. Did she know about that dinner the night before, then? Sweet of her, if she did.

We hastened to pack.

I had to wait some time for the bill; no one apparently was up. I was shown into a ceremonial and musty *sala,* a very Italian apartment with ponderous brown carved furniture —shabby, however, and with dirty yellow curtains; but it had the view.

Not much view this morning except wet palms; for it was raining. The sky was sadly gray. The Spider, just out of bed and not too heedfully dressed, with a bit of soiled nightshirt protruding from his bosom, came stepping softly in from a den he had next door. I caught sight of appalling confusion—heaps of dingy bedclothes, utensils, garments; unspeakably watchful was his eye, as he sat down at an immense brown table and began to write. He wrote and wrote; I felt a foreboding. What in the world was he doing at such length?

Briskness suddenly came upon him; with a look of subdued triumph he laid a long document before me, then, not quite rubbing his hands, stood back to view the effect. Ha! as I thought; the bill came to nearly twice the amount agreed upon. (*Pranzo,* 40 *lire,* I read; that feast, last night.)

And then the battle began. The Spider was majestic. Oh no, madame was quite mistaken; he would call *mia figlia. Mia figlia,* in a very soiled dress, came, and corroborated him. Everything the old villain said was just right.

"Si si, signora—si si!" with virtue unutterable.

To my great disadvantage this part of the combat was in Italian. I was fairly good at Italian figures, however, though not at repartee, and kept right to them; *camera* this much, *colazione 3 lire—*

"No, no!" screamed *mia figlia. "Cinque, cinque!"* and she held up five stubby fingers—or rather, cast them dramatically at the air.

Yes, it ought to have been that, young woman, I thought; but that's not what you *said. "Tre lire, signorina,"* I rejoined, silkily. "You told me so, many times."

"Cinque!" she screamed again, with an apprehensive glance at her parent.

They conferred, whereat daughter ran off and returned with Maman, also inadequately attired; very draggly and unhemmed as to skirt edge. . . . A rainy Monday morning was evidently a slack time at this establishment, since not a car was out, and they doubtless relied for sustenance on the passing motorist. They had a pretty garden; no wonder the Spider kept watch and ward at the gate.

And now I had three of them to combat. I felt like calling Babs in from Nicolette—but at any rate Maman could speak French. That was a relief. She had come in, composed but acid, and now took a lofty tone. . . . What was this? Madame objected to the bill? This was unheard of. Of *course* those were the figures agreed upon . . . and we went through the items again; daughter, when it came to breakfast, throwing her eyes to heaven and her fingers at the ceiling as before. Had there been a gifted but mistaken parrot somewhere in Mademoiselle's ancestry?

"Cinq, cinq!" cried she, also shifting to the French tongue; but she and her mother exchanged an uneasy glance.

"You told me three lire, mademoiselle, and you know perfectly well you did," I said, growing angry; it was only a slight link in their chain of lies, but this barefaced repetition of it was annoying. And the obloquy of having to argue with these worms. I strode to the door.

"Babs!"

My ever-blessed and loyal defender came in. With scarcely a word from me, she understood; and her young brow darkened. Anything my child hates is a row of any sort—she also loathes using a foreign tongue; but here was a clear case, and A.B. with her back against the wall. Worth rowing about . . . and one could see these things darting through her mind as in very good, grammatical, if halting French she told those three harpies exactly what I had told them, repeating my figures with precision.

I looked at her devoutly while she did so; pleased with her clear mind, touched by her loyalty (I am always that), but also very much surprised. I never knew she could speak French like that! And I that had been laboring with garages all the way down through France. . . .

But a conference was taking place. The harpies had listened; had watched my child's coldly-disgusted eyes in a contemplative silence tinged with something new. What, I could not tell; but it was new. The Spider, after a whisper in his spouse's ear, tiptoed away with an air of lofty detachment, while Maman, pursing up her mouth, seated herself before the document. . . . Since madame was so unsatisfied with the terms, a slight reduction might possibly be made.

"Voilà, mesdames!" and with an air of indescribable moral loftiness she put the bill before us. It was scarcely reduced at all. I gave it back to her.

"I will not pay it like this, madame," I said.

"Non voulez—you will not pay it? You *will* not?" suddenly shrieked Maman, rising and rushing to a bell in the hall and ringing it frantically. "Marie! Marie!" she screamed—though I noticed nobody came. *"Va chercher un gendarme!* Get a policeman, Marie! This food that I have given—we will see if I shall give it for nothing. Marie! Marie!" and she ran crazily up one flight, down a flight toward the kitchen and back, chattering and shrieking, doing the demented with

great success; daughter careering after her saying, "Maman, Maman!" in soothing tones, taking to perfection the part of the reasonable and interceding *figlia;* but still no maid appeared.

"Do get a *gendarme,* madame!" I said, as she collapsed, panting, on a chair. "That is just who I want to see. Get one —or I will go for one myself!" and I turned very purposefully toward the door. Disgusting apes! Why hadn't I thought of this before? I would *walk* to Camogli, if necessary, and get a gendarme—

"Non madame, non!" implored daughter, clasping my arm.

"One moment, signora," interposed the bland voice of the Spider, now reappearing powerfully on the scene. "My wife is a little overwrought;" and between them they conveyed her into the *sala.*

Babs raised a sardonic eyebrow at me. Yes, it was time for him to intervene; their best card had been played. Maman was splendid on hysterics, but the Spider's rôle was to be, throughout, that of the benevolent host; slightly pained, but benevolent.

His wife removed, he sat himself ponderously at the table, and once again we went over those infernal items. I stood over him this time. Every lira was a scene of battle; at last the Spider sat back, surveying me with arched eyes of wounded virtue. (He reminded me of a whiskered old Polish drawing-master I had once had.) Now for it! The bill still stood at far more than the original figure; expecting uproar, I told him we would drive to a bank in Santa Marguerita for the extra (and extorted) francs.

He was quite calm.

"Zo!" he said; and I knew he was German. "Well, pay me what you have, madame." I counted out almost our last lira. Anything, to get out of that stifling place into the fresh air; but Maman, now recovered and watching us from the doorway, was not so calm.

"Mais—vos bagages!" she screamed. "You shall not go, with all your luggages! No, no! Give them to me!" and she rushed,

panting, at Nicolette. "Give me—" and she seized the handle of a suit-case. Babs pulled it helpfully out for her; *mia figlia* was now to the fore, handling luggage like a female porter.

"Here is the steamer rug, madame; would you like that?" I politely inquired, passing it to her. She snatched at it, muttering, with a strange look. "And the coats. . . . You'd better have those, don't you think?" I piled them into her astonished arms. "All right, Babs," and I banged my door. . . . Nicolette, who had been consuming petrol for some time, leaped away.

"Pah!" I said, and took a long breath.

"Exactly," said Babs, giving me a feeling glance. "Hope we'll find the stuff there when we go back!"

Up the hill and through a dripping tunnel; mud and mud; wide puddles everywhere. We sped furiously through them, and along a wood-bordered road, then down a long twisting hill on the other side of the *punta.*

How unspeakably sweet the kind, sane, outdoor world seemed once more; how wonderful the wood-fragrances. We gazed around with hungry eyes . . . though we couldn't really enjoy anything yet; we still felt the fingers of that place in our necks. . . . Soon came the clean gray sea and a very wet little Santa Margherita, with streaming pavements and awnings. A few brave Englishmen in macintoshes were striding about its streets.

Really a picturesque little ancient town, Santa Margherita, with fishing-boats, and a park by the sea; but bank, and nothing but bank, was in our souls. We wheeled, questing, along its little sea-front: this *banca* and that, fruit-shops and a *farmacia,* but not the Banca Italiana.

"Just wait and I'll ask," I said, jumping out; and assailed a large, elderly Englishman in a yellow mac.

Regarding me very kindly, he not only told me where to go but took me there himself; into a little roofed arcade containing a market, with cabbage-leaves thick underfoot—I can still feel them scrunching under my astonished feet—and to some stately steps beyond. . . . No wonder we could not find our *banca;* it was beautifully tucked away. My tall guide, conversing pleasantly all the time, and explaining what a nasty wet winter it had been in Santa Margherita, even went with me into the marble interior and introduced me to just the right person. Balm and benediction! I thought it extraordinarily kind of him; and the young Italian in the brass cage, beside speaking excellent English, was so honest-eyed, normal, and kind-looking, such a contrast to the vicious hysteria we had been dealing with—that before I knew it or really meant it, I was telling him about our hold-up.

His smile faded; he listened intently.

"*Where* did you say that was, signora?" he asked.

I told him, and he nodded grimly; seemed to have heard of the place before.

"But that was robbery!" he said; and his face was grave. "This must be looked into!"

"Oh, thank you—I wish it might be!" I said, astonished; and hastened away.

Comforting, to know that somebody else felt about it as we did . . . and there outside was the nice Englishman standing by Nicolette and entertaining my child. It was good to see an amused look in those eyes again; thanking him, and regretting our haste, we whirled off.

"*What* a nice little town," I said, looking gratefully back at its yellow houses, its terra-cotta awnings against the sea; Babs was greatly comforted to hear what the bank-man had said, and Nicolette, as if to do her bit toward consoling us, ground bravely up the three miles of slimy hill.

"Think of having to go *back* over all this," said my child disgustedly. For it was rarely that we retraced our steps.

"Yes, but we shouldn't have seen Santa Marguerita if we hadn't. This road must be a sort of loop, and we were going straight along. . . . Besides, we've learned something, darling."

"What?" said Babs interestedly.

"Not to deal with a white beard," said I.

"Quite!" and my child grinned all the way up the rest of the hill.

Here was the tunnel again; the detested garden-front; indoors the Spider, magnificently moral as ever, and eyeing us, I thought, with regret.

"So you return, signora," said he.

"I return," I answered, laying notes on the table. He counted them. Madame, from her doorway as usual, looked languidly on.

"Nos bagages?" I said, wheeling to her.

"Ici, m'dame," said she unemotionally, opening a door. It was all there; but madame still eyed me, as I brushed past her down the steps; pensively blinking her little eyes. That look was just one straw too much.

"Vous êtes une—voleuse, madame!" I said with calm, collecting my epithet after a second's hesitation; then I wondered what happened when you called somebody, in French (or thought you did), the feminine of a thief. . . .

Nothing happened. She blinked at me thinly, mildly; without triumph, without malice, without regret; the face of negation, pensive still . . . poker face! I thought; and climbed swiftly into Nicolette, who again, like an angel, leaped forward. Something made me look up, and in a window above us was the nice maid, looking out; guardedly waving to us, and smiling so!

"Look, Babs!" I cried, and waved back. I felt like kissing my hand to her—sweet soul, at the risk of a berating, or perhaps of losing her job, leaning out to show us we had one friend at least in that beastly den.

In a moment we were up the hill and out of sight; what a liberation. But how tired I was; as if I had been pulled through a dozen knotholes.

"Not bad—to get away from that hole?" said Babs, reading my thoughts as usual, and laying a hand on my knee.

It wasn't. No medieval soul emerging from *purgatorio* could have been happier than we two, speeding down a long delightful hill toward Rapallo with a free little Nicolette doing gay things under us, and the free winds from the sea blowing over us.

An artist had once raved to us about Rapallo as a charming place to paint in, hence a shade of disappointment crept over me as we drove down its very neat streets: streets that were so freshly pink-and-yellow washed, so faggot-broomed and scrubbed. . . . All the little towns along here are desperately neat.

But the great thing about Rapallo is that it is nearly in the water. Deep, green sea-water was swashing it everywhere; deep, right off the rocks, deep down from a small stone jetty, or under old houses that jutted (sketchably) over it; especially deep and swashing, round Rapallo's rocky islet covered with an old brown castle, only a few rods off shore. A lovely islet, walled, cliffy, and romantic. Rapallo's little roadway ran around the water-front, which was well-decked with inns, horse-cabs, pleasure-boats, and flowers; across the green water of the little bay rose the Punta, wild and purplish; altogether the scene was an enthralling one—mountainous, pink-villaged and blossoming, yet with everywhere this lively swash of active—unusually active—Mediterranean.

Rain was now dancing hard on Rapallo's pavements, and we bolted into a prosperous-looking restaurant with steam on its windows. Here were pleasant waiters, and fresh little tables with flowers; also mounds of most superior spaghetti, smoking hot. . . . It was good to see a fat pink plateful of something decent; and the nice Italians, eating near by at little tables, beamed at us and looked benevolent and appreciative—of what, we had no idea, but after Ruta it was heavenly to be looked benevolently at—and when we dashed out to Nicolette again, behold she was standing in a pool of yellow water.

"*Very* bad for tires!" said Babs, beaming at me.

"Frightful," said I; "but her top is washed—all lovely."

"She needed a bath. Nothing else we ought to see here, is there?"

"Not a thing, thank goodness," said I.

And then I discovered from a chance sign—our map said nothing about it—that this same little road would lead us to the village of Portofino. A ray of sun arrived like a gleam of approval on our undertaking, just as we were meditating what to do; and though we should not have, we took that wonderful drive along the twisting shore.

It seemed to us, with our convenient *penchant* for the present, quite the loveliest yet. The most concentrated little drive; excitingly narrow, wooded and wild, and right beside the water. Through our Santa Marguerita again (we looked at it with pleased attention, now), close by its little walled *molo,* cram full of storm-bound fishing-boats, then along more wooded shore; up and down the sharpest little hills—hills that landed you almost *into* the deep, splashing water at the very scariest of their down-dipping corners.

"Awnk!" said Nicolette, putting a serious little nose around them.

But we met nothing, and soon turned down a lane of old houses to the little square-ended harbor that is Portofino. At a corner rises Portofino's church, its twin belfries sociably against the wooded cliff . . . for except for a small gap outward to the light and infinity of the sea, the walls of the promontory leap straight from the little harbor, towering above it like "the mountainsides of dreams."

Stay? This was the place to stay in; what was Rapallo to this, said we, abandoning Nicolette on the first inch of the quai and leaping down on the beach. . . . Here were actually awnings, and orange trees in tubs: a little *ristorante,* with a pension attached, all freshly painted and everything.

And we had no more time for Rivieras.

Rather maddening, for one could spend a year here; the finest spot we saw, along this coast. The cliffs were all boulders and flowering shrubs, below them the same depths and deep-sea colors we had watched from the cliffs of Ruta. (The *punta* specialized on those.) On their seaward points white foam was splashing, but in their pools, leaned-over by gnarled cedars

THE UNEXPECTED ENTRANCE TO SARZANA

and tropic shrubs, was mirror-like calm. Little harbors they are, into which with care a fisherman can squeeze his boat. And in the pools were deep-sunken rocks, violet where sea-water was green; purple-gray water mostly, with (deep in it) the backs of big fishes barely moving. When they moved there was a flash of crystal—of blue and emerald and crystal, if a sunbeam broke from the clouds and shot across.

We did what we could, in our blink of time; climbed around, up the path, and back again. Reflections in that harbor were enough; reflections from the colored boats, from beautiful arching shapes of shadow under the old houses. Bits of the belfry waggling at one's feet; slits of scarlet and silver, of mountainside purple; bits of blue dancing about, and green, and gold. . . .

Nicolette took us hastily up the lane, and as we drove again out of Rapallo, "O lamb!" I shrieked, "look at the *roses* climbing up that palm tree!"

For it was the best smother of pink and yellow we had seen. And they were large, pedigreed-looking roses; not just ramblers. . . . We climbed a hill with a wall above a high bank, where flowers lapped on vines, and blossoming vines ate up trees; I was quite mad with the little banksia roses—the apricot-tinted ones. They climb up tall elms, and hang down in streamers over one's head; they frolic and rollick over everything. The scent of them, as we drove, was ravishing; rather like wild apple blossoms.

A sort of Corniche, this road. Very near the sea we went, for miles and miles; sometimes delightfully high up, looking off over its red sails and green shore; sometimes close down beside it. Zoagli huddled at the mouth of a wild ravine, with the sea splashing almost into its woods; beyond was a region of slate-quarries, and then Lavagna. . . . I managed to remember that a black-board is called a *lavagna*—from the slate in this village, of course—and how thrilling that was. Or perhaps the village was named from a black-board?

"Charming drive, on a bunk road," say my notes. "Coast very rich and floral, to Sestri."

Nicolette was brisk and able, and she needed to be, for beyond Sestri Levante, a pink-cliffed spot with an old Genoese castle, the railroad plunged itself into a tunnel apparently for good and all, but we turned inland and began to climb. Was this good-by to the Italian Riviera?

"Good-by, Riviera!" cried we, most torn at leaving it—and scrabbling round in our seats to stare at it. "There's a red sail—good-by, good-by!"

And we swarmed and climbed, coming out again on the swell of an arid mountain—and there it was below us; and we swarmed and swarmed, and saw it again and again . . . just as lovely, though smaller.

We took a generous swing up a wild valley to the northeast, only to swing generously back again; folded around great folds of wild rocky hills with the sea falling below—and behind us a blue charabanc, full of girls, trying to get by.

"Climbed a wild pass," my notes remark. "Gorgeous bushes of white heath-like flower; lavender bushes too. Nice girls, in despair; shut in behind curtain. Rain. Mountains the more gorgeous. Water for N. Hot work!"

For we had got well beyond the charabanc now—it had been intermittently trying to pass us—and stopped at a little dashing brook that wanted to hurl itself into the road, but only succeeded in hitting a stone culvert. We filled our water-bottle and Nicolette's radiator, and she hissed and sputtered and said "Ha! Sst! this is like old times, isn't it!"—but she didn't boil; not she. This was one of her magnificent days on hills; so after gazing at the unforgettable mountains, and collecting a violet or two, we went churning valorously over the top of the wild divide.

"We're up, by jinks!" muttered Babs.

We were indeed; very high up, I told her. More than two thousand feet that little red bonnet, with drops still on it—"Ha!" I said, "that's a rhyme!"—had climbed, in what seemed a few minutes.

And wildness still kept beautifully on. It seeemed a long time since we had been in real wildness—as much as six days;

with our usual inconsistency, we were rejoiced to be doing something arduous again. We had had quantities of rest on the Riviera, flowers and foot-trips and lulling waves; now we were all for adventure . . . and Nicolette—flinging up, as it were, her tail—set off with arrant joy along the tops of things.

Where were charabancs now? After grinding, it is fun to fly. And the sun had come out.

Nothing in sight on the little road but us. How one does love to be a pig, when traveling, and have it all to oneself: villages, animals, scenery, everything. (For we were beginning to have peeps at the Mediterranean again; blue now, with wooded depths plunging to it.) And a high mountain road in Italy, in April (I can vouch for no other time), is a fine spot for these egotisms. We met scarcely a donkey-cart.

How blue the sea was, now! We wanted dreadfully to go down a lane of deep red mud to Levanto, which has a fort on the romantic sea; but refrained. . . .

For we were going to Spezia, and there was doubtless any quantity of dramatic road between us and it—but all of it might not be as good as this. This reminded us of our beloved G.C.s, in France, that were so tiny and marble-smooth; only this little Italian *scorciatoia* was blue-gray, not marble white. . . . Along it, even without going down to the sea's edge, there would be quantities of charms; Babs consoled me, and I consoled Babs, and every other second there was a new burst of Corniche-like scenery; altogether, we decided we weren't too badly off as it was. My notes say:

"View of the sea. Perfect village, with church tower, on wooded point. Looked so complete, with its church to take care of it, like a brood of chickens with a nice hen-tail sticking up among them. We felt very comfortable about that village. . . . Wild, rolling, pink and purple country; distant spots of dark woods.

"Strange craggy village (Baracca), great old stuccoed houses stained a violent pink or bright blue, stables below, dilapidation above. A woman and about ten children in fantastic colors stared at us from great dark place like a blacksmith's shop; a red fire blazing, everything all smoke, two cows in rear, straw on the floor. Tousle-haired youth gazed at us with a barbaric stare, like an animal.

"In another village a virile woman in blue, wonderful color, strong and graceful as a panther, her black hair in her eyes, was splitting wood on her stone step. About her stood various children in red, orange, and pink, very dirty; fire blazing in legged black pot, wet clothes in basket. . . . She was going to boil clothes on that fire, or know the reason why! She gave us one glance from her superb dark eyes—scornful, half-savage; then raised her ax over her head and went on splitting."

A mountain Venus, that woman; she should have been a masterpiece in a gallery. The pictures that were wasting, along this road! yet who could stop and photograph this sort of thing? That mountain tiger of a woman would have hurled her stick of wood at us; maybe the ax. But she should have been preserved in some sort of very permanent art or sculpture, at once. So many of the peasant-women one sees, should —yet they are apt to be thicker; few had that victorious, long-waisted build. It did seem wicked to have her wasted just splitting wood—though she was sublime doing that; the stained pink of the house behind her, the fire, the pot, and the fury of her, all helped . . . though I should have hated to be at her mercy just at that moment.

"It *is* Monday, isn't it?" said Babs, steering us carefully up a rocky hill. "Wash day . . . huh!"

"Yes, my dear; 'the day of dolor.' . . . Everywhere apparently—even in the Apuan Alps!" and Babs smiled.

"Italy should wash on Wednesday," she said. "Just to be different!"

We gained the top of the hill and a descent at once began; though we did not know it, a great descent. "Road winding down through mountains," say my notes; "peak after peak, sharp and clear-shaped. A wilderness of peaks, all olive trees and terraces; often capped with a village." The sun came out, cutting across one of them, lighting up the mellow colors of the old walled town on its top, its terraced and vineyarded base deep in shadow. An exquisite sight.

"Tiny, intense valley," the notes continue. "Lovely natural brook, golden brown, with fringes of untroubled trees. Natural bushes; so sweet and restful! Especially grand village, as we wound down a long hill, crowded, slapped on the hillside below us."

I think that village was Tago. It had a belfry, and rare old color; its huddled roofs were of purplish tile. Across a stream that ran at its foot, we swung up a hill of noble and ancient trees in earliest spring leaf.

"*What* are they?" asked Babs; then, "Why, they're chestnuts!"

The first chestnut woods we had seen in Italy. Rough-barked trees, pictorially branched, holding fast to that hillside; heart-melting now with that airy foliage—and with anemones in the grass below. Italian thrift it is, to have the profitable chestnut tree clothing these impossible slopes of which Italy is full; besides, they help hold the hillsides together.

But the spring beauty of that climbing wood. We were inexpressibly moved. . . . This was the *real* spring; the mountain sort we knew, with sharp air and rushing brooks, reluctant budding, and fragile little wind-swayed flowers clinging to the slopes.

The top of the climb—a curve—the chestnut wood was gone; but Babs' hand was in mine . . . till the next precipice of a grade. Strenuous driving today, sharp moments with a little slipping Nicolette; but when is it not strenuous, in the hill-country?

"On and on," say the notes; "endless valleys. A walled town, overlooking the wide bowl of a valley; the River Vara and its stony gorge; waste land. Floods, probably . . . rare, here, to find even a foot of land not cultivated. Pine woods beyond."

Again we climbed quite high, only to slide down an immense descent toward Spezia and its bay. Literally slide, for the road had turned to slimy yellow clay with Nicolette doing a rather frightening "shimmy" across its surface; and a gentle rain had come on. A very scared G.B. met us, crawling down a pitch, with two nice-looking people in it; they gave us a distracted smile and bow.

"To Spezia via a romantic col," says my child's diary. We felt as if we had been over six cols.

There should now have been a huge view over the Golfo di Spezia, but the drizzle of rain had thickened it. "Top of hill," say the notes; "lovely bit of snowy Alps, very dim. Pinkish. View of bay, dim and smoky. Battle-ships in bay. Smoky chimneys, biggish town."

We didn't like Spezia . . . smoke, and battle-ships, and a large, appalling look; *and* outskirts? We abhor outskirts. Stay here? No, we would stay at some little place on the coast near by; but first, oh first! let us find a *pasticherria* and tea.

Spezia looked large enough to contain both. We slipped and slid past naval warehouses, through black mud and over tram tracks, finally reaching the town's clean flat paving-stones, which we were very glad to meet. We drove inquiringly through its late-afternoon crowds—busy black-clad men, deep in talk with each other, who had too much to think of in their metropolis (foremost naval harbor of Italy), to waste glances on a little prowling G.B. They were all over the street, but not concentratedly; Spezia's traffic did not approach the mobs (or the noise) of Genoa, so we found a *pasticherria* very easily—a nice little marble-floored bakery-place with a shining coffee-urn—last word of progress, in Spezia!—on a counter at the far end.

In spite of Spezia's size and smoke there was no tea to be had, but *caffè latte* would do; we sank happily down before a marble-topped table which was being strenuously, indeed feverishly, wiped for us by the young padrone and his chatty little wife.

Never was anything so hot and reviving as that *caffè latte;* also it is pleasant to be received by perfect strangers with enthusiasm. They beamed as they dashed about recruiting our supplies; they stood, arms akimbo, admiring the mere fact of our being there. Such a warm, cake-scented little haven they made of it—with Spezia surging by outside; we felt beautifully protected. After a bit I opened the map—we always take it with us into these places as a sort of mental dissipation, to match the cakes; was there a place we could stay?

Ha! Portovenere, at the point of the bay, looked nicely out on the tip of things. We had never heard of Portovenere, to be sure; the guide-book mentioned a day-trip down there by boat, but said nothing about hotels. Greatly daring, I asked the padrone and his wife.

"Si si, signora! Un' albergo, si!" in tones rich with reassurance.

They and their friends gathered round, deeply interested; they appealed to other friends who came in. *Wasn't* there a hotel at Portovenere? Animated discussion followed; much affectionate jargon and many beaming nods. *Si si si!* Portovenere was *"molto bello; bellissimo!"* We were advised—yes, begged, to go there.

How nice. We would go. It didn't look far on the map. We paid our microscopic bill, bade our hosts farewell and departed into the dusk of Spezia, feeling a little lost.

Dusk had fallen with strange speed; but Babs seemed to know where to go, and took one dark turning after another. Then we swung harborwards—and into black mud, with a fat dog persistently in our way.

Nicolette and he floundered out, and up a little rise we had a sudden look-out over Italy's naval preparations: acres of military yards, docks and derricks, and a strip of harbor amazingly thick with naval craft.

Annoyingly thick; we could hardly see the water; and what a lovely bay this otherwise might have been. The old Romans called it the Harbor of the Moon; apparently even they thought it was pretty.

Soon came the Arsenal and its high wall, with sentries peering suspiciously down at us from their boxes; then we climbed a hill. Firm red gravel arrived under us, there was a view of bays and islands, and it was suddenly lovely.

The air was clearer out here; daylight again, with sweet sunset tints on the dim Alps beyond the bay. We wound in and out, above little coves and beside olive groves; through a soiled old salmon-pink village curled very possessively round its fishing-boats, which lay in a deep lobe of harbor below.

Another deep lobe of hilly-sided harbor had two villages on it. One looked uncommonly steep and precise; we stared at it, then burst into laughter; that village was camouflage! just sheds for sea-planes, painted on their fronts to look like a village and on top to look like modernistic meadows, great strips of green and pink. As we looked, a dark hole arrived in the village; a door had opened, and a sea-plane floated out.

Then real meadows began again.

It seemed longer than we had fancied to Portovenere, but it was still pretty . . . with low hills, reddish-purple rocks, and groves of silvery little olives; and our red-gravel road was almost good. But was there ever such a winding shore?

At last, behold a widening of the gravel road. It ran high above the water, by a cliff; descended, widened again, and —*what* was this?

Surely the Middle Ages. No place in the world still looked like this.

Just an old gray *porta,* with a peep through its opening at a cobbled lane going uphill, and houses leaning over toward each other as if offering the gay pots of flowers on their window-sills—the loveliest shamble imaginable; masts rose from a tiny harbor at our left, sails were drying, nets and more flower-pots hanging from balconies, bare-legged fisher-people running about.

This must be Portovenere—*"molto bello; bellissimo!"* a jewel, through its arch, of medievalism and swarthy color and real-thingishness, all jammed together in an unutterable huddle; but its foreground was what was making us gasp—two fortified towers that made each side of the *porta.* They were both very solid and battlemented; one ran its fortifications back into a grassy cliff, the other down to the harbor, and the inland or right-hand tower that ran into the cliff was the intriguing one. It was all ramifications, housekeeping, and balconies. Up aloft a sort of pergola-roof projected, with a fresh green grape-vine airily growing; from behind this pergola, romantic steps in the tower wall led up to a flower-trimmed balcony—and what looked like bedroom windows with white ruffled curtains.

From the bulge of the tower shone more windows, and they too looked prosperous and inhabited; part of its thick-walled lower floor was a gaping, open fronted, but very clean butcher's shop with big white marble slabs, and a row of carcasses hanging up.

The other, more sea-going tower had a fish-shop, and fascinating glimpses of water and boats beyond, but on the whole was barer and more warlike-looking . . . while this right-hand one—yes, there among the grape-vines was its sign. It was Portovenere's hotel.

And we had come to this place by a mere fluke.

We looked at each other, silently—but about Nicolette by this time a crowd of about twenty little boys had gathered. Gesturing, handsome, sunburnt little boys, all desirous to assist; and a torrent of questions assailed me as I stepped out.

"You think it really *is* a hotel?" asked Babs—quite dazed by medievalism, surprise, and fatigue, but dismounting to deal with Nicolette's top. " 'Think you'd better go in?"

"Better?" said I gleefully. "Well, rather!"

But one would need more Italian here than ever before. I rehearsed as I climbed stairs, then ducked through a fort-like wall and entered the bulge of the tower. A restaurant, it was—and the hotel office too: a large, light room with a wooden floor scrubbed very white, and its tables decorated with fresh-looking white linen and charming bouquets of spring flowers, arranged with skill and taste; a nice respectful padrone and two slim, dark-eyed daughters at once came forward to greet me.

Italian, Italian! Not a word of French did they possess, but I managed to make them understand; and relief seized me as the elder daughter, with something kind and protective in her manner, as if she knew this was a strange sort of *albergo* and hoped I wouldn't be afraid of it, took me under the grapevine-arbor, round tubs of shrubs and boxes of brilliantly-blooming flowers, then up a flight of steps to a balcony on which fronted three curtained windows and three little green doors.

These were the windows we had seen from below. There was Nicolette, beneath me; and Babs, surrounded by helpers, strapping down the top . . . but the daughter proudly motioned me to enter, and I stepped in.

No wonder my hostess' gesture held pride as well as courtesy. Such spotlessness and rosy silk quilts; such charm of old furniture, fresh white muslin, and surprising great gilt mirrors; an interior a museum might be proud of . . . might indeed wish for in vain, because no museum would smell of soap like that, or exhale comfort as those plumy white beds did, or have whiffs of salt air and flowers coming in at a little romantic door that looked out on medievalism and bays and fishing-boats—and beyond that on infinite sky and sea and Alps; and down on vine-leaves, and backwards up a cliff bright with poppies—and nearer still, into the charming and trustworthy face of a quiet-voiced signorina, now awaiting my verdict.

"Va bene!" I said, smiling at her—insufficient, but all I could think of at the moment; and we went out on the narrow balcony.

I could not resist it: there was unconscious Babs far below me—and I cocked up here in medievalism, with ruffled muslin at my back; it was too absurdly delicious. Leaning over, I whistled a bit of our tune—Siegfried's bird. She looked swiftly up—I could see her astonished face; I waved and nodded, she smiled and waved back . . . and I wanted to go leaping down to her, but crept instead. (Not for hastening, these lighthouse-like steps.)

But it was lovely, going down into the fluffy, bright-green top of the grape-vine . . . I fancied our waking, in that high nest; in an ancient gate tower, under battlements—with birds singing on that cliff, poppies waving, a soft air blowing; the tide sloshing, and fishermen going out to fish. . . .

Daughter had told me the terms and the nice padrone corroborated them—an honest place, this; with everything settled and beams on everybody's face, I happened to mention a garage.

Oh no, they said pleasantly. There was no garage.

I stopped, transfixed. But surely there was one *somewhere?*

Oh no! They were sorry, but there wasn't. I simply couldn't believe it. I managed to stutter:

"Non vi è—nella città? in *questa strada?* in *altra strada?"*

"Niente!" Not in the whole town. Not in this street, not in another street! Nobody in Portovenere had a *macchina.* They stood there, sadly shaking their honest heads.

"Niente! Nessuno!"

Shutting my mouth hard, I tramped down the flight of stone stairs. . . . Of course we'd stay here; I'd fix it somehow—confound Nicolette anyway. Good gosh, couldn't we put her in the butcher's shop? The mouth of it was certainly wide enough, if it wasn't all filled up with pigs and things. . . . For never yet had we come across just this combination; a possible, indeed an enchanting *albergo,* and an impossible town with no place for Nicolette.

I strode swiftly to Babs. Rather pestered by little boys, I saw; very tired, and hopeful of harborage. (My lamb; we would anchor right here.) Dash Nicolette, I thought—and said; couldn't she stay in the street?

But Babs was horrified at the mere idea. Breathlessly I unfolded the whole story—she just needed to hear some details, I thought; and to my amazement saw she was not greatly moved.

In desperation I even unfolded it to the little boys. They were inexpressibly moved, and surged forward with tumultuous suggestions; really quite nice little boys, only full of a most fearsome vitality—one of them, with a winning smile and bright brown eyes, mounting on Nicolette's step and insisting on bouncing up and down and shouting, just when I wanted a quiet moment to think in.

For Babs was still quite without her usual suggestions—I could see the mobbing hadn't helped; she was ready, though with regret, to bow to circumstances and depart.

"*You* haven't seen that hotel," I burst out—my heart ready to break. "It's simply marvelous. We've never *been* in such a place. It's the chance of a lifetime. *Why* can't Nicolette stay out?"

" 'Wouldn't be a thing left in her," stated my child mildly.

"They're *quite* nice boys!" I pleaded; somewhat dashed, I admit, by the idea of a rifled Nicolette in the morning. She was pretty precious; in fact she was everything. She was the trip. "But, take all our stuff out, put on the curtains and button them up tight—and this biggest boy says he'll take care of her?"

For indeed he was pressing his young hands on his heart, swearing to sit in her, to sleep in her, to keep the other boys out of her; to guard her like his mother. . . .

But Babs was unshakable. Not in the street; not her Nicolette. If the mob was like this now, what would it be when we went in? Nicolette would be picked bare in five minutes. And all night? Simple lunacy.

The clouds were lighting for sunset. Rose-color lingered on the old gate, the grape-vine was glorified; battlements, on our tower, smote the sky . . . I felt—well, just up against it, as we say. (Queen Mary with Calais written on her heart—myself with Portovenere?)

Desperately I argued, calmly I was withstood. I knew in a way that Babs was right—that was the worst of it; she *must* be right; yet with a hunch I have sometimes, and can't always trust, I felt in my bones that she was all wrong. That

Italy was an astounding place where you found honesty when you least expected it; that that boy (if he wouldn't clamor so) had honest eyes, and that Nicolette—I'd stake a good deal on it—would be there in the morning, wet with dew and hard to start—she hates dew—but quite untouched.

Yet supposing she shouldn't be? Babs' hunches were usually better than mine; she had a psychic sense and I hadn't. . . .

Misery, misery; to leave this enchantment and go back to Spezia—noise and crowds, hotels that were just like all other hotels—with no birds singing, no tower to sleep in. . . . Thunder-storms and cataclysms went on within me; I never was so rent. This was indeed one of those moments Emerson mentions, when "nature says 'no' to some 'yes' in you"; though in this case it was an over-enthusiastic *pasticherria* that was behind our débâcle, not nature.

But Babs was already sitting in Nicolette; with feet like lead, I climbed in. At this the shouting redoubled; boys danced here, shrieked there, but we swung slowly round; across the cobbles . . . away from Portovenere.

I felt like lead all over now. Nobody said anything; through dark orchards we drove what seemed the endless miles back to Spezia—much hindered, as we roared through the mud, by strings of four-horse teams also laboring in the morass, which this time had a row of lamps shedding gleams on it.

Spezia, beyond, looked very large and dark and unknown; where should we stay? (Not that it mattered much.) My lips were actually stiff, but I managed to move them.

"Let's ask at the *pasticherria.*"

"Good idea!" said Babs cheerfully, casting a glance of hope at me. Poor child; never in all our mutual history had she had such a swamped parent.

"Don't be a beast!" I said to myself; for that hopeful glance had touched something in me . . . deeper than all the Portoveneres in the world. I sat up, unlimbered my face; tried very hard to "come to."

The *pasticherria* was brightly lighted, full of friends and sympathy. Every one was desolated, horrified, petrified with amazement about there being no garage in Portovenere. The padrone and his wife ran out into the street with us, directing us to a hotel they were sure we should like; they smiled and gesticulated, did all that two humans could—fancy an Anglo-Saxon bakery making a fuss like that about two passing strangers—and into dark traffic we wheeled again.

Honk honk! Down through worse crowds, for all Spezia was out now; tremendous puddles, clanging trams, then a turn into a very dark by-way. *Could* this be right?

Yes, there was the sign; and I was ushered upstairs by a talkative page-lad in red and green livery.

Dull, everyday stairs with church-matting on them, and a red velvet rope to assist. . . . Portovenere didn't think you needed a velvet rope. But the nice girl at the desk was most kind, and when my Italian deserted me (as I knew it was going to, out of mere weariness) instructed the boy to take us to a garage.

He was *"le petit garçon de la restaurante,"* he told us, and there was combat at the door between him and a bigger lad as to who should show us the way; it ended by their both going with us, *petit garçon* on the running-board, his plainer rival bursting along the sidewalks to escort us. . . . Nicolette was soon backed into a superior locked house all her own, and the pleasant Italian garageman bent over her, reading, examining.

"Ah—Sheetroënne!" he said, smiling; then inspected our G.B.

"Inglese, Inglese!" cried the boy, dancing up and down. And we all walked toward the dusky exit, talking busily.

"La via di Genova—è brutta, non?" asked the garageman sympathetically; wasn't the road rough, from Genoa? I hesitated an instant, seeking adequate words, and—

"Bracco! Bracco!" broke in *petit garçon,* dashing his arms violently up and down to illustrate bounces.

"Si, si!" I said cordially. *"Molto!"*

And dinner that night was a surprise. We descended to a very glittering *sala*—the hotel as a whole did not glitter; there were naval uniforms brightly dining, and two large and efficient head-waiters charged wrathfully about, waiting on us personally—melting into angelic smiles as they approached us, but very fierce to their subordinates.

It was pleasant, in our state of weariness, to be thus terrifically taken care of; we ordered an extravagant yellow wine; and as we looked out of our window later, listening to a beautiful tenor voice singing somewhere in the gardens—Babs very content with one of her English cigarettes, I with the achievement of a fairly decent frame of mind—we saw that the rear aspect of Spezia, at least, was picturesque. Quaint blocks of balconied houses with irregular, orange-lighted windows, and dark rustling gardens below: above this a large white belfry, its marble turrets and angels softly lit from below, surmounted the dusk and quaintness.

The belfry also had a voice. Ten enormous dongs we had just counted—with marvelous elaborations on the quarter-hour; for though I had asked for a quiet room, to an Italian church-bells are not a noise.

But it was a nice noise. It was not wheels going round, or motors whirring, or any of our daytime sounds; we decided, with pleasant sighs, that we liked it, quarter-hours and all. . . .

For we had had a day.

A bird sang presently—two or three of those mysterious and solitary notes in which birds elect to express themselves, after nightfall; a breeze rustled the pear trees and the one conspicuous palm that stood in a center garden, and the beautiful voice kept on.

"After all," I said, moved by a sudden desire for truth, "it isn't too bad to be here!"

And Babs, gazing outward, gave a contented grunt.

CHAPTER VI

TUSCANY AND WHITE OXEN

How we slept, that night. Church-bells did not exist. I awoke before my child, and lay staring at the ceiling of our room; a sort of brownish lavender, with frescoed blue flowers. "Truly Italian," say my notes.

Excellent honey and rolls, Spezia provides. There is all the difference in the world between the rolls of one *città* and another, we said, consuming them with approval; for after months of rolls and nothing but rolls, one becomes, as a mere matter of intellectual interest, a critic of them.

Such a morning! There had been clouds earlier, but they were breaking away; the belfry was sweet, in sunshine.

"Spezia, Massa, Pisa, tea, sights, beggars, to Lucca, Hotel de l'Univers," says Babs' diary in a splendid burst of information; but first there was endless palaver at the garage. Nicolette had had this thing and that done to her—quite a bit of wiping, which had to be honorably explained at length; also the *petit garçon,* very full of enterprise this morning, had come with us and wished to monopolize all the tips.

But the nice girl at the desk, when we called for our bags, said *"Italia la piace, signora?"* so very sweetly, I had to assure her that not only Italy but la Spezia pleased us; and she smiled meltingly.

"Strange, earthquaky roads out of Spezia," say the notes; "Good-by, my Portovenere! No time for another night. I looked and looked, and on the very tip, by the sea, thought I saw it."

For we were jolting at the moment out a cinder road full of gullies; a wrong road, as it happened, which twisted us into puzzling small suburbs, finally landing us in a freightyard, where we had to ask our way of lorries. They shouted genially at us. One of the drivers even leaped from his high seat and ran to the next corner with us, laughing and waving us on our way with exultant good-will; then raced gloriously back to his lorry.

We soon sighted open country; crossed the historic Magra, once a frontier between provinces, now merely a pale-blue stream in a wide stony bed—and came to Sarzana, a clean, interesting, old fortified town with a fine gate, wall and moat.

The sun shone hot and white in Sarzana, we liked the old place so very much; yet who hears of it? We merely thought, as we looked at the map the night before, that there was a town we should have to go through; and here it had the most ancient great paving-stones, the kind we love to drive over, and was clean and empty and classic. We were thrilled by it. The great gate was as beautiful as any we had seen. The colonnaded piazza ran itself to a point, and was most original, and we nearly got lost in Sarzana but not quite, because of some agile boys who ran at least half a mile to direct us, and thought it all a joke.

We took pictures of the wall (with things growing on it) and the moat—which was dry, they mostly are—and drove on, impressed.

We do love to be impressed when we don't expect to be; so Sarzana burst most beautifully upon us. But a great and learned Pope who founded the library of the Vatican, was born here—we thought Sarzana had a literary look; a sunny, contemplative look—with tall old stone houses that would hold cool shaded rooms, good for study . . . "and pop. 10,000," said Baddy.

Ten thousand wouldn't make very much noise, I remarked, unless they were all out in the pointed, echoing piazza at once; in which case, if you were an Italian, you would be out there too.

"So that's that," said Babs, smiling at me. "Oh—look back at the bay!"

La Spezia, from here most picturesquely smoking; the harbor very blue. What a morning! we said again.

Along and along a fertile valley, with white clouds streaming up from the Apuan Alps—lovely soft moss-rose peaks; we had not had a day like this, in country like this, since our drive to Forcalquier a fortnight ago. A mountain-range to keep us company, all sorts of colorful things on the road and beside it; Nicolette took the bit in her teeth and skimmed! We covered ground! It was astonishing.

And peasant life, here, was endlessly entertaining. A whole family were decoratively tilling their small field beside the river; father, mother, and daughter hacking at it with mattocks, son ploughing with two little brown cows—they wallowed along so nicely; an old grandsire in a black blouse was picking up stones. They looked brightly up at us; daughter (in an orange kerchief) waved her hand.

Charming vine-arbors were at the edge of every field, poplars were shaking their leaves; ditches had clear brown water in them, flowers were in the grass; everything, in this district of la Luniziana, looked as if it loved to grow. They'd had our rains; and now one could have lived off this sunshine.

Our road began to be full of white oxen with red tassels on their snowy foreheads, drawing wine-carts; the first we had seen on our way through Italy. Tuscany is the home of these creatures, we knew; were we in Tuscany then?

We had a great thrill on discovering that we nearly were. The famous province takes a loop up north of Spezia, not quite including it (Spezia must be forever deprived of that glory), then drops to the coast by way of Carrara and Avenza.

Toscano! Yes, there were the big letters, the pink-shaded line, beginning on our map; that line we had so dreamed of crossing.

Now for towns full of art, for hill-villages—art and landscape mixed; now for white oxen. France had had villages, France had even had oxen, but yellow or brown ones, never oxen like these; immense silvery creatures with dark melting eyes and silver eyelashes with positively a dew upon them.

. . . They stepped placidly along, unhurried, ruminant, a benediction to the passing eye, their carts gay with bright-painted casks. But by a bridge, under some great poplars, we met two of the carts with drivers asleep, and were amused by the inimitable slow pace of the astute oxen. In perfect unison they raised one fore-foot, leaned imperceptibly and by degrees forward, and by and by the foot came down; then, with equal grace and deliberation, they raised another. Their faces were mild, their expressions conscientious; they were progressing, ah yes! And their bare-legged masters, each curled uncomfortably over a sharp-edged cask, were having, I suppose, a legitimate siesta; it being nearly *mezzogiorno,* the sacred hour, all over Italy, for sleep.

But those casks would be a long time getting to Spezia, or to the wayside *osteria,* not so far away, where they were bound. The drivers never stirred as we passed—a tribute to their beasts' wisdom. The oxen kept intelligently to their side of the road; and before the poplars cut them off I saw them deliberately swinging the curve and, with the same excellent judgment, crossing the little stone bridge above the dark-brown water, with its border of blue flag.

But out of a side-road came a boy driving the smallest of donkeys—or was it a donkey colt? Its little legs were about a foot high; and it was drawing a load of *stone.* The boy jerked dreadfully at it, and beat it with a stick—for they were on the wrong side of the road; Nicolette swerved indignantly out of their way.

"I'd like to buy him and put him right in here—between the brake and the gear-shift!" said Babs, gesturing wrathfully downward.

Poor tiny thing; it had such patient eyes.

At Avenza there was the old castle of Castrucchio Castacani, "perhaps the most illustrious of Italian soldiers of fortune." It rose finely above the town, with its bold towers and pinnacles; and now it was that we began meeting endless loads of marble coming from Carrara. Everything began to be marble. "Marble mountains!" say my notes. And we had been so lately in the French Alps, that when we saw these little Apuan ones crowned with white, we thought of course it was snow. It was marble dust! A beautiful and striking sight, those peaks suddenly pearly, against blue; one does not dream marble can fly so far or be so pervasive, but it made very convincing snow; cool and permanent for summer.

"Road now perfect," say my notes. That is, it was smooth as marble, and blinding white. The oxen drawing great blocks along it were lavishly trimmed with scarlet, instead of bells, to make them visible; and every self-respecting villa had marble window-sills, steps, fence-posts, and foundations. Shops and sheds were frequent, with the names of New York firms on them and with workmen sawing, chipping, and otherwise manhandling great chunks of the stuff—usually with sad results. For every village had its war-memorial, glaring white and terrible.

The most remarkable one we saw was of a nude infantryman in a helmet, a well-fed infantryman—Italy likes them plump; and the helmet was a thick-edged, smeary affair, running into the man's ears.

It could have had sunbonnet-strings depending from it, for all the martial air it had; whereas there is a frightful vitality about a bronze helmet.

Carrara, in spite of these sad samples by the wayside (I discovered after we had passed it), has an Accademia delle Belle Arte and a twelfth-century cathedral; but were we not on our way to Florence, the home of art? The mountains swept us along toward Massa. . . . It was deliciously warm after the damp chill of yesterday, and we took our coats off; strange, to see Babs driving with shirt-sleeves fluttering in the wind. We careered along blissful, oblivious; shone on by the sun, blown by the breeze; the road soon forked, amiably heading us at the charming little green Alps—for Massa nestles in the edge of them. Another sweet clean old town with sunshine very hot and white in it; Massa is on the *Frigido,* but you wouldn't notice it. There are quarries here, but invisible in the mountains; we didn't mind their being a little farther off, and stopped in Massa's sunny uphill *piazza* by a neat-looking, white-fronted *albergo,* very dazzling in noonday light.

Nicolette had to sit out there in the heat, poor dear, and soon became a center of interest to noontime Massa. Strolling populace looked her thoroughly over; our nice landlady dashed to the door several times to be sure she was all right. A domestic-looking dining-room received us, a cosy *sala,* ending in a crimson portière; one or two Italian worthies still lingered. Its one table was adorned with the plates and wine-stains of those who had just finished; but the shade, its home-like air and coolness were most welcome, and in spite of the attentions of one very intent fly who got in everything and refused to move, Massa gave us a delicious lunch. Rosbiffe, plenty of green things, and *spinacci* in oil; also some delicious snow-white cheese in a great bowl—a local delicacy made in their *latteria,* the landlady told us.

A dashing-looking young woman came in, had a moment's dashing conversation with a middle-aged Italian who was just leaving, and, looking over her shoulder for a last bon mot, wafted brilliantly away behind a portière.

"The town wit!" murmured my child; for laughter had greeted every one of her sallies. Indeed this brilliant visitant, with her height, her resilience, her air, and her humor, reminded us not a little of London's favorite comedienne, Edith Evans.

Even our hostess, tired as she evidently was, smiled reminiscently as she went about removing glasses and plates; then, her duties over for the moment, sat cosily down for a little chat with us. She was so nice; encouraged me with my Italian, corrected me when I said anything wrong, and watched for my forthcoming words with anxiety and interest. I found myself talking more than I ever had before . . . in that atmosphere, so friendly and favorable, and with Babs beside me, so pleased and rested and amused.

Our new friend asked us where we had come from; and was thrilled to hear, from *Londra.* . . . By a boat, yes? And then all the way down through France?

"*Benissimo! signora.*" She thought it splendid for a *madre e figlia* to travel all that way together—*insieme.* Together.

"*Insieme!*" she kept repeating.

It pleased me more than anything she could have said; I translated it to Babs. . . . She understood—this thin, careworn woman of the inn at Massa. Perhaps she had a daughter herself. . . . At any rate she took the trouble to understand; and that again is Italy.

She beamed more than ever upon us after this; and stood up, most unexpectedly, for Nicolette.

"*Piccola* automobile!" I had remarked, though with a fond and foolish smile, walking to the window to look out at our treasure. "Just a small car, signora!"

"*Ma comodo,*" she said instantly; "*molto comodo!*"

She smiled, drawing the curtain back and noting all our rugs, tea-baskets, and other traveling matters, with quick-glancing appreciation; we were touched. Nicolette *was* convenient, the darling, but most people didn't notice it.

At the moment she needed water, however, and the landlady herself brought us out some, in a copper jug that poured beautifully . . . Ouch! what sizzling sunshine. Nicolette's tin pocket, when I laid a hand on it, was burning hot.

Massa continued to be delightful, as we drove out, showing us the great castle of Montignoso; an imposing thing, partly ruined, but with rows of terraces, frowning walls, smiling grape-vines . . . all the accompaniments of castles; too high overhead for a picture, but I took one, and just as I was winding up the completed film, along that road came the pearl of all wine-carts—romantic Italy at its rarest . . . and we could only watch it pass: a very brown, musical-looking Italian, in a gentle shade of brown corduroy that just matched him, driving two little brown oxen much decorated with crimson tassels, their coats satin-smooth. Behind them they drew a slender, crimson, two-wheeled wine-cart with a very long, beautifully-tapered, bright-crimson cask, slightly bound with primrose-yellow straw, for its sole load.

I never saw such a cask. It was a poem, an *objet d'art;* it might have had the King's wine within.

The handsome Italian was in front, of course, but on the swinging tail of the cart balanced a *contadina* in brown skirt and crimson blouse—again, an absolute harmony; one bare brown leg hanging below her, her charming toes just tucked into a heelless wooden slipper. These young people, with their high foreheads and romantic, waved-back hair, had an innocent nobility of mien that made one think somehow of the Garden of Eden. They looked at us with gentle and happy smiles.

Did they know how beautiful they were—composition, color, feeling and all? Brown and crimson, bits of primrose yellow, more crimson and brown. . . . And the bewitching *Italianness,* the grace of it—beautiful woman balancing beautiful man; for the young woman, swinging her foot and smiling at us, her hair loose and waving about her face, yet smoothly coiled at the back of her head, her eyes large and lustrous, her features more than Raphael-perfect, was (as we carnivorously say) a morsel to melt in the mouth. Even the little oxen, with their delicately nodding noses, their dove-brown legs fading to silver, like a deer's, planted their sharp feet in silent harmony on the marble road.

Well, that went by. It was like a picture, it was like a dream; I can still see—if nothing more—the exquisite expressions of those two.

But the mountains were leaving us; bearing off more to the north.

"Stippled in sunlight and soft shadow," the notes regretfully say; "a perfect picture across soft fields. . . . These fields were growing oats, or grass and flowers in delicious mixture. An unexacting scene, full of peace. . . . Damp land; unusually vivid with tall, royal-purple orchids. Some meadows were mixtures of pink, green and gold: buttercups, ragged robin, and the lovely fresh grasses. Land too precious here to be given all to vineyards, must produce at least three crops; grain or vegetables, cherries or other tree fruit, *and* vines."

Ancient soil; yet it looked as if it grew richer every year.

A town with a pretty name approached; Pietrasanta. Babs stopped short on its old bridge for me to "snap" a heavenly woman in dark-blue, striding along with two big brown-willow crates on her head; but she just stepped aside. It was certainly not our day for pictures. I sat down—grasping the top of the wind-shield, which one shouldn't do—with perhaps a piece of her on the film; and there had been a bit of old castle behind her!

Babs, sympathetic, though not quite approving of these impudencies, drove swiftly off.

A nice clean stony old town, Pietrasanta, but with no signs; we became completely lost in its windings. By a very hot piazza we inquired of an ice-cream woman and a boy; the stout purple-faced old woman wore a knitted shawl of crimson wool, and looked extremely hot too—I can still see the stitch it was made of, I was so astonished at any one's wearing wool in that sun. . . . Mouths open, they both gaped at us; apparently they had never heard of Pisa.

Up the hill, farther on, a nice Italian was sitting in the shade of a gateway, doing his accounts; he jumped up and explained beautifully. We thanked him; Babs swung Nicolette around to the boiling piazza again . . . and *that* was the road, going to the right, toward the sea.

* *

Of course that was the road. We felt we should have known.

A sea of pine-tops suddenly loomed; a wood. Sun-spotted sward, little pink-tipped daisies, purple shadows, and clumps of live-oak underbrush.

What could this forest be?

Then we saw a small, select, dark-brown sign high on a pine-trunk; *"Riservata de Caccia"*—with the royal arms in one corner, a yellow crown. Ah, this was the King's shooting, then; charming place. What would he shoot? Rabbits? Birds as a rule don't like pine trees. And this was a romance of huge pines, stretching duskily away; stone pines with flat-topped heads, the branches beginning high up. A little way in, we passed a man going along on a bicycle, a gun across his back and two setters, on leashes, trotting beside him. One of them lost his footing in a deep rut and fell against the other dog—who, quick as a flash, ducked his nose behind the wheel and took up a place on the other side; neither hitting the bicycle, nor upsetting his master by the slightest change in pace. . . . Clever dog. Bicycle-trained. They must have been the King's setters, going out to practice; for if hunting was *riservata,* that was an open-hearted gun on the man's back.

And here was a family picnic-party on the sward, well back under the pines; two curly-headed cherubs ran out to see Nicolette—pictures of fat-legged little Raphaelesque boys, with wads of daisies in their fists—and ran back again in a panic. Laughter came from the woods. . . .

Our road, now in the duskiest depths of the forest, was a swamp of orange-clay mud, with wide pools and soft-bottomed ruts; Nicolette splashed and floundered. I wondered once or twice if we should get through, but after a time there was a merciful uptilt to the land about us, and the wettest of the swamp dried up. . . . Forest and forest; to our regret its great solemn tops gave way to a clearing, and here was a horse-farm with mares and colts; also an extent of very special-looking vineyard, all under the King's arms.

"I didn't know the King raised his own wine," said Babs, and we speculated about the rare white grapes that probably grew in those meticulously-kept stretches of vines. But the colt-tails, short and curly, frisking about bright-coated mothers, did us any quantity of good; if I were Vittorio Emanuele, I should visit my horse-farm often.

Flat country rimmed with blue mountains was now before us; the road across it almost straight. Somewhere across that exciting plain (said we, peering) should be—ah! a tiny dome, pale blue; a leaning thing beside it! Salutations, leaning tower! Babs was thrilled; she put up an arm and waved to it. This tower had been one of her great expectancies.

It and the dome grew—I love speeding across a plain to

something; they were on our right now, also a long wall. A stunning wall, purple-brown and battlemented, going on and on above flower-spangled fields, angling and crooking round corners; Pisa's wall. And nobody says anything about Pisa being a walled town.

It is very much walled.

A very sweet *dazio,* chewing his mid-afternoon meal (bread and chocolate, a hunk in each hand), let us by with exquisite Pisan smiles. Nicolette ducked under the plain old gate in the wall and ambled surprisedly over great blocks of paving stones. Cream-yellow stones, some six or eight feet square; and they sounded hollow.

But Pisa does not conceal her charms; across an open field, there directly before you is the Group.

It was nice to come in from the country and find them so easily; a whole square away from the town. Too new, the cathedral seemed at first glance; quite annoyingly spruce. Yellow things always keep too fresh, we told each other. Gray, Gothic things in France look old and hoary—as they are; in England they look older than they are; not so this *duomo,* "begun by Buschetto in 1063." "Toned on the exterior to a delicate gray and russet," says Muirhead: but it isn't russet, it's primrose. (It was black and white marble originally.)

And Babs was much disillusioned in the height of the tower; it does look squat compared to its pictures.

"And the one I'd seen most, in London, was a poster," she explained. "Done with moonlight and sunset mixed, you know—clouds and melodrama and everything, and the tower vanishing into it, miles high. . . . But that was always my idea of it," she said plaintively, "and now it's shattered forever. . . . That's why I hate seeing Sights."

"Sorry, darling!" I said, as we parked Nicolette on comfortable yellow gravel—"it's not a bad tower, you know . . . though Arnold Bennett *did* say it 'looked just as idiotic' as he thought it would! Well, I hope they're still making echoes in the Baptistry; that's my one memory of it."

Inside the great door there was a man quite ready for us; a

sweet and cultured Italian, who stood himself in the proper spot, and us in the proper spot, and made "not echoes, signora, but gliding resonances!"

He was quite right. The notes slid round and joined, in a heavenly chord. We could feel them going round; fitting into each other without a jar. . . . We listened raptly. There are so few things one merely *listens* to, on one's travels. And it was nice to stand very quiet, while doing so.

The last resonance faded; we walked around, in all dutifulness, so that Babs could inspect bronze doors, then the Pisano pulpit. There is one in the cathedral too, modeled from fragments of Giovanni's original.

It should be seen; the tireless workmanship makes one ache; but elaborate pulpits, like ornate language, leave us a little cold. . . . A sculptured lump of something out on marble pavement (a pulpit, from the nature of it, has to be rather a lump), put there to hold up some one in embroidered bands who will say Words, suggests to me merely the ecclesiastical fuss and trappings that are far from the Man of Palestine. . . . I *have* seen Puritan pulpits, out in the country, a lean and simple one in a little white meeting-house on a hill, that spoke to you at once of the spirit, and quiet thought of other worlds; but every sort of lamb and bird somehow do not. Sculpture on the cathedral itself seems to belong; clerestories as exquisite as you please, columns flaring into ordered foliage, jewelled form in the great rose-windows . . . but simplicity in all that pertains to man. And as we looked around this superb, unshadowed, too-explicit building, how we missed our Gothic.

Nothing else, to us, seems like a cathedral.

For we had been seeing Chartres, and Amiens, and Beauvais. . . . We were sorry to have preferences, but soon went out—though not as simply as that sounds. Very firm of lip—from our effort not to be shaken in the spirit!—we made our way past those who angrily rattle alms-boxes in the portico; waded through the rows of old creatures basking on the *duomo's* edge, evaded others who sought to follow us and bent our steps—unaccompanied, by heaven's mercy—toward the lovely tower.

For it is lovely. Even Babs was becoming reconciled to it; to a new idea of its shapeliness and beauty. After all it *is* Giotto's tower; and though, when you say "Giotto," most people curl up in a sort of traditional ball of reverence no matter what they really feel, yet you can think as hard as you want to while you look at this work of his—as intimately, as truculently, even, as your mind demands—and it is still exquisite; a bit of faultless grace (though I *should* like to see it stand up straight just once) with a soft luster, a pearliness of tone that reaches perfection only as you come near. Clear little columns in delicious groups, looking as if they were made of alabaster . . . marble cherubs should look out of them, or a lady *"d'un clair visage"*; birds might go through them, flying on beautiful wings—and here were overcoats passing dingily up and down. A patient tower.

It leans dizzily too; more than one remembers. It was only thirty-five feet high when the ground sank—or, as guide-books elegantly say, "subsidence of the soil threw it out of the perpendicular"; fancy working on anything at such an angle. One would think the mortar would have fallen off the trowels, the masons off their ladders; and suppose the soil had "subsided" a little more?

It sounded hollow enough on that pavement we drove in over—though we laid it to the rumbly nature of the great stones; one would have liked, however, to poke down and see what Pisa is really founded on. Honeycomb? A river, hidden from the eye of man, even a walled river like the Arno, does queer things sometimes.

But the generations of tower-builders were two hundred years finishing their difficult job; with intervals for wars, of course. Pisa battled and battled with this enemy or that enemy, for that thing every one seems to want so much—supremacy on the seas; at last for her very life. Florence possessed her in the end; and not a vast deal of difference would it seem to make to anybody today, whose she was . . . or how much she battled. Pisa has a wall, and the yellow Arno flowing through her, Florence has fragments of wall and the Arno; it is hard to see a desperate personal war, such as that play in Paris tried to persuade us there was—with noise and blood and body-armor, and generals sitting in tents, going on between the two close and now amicable neighbors.

At least if they still hate each other they don't mention it.

But Pisa soon became "a quiet refuge of scholars and artists." It is easy to believe that; Pisa is very quiet. We drove exploringly into town by a bare, solidly-built street that curved slightly and had not enough windows in its walls; an earthquakey street. The pavement sounded hollower than ever. Suddenly it scooped down with us; for one awful minute I thought we were going *through*—that the Arno had undermined it, and we should crash downward into heaven knows what—when the stones curved up once more!

We breathed again; stared back at the innocent-looking pavement, and laughed at our fright . . . but that scoop is invisible as you approach it, therefore all the scarier when you dive in. Maybe they have propped it up, now.

But here was a crowded corner, and the Arno. Beloved Arno; we were rejoiced to see it again. It seemed very far down between its quai walls—much lower than in Florence; but as the Arno should have, there was a street along each edge with a wall of yellow-brown houses looking down . . . and though not exactly a familiar one, a long, long curve the river made, vanishing in bridges.

A cab or two, a few pedestrians, made helpful black spots upon the yellowness, but the old house-fronts along the quai seemed to us needlessly, stupidly plain; not beautiful, as in Florence. Browning brought his bride here, but they did not stay; Shelley lived for three years in the Palazzo Chiesi—"from 1819–1822, the period of the Epipsychidion, inspired by the Countess Emilia Viviana"; one cannot somehow imagine Shelley otherwise greatly inspired by nineteenth-century Pisa.

In medieval days, Pisa was considered artistically precocious, but that preëminence soon faded; "the mere fact that

Cimabue was invited from Florence to embellish the apse of the cathedral, indicates the decline of native art." So we drove on across the Arno, looking affectionately down into it; admired the little Gothic church on its edge, built in 1230 "by the senate and the noble families Gualandi and Gattosi, for sailors about to go to sea"; then looked about us for more "native art" and didn't find much. Pisa is barer than most Italian cities.

And it would have taken so little to make the old house-fronts fascinating. A green shutter now and then, something done to cornices, doorways ornamented a *very* little: one could "do over" Pisa with such pleasure. . . .

Tea-time. We drew Nicolette into the gutter beside a pleasant-looking but characteristically empty restaurant. An old beggar-man wished to stand by her; feeling amiable toward all the world, I nodded to him, and we went in.

A weary though cosmopolitan waiter spoke four languages —or told us he did; by using three of them I was able to discover that there was no cake in Pisa. *Biscotti* were our resource as usual. Is there a cake in all Italy? We began to doubt it. But there was *del tè,* here, which there had not been in Spezia. Progress! It was a nice tea.

We heard people laughing outside. Sensing that something was happening to Nicolette, we flew out, and there was the old beggar rubbing her grittily off with a *dry* checked blue gingham cloth. The old villain—I had seen it hanging out of his pocket; this was his regular program then. He had scrubbed the mud from her bonnet and doors and now demanded recompense. We were almost speechless, but—

"Perchè?" I managed to stammer. *"Non l'o domandate. Troppo secco!"*

For indeed I had not asked him to. Indeed it was too dry! A young Pisan, smiling but indignant, helped me to get rid of the old rascal, and the little crowd drifted away. Nicolette, we were sure, was furious—being scratched over with a beggar's rag; after patting and commiserating her Babs and I climbed wrathfully in. She had had such a nice refined shine on her bonnet, and we were going to have her beautifully washed in Florence; had the old villain spoiled her forever?

She snorted angrily as she left the curb.

We had one more look at the cathedral ("Let's give it a chance after tea!" I suggested); but it really needed more than tea.

It was a nice time in the afternoon, the tower had a shadow, the turf under our feet was thick and soft, even harboring an anemic daisy here and there—daisies whitened by the Pisan sun (or overcome by architecture), for they were pink in the forest . . . yet, try as we would, we could summon no real feeling about this Group.

Perhaps, for all its agreeable ease of approach, it has *too* much room. Cathedrals don't need much. Chartres has only a cobbled square, Amiens scarcely that, Bruges is best seen through the slot of a little street, but here is this one, plain as your thumb; its own mountains skulking to the north, even the town turning its back—rounding away as if to leave these, its chief treasures, in isolation. They should be somehow juggled up, jammed around into each other; if there were only a hill, we said, or a setting of trees.

In England there would be. In France, a hunched-up old town does instead of trees . . . for Gothic is different. Gothic is a forest in itself. But imagine here a few stone-pines towering against that sky.

The world would abase itself before the beauty of Pisa.

We swung Nicolette very cheerfully around—that piazza is a grand place to turn in; drove back into town and decided that its blankness bored us. (This may have been an unusually blank day.) Lucca was not far; we could stay in Lucca—brilliant thought. Halting enthusiastically, we took out the map. Below us the Arno burbled very quietly; dear Arno, we said, we shall see you soon again.

But Lucca: twenty-two kilometers and a bit north, but it's more toward Florence than any other town of any size. Taking us back on our tracks rather, it'll be—we'll land about opposite the forest. Well, *let's* land opposite the forest then. (We adored forests.)

"Righto," said Babs, sitting up briskly. "Gangway, A.B.! Sorry, but your map's in the gear-shift. Come along, woman!" and Nicolette slipped blithely away from the wall.

All we had to do now was to find the gate to Lucca; north-east, that would be.

And we nearly did find it. We crossed the Arno by a wrong bridge, crossed back again and, not asking directions of anybody, came to what we *thought* was the north-east gate; for in a walled city you must go out the right one, or you proceed gaily to the wrong town. These old roads go unfalteringly the way they were laid out, from the fortified entrance of one city to that of another; and between them, as a rule, is a great gulf fixed. . . .

So we asked another sweet *dazio*-man, *"Questa è la via à Lucca, signore?"* and he ran all the way across the road to help us. No, this was not the way to Lucca; nearly, but not quite. One jog to the left!

"Sinistra, sinistra!" explained the *dazio,* smiling and waving us along an expanse of pink mud. If we had only known the way to the proper gate we could have gone this stretch on good pavement, inside the walls; but never mind. What should we do without *dazio*-men to inquire of? And we sailed happily out into mountains, and a Roman prospect of old machicolated walls; also a viaduct of most lovely color, a sort of warm purple, stretching away to blue mountains across buttercup fields.

Late sunshine was on them; it was beautiful, outside Pisa. Beside us, a little turquoise-blue canal was sunk deep between grassy, flowery banks, with golden poplars on the banks, and a pink path beneath. . . . The poplars were golden, because they were in early spring leaf. . . . How lucky, we said, that we were going to Lucca; we wouldn't have missed this for anything.

But under Nicolette arrived mudholes; fearful, red-purple

DREDGING-BOATS BY THE PONTE VECCHIO
Florence

"SAN SPIRITO WAS VERY QUIET; NOTHING HAD WAKED UP YET"

ones, through which entirely too much stone and marble had been hauled. A big old white horse drawing a load of blocks, tried to turn out for us and nearly stuck in a mudhole; Nicolette swung out to avoid him, banging herself into a poplar tree—the road was closely lined with them. The poor things were scarred with knots and wounds, where previous hubs had hit them.

"More mud; villas; ancient distinction," say my notes. "Castle and crag; great trees and gardens. Bagni with jolly old Roman gate; wall 16 feet thick."

For there are warm springs along under the mountain, and the Romans (who knew all the nice spots) had country-houses at the foot of Monte Pisano. The sight of great trees in their gardens was refreshing. These Romans surely traveled and did themselves well—going wherever climate led them and a new sort of bath could be had; their lives, it seemed, revolved around a sort of centerpiece of bath, with meals, sports, and politics attached.

Columned villa-fronts, a few hoary garden-statues, are what remain of their magnificence . . . but Monte Pisano still looks down, the viaduct goes its way across the buttercup fields; and today a fine flying sky—that we had had since morning—the rich late light, were glorifying it.

Through Bagni's old gate (one fat tower, and a twist around another) and a drunken man lashing his galloping horse almost into us. . . . Babs looked back, in fury; but he was gone, beyond the twist of the tower.

Nicolette sped us up a little hill into better road, gray and wind-dried, leading away into golden-green country; with dark-blue hills jumping up, ruins on peaks, and snowy Apennines to look at; beautiful! A pure white peak was in front of us. A cool wind blew, there were almost no motors; just the fertile beautiful country. . . . An old *trattoria* with grape-arbors by its door was gay with mule- and donkey-carts and their scarlet trappings; there had been an artichoke market, and the gray-purple leaves were thick about the yard. A crowd of gabbling peasants was seated on the ground counting the purple artichokes; two or three donkeys were munching at piles of leaves.

Nothing wasted, here. Artichoke-leaves look like prickly eating, but the little beasts seemed content; it was probably a treat. The donkeys who were tied gazed enviously.

Round a hillside we were met by the sudden sight of walls and a moat; golden poplars shaking their leaves on top of the reddish-purple wall, water in the moat, a Roman gate; Lucca, a walled city. Lovely in sunset light, as everything else had been; lovely with the golden shimmering of those trees on the old wall . . . I wish I knew what color to call it; red-purple doesn't quite do it. It was the color of age, I suppose. Rose-red cities, half as old as time? Only poets are so inaccurate; the mere truth of this wall, and gate, and moat was enough to make one mad with its perfectness.

But Lucca, distinguished, ancient, uncrowded; we were delighted we had come. Still another nice *dazio*-man, who had a little wooden coop beside the imposing gate, told us how to get to the hotel—we had picked one out beforehand, this time; and as there was a good deal of mud at the gate, we were glad to drive inside upon paving-stones.

This was the narrowest street we had been in, except the one at Laigueglia. Pink walls, green doorways, a little piazza suddenly thick with people; then the narrowest of all turns, round which Nicolette could barely squeeze herself, and a larger piazza. At its far corner was our Albergo Reale Universo—looking forth on a fountain, public buildings, and many large Italian flags . . . a once regal place. An old porter came out to take care of things, so Babs and I both went in; a great treat, to go together.

Under the lofty, palace-ceilings of the hall we were greeted by a young signora—tall, languidly fashionable, and interesting, with a long, pale face and haunting eyes. Murmuring hospitalities in beautiful Parisian French, and eyeing us, meanwhile, with a very pleasant sort of liking—which from her Bernhardt-like type one did not somehow expect—she led us up the ex-princely stairs to a room like a salon, with coats-of-arms on the ceiling and huge pieces of furniture at immense distances apart. It took time to dress, in that abode; we were amused at the long walks between our wardrobe by the door, and the tin wash-stands by the windows; our two enormous beds were islands between—and very much in our way.

But we liked it. We liked it all.

Dinner was in a princely though not too huge *sala* all dark-green and gold, with another heraldic ceiling even more gorgeous than ours. There were intricate, cut-velvet-and-brocade drapings at the tall windows, looped and arranged with the tireless ingenuity of past centuries—we were positive those hangings were medieval; and exquisite tea-roses on our table. Asparagus being on the menu, we ordered it; the pleasant Italian waiter, with a most inconvenient starched napkin that wouldn't hang on his arm, looked a trifle nonplussed but instantly recovered, bowed, and said with the greatest gallantry. *"Si si, signora. Subito, signora!"*

And that asparagus was three-quarters of an hour coming.

We were amply entertained, however; and had a basket of bread to play with, besides. Townspeople drifted in to dine; many Italian officers—for Lucca is a cavalry post—came clinking in with swords and spurs, their tunics gay with decorations. One arrived late, and very cross; sat heavily down, and inspected the menu with darkest frowns. . . . There wasn't this, there should have been that; he tossed his head in despair. Waiters flew hither and thither, but nothing could clear the brow of the discontented one; he pushed his plate away, and fatalistically ordered dessert.

Babs eyed him with humor.

"Poor man," she said. "He looks as if 'Nothing's right in this hell of a world!'—as Jibs used to say," she added, smiling. (Jibs was a Provincetown acquaintance.)

Then at the end of the room was a cheery and sunburnt tableful of N.C.O.'s; jocose young things, obliged to jump to their feet and salute every time a superior came by, which they did with great spirit and humor; and beside them an even merrier table of three young lieutenants, or captains, who were positively curling up with laughter over their food. In stalked a fourth, cold, gray-eyed and grim, and sat down with them.

"Disagreeable enough to be commander-in-chief!" I thought; and scrutinized his uniform for signs of superiority, but saw none.

A pleasant, merry place, Lucca.

CHAPTER VII

WE ARRIVE IN FLORENCE

Breakfast with one roll each did not match our immense room, but outside the window was spectacle enough to make up; the Festa Nazionale was beginning. Flags gathered in the piazza; gay uniforms, soldiers, dignitaries, much prospective excitement.

It was a gray day and soon began to rain, soaking the flags and making large, shining pools on the pavement.

But Lucca is nice in a rain; as it began coming down rather hard, we let Nicolette take us round the wet streets. Some were too narrow even for her to enter; some had chains across their fronts—concentrated little shopping lanes given over (as in Venice) to walkers. Men and women of Lucca were tramping gaily through them on this holiday morning, chattering indefatigably, diving to this window and that, pointing and chattering still more: it is pleasant to walk undisturbed, and the little shops were charming.

For we shopped too; tramped up and down, bought—what did we buy?—stockings, an old print; looked everywhere for a tie to go with one of my blouses and couldn't find one.

No monotony here, or bare yellow-brownness, but aged pink walls, lovely doorways, carvings, and concentration; Romanesque fronts, fountains, faded frescoes—and charming window-ornamentation everywhere. Round any corner—and Lucca is all corners—was an odd little piazza or an original-looking church; the tall façade of the *duomo,* very different from any we had seen, and the "embattled" campanile beside it, were both covered with most primitive stone-carvings—beasts of every sort. We left Nicolette, stepped into the portico, and stared as long as we could.

It was a sweet piazza, peaked, and with ramifications rambling off here and there: pink or orange walls, a bit of a fountain, an old church-front wedged in where you didn't expect it; flowers drizzling from boxes, or from the black lace of a balcony. . . . All the little piazzas were like that; buildings were low (except the towers), there was plenty of light, and everything was clean; it was grand wandering. And Lucca has a nice patron saint, St. Zita (mentioned by Dante!) who has a chapel of her own and was the "special protectress of maid-servants." I was glad to know they had one.

Lucca, though a little city, is specially rich in towers; yellowish towers, reddish ones, a gay red-and-white tower with little columns. Almost every one of them has had an extra story added to it by ambitious generations—one can see, plainly, where the new bit begins; and one very old palace had a tower with a tree growing on it.

We drove up on the ramparts—what a view!—and from under its rows of poplars surveyed the tops of everything. From here the town is wonderfully sketchable. You get a fine look at the towers, or down on the roofs of church-naves—which one doesn't often see; into new little piazzas one didn't know, down picturesque streets into great empty barrack-yards with soldiers grooming bay horses; down into lovely gardens with great flowering trees and arbors and fountains—in short into all sorts of places you don't ordinarily see. The old colors were marvelous. Lucca is in a circle of lively hills, or little peaked mountains; one does not realize, from inside, how beautifully they jump up around her. The hills were deep blue, Lucca's gates and walls red-brown; there were golden poplars outside as well as on the rampart, and you looked down from it into the silvery-green water of the moat. (Nice fresh water, it looked.)

The town being tightly built, the ramparts are Lucca's park, roomy and delightful; a good place, if one lived here, from which to decide where to take one's afternoon drive. There is that winding road across the lovely plain, or a bright pink one toward the mountains; yes, that looks nice for today!

Much simpler than trying to think which road you want, or look it up on a map. Maps don't say how blue the mountains are.

An officer came by exercising his horse—a fine creature, who looked hard at Nicolette but didn't *quite* shy; and in a large loop of grassy bastion, dogs and children were playing. . . . Babs and I drove on, completely charmed with Lucca. You can almost put an arm about it, it is such a tight little bunch of fascinations; a round town, like a kitten curled into a ball. . . . *"Lucca l'industriosa"* used to make silk—and fezzes! which were then exported to the Levant; I don't know what she makes now, but she is a picture, from any inch of her.

But Florence was an unexplored sixty miles away, and sixty miles is sometimes a day's trip in Italy; we felt we must be off. We were impatient to be getting at those Florentine interiors. Also we were to take no well-marked road from Lucca, having chosen to go not through Pistoia but by little inarticulate villages and signless country, probably meeting much mud and getting lost.

We did both.

It was raining; we looked back at the beautiful warm-colored ramparts and started. So far this was gentle storm, but there are regions, even in Italy, where one likes rain less than in others. At first we passed charming old houses, pink and blue and yellow, set back behind fields with trees and vines; one very old one was lavender; the mountains were behind it and a sweet gray sky. "Simple style of house," say the notes; "plain long shape, only nice because old and weavery, and colored."

And then we were quite lost in muddy little roads. "Mud and monotony," say the notes. Rain, ditches, wet oats, bright wet wild flowers: the grayness brought out their color. Nicolette sent yards of yellow mud flying but slithered steadily along, meeting men-peasants marching under great green umbrellas. It being a *festa,* they were bound to some *osteria,* and looked most contented under their huge green tents; but when they saw us coming consternation fell upon them and they hurried into hedges or gateways. We always slowed down, but Italian cars shoot through landscape like bomb-shells, so the peasants are trained to expect a deluge.

Two beautiful little girls indeed fled in piteous confusion; one crawled half under a wet grape-vine, and was so cross and worried about her nice clean holiday apron and little red skirt, that she lifted her lip and snarled at us.

And then we overtook a woman on a bicycle, who quickly dismounted and crouched behind a stone-heap, smiling bravely at us; such a neat woman with wooden heelless slippers and a fresh-looking light-gray skirt.

I saw her mounting again and going very carefully off, dodging the puddles; on her handle-bars she had the neatest little basket with knitting in it, a pair of shoes, and a parcel.

"She's going to spend the day with friends," said Babs, "and have a grand knit!"

After splashing through unlimited country, feeling steadily wetter and more lost, "found Altopascia at last," say my notes. (We should have come into it by quite another road.) A wet four-corners was Altopascia, looking shiny in the hard rain; with a *banca,* a steamy *ristorante,* and a blank appearance. Fringes of citizens with their collars turned up were crouching under its eaves or in doorways; it was a holiday and they had time to be out, so they were out—though rather quenched and drippy. They stared hard at us; something to see, anyway. They had evidently had their *colazione;* we were hungry enough, also cold and stiff enough, to stop for ours, but Altopascia with its blank drip and its starers did not attract us.

Which way? After turning around some three times we stopped, suddenly: so high, on a corner building, that you could hardly read it, was a sign of the Touring Club Italiano, bless it! our first sign of the morning. Passionately appropriating its lofty information, we set off for Galleno.

Wonderful, to feel that this was really our road.

"Bleak—wild wind and rain," say my notes. "Wrestle with curtain. Nice, after Galleno. Flat country ceases; pines; a hill!"

For Tuscany was obviously upon us now; dear Tuscany, with its rough little mountains. We were joyful to see them. The road twisted, and was full of variety—ducks, goats, and farm scenes; but we sped on as fast as pitches would let us. "*Very* hungry," say the notes. One is, on a cold sopping day like this, when everything whistles and pelts and smells of wetness, but we managed to appreciate an old village we suddenly dove into—as one did dive into things on this road; and downhill, beyond meadows, came upon a real "sight": an old Roman *porta,* thick and plum-colored and romantic; a bridge, and the Arno.

Odd to see it in fields, when it had always been inside walls; but it was sweet, in fields. The rains had swollen it. (We found later it was a tributary of the Arno.)

Just here was a fork in the road. Either branch of it looked equally promising, but now there was some one to inquire of; as we stopped in perplexity a tall, fatherly-looking peasant standing there under his green umbrella waiting for some one, told us the way to Fucecchio.

The haughty Roman *porta* did not bother itself with signs. . . . In the early days of Rome's glory, when it was built, there were not so many roads that wayfarers got lost on them; neither were there ladies cruising damply around to see sights. The world, unless it had urgent errands abroad, stayed tucked inside its towns and castles, only too glad if they weren't wrenched away from it.

The world has advanced—pessimists needn't talk to *us;* I wanted to take every one of them through that old gate and see what he would say. That tall peasant with his shrewd, lined, honest face not only looked at us fraternally while giving us those intelligent directions, but did me another great service. He taught me how to pronounce Fucecchio, about which I had been in doubt for days. (Soft c; foo—shakio!) For you feel better, when approaching a strange town, if you know what to call it.

We ran along the valley a little, and there, high above us, it was. We had no idea Fucecchio would look like that. . . .

But this was Tuscany.

"On a hill; nice thick town, in perfect hill style. Walls, turrets and everything; gray, battlemented, medieval. We explored the base of it, looking vainly for a restaurant—through narrow streets winding uphill to the grand old citadel, all gay with flags."

But it looked too ancient for eating, up there, and Fucecchio wasn't in the guide-book. (It should have been.) The rain slackened and gleams shone on the old pavements, all hollows and great pools; at last, in our splashing, we swung into a most unlikely lane and caught sight of a small establishment with white, uneven letters across its steamy window; a dark face or two stared out.

" 'Looks pretty bad,' said Babs. Went in. Fine!" Thus the notes.

For as we hesitated the door opened and a nice-looking padrone peered out; holding the door, he courteously welcomed me in.

Sawdust was thick on the floor, on one side was a counter with wine-flasks; a few citizens, at long narrow tables, were very quietly playing games. At the back the room opened pleasantly to wide windows and a streaming garden.

I called Babs, who gladly though stiffly alighted. (We *were* stiff.) The padrone led us past the players and seated us on a bench against the wall (I love sitting on a bench) whence we commanded the room and the garden; then bent and suggested food. Minestrone first *si si;* then a jumble of Italian which, however, contained the word *fritto,* so I in my turn said *"si si."* The padrone's expression was trustworthy. Minestrone arrived blazing hot, and when the unknown *fritto* came, behold it was a compound of roast and delicately-browned kid with tiny artichokes and brown gravy; sautéd *patate* we had, and white wine. We glanced admiringly about us at our pleasant, homelike shelter: sawdust was simply splendid on floors on a wet day, we agreed . . . and what a jolly garden that was, with its neat plots of gravel, trained rose-bushes, and white iron tables set invitingly about.

The sweet Italians playing their games tried so hard not to stare at us; when one of them did glance shyly up, it was with the nicest expression of friendliness. . . . How grand this heat felt! for there was a stove near by. We were unstiffening fast under its genial rays; between us we finished that inspired *fritto,* to the last savory petal of its last artichoke. . . . A bowl of figs, oranges and nuts was then set most cordially before us—there was a fig tree out in the garden; and at the mere mention of coffee, the padrone bounded athletically away.

"Subito, signora—subito!"

This time it was *subito.* Drip-coffee in pretty glass-and-silver was at our elbows in a second, dripping valiantly; for everything this padrone had worked properly and well. It had to, he dashed at it with such energy and spirit.

The kitchen door opened softly; the padrone's wife came in, a waft of good odors with her, and sat quietly down in an arm-chair near the door. Her apron was very fresh, her good brown face (a peasant's face) shining with satisfaction. Evidently the padrone had told her the signore were pleased with their meal; there was nothing for it but that she must come in and see them—and on went the clean apron.

As we passed her we bowed and smiled, and she bowed and beamed back; the padrone, standing very straight beside her with a hand on her chair and a nice pride on his pleasant, good-looking face, beamed too. . . . I made to open the door —but should I? Never! He made a dart and had it wide open, bowing, at which every Italian in the place jumped up and, with a murmur that was almost a cheer, rushed to the front of the room to see us go. The window was full of dark faces, cordially smiling. We ducked in behind our curtains, then looked out again; everybody waved and laughed, showing white teeth; the padrone, once more monopolizing the doorway, cried *"Buon' viaggio, signore!"* and Nicolette, with many backings in the little via, backed herself around.

Dear Fucecchio; that had been a welcome indeed.

"Warm, fed, and cheered," say my notes. "Happy wet drive

to Firenze; two lovely walled villages. 'Shell' at one of them; honest, red-haired boy ran out of sight down the street with a hundred-lire note, to get '*cambio*.' Brought it back, panting. Tremendous roll, all in one-lire notes. . . .

"On, in awful mud; tram-tracks—a tram: 'Pzza. Duomo.' Sounded good to *us!* Florence—we were at home in Florence; we knew how the Piazza Duomo looked!"

This was the first town since Paris that both of us had been in before; our hearts warmed to it. The rain poured down; a wet *dazio*, briefer than ever, took one look through our curtains:

"*Niente per dazio? Bene! andare!*" then dashed back to shelter; and we were in a Florentine street.

"Muddy street, mud-colored town," I said.

"Yes, if it weren't for the flags—"

"And the shutters!"

But there *were* the flags and the shutters—the latter of a soft, faded, yet clear green. It was Italy; it was charming. The street widened to a great blank-looking brown gate, standing alone; the Porta Romana.

"As blank as the inside of the *duomo*," I said, remembering our surprise on first seeing the interior of that famous building.

We bumped irreverently through it, trying not to splash two women and a cowering bicyclist; navigated narrowness, saw the Arno ahead and crossed it; turned up beside its low wall (pouring rain!) past the Bierchelli, where we had stopped before, inquired for the Piazza Cavagliere of a horrid *carabiniere*, then of a nice one—who told us about its being "near a building."

Strange, to be driving along the Lung'arno; we felt we must be in a dream. A cab with great yellow wheels nearly banged into us, the darling Arno was beside us but we couldn't look at it; we crept through the terrible tangle at the mouth of the bridge, attained the merciful little rise to the Uffizi, then a bit of clear driving over wide white stones with great cracks between them . . . and beyond the Ponte Grazie, a triangular gap containing a great structure with scaffolding.

Was this the "building"?

It was. Our recommended pension being full, we were referred to a near-by one with the same view. Our room was stately, our signora charming; her prices seemed a trifle high, but—

"Nawt for that which I geeve you!" she said in her soft voice, smiling at us. "The vairy best fud, signora; much sheecken! A real desairt—a pouding, every night!"

Admitting that this somewhat altered the situation, we drove happily off to hunt for a garage. It had to be a very special one this time, vouched for by the Touring Club, for Nicolette needed things done to her; after navigating some forty streets, we found it. A tiny sign it had, high up, but it was It; and that dark-eyed little mechanic simply leaped to understand us. *"La graissage?"* I ventured—whereat, translating perfectly, he snapped back a brilliant *"Grassagio! si si!"* But a horrid great chauffeur who belonged to a Rolls was sauntering about the place, and stared most slightingly at one of our tires. It *had* an outside patch and a sad expression, but he needn't have tapped it scornfully with his boot-toe and said "St—st!" when we knew perfectly well it was going to blow up pretty soon, without his telling us.

We went very haughtily out.

A homelike, rambling place our pension, with thick English carpets in the halls, and bookcases full of English books. (A great item.) It was good to feel settled; to unpack fundamentally, and shake out frocks we had forgotten. While dressing we gazed enjoyably at the Arno, at Florence going home, twilight settling down on San Miniato, and the few lights on its dark hillside coming out, then, feeling nice and silky, strolled to the *sala*. A brightly-lighted room with cheerful yellow walls and (to Babs' disgust) a sign *"Vietato fumare"* on one of them; old ladies in pensions don't like smoking.

"Sheecken" night, however (very good sheecken), and a

yellow pudding to end with; a fair meal, though not approaching the one we had in little rainy Fucecchio on a sawdust floor.

"Assembly of chumps at dinner; blameless frumps!" remark my notes. Coffee in the drawing-room; much gilt-framed art, much bric-a-brac on small gilt-and-onyx tables; red brocade, mirrors, lace curtains, a terrible piano; but the chairs were comfortable. Two ladies approached us, bridge in their eyes; we graciously declined. Our room allured us; those English bookcases; the lights across the Arno. Sanctuary!

Late at night however we were roused by a subdued tramping; the Italian flag going by. Just a shadow, flitting darkly . . . gray shapes marching silently, along the half-lighted Lung'arno. Romance of fortified Italy! . . .

It made one, lying there in the darkness, very conscious of being in a different country.

CHAPTER VIII

A FIRST FLORENTINE DAY

AWFUL noises on the Lung'arno in the morning; trams seemed right in the room. Horses and mules were clattering by to market. It was a wet morning, and all the cab-drivers had umbrellas up; every horse was under a scarlet blanket.

The red blankets were delightful against the gray morning. For there was atmosphere, today; San Miniato's hillside was dim, the river yellow and babbling. We walked along by it—a very full and rapid Arno—bound for a tiny alley off the Piazza della Signoria, where the biggest film-shop was; important shops in Italy usually are in alleys. Our camera was not working, we feared we should have to leave it for indefinite repairs; but the smiling padrone gave it one look, a shake, did something skilful inside, and handed it back to us, cured.

"Ec-co!" he said genially; and would take nothing for this bit of honesty.

We bought some field-glasses to reward him. "They'd be wonderful for frescoes," said Babs, picking up a pair; "and things in a bad light, high up. I always want to read inscriptions, and can't. . . . Goodness, I can see all sorts of things! I can see Cosimo's buttons!"

For she had focussed on the bronze Medici in the square outside. So we went off, feeling vastly extravagant, with them in a burberry pocket; tried them, with immense success, on the battle-frescoes of the Palazzo Vecchio, "in a very dark light," as my child said, and came out beaming. The old palace, from the squat columns of its dusky courtyard, up, had been unexpectedly fine.

But it was good to be out again, and strolling past the loggia; hearing the play of the fountain and being drawn over to look at Neptune's curly white-marble steeds, curvetting almost over the edge of their wide marble basin. . . . A fiercer Neptune than at the fountain of Trevi, very conscious of the powers of the trident in his right hand; and the horses just match him. We loved their open mouths.

The fountain was in great form too, hissing and spraying, sending white water high in air or dangerously out upon the paving-stones—a grand thing, we agreed, to have in summer in a hot square. On an April morning, too, it seemed exactly what was needed in the Piazza della Signoria. Even sculpture is the fresher for a wetting—which is perhaps one reason, beside their own melodramatic activity, why the groups under the loggia never grow dull. Rape of the Sabines—unclad ladies in difficulties; Ajax nobly rescuing a friend, Judith and Holofernes, not so noble; the horrid Perseus of Cellini—the one he had such a time casting; and behind all, a calm row of Roman matrons "or empresses."

But the heavens were descending, and it was noontime. The loggia was black with men arguing, prattling, having a wonderful time under shelter; we climbed its steps and took shelter too, not realizing that it was like a Stock Exchange and there wouldn't be another woman there. We had to edge our way in—but we didn't see why we shouldn't; the Italians didn't either, bless their hearts—or else they were so intent on their affairs that they didn't see us, which was better yet . . . and something, we assured each other, that wouldn't have happened in la belle France. A petticoat in that land is a petticoat, and not to be ignored.

One rotund citizen, to be sure, rolled a very fierce black eye at me as I slid between him and a pillar against which, at that same moment, he had intended to lean; but this childlike fierceness was nice. We peered blissfully under their elbows at everything; not forgetting the loggia's seated but defiant little lions, four of them round each column and every one different—a simple *deluge* of little haughty lions with their tails curled round them—while across the piazza the neglected fountain played, and the gray rain fell on the bronze horse of Cosimo . . . on Cosimo himself, very blue-green and pleasant against the yellowish palace wall behind him; growing greener, maybe, in this very rain.

But Babs needed cigarettes; and across the piazza we saw a sign.

Sacreligious it seemed, even to think of tobacco here, but I at least found out the way to buy them; the terse, proper, Florentine way. We followed on the very heels of a man who stepped into the booth, said *"Pachita-Macedonia!"* very fast, and was out in the square with a package in his hand before one could wink; so murmuring the magic syllables, I also drew a prize and stepped out—feeling powerful. These were the first cigarettes we had had to buy abroad, and now Italy, as far as *pachita-Macedonias* went, was at our feet. . . .

It was still raining; we decided to look for an umbrella-shop. The street leading up from the Ponte Vecchio seemed promising, being full of gay little shop-windows; ah yes—in one was a rainbow of Florentine umbrellas. The nice little signorina willingly shot up a dozen for us; last, a generous green one with a narrow border like a bit of Roman ribbon. Hilarious, that border; and we wanted something big enough for two. It was senseless, also very separating, each carrying an umbrella in a crowd.

"We'd *never* be near each other, then!" said Babs.

Great fun, trying to keep under one umbrella in a mob.

We had had a pet umbrella called Chubby, large, like this one, that we lost somewhere in France; but this one was really gayer. We went out, fond of the thing already.

"It'll do for the sun, too!" I said, putting it triumphantly up.

Under the "celebrated Tuscans," again; back to our yellow Arno. We were always freshly glad to see it. There is a bit of swollen sand with marsh-grass on it that you can see, if you lean over the wall at this point, round which the water madly rushes; it came to be our favorite leaning-place. The bridge is nicest from there, it sags so beautifully and alarmingly over the current; and its three holes show bits of sky through. . . . Fascinating fishing was going on below us—and fishing is becoming to the Arno; it is done by men who wade—or row hastily about in black, shallow, long-nosed skiffs, with one of those blond scoop-nets caught up at the corners to a pole, by which it is plunged into the water.

Thick, cream-yellow water; what kind of fish would be happy in it?

But this is classic fishing, shown in many an ancient print; and we never tired of that glimpse through the Ponte Vecchio. Florence without that bridge, or the small badnesses and sociable rushing of the Arno below it, would be Florence only half charming. It comes from mountains—bumpy, blue-green ones—and goes, not far away, to the sea; a hasty, confidential little river one could hold in the crook of an arm, yet with something eternal in its flowings, something mysterious and unspoken, that rises and assaults the very soul.

Ancient days seem to hover over it; no traffic confuses it. The Seine, on the contrary, though a delight and a charm winding through Paris, is gay and self-sufficient; besieged with river-business of a sandy or barge-drawn sort, and not like this at all; only in one spot does it have, or communicate, its meditations—where the green-topped stalls of the book-sellers lean over the quai wall and the miraculous apse of Nôtre Dame rises opposite. As for the dear Thames, it is afflicted with tide. It hurries up and down, washes steps here, hastens a tug there; has monuments on its edge, sea-gulls clamoring, Parliament at one end looking down on it, and goodness knows what floating by; and though one loves it more than any of them, with all these things it is a little mixed in its meditations.

The Arno is all meditations. Babs never once rebelled at seeing "sights" on its rim, for nothing one does there seems hackneyed; beside it Florence forever renews herself, and a hundred novelists cannot wear her out. The Arno may grow shallow at one end, with a shallower dam making a silly frill across it, it may run to quietness and a sort of charming inconsequence, in the Cascine Gardens; but to us it is The River, as regards romance and flowing through a town.

And we are fussy about our rivers. Nicolette has made us so. The Rhône at Avignon, the Loire at the foot of a château-dominated Blois, have something of this quality . . . but they have not Florence hanging over them; and not all the thick-walled palaces of the popes or turreted fortifications with sunset on them, can make up. There is a delicate art hanging over the Arno, such as hangs over no other stream—delicate cornices, a perfection of grouping; delicious underpinnings!

Even the dredging that goes on in it is delicious, done from a group of the same black, long-nosed fishing-boats, with wooden scoops set on long handles; done primitively and by hand, a scoopful now and then, with much laughter and sociability. There are two or three bare-legged Italians in each boat, dipping and gabbling lightheartedly; and if modern Italy ever disarranges this in her zeal for improvement, something very charming will be gone from our Lung'arno. . . .

"P.M., Uffizi, tea, and a general wander," says the three-line diary.

Not as much Uffizi as we wished, for we were "shooed out at 3:30"—an unjust and wintry hour for any gallery to close; but we had a beautiful time with the Botticellis and their neighbors . . . Titian's men are invariably so marvelous; and so real. Scorn, craft, or benevolence—there it is; even their dress is a sincerity; so obviously what they wore. And Titian may have tilted a velvet hat so that the shadow fell, as we see it fall, divinely, or brought a hand, with one great jewel on it, into the light; but he let souls alone. None of *his* people were told to look at the canary-bird.

And the Botticellis. A blaze of mild but most individual glory comes from that room; it is alive with line, held down by the creator's wonderful, strange, yet soft and almost dead coloring.

On the right, beautifully hung, and taking up a large amount of wall (the Uffizi treats all its pictures well), was * the Venus, that "chaste and slender figure with dreamy eyes"; she looks so comfortable blowing along shoreward in that roomy

* I say was, because things are so often changed about in these galleries.

shell. Such a nice flowered cloak is discreetly waiting for her, likewise blown by the breath of the two deliciously earnest Zephyrs—one can't blow if one isn't earnest; while on an adjoining wall is the Primavera, quite bewilderingly full of chaste and slender figures—with melancholy eyes—and also covering a delightful amount of space.

Percy Dearmer says that, of all pictures, this is his favorite, and sometimes one feels that way; but we were transfixed before the Venus because it was such a surprise. Her hair is yellow! and all the reproductions make it dark; whereas the mild, somehow patient, radiance of it seems to pervade the room. I wrote pages, in my notes, about the "dead pale gold" of that hair; how, "casting itself upon the wind in modeled masses, it is the color of Botticelli's Venus's hair and no other pictured woman's"; about the "marvelous intention of line" in the whole picture, and how the "pale old pinks and soft dead greens seem somehow to balance it, to give it weight, so that no one who has not seen the original hanging there under its skylight can conceive the charm of the thing": how (in short) to know anything about these Botticellis with which you think you are so familiar, "you must climb those Uffizi stairs."

There is a lift; but one should climb, to a gallery. It brings one to a frame of mind. . . . It undoubtedly does; they are tall flights. . . . Expectancy grows with each step; I have seen people go leaping up those long stairs.

On the Portico once more, with the gray rain coming down and making everything soft and lovely (it is always lovely, but usually not soft), we were about to step out into the dampness but two ladies, evidently mother and daughter, likewise evicted from the gallery, and attired in light and lovely stockings, were vainly looking for a cab.

"Ask that old mon," said the elder anxiously. "Tell him, *'un toxi'!"* (Ah, they were Scotch.)

But the old man was a beggar; they waved him off, with annoyance. Then they waved, summoningly, to a youth. *"Garçong!" Garçong,* being an Italian lad, went his uncomprehending way, so Babs, compassionate, stepped out into the rain, gave one whistle, and a cab came hastening.

"Why couldn't *they* do that? Didn't have an umbrella, I suppose," said she practically, as we went off under ours.

"No," I said, "they had an umbrella. . . ."

"Well, then, it was just their stockings!" and we laughed—rather faintly.

But then we had never seen in the London papers any joke about Scotchwomen on the steps of the Uffizi; no, that was new. That was ours! We crossed the piazza, inflated.

Winding out of it by a populous street or two we made for the Piazza Vittorio Emanuele; gazed at lovely things on the way, bought flowers of a flower-man (some exquisite yellow rose-buds—for a lira), and established ourselves on the sidewalk of a corner café. Sunny *caffès,* shady *caffès;* just now one made for a sunny one. A great observation ground, this *caffè;* with the *duomo* almost in sight round another corner; we never cared to sit on Paris sidewalks, especially in the cool season, they are too narrow, the streets noisy, and fumes from the braziers disagreeable; but this was pleasant.

The rain had stopped, and waiters were having drama getting the red-brown awning up. . . . Ah! at last it was secured, and everybody basked in a sudden sunray that streamed down at us from a blue place in the sky. . . . *"Tè, per due?"*

Yes—and excellent tea; superior little tarts and cakes. Teas in Italy were mounting up, we told each other; tea in Laigueglia, Genoa, Pisa, and now here . . . oh yes, and in Noli. Our fifth, this was. Doing well, when Italians hate it so. In France at this hour the people of a town go into a *patisserie,* stand up, or walk nervously about, and nervously eat little cakes. Just dry cakes, and nothing more.

But this place was an international assemblage. Three Germans seated themselves near by us, rather uneasily—two young men and a young woman speaking French; but something thick and harsh in its pronunciation gave it away at once.

"Besides, look at their boots!" said Babs scornfully.

A nice little Italian officer, his bride, and their very happy and indulged police puppy were at a table beyond; a sweet puppy, licking out a cup. After that he very much wanted the frosted cakes of a big Italian next him. The bride, horrified, called him away, and he lay down at once; very sweetly arranging himself among table-legs. Such a proper little dog! The couple smiled at him.

The female members of an American family, finishing a large tea at a table by the edge of the pavement, rose, leaving Papa and a young son still seated. Smiles and gay farewells flew between them, and "Don't forget to pay the bill!" they called back; evidently a family joke. Papa, a hand already in his pocket, grinned.

"Cabbies we want to shoot!" say my notes. Two went by just then, slashing at their thin old horses; Babs frowned.

"I'd like to pick 'em right off . . . bing!" said she.

Strolling now allured us. Down an old via to the market for cheap straw hats and debatable, half-mussed linen, in that pearl of a sixteenth-century arcade of Bernardino del Tasso's—once the market-place for *gioielli;* its somber, almost bronze-tinted little columns as exquisite as ever, the Bronze Boar still faithfully showing his tusks, and jars of tall crimson roses becomingly on the steps below him. (How the rubies and sapphires must have gleamed in that shadowiness.)

But down a side street a crowd was gathering. Every one was staring upward.

Feeling gossipy, we went to see; and there, to our stupefaction, was Mary Pickford, with Douglas Fairbanks behind her, saying farewell to dignitaries at the top of a roofed and columned staircase in the rear of an old *palazzo*. . . . Yes, there was the little figure, descending the staircase now in a dark suit and great white furs (what was *she* doing in Italy?); she had a small hat on, and only a bit of the famous curls visible. We could hear the voices of camera-men imploring her from below; gallantly smiling, she stripped off the hat and there, in a ray of sunlight, shone the bright hair. (We had never believed it so lovely; it really is.)

A small cheer rose from the bystanders; then the two hastened into the car waiting for them, police escort and all. Ah, Florence was honoring her visitors; Mary and her smile, we heard, are beloved in Italy.

Perceiving the escort swinging round the now empty *mercato,* with one look at each other we dashed across it, arriving breathless just as the two stars, somehow alone again, came slowly by—not a foot from the curbstone where (feeling deliciously vulgar) we stood, staring hard. Douglas, in a magnificent frock-coat, was amiably lighting a cigarette, Mary with languid fingers putting on her hat; both their expressions seemed to say, "Well, we've been through something today. Thank goodness *that's* over!"

Storms of Italian, such as had come from the top of that staircase. . . . I knew what that meant. For the dignitaries had been doing their best; eloquence, hand-kissings, boutonnieres and all. . . . And Doug and Mary were touring the cities of Italy. Having weeks of this.

Well well; feeling pleased with the sight of "our Mary" actually walking down steps, we turned up, or rather down, the dear Arno again to see Santa Trinita; and it was shut. Rude of it. Church doors should never be shut . . . especially after tea, when we like to wander; though they often are. And these hoary old ones, picturesquely studded with knobby iron, were not only locked in half-a-dozen places but bolted with stupendous medieval bolts; enough to repel an army.

So we leaned on Santa Trinita's bridge, looking back at the Ponte Vecchio in the rosy light; old houses all shadowy, the river very calm. I took a late picture (Babs said it would be *too* late, and it was), and we strolled back in great content, squeezing along the eighteen-inch footway by the river's wall. . . . past the row of little art-and-linen shops we always think we'll go into and don't, through the late-afternoon streams of everything crowding off the old bridge—people, bicycles, mule-carts, cabs; past our bit of marsh-grass, with the Arno rushing very hard—and home.

Nice old porter, coming out to greet us; nice room, with

hot water waiting for us and everything laid out; nice lights coming out on San Miniato. I wrote notes for a while, then joined Babs at the window. We could scarcely keep ourselves from that bit of view, somehow so precious—just the way the hill and its cypresses go up against the sky, the columns of San Miniato, still faintly bright, and a few lights scattered on the darkness below.

One knows the darkness is foliage; and that is a great deal.

A lovely note came from it. Was it a nightingale? breathed Babs. Yes, it was time for him; April. Out of the darkness he sang; and we could not stir.

My daughter was borne off to a bridge-table that evening, and I fell into talk with two young women—Americans, traveling together; a Swiss gentleman, who had been sitting alone over his coffee-cup, timidly joined us. Thin-faced and intelligent he was—somewhat hard of eye, as the Swiss are, but hungry for talk.

"We Swiss are gr-reat travelers," he confided.

Apparently he lived in Geneva when that city was at its best, and wandered in Italy the rest of the time. He simply babbled Italy. Did we know this place, that place? Viareggio, such lovely pine woods; Lerici—he had a little pet hotel at Lerici, kept by a Swiss who was brother to his own valet.

"Zey do anything for me, zere!" said he, with satisfaction; and when, in his cataloguing, he veered across the bay to Portovenere, I fairly leaped from my chair with the tale of our not staying there—the woe of our missing it; at which our friend's eye lighted with interest, and he proceeded to make it much worse. Portovenere—ah yes, a wonderful spot. Byron wrote his *Corsair* there—the waves and rocks gave the needful color for his use.

Byron? If I had known that, I thought (though I am no Byron addict), Nicolette would have sat in the square for a week.

"Byron always picked out the loveliest places," I said, gritting my teeth.

"Palaces in Venice, yes; a villa at Lerici," said the Swiss gentleman helpfully.

"Byron *and* the Peace Conferences," I muttered—and he gave me a sudden, keen smile of intelligence and assent; then spoke of past and present Italy.

"I miss ze gayety of ze people, since ze war. Now, zey are see-rious. Zey are made to work. . . . Zis wall, here by ze Arno, used to be full of Italians lying asleep in ze sun—oll day. Happee! so happee. Now you don't see one. And ze costumes—so lovely—zey are going too. A pity!"

We agreed with him; and then discoursed, in what connection I quite forget—it is a topic that is always cropping up in Europe—on central heating. Italians are the healthiest people because they live in a draught, said he—and maintained that most heating was too hot; that houses in both Geneva and Paris were "frightful."

"I go to a . . . to an afternoon tea, zere," he said carefully, "I cannot bear it. I am burr-sting of ze heat."

After which he showed us a collection of old prints he had picked up, to our surprise presenting us each with one; a modest little one. "American ladeez—have always been ver' kind to me," he said, bowing severely.

CHAPTER IX

CLOISTERS AND SUNSETS

DURING the five succeeding days we did the things one does in Florence, things trivial or momentous, but always satisfying. It was nice to have the dear place in a state of quietness; on our previous visit Il Duce and ourselves had arrived at the same moment, and we had had to fight our way out of the station.

The morning we went to the Pitti it rained; the flooded Arno, very yellow-brown, with creamy froth, swirled high inside its walls.

Crossing it, we made our way through a tight little via thick with people, umbrellas, and shop-windows containing Art, and struck upward across the Pitti's expanse of yellow gravel—which was grooved with little streams—to the palace. . . . Arnold Bennett says it looks like a rather expensive barracks.

Inside are fine stairs, with a roomier setting than those of the Uffizi; then the rich tangle at once begins. Just palace rooms, with too much palace furniture in them; often quite annoyingly too much. A "tour" was surging through the rooms, being halted before every tapestry, every notable painting, with an Italian guide patiently, smilingly, abominably explaining.

" '*La Bella,*' that means in Italian a handsome woo-man," etc., etc. ("Tired faces of the mob," say my notes.)

We lingered, to get well behind them; but the Pitti was not the best place for us to linger in. Masterpieces were there—and so was a crimson velvet throne draped with bright pink brocade. . . . We fled; only to hear in the next room the raptures of a girl exclaiming to an elderly man, "Oh *look* at the green cushions! Aren't they *sweet?*"

And then there was Babs' lost gallery. Somewhere, she said, "in one end of the place," there had been a really nice gallery; long and simple and well-lighted, with some of our favorite pictures in it.

"That little Raphael, you know!"

We searched and searched. We tried bedroom doors that were locked, we inquired of guardians, who stared at us in bewilderment, we went round and round and in and out, trying not to see that brocade; for I thought I remembered the gallery too. My visions must have been colored by my child's, for it was not there; nor the pictures that belonged in it.

It was just Babs' lost gallery. The Pitti will always hold it for me.

Mystified, mildly bereaved, we went down the wide stairs. Gold cups and things? No thanks. We had had enough of gold upstairs. Relievedly we stepped out on wet gravel. Ah, the clouds were breaking. . . . The entrance to the Boboli Gardens attracted us, its stately foliage dripping with rain; but it was not the day. One did not enter on a Wednesday . . . or was it Tuesday? Three cabs thought we ought to take them, and wheeled attractively before us; but we walked obdurately away.

Everything is near everything in Florence, that is one of its charms.

Lovely mules with red blankets were coming off the Ponte Vecchio. One had a pony to help him, also in a scarlet blanket, and both wore brown-wicker nose-bags with hay still in them. Unpleasant, we both thought, to go along with your face in ex-food!

But at the foot of the slope near Machiavelli's house was an appetizing little *pizzicheria;* its window showed the most fascinating cheeses, and boxes of things wonderful for lunch.

"We never seem to lunch outdoors, here," Babs remarked; "I wonder why?"

Of course we had been going through populous regions a good deal, also through rain; or was it because good little *ristoranti* are easy to find, in Italy?

"We've certainly had luck eating in little towns," said my child, as we dove into the shadows of Via di Bardi; "but someday, soon, A.B., we must try these Italian cheeses!"

The narrow Via di Bardi is now, in spite of grave buildings, an almost frivolous little spot. Could Romola once have lived here? Muirhead merely speaks of it as "named after the family of which George Eliot's *Romola* was a member." A lively smell of baking was in the air, there was a brightly-lighted, tiny hat-shop with just one window, and one very gimpy hat on a stand in front of red drapery; there were wood-cellars with grimy doors opening downward, and push-carts of flowers, and a hearse standing by the curb . . . but even that was gay with decorations.

A step more, and we were on the Lung'arno Torrigiani nearly opposite our pension; crossing the Ponte alle Grazie, and feeling at home once more.

It is nice on that other side of the river, but one somehow feels wrong-side round. (In Paris one doesn't; one bank seems as natural as the other; and again we wondered why.) One sees more mountains from the Torrigiani side, and fewer cabs; but why the Arno should not look itself from there has always been a puzzle. One seems behind its rushing—as if it had turned its back—and hurries across the nearest bridge to look it in the eye again. Must have the Arno looking at you!

Staccato steps clattered behind us. Italian officers are fond of driving themselves about Florence in smart little two-wheeled carts drawn by a dashing, high-stepping pony, and one of these outfits passed us now; the pony, with a very bright eye, apparently having the time of his life.

After lunch it rained, and Babs had letters to write, so I went for a lone walk. Rain is company, of a sort; I am fond of it, and of the feeling it gives you—the self-sufficient little island you and your umbrella make. Straight to Santa Trinita we went again, and it was shut . . . and this was early in the afternoon, instead of late; didn't Santa Trinita ever want to be looked at? Onto its bridge I turned, obeying that something about a bridge which says "Cross me!" The old houses were beautifully gray along the river, the Ponte Vecchio a sweet ghost of itself.

Out the Via Maggio we turned; it was raining streams, everybody was stolidly trudging. No one but myself, it was very evident, liked rain. Hurrying men plunged by me, off the footway and back on it again; old women padded sadly, with drooping, voluminous black skirts.

But this was an *antichitè* street; windows of antique mirrors, brasses, delicate ironwork, bronzes, marbles, dusty and dingy, but refreshing. Art, mixed with junk. It was pretty wet for staring, neither could one block the one-man sidewalk too long; but as much as possible, I stared—and the rain streamed down.

Little vegetable-shops or an occasional market alternated with the antiques; these shops were clean little places, with the freshest of vegetables prettily arranged in brown wicker baskets. In one or two of them a woman was shelling peas; lovely little new peas. . . . In the morning, every pea in Florence was in its pod; they were sold shelled only at the end of the day. Was this as an aid to hasty or belated housekeeping? I was sure there was no such thing in Italy. One young woman, thus occupied, sitting in the dusk of her tiny shop with the baskets all about her, and her dark head bent down over a wooden bowl in her lap, made a charming picture. . . . One liked the Via Maggio.

It soon brought me (sloppily) to the Porta Romana; which has a fresco on its inner or city side, that we had not seen as we drove in. Their art was not for invaders, it was for Florentines only; and the weather-worn colors of the figures, on the vast brownness of the old gate, are delightful. They should be; they were put there by that great soul (and great painter) Orcagna.

Returning along the Via Romana, which is a shade wider and more architectural than the Via Maggio, but with the same flavor of art and *antichitè,* I observed a new use for the great iron rings—or are they bronze?—that hang from almost any Florentine door. Little boys were using them as a gymnasium on this rainy day; sticking their small legs through, hanging head down, writhing and squirming, having a heavenly time with these classic rings. . . . Were they knockers, in old days? They looked strong enough to tie chariot-horses to.

But here was a rich garden, hanging over an old wall; a sculptured wall-corner and nook. Another Boboli entrance, with a glimpse of dripping foliage-beauty. Farther down the street, set back a little on its stone-paved corner, was a church, small, but with a beautiful Renaissance doorway; San Felice; and across the way, high on the wall of a rather blank-walled house, was a marble tablet. Having, like my child, a passion for tablets, I stopped; and suddenly the world turned to music.

> I heard last night a little child go singing
> 'Neath Casa Guidi windows, by the church. . . .

Their house! And under this was the Italian translation. . . . Sweet of the Florentines, to put it into Italian. And how beautiful it is; how a couplet like that stands out above noise and stone. This old yellow San Felice, then, was "the church." Mrs. Browning had looked out of those windows.

Not meaning to in the least, I stepped softly by that house. Odd what a difference mere association makes; that bare and commonplace corner was hallowed now. If Byron had lived there, or Tennyson, or even Shakespeare, it might not have been; but there is something about the Brownings infinitely touching and affecting—as there is about Shelley and Keats. . . . And that bit of song on the tablet, how wisely chosen. I wondered who chose it. A Florentine?

It all made me feel like going straight home to Babs.

I did; as straight, that is, as a lovely mess coming off the Ponte Vecchio would let me; two donkeys with carts loaded high, and hay-baskets on their noses, a poor handsome big mule with the heaves. He had a red blanket to his ears, thick trappings over his face, and his nose tight in a hay-basket; bad for heaves, I should say. So smothering. . . . But first I had to pass little marble markets with red chops on white marble, and white marble counters, very clean; food in Florence certainly looked propitious, and our *pizzicheria* by the Via di Bardi more attractive than ever.

Goodness, nearly tea-time. I hurried, or tried to hurry, over the bridge, but the crowd was extraordinary, and I against it, so the goldsmiths' shops had me for what seemed a long time. All that jewelry is so sickening.

Ultimately I and the wall by the Arno achieved each other, also a comparative breathing-spell—it is nearly always peaceful under that arcade; and when I reached the Via Tripoli I found Babs had something waiting for me . . . *The Shadowless Past*. (Odd; when I had just been thinking about poetry.)

But—tea-time! With tremendous feelings of reunitedness after being separated an hour or two, we set briskly off for the Piazza Vittorio Emanuele. "O lyric love—"? I thought, almost derisively; *I* had my lyric love beside me that day, looking lovely in a burberry; her profile against Florence in a rain. Italy was somehow the background for her, I reflected. . . . Dodging puddles and the shearing edge of trams—those by the Arno nearly take your ankle off—we tramped blithely along; that walk into Florence was one of the pleasures of which we never tired.

Crowds; black streets; a black Piazza della Signoria, with the fountain's splashing nearly drowned in afternoon chatter; an amusing world today. On every hand were Fascists with different caps; caps with colors, caps with little plumes. Fascists, as it were, for every need. . . . One hears of them as "blackshirts," which sounds dismal; not so the reality. Bits of scarlet, bits of gold and blue, a piquant collar: what Italian, with the genius for costume they have (and centuries of it behind them), but could make something fetching out of a somber garment? Black, in this case, just gives the necessary background for adornment; and if you meet, as you so often do, a pair of armed Fascists patrolling a lonely country road, the bright addenda—apart from the politics of it—are what you notice.

The politics seemed to us a trifle sad.

But today we had seen soldiers marching over the Ponte Trinita; excited officers in crimson-lined capes were stationed in the piazza giving irate orders to subordinates, who saluted and hurried feverishly off. I asked a nice-looking Italian whom they were expecting.

"The Principe of Pistoia, signora," he said pleasantly.

I didn't know who that was; anyway he didn't come.

The flower man, however, was in splendid form that day. He had got us yesterday; got the two Germans to buy a bunch for their young woman; today the Italian persuaded a lady in velvet and white furs, with a little white dog on her arm, alighting from her car with a husband and three dressy daughters, to buy a great bunch of long-stemmed roses. She wasn't going to; oh no! She swept by, turned a shoulder to him, applied all the defensive arts; but he shook the flowers (they *were* lovely) and persuaded, and followed, and shook more flowers; and lo, the tea-roses were on her velvet arm, along with the little dog.

The younger flower-man was also an expert; meeting the other one he stopped, while, laughing and gabbling, they compared baskets.

"Ha! Sold more than you did."

"But *you* have only those horrid little short-stemmed bunches. You don't get any price for *those*—hoo!"

"Well, I sell 'em anyway. Hee hee!" and they parted, the best of friends.

Just then a little anxious boy who was always too late, came hurrying along with his basket of red and pink roses, but found few customers. . . .

Bright and early one morning, we started for Santa Maria Novella. A little lost lady, in the beautiful gloom of a transept, was looking for Cimabue's Madonna, and appealed to us; a nice little Englishwoman, conscientiously sight-seeing.

THE TWO BALLAD-SINGERS ON THE LUNG'ARNO
Florence

"Up the stairs, you know, the book says!" she told us anxiously.

And she had climbed steps, but not the right ones; poor dear, she must have a silly guide-book. Baedeker said just *which* stairs. Meanwhile she was staring hard at a Last Judgment, trying to make it into a Madonna. We glanced at the description. Heaven—yes, on our left; Last Judgment in rear; "right, Hell," remarked Baddy in his brief way. . . . Just so. Hell in sections; a very clear-minded analysis of that well-known medieval region:

a) Flames
b) Pitchforks
c) Hurlings
d) Snakes
e) Being tied in chains, etc.

After sufficiently digesting this, Babs, in her casual, kind way, took the little lady across to the other steps; and there was the Cimabue Madonna, lovely in the gloom.

Doubts have been thrown upon its authenticity, of course—the thing, to us, that matters least about a work of art; and Professor Gardner, mentioning "the Tucellai chapel where, half-concealed in darkness, hangs the famous picture once supposed to mark the very birthday of Florentine painting," says: "That Cimabue really painted a glorious madonna for this church, which was worshipped by a king and hailed by acclamation by a rejoicing people, is to be most firmly and devoutly held. Unfortunately, it seems highly doubtful whether this picture is Cimabue's Madonna."

They think, he says, that it "closely resembles Duccio's authenticated works at Siena. . . . But there are still defenders of the old tradition."

We hoped there were. Why not, when he has had it so long, let Cimabue keep the credit of it—"a noble picture in the truest sense of the word." Nobody can be sure it isn't his;

as my uncle Henry, a Massachusetts judge, once said to me about one of those exasperating, didn't-know-it-was-loaded, cases, "If the boy didn't know it was loaded, he didn't know it wasn't loaded—" which appeared to me good reasoning. . . . Poor Cimabue, every guide-book to the contrary, has been "reduced to a shadow by modern art-criticism"; and I can't think the better of it for that . . . its one mission seeming to be to knock down comfortable suppositions that the world has cherished happily for years.

Why shouldn't it cherish them . . . especially in a take-it-or-leave-it matter like the history of art? What essential good does it do anybody to think Duccio did the Madonna in Santa Maria Novella? And my child, though really agreeing with me, here had a somewhat doubtful eyebrow—on behalf of her friends the critics.

There was a time, I confess, when I should have entered with some passion into an intellectual quest like this. Now the main point seems the sheer pity of it. "Pity is tosh!" I suppose—as one of Galsworthy's humanest characters, young Michael, had to keep reminding himself; I am not entirely certain what is meant by tosh, but it seems clear that our Cimabue, who in his heart of hearts deeply craved recognition—yes, Mr. Critic, there's "documentary evidence" for this! —and was very possibly one of those temperamental souls who need it in order to do befitting work, must have had, in a way, a particularly sad and frustrated life . . . selfishly, if you like, but quite in the unfortunate human manner. One of his pupils, a lad whom he had rescued from poverty and "done everything for," as we say, proceeded to outstrip his master—in the estimation of a facile public—and the elder artist had to see his own great reputation waning, while young Giotto di Bondone surged to the front. . . . The poet Dante, a "friend and contemporary" of Giotto's, took (it might seem to the jaundiced eye) quite malicious pains to mention this—I quote Professor Gardner's translation of the "immortal *terzina*":

In painting Cimabue thought that he
Should hold the field, now Giotto has the cry,
So that the other's fame is growing dim.

Cry, indeed; a pack, yelling at each other's heels. And what a thing to say of somebody you know!

Entre nous, I never could see why that terzina was so marvelous. Considering the life-work that it attempts to demolish at a stroke, it is quite heartlessly light in tone: a perfectly simple remark, even though containing the aged image of the hunt, which any one feeling malignant enough could have made. Dante of course was the most inclusive gossip of his day. . . . And though Giotto may have been the "first modern painter," to us Cimabue's ways were a thousand times more precious; his work, imaginative and not literal, the higher art. . . . That little ingrate of a Giotto was found by Cimabue among the mountains, Professor Gardner says, a little goatherd "drawing upon the stones the movements of the goats committed to his care"; we were amused by this description, but inclined to wish that Giotto had stayed up there on his mountains, among the goats, and continued to beautify stones. Nothing he ever did moved me a trace as much as that lovely thing in the Rucellai chapel; and I have, besides, the somehow unforgettable picture of my child and the little old Englishwoman going over to look at it.

I watched them with such pleasure. What a thing it is, I thought, to be casually kind; and felt then, as I do now, with heaven knows what warmth and security at heart, that there was something of the shadowed beauty of the Cimabue in that little act.

Full of riches and wonderful old color, this Santa Maria Novella—the art for once as interesting as the church's self; we went out at last, quite blinking in the piazza's light.

Lovely, the loggia opposite, its pale, stone-colored cornice (or rather its "spandrels between the arches," one should say) enlivened by bits of blue-and-white that looked exciting:

nothing less, we found, than the terra-cottas of della Robbia. That touch of color quite makes the loggia, though its slender and delicate columns are delight enough. They are supposed to be a copy of those that adorn the colonnade of the Innocenti—which was also one of our joys; for when you come up that long uninteresting street and it spreads out into a square with that graciousness all around it and a fine gesticulating fountain in the middle, and enough della Robbias—really as many as you can take in at once—looking down on you in their shining baby way; and when the springing of those columns, each like a single lily—a Regal lily, in our border under the old apple tree—is enough to make you hold your breath . . . well, in its pale color and all, that square of the Innocenti is as rare as woods in winter, with branches against snow.

Loggias are a special love of ours. I think the thing in all Florence, besides the Arno, that gave us the most instant leap of pleasure, was that lofty, brown-columned one in the great piazza, under which so many Italians chatter obliviously every day. The surprise of it never failed us, though we saw it so often. . . . Oh, of course there is the courtyard of the Bargello, a most moving thing; or just its poem of a covered stairway leading to the open galleries above, where Donatello's lion, erect and sinewy, is being the sweetest thing in the world sitting there on his pedestal; so gimpy, so stylish!

All Donatello's work, we were discovering, had that quality; spicy Davids, slim and perky saints; a muscular and respect-prompting infant Cupid, fierily spurning a snake. Vivacious, super-modern creatures, all; and of course Donatello had to do a lion. Everybody did them, then, just as sculptors do now; though why the poor misplaced creature must illumine the steps of all our libraries and museums, it is difficult to see.

But lions are logical enough in a medieval city; they belong on any loggia; and Florentine streets are full of rivals to their own beauty. Exquisite if smaller loggias—one on such a trafficky corner near the *Duomo;* façades like that of Or San Michele's on the Via Calzaioli (the Street of Stockings) where one is frankly looking at stockings and does not expect façades. . . . I even found my tie in that street, the one I couldn't get in Lucca; it has been a blessing ever since.

But most of these things we loved so had columns; I came to believe that columns were at the root of one's deepest admirations.

Is it because of what a friend of ours calls their "rhyming repetitions"—or simply because they are round? George Eliot says we are "slaves to roundness"; but a column is far more. It carries the eye up, it has spiritual significance—it flowers into something beautiful; a row of them, diminishing perfectly away, suffocates one with pleasure. For all their immobility, they are like the stony echoes of trees; and for me, that explains everything.

But a gleam of rare, Florentine sunshine came out, and sauntered across the piazza. A pinkish piazza, somehow; was there pink in the old pavement? The sunbeam lingered on Santa Maria Novella. . . . Two obelisks, at each end of the piazza, amused us: short obelisks, supported on somebody-or-other's brazen turtles, green with time; solid, realistic turtles, fit to hold up obelisks. Their expressions are doughty. Each turtle, with bulging eyes, one paw raised and head lifted alertly to one side, shows just the look of startled enterprise one of these creatures has, when he gets his legs unlimbered and really starts for somewhere.

But the piazza of Santa Maria was formerly used for games and festivals; the obelisks were goals for chariot-races. Four four-horse chariots ripping round that not very large piazza would be exciting to watch; they might so easily crash into an obelisk, or into Santa Maria. Doubtless they did; we could quite hear their frantic axles bumping upon the steps. . . . And over it all, on the Eve of St. John—above the tumult of citizens, and the flying of the four chariots, blue, yellow, red, and green—the *bambini* of the della Robbias looked down.

Gentle *bambini,* with gentle arms outstretched on a background of blue—*azzurro,* the beautiful Italian word is: perhaps they did calm, a little, the excitement below.

And now we must find San Lorenzo. It was not far from the piazza; we felt its drawing power. One reached it by the Via Giglio, an Italian lady sweetly told us; but where was the Via Giglio? Streets were complicated; we navigated muddy puddles, strode here and there; finally found it. . . . Something of an achievement, in foreign towns, just to find things; our compatriots usually hailed cabs . . . but we liked our blundering about.

A nice, duskish little street, the Via Giglio, distinguished in a nameless sort of way, as so many Florentine streets are, yet with something *sotto voce* and parenthetical about it. If I were a small via and led to San Lorenzo, I should feel parenthetical. Michelangelo hovers over these regions. He designed things; inside, he did sculpture and painting. There is an air of mightiness; not always of beauty, but of power. In a small chapel are his Evening and Dawn; he designed the whole of this little Sagrestia Nuova, which Baddy says is "a congruous whole of greatest beauty," but not, as I had always thought, the Chapel of the Princes adjoining; a domed octagon containing huge and depressing sarcophagi. The Medici family spent 22 million lire on this chapel, but that does not make it cheerful. One was relieved to find that Michelangelo had nothing to do with it.

"Awful Medici chapel," say my notes: "marvelous marbles, gloomy color. Dark-green and plum. Mich. Ang.'s little chapel a relief, in simplicity of sculpture-color."

For it is all in clay-color, like a master's first model; most soothing. A trifle pallid, it seems at first, with a hint of being unfinished—as indeed it is, Angelo having worked on it "full of bitter feelings at the abolition of the Republic by Alessandro de' Medici," and left it thus in fear of that tyrant's retaliation. One wonders what, in the magnificence of his dreams, the master would have done with it; if even he could have made those great figures more marvelous than they are. One feels as thoughtful before them as Il Pensiero looks, his helmeted head resting so comfortably on his mailed knuckles. Elsewhere, in reproductions, one sees that figure—and sees it and sees it; here in its own shadowy home it seemed more than ever divinely at rest.

There is a fixity, however, about the lines of the chapel; my notes continue, with a sort of irreverent fretfulness, "But Mich. A. can't make anything melt! Refreshing to get out of its setness into the robing-room, plain, tall, dignified, with fine dark woodwork, and see Donatello's San Lorenzo, young, stylish, perky; very charming, as always. Lovely color in 15th cent. painting on the wall. Just the touch. Little glowing stained-glass window over a soot-black chapel. Rain of heaven on a round marble table. Refreshing bit of naturalness."

For down upon the marvelous inlays of the marble the Florentine rain had fallen in a little round pool. The air here was fresh and soft; one looked up through the opening at the sky, and felt fed. A rare bit of atmosphere, that robing-room; the last thing you would expect of it, but it moved us very much. Now and then we sent grave glances at each other, glances in which, even between frail humans, there seems something immortal; for thus did beauty affect us. I have seen Babs come out of a wood with the same look.

Very quiet at heart, we went out.

Even a somber little street seemed giddy after that, but our purpose was gay; "Let's go and get the woman!" Babs had said. So long since we had seen her! Map in hand, so that we shouldn't get lost in that maze of streets, we walked very fast.

Ah, there was the tiny sign above the big doors. Inside sat a prosperous-looking Nicolette, clean and happy, polished and gleaming, with her top smartly strapped down; really looking very nice. Turning cautiously out into noonday Florence, we made our way back. Street-corners were knotted black with pedestrians, but we chose unimportant *vie*—"a series of those gray-brown streets," as Forster says, "neither commodious nor picturesque, in which the eastern quarter of the city abounds." We went down one long one we had never seen before, and were quite sure we were getting lost, when there was the wall of the Lung'arno, only a block away. How sweet of it. And Nicolette was running beautifully.

"Listen to her—so quiet," said my child, with satisfaction. "She does run quietly, if you give her half a chance."

"She must feel better, with all that mud off her! And apparently she did need that *grassagio,* poor lamb."

"Yes—three days overtime, by Jinks," grunted Babs, as she reached down to her brakes. "Mustn't treat her that way again!"

Almost hating to leave our comely treasure sitting in a Florentine gutter, but knowing that the cabbies would discourage beggars far more bitterly and efficiently than we ourselves—I had once heard their roars at a lone specimen who had rounded our corner—we gave a last glance at her and hurried in. Cheese-cakes, a réchauffé, salad, great juicy oranges; pleasant lunches the signora gave us—and only a few of the dear frumps were in at noon; collecting maps and books, we came out to Nicolette.

Great, at this (if slightly sardonic) was the interest of the cabbies. They had not known we had a *macchina.* Silent they sat—they usually shouted at us; but as we moved off a muttering began which grew to a chattering. *Ec-co!* the young signorina drives! Behold, they safely reach the corner!

And as I looked back every purple face—whether its owner were on his box, or on the sidewalk feeding his horse—was staring benevolently after us. Good, crusty souls! For these were decent cabbies, that stood by our door. One of them, with the chestnut mare, we had employed several times; and liked him, crustiness and all. He was quite rude and domineering, drowning all our tentative ideas as to routes with bursts of hoarse scornful Italian—Florentine cabbies are almost always hoarse; but he was as honest as he was rude, and took good care of his cross, good-looking mare, who had bitter ears to match her master's glances.

Out along the Lung'arno we steered, dodging crevasses between its wide white stones, loving the warmth of the sun now full out, and glorious in the blue; then into the wider calm of the other side of the river. Fishermen with their tan-colored nets were industriously fishing, horses and mules had their blankets on, though they didn't need them; we swarmed, rejoicing, up the magnificent curves, bordered with cypresses and roses, that lead to the Piazzale Michelangelo. One Poggio did it; Viale dei Colli, the Road of the Hills, it is called, and without it one would not have had, so easily, "one of the most delightful views in Italy." A finely generalized view—Florence en masse, hills and distance all in one; and a deliciously itemized one as well. All the shapes you know, and a hundred you don't; a new intimacy with the Arno—blue, from here, and its bridges all bunched together. . . . Far away it is a mere hint of silver in the plain, with rough little Apennines about it; that must be nearly Pistoia—off there.

But what deep reds and purples and pearly gray of the city below one; shapes of pink or pale yellow, some in sun, some lightly shadowed, fading charmingly away into the blues and greens of a Tuscan landscape.

Beloved blues and greens, one thinks; beloved silver ribbon; even beloved dome—which one sees from here, as from Fiesole, in quietness.

From here, too, it is very much its architectural self; just that would give thoughtfulness to any landscape. One does not look lightly at the dream of a man's life. A dome may seem an odd dream, but to Brunelleschi it was all-possessing; and one likes to read of his victory over "the jealousy of rivals and the doubts of the *cognoscenti*."

The *cognoscenti;* how they must have wrangled. A public competition for a dome 300 feet high, announced in August but with decision long deferred: one can see the good burghers, in their enviable, Renaissance clothes of the rich warm-colored wools that Florence was famous for, halting on street-corners of a chill autumn morning . . . clasping their cloaks about them, loosening them at last, and thrusting hands into their tunic-belts, in the very warmth of passionate argument. "Art belonged to the whole city," says Blashfield, "and was a matter of personal interest and pride to each citizen; the façade or the monument was his, and he walked out to see it uncovered in a flutter of pleasant excitement, and quite prepared to fasten his epigram or his sonnet at its base . . . all Florence became at once customer and connoisseur, and fairly went mad with enthusiasm over its new masterpieces. . . ."

Their judgment in this case was confirmed. A hundred years later, says Gardner, "Michelangelo imitated it in St. Peter's at Rome, turning back, as he rode away from Florence, to gaze upon Filippo's work, and declaring he could not do anything more beautiful."

We were glad once more to see the David up here, nice against the foliage of the hill behind him. To us, in this big bronze copy, he has always seemed a trifle mature—far too old to be throwing stones; and as he stands there with his mature muscles, and a fragment of something largish in his hand (Michelangelo had too much sense to arm him with a pebble), he looks manfully out over Florence.

Perhaps that is why he hasn't more appeal. The thing that actually charms you about him is the line of his mouth and chin; *that* is boyish. One thinks of the little David in the Bargello, and this one isn't David at all. For if it weren't for that laurel shrubbery—and a sense one has, in the back of one's head, that behind one are belfries and the green-and-blue view . . . what would this large piece of sculpture be? Even Professor Springer murmurs that Angelo's figures are sometimes "anomalous, exhibiting a grand conception but no distinct or tangible thoughts."

That's it. This rather lovely young man would never throw anything, even with Goliath raging on the other side of the brook.

The original, of course, is in a room of the *accademia,* and becomes more interesting when one finds that Michelangelo was young—only twenty-six—when he did it, just back from his first stay in Rome; it was "shaped by the youthful artist from a gigantic block of marble which had been abandoned as spoiled." "No plastic work of Michael Angelo," says

Springer, "earned such a harvest of laudation among his contemporaries as the David. Vasari sings the praises of the miracle-worker who raised the dead spoiled block to new life . . ." etc., etc.

(And what about Vasari's taste, said we—he who nearly ruined the dome of the cathedral with his intolerable frescoes?)

Well, David, well. At least, against your shrubbery, you remind one that this is the city of Michelangelo; and there are later works of his that do not lack in appeal, or in poignancy. World-thought; magnificent mournfulness; has he ever been approached in those? The Adam; the Night? Forgive us, David; we will look at your chin and be charmed.

We had been sitting in Nicolette all this time; we now ran her against the curb and dismounted. The little Italian photographer who haunts the *piazzale* was in his element today, taking pictures of a bashful young bride and groom; shoving them here and there, under a tree, against the wall; evidently just in from the country, grinning and blushing, and very stiff in their best clothes, they were as wax in his hands.

So we easily escaped him; felt quite taken care of in fact. Michelangelo's great sculpture looked down on the foliage of the hillside, on the wide gravel of the *piazzale*—and on us leaning over the low wall, luxuriating in sunshine and domes and each other, and the blue-green plain; also in a sense of being able to scud anywhere over it, now that Nicolette was with us again. . . .

"Shall we go?" I said.

"Let's!" said she happily.

Br-r-rrr! very energetically this time; for we were going up a steep wet hairpinny hill in second. Oh, very smart after her cleaning!

"She wouldn't have done this in second before!" said my child, steering round shrubs and a grass-plot and up to an old wall. A bearded beggar in a green hat was there to wave us to the right, graciously permitting us to do what we were going to do anyway; parking Nicolette with her nose in a white-blossomed shrub and her left mudguard almost touching a huge Rolls, we approached the custodian's gate, "where" says Baddy, "we ring for admittance."

"Indeed we don't ring," I said; "we go in!" for the little thick door in the wall was open. Gravel and grape-arbors, then out upon stone terraces; a rose-garden, flights of lovely steps—and the columned front of San Miniato.

Unexpectedly lovely, all of it; including the cherub child belonging to two proud young English parents, who was climbing upon stone urns and sliding down balustrades, and making a picture of himself, with his gold curls against the view. . . . There were seats, there was leisure, there *was* the enormous view; there was also the interior of San Miniato, with its pavement, and its age. A fresco of a lady, used to cover up a square hole for a timber, in the old whitewashed brickwork, pleased us. It was a sweet, wan head; and somehow you didn't mind the hole.

We slid down by more curves and gardens, coming at length to the Porta Romana and San Spirito again. Shut! at two-thirty. Its square, with a long thin grass-plot and four or five tall thin palms such as grow in a desert oasis, is nice.

Horses and mules were having their dinner, Casa Guidi, as before, was very quiet; nothing had waked up yet. We wheeled up the Via Romana to look at Orcagna's fresco; also to acquire *benzina*. It was brought us in a two-gallon tin, small boys gathering closely round and watching Babs' every move. When it came to making change, their eyes—the beautiful, long-lashed eyes of Italian children—almost fell out of their heads; they peered intensely into my hand, and fairly a sigh of relief went up from them when this transaction was safely over.

Nice, quiet, little Florentine boys! Babs, who dreads noise, and therefore does not usually care for little boys, gave me a quick smile that said "Rather dears, aren't they?"

Masaccio's frescoes in the Carmine were quite near; thinking we would give San Spirito plenty of time, we drove out the Via Mazzetta.

The work in that cloister is soul-shaking. Percy Dearmer in London had prepared us for this, as much as a lecturer could, but we quite shivered before Masaccio's conceptions. Their young creator died in Rome when he was twenty-seven; already, on the walls of the Carmine, he had painted "all the leading spirits of his time." What would Masaccio not have done if he had had a little longer to live?

"Those whom the gods love . . ." again; and that does not help one over the pain of it.

But these "mighty" frescoes—mighty, and yet not objectionably so; heavens, the lighting of them! the great swooping shadow—were to become "the school for all future painting," and Cellini tells a tale about his showing Pietro Torrigiani, the sculptor, a drawing he had made from a cartoon of Michelagnolo Buonarroti's, "that divinest painter," and Torrigiani, instead of looking at the drawing, began telling him how "this Buonarroti" and himself, when they were boys, used "to go into the Church of the Carmine, to learn drawing from the chapel of Masaccio." There is more to the story—of a brawl between the two lads; but the point to us was that Agnolo had learned his stupendous drawing from young Masaccio . . . and that up to last winter, we had known little of this master.

Down past old Florentine doors; and now the church was open. San Spirito has transepts, which San Miniato had not. The church is by Brunelleschi; a nobly-vaulted, hugely-columned thing, rich with art. Frescoes and sculpture, niches and chapels . . . but what we loved best, except for a bit of colored wood-carving and a simply darling madonna by Filipino Lippi, was the cloister.

Any cloister is charming, and goes to the heart, but this one had a garden, and such a nice robust-looking saint in the middle. . . . Spinach and radishes grew in neat beds, the spinach hidden in a border of sage, with bunches of lavender here and there.

It all smelled just as a cloister garden should—sunny, herby, rich, and a little damp, with a slight perfume of roses; for there were rose-bushes in the border too; just budded crimson. The Saint was surrounded by radishes and more young spinach, muffled by iris and a few hollyhock plants; little violets were doing wonderfully under everybody else's leaves. The sky was beautiful, above; and the Saint's inscription, if not alone his good, uplifted face, was enough to make anything blossom. Laboriously, while the herb-scents and the slight crimson of the roses came to me, and Babs wandered dreamily about, I copied the Latin words.

S. Nicalao

Hospes leva puras manus
Cementarios arundine
Eliciens aqua
Solatus est—
Nunc virga crucis
Cor feriat
Fiet in eo
Pons aquae vivae
Coelio salientis . . .

"May there be established in him a bridge to the living water, springing to heaven. . . ."

Babs put her arm through mine. "What does that say?" she asked, looking up with trusting eyes, like a child. I tried to render it—a very free and bad rendering; but Babs was struck. Her eyebrow lifted.

"Had a flight, didn't he. . . . Poetry!"

"Yes," I said; and pressed her arm. We stood there. How sweet the sunshine was; the faded frescoes behind the old columns, some sunlit, others in shadow. I had discovered some flowering thyme, Babs some strawberry plants in blossom—doing well, as usual, under something else; marvelous, how a cloister made things grow. But then monks were splendid gardeners, weren't they? And probably the Saint helped.

"If I were a radish," I murmured, "I'd do well for San Nicalao."

As for the violets, they were the finest purple I ever saw; and we *thought* we had violets in our woods at home. . . .

Suddenly we heard voices, and laughter. Part of this monastery is a barracks, and soldiers were looking down at us from one of the windows; a typewriter was clacking. Sacrilege! Retreating under the gallery, we read inscriptions on little tombstones of English babies. "Remains of George Ferdinand Radziwill Walker (what a name for a poor child), son of Sir George Walker, G.C.B., and Lady Helen Walker, his wife, born at Florence, April 1823, died August, 1824"—and that of a female infant, one Harriet Elizabeth, "the stone set by her afflicted parents." It all sounded so lonely and sad. Too much stone and winter damp; palaces are chilly places for the young. . . . And yet Florence Nightingale was born here—she who lived to help so many others survive; we walked away, refusing to be depressed by tablets.

A nice little black-robed sacristan met us: *"Gli chiostri la piace, signora?"* he said smiling.

I assured him the cloisters did please us; how chill the shadowy church seemed, after their sunshine.

The little sacristan's smile was sweet enough for a benediction; yet he didn't want anything. Strange! He hurried away as if afraid we might think so; disappeared through a little door. We put some lire in a box out by the holy water. . . . A sweet place, San Spirito. A book by Madame Alexandra David-Neel, that eminent traveler and adventurer, speaks of "the greedy sacristans of old Rome" in contrast to the absent-minded, unworldly ones she found in the wilds of Tibet; I have forgotten about sacristans in Rome, but those we saw here were unworldly—like this one.

Outside, the campanile was pointing to a sunny sky; for a moment we could not find Nicolette. She had not forgotten her way of melting into things so that you don't mind her being there (I should hate to go about Florence in anything large and glittering), and was now almost hidden in the iron railing of the grass-plot. Such taste! We felt more than ever fond of her, as we climbed in. Her door shuts so nicely too; a really cultured bang for one so small. It did not injure the old fronts of things around us, or the palms, or even San Spirito.

Moved by the nearness of Casa Guidi, we set off to find Mrs. Browning's grave in the *Cimitero Inglese.* It is reached by a succession of broad avenues, or *viale,* built on the site of Florence's wall; hence we, and all wall-lovers, owe the *viale* an undying grudge. . . . Broad avenues—any raw town in the prairies can have those—and a twelfth-century wall? Maybe it was only fourteenth or fifteenth century, but that is something compared to a bumpy, light-colored thing with tram-tracks in it, uninteresting low buildings on one side and half-grown trees on the other—for that is what the *viale* is . . . or are.

I am not sure how much of the rampart was pulled down, and how much merely fell down, but we had seen bits of it here and there about the city, and felt that every stone should have been cherished. It was before my day and I don't remember screams on the subject, but the laying-out of the *viale* caused a considerable international disturbance, the Swiss person told us; the Florentines wanted the line of it to run straight through the Cimitero, which it naturally couldn't do, and such protest arose from England that the boulevard was finally made to divide, a piece of it running on each side of the enclosure and being called, possibly as an artistic sop, the Piazza Donatello.

For many an age-loving English heart, as ours were at the moment, was doubtless saddened by the vanishing of the lovely old wall. Battlements, and little towers, and a plum-color like that of the old gates?

We should never forget Pisa's wall against the buttercups.

And Rome's old warm-colored one, in the springtime, with the young sunlit leaves of sycamores fluttering against it, is one of her sweetest charms. I remember turning toward the Pincian Gardens from that gate at the top of the hill we used to call, when we forgot its other name—and why shouldn't one forget names, in Rome?—the Street of Cinerarias, because they were planted in the most heavenly way all up it; and there, over our heads, was the old wall and its spring greenery.

But here we were, bumping along with little thought of cinerarias; trembling, in fact, for Nicolette's axles. A tough and sinewy Italian car now passed us, going at least eight miles an hour, a reckless speed for the *viale,* and throwing its occupants a foot or two in the air as it did so—the four young Italians were laughing, shouting, and clutching at their hats; and when at last we saw a tree-clad hillock rising before us, artistic, semi-neglected, and altogether heart-melting, we drew up in its soothing shade.

The gate was closed, but blossoming shrubs drooped at us; roses climbed about the old cypresses or lifted themselves on the grassy hill—pink roses, red roses, yellow and white ones. The air was sweet with them.

"Veree pretty!" the Swiss gentleman had said.

It was; and strangely full of repose. After the *viale's* insipid brightness, the shadowing of those trees . . . the sweet color and scent, the rough mounting of the little hillock; above all, the generous, untended luxuriance of everything—of those roses, lavishing themselves with what seemed like love, in this bit of peace.

Only Browning should be here, we felt; not under fat écru cherubs in Victorian stuffiness, far away . . . the part of Westminster one likes least. We sat there, feeling this very much; and just then a tram came nosing round a curve, with a red and white sign which said *"Oggi Galop!"*

We burst into giggles. Oggi, we knew, meant today, and—

"Why, it's a race!" I cried. "A horse-race, at the Cascine Gardens. I didn't even know there was a track there."

Babs whirled Nicolette vivaciously around.

"Let's go to the Oggi Galop!" said she with sparkling eyes.

A grassy field, with white posts marking the track; a small grandstand, built over quarters for horses.

"Want to go in?" I asked; stirred in spite of myself, by the sight of a sorrel ear in a box-stall window.

"Don't *think* so," said Babs, looking at me. "Do you?"

"Don't—think so!" and Nicolette slid us quietly by.

"Ah, this is nice," murmured my child.

For we wound through a glistening, earth-smelling woods, in and out of meadows bright with buttercups and backed by curving woods; there was a small blue stream winding through fields on our right, and wild roses on its banks. (This garden was once a dairy-farm belonging to the Medici; de luxe farmlands. The Medici *would* have that sort.) Everything was fragrant and fresh from the rain; bright drops hung, birds sang, and Nicolette glided softly along.

All too soon, for the gardens are not long, we came out of the woods upon a tea-house quite near the Arno, with little tables set under tall trees. The sun broke brilliantly out again, as only an April sun does; a line of poplars glistened, the meadows were very bright . . . and after the various emotions of the day, we needed tea. It was so seldom, in Nicolette, that we found it just when we wanted it, and in a charming place—charming places and tea being, as a rule, two distinct events. We gratefully dismounted; leaving Nicolette's little nose pointed so that she, too, could see the Arno and the meadows.

Such a happy tea; "tost!" Not as good cakes as in the piazza, but the bare-headed waiters in dress-suits, with napkins on their arms, did not look too funny under the tall trees. The ground here was hard and experienced, tree-roots stuck out of it in a veteran, hard-boiled sort of way . . . yes, a tea-table was all right in this place. "And we had our choice of blue, pink or yellow napkins; fringed ones!" my notes exult.

We chose yellow. It seemed best for spring.

Oddly quiet it was here, after the babble and clatter of the piazza to which we had become so accustomed; we almost missed it. Actually, it seemed strange to hear just leaves rustling—and from somewhere in the wet woods, a bird or two rapturously singing.

Presently one sang almost overhead. Could it be a nightingale . . . with the sun still on those meadows? It was not any thrush that we knew . . . and then we remembered hearing nightingales, at about this hour, in Hadrian's Vale of Tempe. "They sing here all day," our nice guide told us.

That voice; it must be a nightingale.

"It was here I first heard one," I told Babs; "we drove out by moonlight, in cabs. It was *the* thing to do. I still remember the tree-tops, and the mass of shadow under them. The bird sang from there."

"Ripping, I expect," began Babs—and just then a wild roaring arose in the wood. Out of it burst a luggage-laden car of fashionable make, its bright new varnish absolutely dripping and extinguished with mud, and from it stepped an obvious honeymoon couple—two young Italians, very dressy and bored. They stretched themselves dramatically in long canvas chairs. The girl, with an almost desperate expression, buried herself in a novel; the youth smoked pensively, eying the tree-tops. Reviving somewhat, after a supply of wine and cakes, they had a moment's romantic eye-play, but that soon gave out; they then strolled, joggling each other a little—half in weariness, half in affection—toward the bank of the Arno.

In a moment we strolled too. The river was clear and green here, running through poplar-reflections; in the sunlight of the meadows it turned pale blue and went twisting away, its banks golden with buttercups, into deep-purple hills.

Sweet Cascine! If it must end, this was a nice spot to do it in. We drove off between laurel hedges. The road was straight here, beside the Arno, and by it a few narcissi were shyly blooming; indeed they were almost under the hedge but had turned their heads, as everybody else did, to look at the clear rippling of the river.

One more morning we had; we spent it having a beautiful time in the cells where Fra Angelico worked, and loving the little Annunciata much better than the big well-known one. The little one (in a darkish cell) is exquisite in faint color; there is much less gold, and a lovely submissive pearl-grayness runs all through it, Mary's pink robe and all. (Fra Angelico was fond of pink; he put quantities of saints in it.)

Amazing how he could have painted in these dark cells, often behind a door, and in his fine-pointed way; did a brother monk hold a torch for him?

No; torches might smoke. Medieval eyes were probably used to it—and up to it; Angelico and the other brothers lived in that duskiness.

Even their cloister is shadowy; though the great old yew that does most of the shadowing was doubtless a twig in those days. But there are yews in England that date to the days of Alfred; our sunny-hearted *Fráte* may have walked or sat beneath the branches of this very one.

We loved this cloister. Its grass was full of yew-needles, it had merely a fountain with a plain stone curb; but by the fountain was a burst of sun, and around it, on three sides, the gracious arches of the monastery. . . . One somehow felt Angelico, in that simplicity; a loving spirit. Savonarola may have dominated San Marco, but it is the humble brother one thinks of.

And the afternoon was for Fiesole—late, that is. We did want another sunset from Fiesole. After a farewell tea in the piazza, we joggled out through the Porta San Gallo, then went sliding up the long curves of Fiesole's hill, beside its garden walls.

Iris leaned rewardingly at us from the tops of walls, the view grew bigger and bigger; before we knew it, we were up, and in the piazza.

Rather barren architecture surrounds it; the high wall and steps of the monastery, a *ristorante* on the view side; a church, and its campanile. Fiesole is very ancient and Etruscan; "for a long period more powerful than its rival, Florence . . . but now of no importance," says Baedeker, making short work of it. And yet Florence was probably founded by Etruscans from Fiesole.

"They came down from their mountains to the plain," says Gardner, "for commercial purposes." Very reasonable of them!

Leaving Nicolette against the wall—a very old and wise-looking one—and trusting it would take care of her, we made for a little lane that led along the brow of the hillside; a most intelligent little lane. It took us exactly where we hoped to go, but had no idea a road would be kind enough to lead us; by ivied walls, then out on the beautiful edge of everything, alone and quiet; a grassy, down-going cliff with bushes and violets on it . . . and all the world spread out.

The outlook is marvelous from Fiesole, but the violets made us think of a scene in a book we are fond of—*A Room with a View*. This might be the very place. Fie, George! a kiss behind that bush, and a discovered kiss, just because you came upon Lucy in a white frock, with the sunshine upon her, staring at violets? "He saw radiant joy on her face, the flowers beat in blue waves upon her dress." These bushes grew too much downhill to be any shelter. Light seemed to love that hillside, to linger on the blue pools of violets; the long-stemmed, fragrant sort. Fiesole is as lavish with her flowers as with her view.

An exquisite place. From her highest hill an exiled Dante waved farewell to Florence; and where else could Andrea del Sarto have lived and been as gentle, as poignant in his sorrows, as Browning makes him? After wandering about his "sober pleasant Fiesole," one has a picture of him.

> But do not let us quarrel any more;
> No, my Lucrezia; bear with me for once:
> Sit down and all shall happen as you wish.

* *

> I often am much wearier than you think,
> This evening more than usual: and it seems
> As if—forgive now—should you let me sit
> Here by the window, with your hand in mine,
> And look a half-hour forth on Fiesole,
> Both of one mind, as married people use,
> Quietly, quietly, the evening through,
> I might get up tomorrow to my work
> Cheerful and fresh as ever. . . .

* *

> See, it is settled dusk now; there's a star.
> Morrello's gone, the watch-lights show the wall,
> The cue-owls speak the name we call them by.
> Come from the window, love,—come in, at last,
> Inside the melancholy little house
> We built to be so gay with. . . .

Narrative music, that is; a tender quietness of despair. It lingers with one.

What indeed would the poets have done without Fiesole as a background—the little ruffle behind the classic head of Florence, the frill of naturalness she needs? A *little* stoniness does not matter. . . . That was Andrea's Fiesole to be sure —"Morello's gone, the watch-lights show the wall"—and old parts of Fiesole are still nice; but oh, the villas. Every time one goes there, there are more.

Must people like sunsets? Apparently they must.

And that tram; they probably commute to Florence. Think of Florence being commuted to.

But from here trams were not, nor villas. What so lovely as Florence drowning a mist of olive-tops, her roofs and gardeny hillsides in a lavender haze; the pale Arno winding, and sunset over the hills of Tuscany? We sat and stared; we picked violets, found more paths, and tramped to and fro and up and down, gazing at the mountain-chain of the Casentino, and wondering if one really did see Monte Albano from here. . . . Never again might it be so lovely—Fiesole, and a perfect afternoon; we could not leave it. We tramped back, glorified.

Nicolette was dozing unharmed by the Etruscan wall. Climbing a cobbled lane that led along the opposite brink, we found an outdoor *ristorante* in a little old pink house perched on the edge of nothing, with flowers all over it, and a few tables and an unworldly bench or two out on flagged pavement in front of it. We sat against its pink wall, still warm from the sun.

The sky was golden above the hills; what purples, what deepening magnificence! Dinner, down in those shadows? We would dine here, and look at heaven. The Arno, in the blues and purples, was bright silver now. . . .

An impressed young girl came out to serve us; some strangely quiet Italian youths occupied another bench, its back likewise against the wall.

It all made us think of English cottages: thatched roofs and little gardens, and jam and thick bread-and-butter for tea. It had that homely charm; and no ravioli, no country bread and *insalata* were ever so perfect as those the rosy-cheeked maid brought out to us. When one eats view—and the gold sky blazes into soft flame, then sinks into crimson and dusky maroon, with the pale gold far above changing into green and turquoise, while the rough mountains go purple-black . . . what more does one need?

And one knows there is classicism beneath it. While stunned by what nature is doing, one feels the art that is there—in those shadows. Arnolfo is there, and Masaccio, and our saint in his cloister; for this is the wonder of Tuscany.

A half-intellectualized aspect of the beauty before us; but intellect helps anything. We loved haze-purpled classicism. Any day can flash gold into its sky, but not always over Florence; and when the Arno went gold, and a thousand jewels began to glitter in that haze, we let them glitter till the guarding hills were really black and the gold thread of the river grew dim, then went leaping down the lane to Nicolette.

For we belonged, in that haze. In all propriety, we should now have been being one of its jewels ourselves—a golden, third-story jewel, close above the river's kind voice, and making one more glitter on its glancing tide.

"Uh?" said Nicolette, waking. "Oh yes. Br-*rrrrr!*"

Coasting into fairyland, this was; with flowers pouring out scents at us and cypresses very black against the jewelled valley. Curves vanished by magic—though we wished them longer: Florence in the gloaming was golden-lighted and sweet, and through that duskiness, while I sat entranced and useless beside her, Babs found our way expertly.

Nicolette had a snug house beside the pension, now. We tucked her in, closed—but only with the porter's help—its ponderous door, and climbed upstairs.

Last evenings are half-nice, half-melancholy; we listened to the night-time brawl of the river, to Florence tramping or rattling by, and were sorrowful. We might have gone to a theater—the Teatro Verdi was just a few corners away, and opera going on; somehow we didn't care to. London had been full of theater—one's greatest diversion—but this was Italy, and April, and either of them put out our feeling for footlights as though it had never been. . . . The smell in the air was enough, one could have lived on it; the purple of that valley, from Fiesole, was still in our eyes; who would displace it?

But we felt at home in Florence now. It was time to go. We could hardly lose ourselves in her worst mazes. Some known bit, a façade, a cornice, even a loved and conspicuous gargoyle, would protrude; and there we were. And we love feeling lost. It is one of life's minor refreshments.

Also we felt, in the middle of a dashing trip like this, almost thorough. We had tracked Dante and Savonarola, Raphael and Angelo and Orcagna, to their duskiest hiding-places, had spent hours going back to things that haunted us—some picture that lived in our dreams; and it is when you go back that you begin to know them a little . . . Santa Croce, for instance; it was our near neighbor,—though we never could get up the slightest fervor about the Giottos, dreadfully restored and pink-and-blue, with hard edges; but its cloister made a delightful back-garden for the Via Tripoli. A tumble of old things surrounds it, tiles and little columns; the sacristan came to know us almost as well as we knew the color of those tiles against the sky.

But there is so much of Florence. If I were a guide-book, I should quail at the idea of cataloguing her. . . . They do take her with enormous seriousness—their job in life, of course; Baedeker gives her seventy-five pages, and Venice forty-eight. Perhaps a just proportion.

"Stones of Venice"! Somehow one is more impressed with the stones of Florence—*as* stones.

In Venice it is color or ornament you are conscious of, in Florence you go about just loving old stone. There is a lightness about the Queen of the Adriatic—an airy something that Dante's more gloomy and battlemented city did not think of; it did not occur to her to be light. . . . One "sat heavy," as Babs always said—and defended oneself against one's foes; one was spare and stark and impressive, and took age nobly. One flung up what airiness one had into *loggie* here and there, or spent love and delicacy on a cloister; but even Giotto's campanile has, for its kind, a squareness. The beautiful tracery of its windows may be Italian Gothic—but neither they, nor dainty columns, nor the pink and green of the marbles, can etherealize the square-topped effect of that campanile.

"The characteristics of Beauty and Power," says Ruskin, "all together, and in their highest possible relative degree . . . exist, as far as I know, only in one building in the world, the Campanile of Giotto . . . that serene height of mountain alabaster, coloured like a morning cloud, and chased like a sea-shell."

It is rather alabastery. But nothing is serene in that piazza, and morning clouds are not square. One cannot imagine that bell-tower in Venice. It would have been Byzantine and bulbous—or it would have soared; gone frivolously heavenward. Giotto intended to crown it with a hundred-foot spire, but would that have helped Florence? One more thing on its sky; something that carried the eye on and up, and did not land it on battlements?

I adore battlements. They may be a bit of this world and its strife, merely medieval wall folded four-square and hoisted upon the clouds; but one loves Florence as she is. It suits history, and it suits her, that her palaces sit ponderously on their pavements; and if anything ever dared soar from that great square of the Fountain except the *torre* of the Palazzo Vecchio, which bristles with battlements, I should simply weep—and run away as fast as possible.

We drew our heads in and began to pack. . . . Siena, next day!

And the old thrill of the road attacked us.

CHAPTER X

SAN GIMIGNANO AT LAST

THURS. 29. *First day of term,"* says Babs' diary. "To San Gimignano and Siena, rather dusty. Lunch Poggibonzi."

" 'Suppose I *ought* to be going back," said she rather soberly, as we drove southward by clayey roads and through suburbs; past the old Certosa on its cypressed peak.

"But term is so short, darling," I said. We had discussed this many times before, but my child had a loyal heart toward her university.

"Yes," said she reasonably; "only six weeks of lectures really, if you cut out the exams. They told me I could get it out of books just as well—the provost said so, and Winifred." (Winifred was the Dean of Women.) "Well, this is jolly!" she decided, cheering up. "Ripping country. And just think, we're going to *see* San Gimignano!"

"Actually. After thinking of it for three or four years!"

For our imaginations had once been inflamed by a post-card showing a great brown wall with a number of square-topped towers against a reddish sunset. For a post-card it wasn't bad, and those towers had been in our hearts ever since. Incredible, it seemed, to be driving toward them; and grand to be driving, anyway.

"I'm glad the poplars are in leaf," I said; for without their quiverings along the stream, or groups of them against the old pink farm-houses, these otherwise treeless hills would have looked bare.

Lovely sharp hills they were, farmed to the very tips. Dismissing London, we talked farming busily . . . always a charming topic when one is driving through miles of somebody else's beautiful work, which one criticizes freely. . . . Some one, at home, once ventured the remark that our farm was "too steep to pay." Hoh! our mild bumps. What would that neighbor say to farming the roof-sides that these Tuscan peasants toil on? *We* put such peaks into pasture; but—waste good crop-land, when you have a pair of cows that will stand on edge, go an inch a minute and plough it?

Animals are not pastured here. Even cows are stall-fed, and see the sky only when they go out to work.

So the peaks were all vineyards and grain. Blue iris was everywhere—not a single purple one; a lovely soft blue like September hills. It grew on walls; every old farm-house had a row of it. There were fields of pink vetch, beautiful against the blues of Tuscan landscape; and in the roadside a pale-yellow thing like a marigold pleased us.

Seeing our garden flowers grow wild, though, upset all one's floral scheme of things. There were many sorts here, all taking splendid care of themselves; no one, in Italy, seemed to pick, or notice, wild flowers.

We now began to climb violently, and in dramatic loops. This was the *salita rapida;* soon we'd be on a *discesa pericolosa.* Hurray! we hadn't done a "descent perilous" since leaving the Riviera. An amusing hill-town appeared on our right, with the stems of a giant grape-vine growing through holes near the top of its wall; it had a great brown gate with rabbit-warrens built over it—story after story of windows and balconies, with things streaming from them. On a peak opposite, eyeing it superciliously, was a *castello* with a grand tower . . . though every farm-house here had a tower, sat on a sharp hill by itself and looked extremely like a castle.

Nobody, in this very scoopy landscape, lived in a scoop. It made the farms most picturesque. The lines of the crops swept downward from the peaks, giving them an air of being draped. . . . We wished our farming would drape.

Nicolette churned very ably up the slopes, and coasted merrily down; picked her way through villages—which today were tiny and far apart. Beside one of them, though oxen were hard at work in the fields, two peasants were sitting cosily together on a wall talking as hilariously as if they had nothing else in the world to do.

"People in these places see each other *all* the time," said Babs, marveling; "and yet they always have something to talk about!"

It did look like a limited village; about three houses and an *osteria;* but Italians can talk, *and* laugh, from morning till night. "It is their nature to." Getting south, we were; the zone of loquacity. A pair of lovely white oxen met us, their handsome drivers walking beside them: *"Gia, gi-a!"* and the oxen at once turned beautifully out. We were always grateful to them when they did that; Babs, who had been preparing for a full stop, or else for climbing by with one wheel up a bank, stepped gladly on the accelerator.

For we were in haste, this morning. Being bound to reach Siena that night and yet have time in San Gimignano (those towers!), we had chosen the straightest road from Florence. Not by Empoli, but by San-Casciano-in-Val-di-Pesa—which doesn't sound as if any one could be in a hurry, but we were —and by doing so we were missing Certaldo, just across a mountain-range from us. I was sorry, for Certaldo is the hill-town where Boccaccio lived during most of his life. He was born in Paris (a fact I didn't know before) but wrote his tales here in Certaldo, and was buried in its church of S.S. Michele and Iacopo "under an inscription written by himself." A later memorial (put up in 1503) "was destroyed in 1783," Gardner says; "in virtuous disapproval of the character of his writings."

Morals in Certaldo were at a high pitch, in the eighteenth century.

Today Boccaccio would not have to write his own epitaph, nor would a cenotaph to his memory be torn down . . . though one does see the drift of his detractors' opinions. But in 1823, when wars had lulled for a moment and literature apparently renewed its appeal, his little *citta* changed its mind and restored the old, bare-fronted, pink-brick house where this gay raconteur had lived; even to the tower, with its beautiful mountain view, and the small loggia where, high above the noises of the street, he used to write. One hopes that his townspeople are yet of the same mind; for Certaldo, unchanged, rosy and ancient at the top of its windings, should be and perhaps is "still haunted by the spirit of him who wrote the Human Comedy of the Middle Ages."

But this wasn't such a hasty road after all. We always aim for a *route dangereuse* just to see if Nicolette can do it, and now were putting her over the worst possible hills—though after our Briançon gambolings they didn't seem much. . . . It was a thick day, though bright with color; we stared and stared for a thing on a peak that might be San Gimignano. There were so many peaks. Once we were sure we saw Certaldo, through a gap in the blue hills that everywhere rimmed the view; but I don't think we did. At last, to the south-west, some distant towers popped up; thrilling towers, blue-gray and bunched. Tiny though they were, we saw their tops were square. The post-card!

"That *must* be San Gimignano!" cried Babs.

It was; but it was late before any lunch-place arrived. Poggibonzi, where the road turned off to San Gimignano, seemed the only possible one; and even then we didn't like its little hotel; picked a bit of *colazione,* and hastened out, for Poggibonzi's little sharp-eyed boys were having far too good a time with Nicolette . . . we had heard their shouts. Up a little cultivated valley we drove. Ranks of hills shepherded it, and not a hint of San Gimignano did they yet give us; but we were beginning to know the ways of Tuscan hills. The valley climbed encouragingly; and Poggibonzi was almost nice to look back upon. It had a castle of its own, on the inevitable sharp peak round which the town is built, and a picturesque muddle of houses; but we hoped its attitude to travelers was not an index to that of other towns we were to meet in southern Tuscany. . . .

One expected extra geniality, in the south.

These fields looked welcoming, with their mists of silvery

olives and big slopes of the pretty, gray-leaved *pacelli;* wild flowers leaned at us with cordial faces . . . everything—vineyards, olives, cultivation, flowers, sweeping on and up as if to a culmination of golden-brown walls and towers.

We swept with it. There they were, our *belle torri,* against an Italian sky. Very Italian today, the richest soft blue; and the afternoon sun, though high, was still afternoon enough to make brilliant edges and shadows. The road whirled, showing us towers one minute and just sky the next; Nicolette, doing her best with the long curves, was getting hot. . . .

Walls growing nearer, more articulate, brighter, more real; *torri* also articulate, taller and grimmer, defying heaven (almost above our heads now) with square-topped invincibility. Very plain, the towers of San Gimignano; scarcely a battlement on them; serviceable, desperate, stark towers—thirteen of them left, out of a medieval seventy-six.

But thirteen towers of every height and size, above a conspicuous wall like this of San Gimignano, have their effect. . . . The wall, built on a stormy peak, goes angularly up and down, in and out: no smooth or easy time have these defences around Tuscan hill-towns. Rock-flowers may grow in them, or iris dulcify their tops, lean trees may peer from behind their aged corners; but agile-climbing, fell-descending, difficult and cruel are they—stiff and stern, for all their peak-evolved agility.

"I'd hate to have to bash a hole in one of them—with things dropping on me from above!" I thought.

"Grand, isn't it," said a voice beside me; and just then the towers whirled out of sight.

"But the flowers, Babs," I said, leaning out. "That iris!"

For a streak of it, blue and white, climbed the hillside. Other flowers, poppies, *bottone d'oro*—gold buttons, as Italy calls her buttercups—decorated the roadside or lighted the mild shadow of the olive groves; tall vigorous anemones, like the Swiss ones, grew in coves by themselves or purpled whole hilltops. Such glowing purple, it was; almost as prevalent, in its field-scattered way, as tulip-colors had been in London.

London in March is solid tulips. Basketfuls held up at your windows, street-corners massed with their brightness, Piccadilly Circus alight with them; tulip-leaves turning yellow on your mantel-piece, tulips being too high-headed for the dinner-table . . . one is positively ill with tulips.

But these slopes were glad of purple. We were too; anemones, in every state of freshness or non-freshness, had not yet begun to wilt on every *ristorante* table. . . . And now we were impatient for towers. Round a bank Nicolette swirled us, up a steep bit and to a level space—a little park; across it were San Gimignano's walls, basking in the sun.

Dreamy, unreal walls, so eloquent of another day; looming above tree-tops, hiding the town behind them. But a gate was in them, with a black donkey and his cart coming through; a load of very actual branches in the cart. A girl and an old woman were filling copper pots from a dripping pump by the parapet; beyond them stretched the lovely Val d'Elsa: pink towns, the blue of the Apennines. An Italian girl and her baby sat on a bench in the sun, and the young mother smiled at us richly, indolently, indulgently—the smile of the siesta.

For siesta was not over in San Gimignano. It seemed to last longer, the farther south we went. We loved siesta-time in these little towns. Churches might be shut, or picture-galleries locked, but streets were possible; poor badgered Nicolette could make her way along the narrowest places, and scarcely meet a soul. . . . Poggibonzi too should have been enjoying her noon nap, we told each other, but she wasn't—another objectionable thing about that valley town; her little boys were never brighter.

And it was *really* noon when we were there. Innate depravity, said we, staring very devotedly at the Val d'Elsa; just natural cussedness!

But San Gimignano was beginning to stir. After basking a bit on the parapet ourselves—I love the top of a low, sunwarmed wall—we began to feel we should like to take Nico-

"DREAMY, UNREAL WALLS, SO ELOQUENT OF ANOTHER DAY"

San Gimignano

lette up into the town with us. She looked so small, so alone-of-her-kind, sitting there with those walls frowning down on her; she *should* go too. . . . She had cooled off a little now; so under the gate, into the exciting intimacy of a real hill-town (our first), we cautiously steered. A wall of old houses made profound shadow in the little via; some little white oxen met us, a pair of two-year-olds, in pretty scarlet yokes; also a few of San Gimignano's citizens, striding along. A church, some little markets: with towers and an archway mounting before us, we began going up a cobbled twist so steep that Nicolette hesitated, and—"Bro-*onk!*" went the gears.

"No start, you see," murmured her owner, with a slightly knitted brow.

"That was a horrid twist too," I said, staring at a tower that loomed astonishingly above us—and there we were, that instant, in a leaning, downhill piazza with a well in the middle. We had whirled sidewise into it—the Piazza della Cisterna; that stone-curbed well, with its graceful cross-piece, was enough to center an old town about. It had charming, shallow steps leading up to it, and a grass-grown tower looking down on it—a very noble tower; a shorter, fatter one just beyond . . . Pale towers, with flowers in their chinks—in the sunshine, against that blue! Children played, and youths lounged, blue table-cloths fluttered in the wind; red geraniums stood by the doorway of a little *albergo* opposite, where a young porter in a bright green apron was wandering about. . . .

But we were not quite up. Round a shadowed curve into the sunshine were the steps of the *duomo*. We could just see an edge of them. "Back he reined his steed, back, back!" and up the cobbled pitch we swarmed, by the gnawed edge of an old *palazzo*. Ah, this was the place. The apparent summit, with towers and palaces—though not as much of a piazza as the other one; more like a sloping space. Beyond it, under dusky arches, the town went down and down; but here were sunshine, and a *carabiniere* to take care of things, little boys with post-cards, and a guide with a red band on his cap lolling carelessly—or was it studiously?—at the top of the *duomo's* long flight of steps.

Nicolette wheeled proudly in; the very first car in the piazza. We wanted to go everywhere at once, but decided on the *duomo*—so near, so Romanesque, so necessary to see; climbed the steps and secured the guide (we really thought we'd like him, for once), and just then a frightful churning came from somewhere downhill. In a moment more a long and glittering nose with a very exploring expression poked itself round the corner—though not any faster or better than we had come—and still another nose, and there were a Rolls and a Daimler.

The little boys at once got very busy, but we swept our captured guide into the cathedral. He seemed to be the only one. Ha! Early birds, we were. The Rolls must have been lunching long and well.

The guide's gestures were illuminating, likewise a few of his torrential words; a pleasant, dark-eyed creature who looked none too well fed, and whose glance at the beauties of his *duomo* had affection in it, and pride. He took us, exhaustively, everywhere; among dusky frescoes, into St. Fina's chapel—with everything very dusky indeed; but beyond the simple little sacristy, light and cheerfulness enter. The cloister is just outside. An exquisite little one, with very old rosy roofs sloping down, two of San Gimignano's towers sprouting unequally into the sky, and a charming plot of iris around a little fountain. One could have sat for a week and sketched those towers, with their foreground of quiet garden; such quietness, such sunny peace. And, in corners, and by the path, a few plants of wallflower and sweet alyssum.

If you have ever been, or tried to be a landscape painter, apparently there is no escape from it. I like dark frescoes in dark *duomos*—and fonts, and ironwork, and clerestories; I adore the sweet faces the Old Masters drew; but the moment I see, down steps or through a little door, a bit of sky and something green in a cloister, I fly to it, and am very difficult to drag away . . . a sweet bit of monkish garden with the sky overhead, sun on its columns, and a clear Italian shadow cutting across them—following lovingly the curve of each little pillar, then whisking off it in a sort of small grayish mist that is lost in the column's roundness. . . . Because the garden is there; and while you stare at columns you hear water tinkling; and one does love sky so, and old roofs—and here were two towers besides. And the purple of the iris was so dark and velvety, and went wonderfully with everything else, and the sky as fresh as a flower too; it is perhaps the cloister's grouping of charms that enthralls one so.

I have never seen an ugly garden in a cloister, though there are some very odd-looking and neglected ones; the cloister pulls it up to its level, I suppose . . . and sky and air help.

The old Greeks knew this, my child reminded me; they also knew how to remove fatigue from their entertainments by staging everything they could in the open air—looking at the wine-dark sea, or Mt. Olympus; perhaps even at Greek wild flowers, which are without a peer.

Babs adored the cloister too, and we went round and round it; finally dismissing the guide, who hurried off to absorb the Rolls.

Then we were in peace. . . . But we had really got a good deal from what this *condottore* told us; Latin is a great help to an architectural vocabulary, and had been thoroughly drubbed into us at school—*ad, ante, con, de!* so when Latinish words came along, which they frequently did, with little Italian tails on them, in cathedrals, I pricked up an ear, said "Ah, got you!" and whispered them to Babs—digging her lightly in the ribs meanwhile, in derision of this borrowed learning. . . .

I, of course, would have lingered here till sunset, but Babs was doing the driving, and time-table was on her mind; Nicolette, she felt, would soon be champing outside, so after a bit I was gently abducted through a little door, out of sunshine, into duskiness again. . . . Some Old Masters, we agreed, would look frightful anywhere but in dusk; like the finest Russian ikons, they were painted for dusk, and belong in dusk, and have darkened with time besides; and as we went back into the *duomo* again, we felt the power of it. The mass of frescoes is amazing. The walls of the nave are one glow of color; the whole interior, though not large, is round-arched and heavy in effect; all gold and richness, and with a terrific Last Judgment.

Outside, we found Nicolette basking contentedly beside her two G.B.'s, so went briskly off to see everything else. Downhill to the Porta della Fonte—with a lovely view, and women doing their washing at the fountain; up again to the Pieve, where litle boys in stout boots and torn, bright-colored shirts at once besieged us.

"Rocca, rocca! Guidare, signora . . . Rocca!"

We were going to the Rocca, but did not desire little boys; their shouting brought no results, so they rushed ahead and posed for us. *"Fare fotografia!"* they wheedled, standing in an absurd row with their heads on one side; and when that failed, dragging in a baby in a red dress, propping him in front, and begging us to take *his* picture.

"Signora, fare la sua *fotografia! la* sua *fotografia!"*

We began laughing, which seemed to discourage them at once; with fragmentary cries, aimed at our retreating backs, they dwindled away. We went on up the yellow path, and three little girls leaped out at us. *"Rocca, rocca!"* One, with a snub nose, bright little eyes, buttoned boots and a very short purple dress, was most persistent, shouting up into our faces till we reached the very steps that led to the fortress, when she suddenly turned and went racing downward, not in the least afflicted by our neglect, laughing in glee, her hair and her purple skirts flying, toward other voices she heard ascending the path.

Children of San Gimignano do not intend anybody to be lost, in their dear town.

A path under masses of ivy took us round the fortress wall to the gate, which a pleasant young woman unlocked for us.

A sweet garden the Rocca had inside; fruit trees and vegetables, and the sun basking down. Under the trees were beds of *pacelli,* that tall, bean-like thing that grows everywhere so well in Italy. It looks even more interesting than a bean, with its height, its silver-gray leaves, and lavender or pink-tinted flowers—tinted just the way bean-flowers are; on our way up we had seen fields of it, banks and steep hillsides of it, doing splendidly in shade, doing pretty well on the driest clay—doing simply magnificently if given a chance in the sun.

Here it seemed very happy, poked in under cherry trees.

In the sun by the wall, borders of flowers alternated with bushes of delicious-smelling herbs; above them, waved onward by the young woman, we climbed ivy-escorted steps—much-worn, stone steps—to a flat-topped tower. With a gasp, we both sank down on the nearest thing; I on a stone table, Babs on the edge of the parapet.

"Oh!" said we. For here was Tuscany in the afternoon sun; near-by waves, far-off horizons of it, gold in the light, deep blue in shadow; threads of road straying off to pinkish villages or being lost in hills. Near by the little round hills were pink, farthest hills were forget-me-not blue; all the villages were exciting because perched on peaks. In that rich spreading light we could see their walls and towers; here and there on a hilltop among cypresses, the pale bulk of a monastery. . . . Cypresses in Italy do not grow miscellaneously everywhere, as novels lead one to think, they mean either a convent or a cemetery; sometimes a lone church, set high above its village and guarding its own graves—or, more rarely, on hereditary hills, the gardens and avenues of the *nobilità.*

In the valleys below us—for this was the very tip and summit of San Gimignano—a keen but misty sunlight quivered over fields and crops the more brilliant for a dark frill of purple-shadowed mountains behind them. Wild, rough, little mountains, waving away westward to fierce Volterra, that ancient enemy of San Gimignano, walled and tremendous on its bleak height. . . . It kept us for some minutes, speechless and staring—but that only one way; when we turned, there before us were all the towers. Our *belle torri,* in sunlight, above the Rocca's wall.

All this time they had been behind us, near enough to look beautifully ferocious, far enough to be just lovely things in a lovely view; some tall, some short, but all rough and warlike and real, with plants growing between their stones. Fascinating, the yellow of wallflowers on that aged gray.

We sat there on the bit of wall, eyes blissfully roving; if the towers basked in sunshine, we surely basked in the towers. Built for fighting, they were, on a height to which it was difficult to drag stone—that might be one secret of their stylish plainness; and built in a quarrelsome age. There is a sense of tragedy about them, as there is about the whole of San Gimignano; one feels its strivings, its feuds, its leapings to and fro among walled and fortified neighbors, to help—or to oppress. The town has had several castles, but seems from earliest history to have been very conscious of its towers, which are used as background in so many of its frescoes. They were always being threatened with destruction; for San Gimignano was a republic in its early days, and a spunky, fire-spitting republic at that.

One would be, living on a peak. There is a certain egotism about peaks. Splendid places to spit fire from.

The town was at first subject to Volterra, and no sooner gained its liberty than it began to look about it, on its hilltop, with a bright and conquering expression, and deprive other people of theirs. It destroyed the small fortresses of lords in near-by castles, it even destroyed the castle of its neighbor Poggibonzi—though at the request of Florence; for San Gimignano by this time had flung itself into the wars of the Guelphs and Ghibellines, and Baedeker gives the rest of its history in a sentence; ". . . in 1353, after having suffered terribly in consequence of the dissensions of the leading families of the Salvucci [Ghibellines] and the Ardinghelli [Guelphs], it became subject to Florence."

Leading families again! They would patch up a peace, "or a Cardinal would patch it up for them," Gardner says, "and solemnly celebrate it in the Piazza; but hatreds would flare out again, and brawls start up afresh." The Ardinghelli, it seems, were always thirsting for vengeance, and doing things just a little worse than the Salvucci: in fact in the narrow limits of this little hill-town they battled so fiercely, appealing to their more powerful neighbor for aid, or secretly bringing her forces inside the gates, that the Florentines lost patience and decided to pull down the fortress, "in order that this castle might no more be the cause of San Gimignano and Colle being stirred up to any rebellion!"

"Very striking," says Gardner, "is the last piteous appeal of Fra Matteo Ciaccheri to his countrymen, to let the dead rest and save San Gimignano before it is too late: 'Among the castles it is the very flower, and we are destroying it with all our might. It is the will of God, our Lord, that it should come to nought for our sin; within my heart I feel bitter grief thereat! Each of us has been hunted out, because we have turned to these factions, and we have been slain and burned and taken and robbed. For God's sake, let us let the past be past, and each one strive to be a good brother, and look upon each other with kindly eyes. And so we shall save this noble jewel, which doth ever move my heart with love, so delightful and beauteous it seemeth to me.' "

But on taking a vote of San Gimignano's people it was decided to surrender to Florence; though as Gardner again writes, "there were so many opposed to it in the secret balloting, that it was only carried by one black bean."

And then Florence behaved very prettily. Most honorable terms were agreed upon, and signed (in our dear Palazzo Vecchio); medieval courtesies immediately went back and forth. Artisans from San Gimignano for instance who wished to be instructed in any art, in Florence, were to be received free of charge, "it being expressly stated that it is lawful to each one of that town to exercise his own art there freely, notwithstanding the ordinances of the Arts of Florence." Rather a noble provision, we felt, considering the usual rivalries and jealousies between the arts.

But the Rocca was not saved . . . We were sitting on its ruined wall, "delightful and beauteous" still.

And we could count only nine towers.

Behind them the whole country-side now melted into pinkishness; the lovely little round hills were blue. Everywhere were the same exquisite interruptions; wee, rosy villages, cypress-pencilings upon the somehow thrilling pallor of a monastery; northward, through gaps in the towers, we saw half a dozen villages that might be Certaldo—rosier, on its peak, than any of them. . . . It was all so lovely one did not need towers; yet when one's eyes returned from roving, nearer still, and defiant in their certitude, sprang the magnificent Nine. The picture I took of them—in which they slant backward like a tug's smoke-stack tilted to go under a Thames bridge—merely serves to show our emotion.

And then we had to go. In the garden, the young woman gave us each a bunch of flowers she had been picking—fragrant ones; mignonette, a sprig of lavender, one or two yellow wallflowers. "St. Fina's flowers!" she told us. Thanking her, we went off, sniffing our little bunches; out under the ivy.

That view! Aged roofs tumbling downhill, a loop of town girt within its wall; the bright country beyond. . . .

But in San Gimignano, if you leave something you love, you very soon come to something else you love. In a few strides we were off the hill and in the upper piazza again. It seemed more like a piazza to us now; its importances were coming out. Italy's greatest poet had been there, in that square, and addressed the people from the balcony of the old palace, for "the young burgher who rode in, with trumpeters and others whose coats were emblazoned with the red lily, was no other than Dante Alighieri, come as ambassador of Florence. . . ." And there is no other town in Tuscany, our guidebook averred, "which presents so faithful a picture of Dante's time."

"A PUDDING-BOWL OF A VILLAGE"

On the Way to Arezzo

That picture, for us, was just beginning to evolve; San Gimignano, though it didn't look it, had had artists and sculptors as well as clashings and wars; also a saint, a poet, and a cosmopolitan *littérateur* of its own. We stepped into the dim church again to realize St. Fina a little better. A touching saint, because she was so young; "the virgin heroine of San Gimignano." At ten years of age she became ill of a dreadful disease and chose to lie on a plank, or *tavola;* when she lay dying—at fifteen—the people gathered at her house to find the room filled with "a fragrance of Paradise," and the *tavola* blossomed into flowers about her.

" 'Hardly had that blessed soul expired,' " the *Story of Siena* quotes from an ancient chronicle, " 'than the Demons in envy and rage filled the air with such fearful whirlwinds, that poor mortals were struck with horror. Against them the sound of the bells of San Gimignano, moved by the invisible hands of angels . . . bore witness to the sanctity of Fina, and caused those storms and whirlwinds to cease.' " "Such are the contrasts," adds Gardner, "offered by medieval life and legend. The town where the streets are still running red with the blood of the citizens, and the remains of houses and palaces are still smoking in their ruin, are visited by beings of another world and have mystical gates and windows that open out upon the unseen."

Babs and I were very fond of that bit; it seemed to express the Middle Ages.

Fina was taken very seriously by her townspeople; "she is the glory, the example, the guardian of her fellow-citizens," says an inscription, and her chapel in the *duomo,* with frescoes by Ghirlandaio, is its particular treasure. One fresco shows her in the room with the plank already breaking out into flowers around her; the other is of her funeral, with all the dignitaries attending, and the towers of San Gimignano playing their part; for there they are, with the angels ringing the bells.

One really begins to think that angels did ring the bells. I should love to think so; and Ghirlandaio surely put them in the fresco! It was painted some two hundred years after her death, but one authority very nicely says that the subject "had probably been settled from the beginning." For how could the good people of San Gimignano *invent* angels doing anything so practical as ring bells? Bells are so specific. And so noisy. And the towers so very visible. Besides, if a saint had conflicts with demons during her life, as Fina did, she simply must come to angels in the end; like the "lived happily ever afterwards" of fairy-tales, that was quite the literary tradition of saints. . . .

Fina is in many more pictures, charming little panels that one finds in odd corners; in the large "Coronation of the Madonna," she is grouped with five very prominent saints, St. Augustine and St. Jerome among them.

As for the town's *littérateur,* his story is most modern. He traveled to Rome and helped found the Academy; became secretary to the King of Poland, wrote several books (in Latin), and went on journeys as ambassador, earning a European reputation; on his return he was given an enormous reception by the town fathers, "in order that his fellow-citizens might be encouraged to follow in his footsteps." Indeed, the little *commune* seems to have been all out to encourage culture and the arts, and to retain the devotion of those who practiced them; for though its poet, Messer Folgore, lived mostly in Siena, in feeling he was a violent Sangimignese, we are told, writing "furious sonnets" on behalf of his favored party, the Guelphs; also a series of more peaceful ones about the life of San Gimignano. "Yet even in these," as Gardner puts it, "amidst the singing and love-making, the feasting and jousting, hunting and hawking," there was a day of fighting to be described:

> To a new world on Tuesday shifts my song,
> Where beat of drum is heard, and trumpet blast;
> Where footmen armed and horsemen armed go past,
> And bells say ding to bells that answer dong.

A lovable way of putting the clamor of the belfries; for as our author remarks (of the Torre dell Orlogie), "When at nightfall its bells, those of the Pieve and the more sonorous one of the Commune answer each other, the Sangimignese assure me that the sound can be heard in Florence."

Coming out from the gallery, into which we had stepped to see the naïve pictures—especially that of good San Gimignano himself, holding the town in his lap—we newly appreciated the rich look of everything; the older palace with its tower and visible bells, its loggia with a dim remnant of a fresco by Sodoma; the two towers rising above the dark and heavy archway where the town tumbles downhill.

It is always doing that. Down steps or through arches, with lovely blue glimpses of sky and country; for beyond it all Tuscany falls and fades.

But no matter how the town drops, the wall neatly receives it. There are no unsightly edges. San Gimignano's declensions, whether gentle or violent, are paintable and sweet. . . . Sometimes we lingered, sometimes we ran—down a violence; but always saw something enchanting. Women were coming from the Roman arches of the fountain, trudging serenely uphill, chatting and laughing, with their hands on their hips and baskets of clothes on their heads—a feat, that seemed to us; children were playing, boys holding mules to graze, boys carrying hay from a yellow rick perched on a bank, its pole scenically protruding. Hens of various colors were scratching in a sunny alley by a stable door, with lovely brooms and things about; and near this there was a walk outside the walls —a pink path with olives climbing against the light, spraying their softness on some of the old towers. There were five or six old churches scattered about, and plenty of streets that were stairs; by one of these, in a warm corner, a painter had set up his easel.

"Nice!" said we, passing meanly behind him.

For the climbing town was before him, a high garden, with roses and an emphatic fig tree bursting over its wall, the lobed leaves of the fig making nice strong patterns on the sky; a woman in blue was going up the steps, a child in red coming down them, etc.

This place would keep him busy, we said. Flowers were everywhere; pots of them along the flat edges of roofs, or in balconies and little upstairs loggias where kerchiefed old women came out to water the plants; but San Gimignano's vegetable-gardens are works of art. A trained grape-arbor at one end, fruit trees at the other, with a swept space beneath for a home-made table and chairs; here and there a tub of special flowers, perhaps a gorgeous shrub of crimson camellia —and vegetables stretched beyond in the sun. Set in the neatest beds, every plant perfect, hilled up, raised separately, tied to a stick (even individual pea-plants were grown that way), with usually an old grandsire in a faded waistcoat to gloat over them—perhaps spend his whole day, with love and slowness, setting out a few lettuce plants, pretty as yellow roses on the dark earth.

How one would love one's garden to look like that. . . .

But it needs the grandsire. I saw one of them doing it; his old wife coming to the door of the little pink-washed cottage to look approvingly on, beam at the vegetables, throw him a sharp, high-pitched, good-humored word or two—which he returned as sharply; bask a minute in the sun, snatch up a toddling grandchild that had attached itself to her skirts—Italy is full of these stalwart toddlers—then duck nimbly in to the dusky *casa* and her cooking-pots.

What a fine, oniony whiff came from that cooking-pot! It made us hungry.

Nicolette looked very good to us, after we had climbed back to the piazza. We strolled toward her partly out of habit, partly to see how she fared, and little boys at once danced earnestly round us, sure we needed guiding somewhere—to Nicolette's step if no further. They opened her door for us with a flourish, and were quite dashed when we did not enter grandly, as signore should when doors are opened for them, and sail off in great state.

But we were feeling quite domestic in San Gimignano by this time. Babs went to buy films, and I dashed downhill to the art-shop, which was under the oldest palace and therefore chilly. Those thick damp walls! The padrona, a thin, competent little woman in a kerchief and dark-striped apron, was standing talking to a customer, holding fast to one of the little screened brass pots with charcoal in them, that the women carry to warm their hands—dear little boat-shaped pots with carved handles; we had even seen them being carried up and down San Gimignano's stone-paved hills.

The padrona went to look for the print I wanted, a reproduction in color of Gozzoli's fresco in the Church of San Agostino: the little Augustine being taken to school by his stately parents, Monica and her husband, and at one side the school-master in his long robes frankly spanking a lazy "scholar"—a child of about four with streaming fair hair, clutched firmly on the master's shoulder, his little skirts thrown back, and the dread bunch of switches uplifted . . . the small Augustine, meanwhile, a picture of an infant prig in his properly pleated and embroidered little dress, looking complacently on. . . . But after vain search, the padrona set down her handstove.

"Scusi, signora! Momento! permess'!" she murmured; and darted out.

At this the shop's other customer, a portly Italian, rose from the chair he had been seated in and with a bow, a beautiful smile and wave of the hand, offered it to me. He then looked grandly and vaguely around, though a moment before he had been chatting rapidly with the padrona, accepted my astonished thanks and stalked out. Such a dignified person. His suit was of very dark blue; he had spats and gloves. Could he be a native? Except for a hasty young man we had met riding a fine young chestnut horse out of the Porta del Fonte, and starting off at a reckless gallop for his afternoon exercise, we had not seen any one of this sort about; and yet—all those families with towers?

Just then the padrona's husband came in—he had the little wine-shop next door; a brown, quiet, bent little man who informed me with great placidness that the visitor who had seemed so established in the shop's one chair—and whose back was now retreating with great dignity down the street—was the Podestà.

"E vero?" I said, rather stunned.

"Si, signora," I was comfortably told; there was to be a procession that evening, starting from the steps of the *duomo,* and the Podestà often came and sat in that chair, to see processions. Now the door of the shop was directly opposite the cathedral—and Italy the most democratic of countries; but it all seemed to me a cheery happening. The historic Podestà, whose title had come down through the centuries (and who was probably an Ardinghelli or somebody), not only to plant himself in a village shop, but rise and give up his seat, with the greatest apparent pleasure, to a stranger; who might have decided to sit in it for an indefinite time.

This, I thought, must be hill-town courtesy; but if anything had been needed to make one fonder of the place than one already was, it was this last touch. . . . Where was the Podestà's house, I wondered. Would it be august and great, or in some democratic nook? Nearly everything *was* in a nook, here.

I bought my print and hastened out, thrilled to see some of the black-hooded *misericordia,* with their long staves, go leaping up the *duomo* steps, and highly-embroidered prelates arriving. A band played in the distance, the stir of preparation was in the air—and a long shadow falling in the piazza; we must be off.

High above us, the two towers were still in sunlight; we climbed into Nicolette, and such was our state of dream as we coasted down the long hills, that I scarcely remember anything about getting to Siena. There were some white oxen in an olive grove—they had a scarlet cart; I remember a cove of anemones, and being glad to get through Poggibonzi. The map tells me we went through Staggia; its river was in the landscape—and probably delightful—also the towers of Monteriggione; but I cannot even recall those towers. Not a stone, not their color, not a wallflower. . . . Our heads were so full of towers, our hearts too; griefs and beauties of towers that the Middle Ages saw and we never should, because the Middle Ages, thinking only of themselves, had selfishly destroyed them.

We drove through something stunning and medieval, I know, because we weren't at all sure it wasn't Siena and drove on in much doubt. There was a great hump we climbed (rather sulkily on Nicolette's part) only to slide wastefully down on the other side; the country was fertile and bumpy, our twenty-five kilometers seemed very dusty and long, and we did hope we should know Siena when we saw it.

For in this region of one perfect medieval thing after another, it becomes rather a problem. . . . How should we know it? Could one really go through Siena and *not* know it? We peered anxiously, yet in some amusement, at the hilltops. It would be so lovely, to lose Siena.

But here was a town on a hill—I well remember the frantic green of the slopes; a mellow, walled town, sprawling irregularly, nobly battlemented and spired. Our road swarmed upward to a great gate; within that was a space, and then another gate. . . . Thorough, this place! but with no name, no sign. Into a close-built and stony via Nicolette took us; down a stony dip; a smiling *carabiniere* with a beautiful Italian flourish waved us uphill into cream-colored buildings and a fine openness, with trees and a garden beyond.

Splendid; but *was this Siena?* We hoped it was. We liked it. It was clean and ancient and satisfactory. . . .

Waved grandly onward by another smiling *çarabiniere,* we drove along an ample, light-colored street which narrowed sharply, becoming full of animation and cabs. Here was a loggia, with people sitting at little tables. Tea! Cups and pots and plates. Marmalade! Whatever the town was, we'd have tea, anyway. With a whirl into a wider spot we parked and came hastily back.

Just one table was vacant. We sank thankfully into its two seats, and a *cameriere* instantly darted to us. (Italian waiters dart so gratifyingly.)

"Due tè? Marmalatte e paste? Si, signora! Subito, subito!" and he darted off.

Some snap to this place. It seemed to be a snappy town. About half the people in the loggia were Italians, gaily drinking cordials or *sirops* and paying no attention to the sights in the street; the straw-hatted English, over their tea, were quieter—spectators like ourselves, and amused with their environment. Almost too amused to talk, I thought, wondering a little at this placid receptivity; I had had the venturous idea of asking one of them where we were, but they looked too beautifully absorbed and sleepy. Besides; *not* know where you were? They would have thought us mad.

And here was our tea; very pretty, all blue and yellow with Florentine pottery. The little tea-pots had dragonish noses. Pleased as two children, we unfolded our choice paper-napkins, delicate almost as chiffon and heraldically decorated in dim soft old red; then looked quickly up at each other and began to shake with laughter. . . . In one corner, inscribed under a device of helmet and feather, were the pertinent words, *"Caffè Pasticerria, Siena."*

We were in Siena!

I tried to pour out tea, but could hardly aim for laughing; Babs' dark eyes were swimming with tears of mirth:

"Very well, paper napkin!" I said, wiping my own eyes; "we'll stay here tonight, then."

Gasping, relieved, delighted, we sipped the hot tea. (We hadn't known how relieved we should be or how much we wanted to stay here, till we caught sight of those words.) Splendid tea; sublime *paste,* piled up in wild assortment, with plenty of the squashy little Italian éclairs.

"See, Babs," I said, bending over them with the remarkable earnestness that motoring induces. "In Florence they were skimpy with that kind."

"They were. Isn't this nice? After all that dust. I think I'll take a fork." For the éclairs were damp.

We leaned back, still reminiscently grinning, and absorbed Siena. Our Siena, this was; not just some unknown place. We felt fond of it already. Cabs, donkeys, bicycles, but mostly pedestrians; all of them walking in the street. Our loggia had an eighteen-inch strip of sidewalk before it, as did another, shallower, loggia caffè opposite, but these small metropolitan efforts could not begin to contain the afternoon mobs of Siena, now flocking enthusiastically by. . . . Young priests leading processions of bareheaded school-boys, in long black coats with white sashes, older prelates in twos and threes, black-coated civilians, officers with their ladies; tourists in sober garb trooping conscientiously along; soldiers, gay young people, noisy Fascist youths with extraordinary hair thrown off their foreheads in a great flopping backward-slanting mop some five inches high.

We found that this was Fascist hair. It seemed to express the ardent youth of Siena, slender and wild-eyed, flying gibingly along; sloped very far forward on their bicycles, with the preposterous hair sloping just as much back, giving them an air of startled, and startling, animation.

And now that we had found Siena, we realized we were very tired.

One more thing there was to find, and Nicolette was soon taking us deeper into the mêlée. . . . Ah, lovely old colors of Siena; the old palaces, the narrowness and quaintness. But we had no time, except for a glance; hooting patiently, we crept along in the solid crowd—not a lethargic one of peasants this time, but a laughing, pushing, out-for-the-evening crowd through which to our horror, every other second, would come an almost invisible bicyclist, shouting, bell-ringing, leaping off and on; trying to think they were riding through that mob.

Sometimes a woman scolded a little in a shrill Sienese voice, or a man frowned, looking crossly down at tire-mud on his coat; but for the most part nobody minded. . . . And then the Via Cavour dipped down a short hill. The shadowy dip was solid black; and up it another motor was trying to come!

Shrieking the horn, fighting her way with a sort of desperation, Babs shoved Nicolette's wing against an ancient front—I heard the wing grind on stone—while the other car, likewise bellowing and fighting its way inch by inch, managed to scrape by us. My child steered straight downhill to a distracted *carabiniere* who was vainly trying to combat the throng.

" 'Better ask him how we get out of this," said she, biting her lip.

He gave us distracted directions, meanwhile waving us quite crossly down another small lane with no sidewalk, and grim old buildings walling it. . . . But it was empty. Bliss! Down and down, past exciting palaces, past shops and shabbiness, all in the same blessed quiet; round a turn into picturesqueness. A gate with a fresco; a bare piazza, a small fountain.

"There's the she-wolf!" I cried, pointing; for the cross *carabiniere* had been good enough (Sienese enough) to mention her. Romulus and Remus are supposed to have founded Siena, and I suppose he was proud of it. At any rate, here they were with their wild mother—very primitive, on an old column; but, "We're getting *too* far down!" said Babs, stopping Nicolette decisively. "We'll be out of Siena soon."

For indeed a bit of entrancing view—sunset country over Siena's wall—showed between roofs of old houses. Lovely, but we had just come in from that. . . . My child bent over the map; pored over it, twisted it about, puckered her young brow. Siena looked like a great spider; a neat spider, with a wall around every bit of him, but which way up did his legs go—from where we were? And where were we anyway?

"Give it up!" she muttered. "Let's get a boy."

The boy-on-the-running-board, sure sign of a car newly entering a foreign town. We hated to be new—to give in to a mortifying necessity we had hitherto scorned; but seeing us hesitate, three boys sprang at us. We chose the lightest one, a ragged-shirted imp who grinned with bliss and hung at arm's length from my door, one bare leg swinging in space; we turned left, into a slot of a lane, went down, went up; then at his behest, set ourselves at a small hairpin turn so steep that the boy jumped off—and *I* felt like getting out and pushing.

But Nicolette, in a fit of energy, made it—she had just recovered from a fading-fit; the boy jumped on, and we went churning noisily up a stone-paved hill.

"Là!" he said suddenly.

It was a palace doorway.

CHAPTER XI

THE SEARCH FOR CAPONSACCHI

THIS, the pension?

Si si! upstairs! waved the boy. Columns, a lovely old grille; I climbed some outside stairs, and a cordial little signora with short, red-brown curls opened the door for me.

Excellent boy. The Duke's palace was below, and this upper floor, a large, rambling place, was rented as a pension. . . . And we only wished to stay one night? The little signora, kind, a trifle weary, was astonished—and pained. One could not see Siena in one day; no, no! There was so *moch* to see. People usually stayed five days—a week! In another day there would be a room on the view side, but at present (and she flung open a door), there was onlee this.

"This" was a largish room with a plaster archway in the middle, and plaster cupids disporting about it, but no outlook; mammoth beds, a huge wardrobe, a small tin wash-stand near the window. Across the street (only a few feet away) and veiled by drapings of Nottingham lace—a dismal fabric much favored by Italian landladies—was the wall of a church, broken by a stone balcony and Gothic casement, through which one plainly saw the padre's robing-room. A devout-looking woman in black (she also looked extremely narrow-minded) was arranging a slim vase of flowers on the ecclesiastical window-sill; but I did not stay to watch her. . . . Babs must hear about all this.

"I must talk it over with my daughter," was my formula.

Downstairs we hastened, through the unfragrant little foyer; and there was Babs, with a hopeful face turned toward our approaching steps.

The signora, evidently struck with something in that look,

lost her little trace of sharpness and became hospitality itself. Usually she did not take in any one for less than five days, at the veree least—but if we would ree-main two nights, why then she would be so veree gladd! She remembered well our London friend; and there was a veree good garage for reparations, just up the hill. Luisa should show us.

"Lueee-sa!"

Whereat not one but two very young, giggling, and adorable little peasant maids who had been peeping at us from an upper window, descended tumultuously and were upon us; heaving out the suit-cases, and *running* with them up those flights of stairs.

"It ees nothing for them!" said the signora coolly—yet with a shade of indulgence in her tone; and back came Luisa panting.

With many grins and bashful hangings-back, she climbed into Nicolette's rear. . . . Never in a *macchina* before! Beaming, but with very red cheeks, she clutched the back of my seat as we climbed to the garage—a splendid big one with skylights and inspection-pits and all the attractions.

In another instant brawny mechanics were peering into Nicolette; pointing and gabbling as if she were the first *machina* they'd ever handled. . . . How gratifying. How adorable these Sienese were, with their fire and energy and simple-heartedness! Even Luisa, still clutching the breast of her not-too-tidy frock, but fairly breathing out approval, astonishment and a sort of childish adoration of the signorina's exploit in getting us up that hill (for in Siena, women do not drive cars), was a refreshing person. . . .

We felt a little limited in our viewless room, though things in the street were engaging to watch; women taking jugs to the fountain, donkeys and their loads coming up the hill, a young peasant going down it with great strides of his wooden shoes; but when six o'clock came (which it almost immediately did) such a clamor broke out from a belfry overhead that we stared at each other in dismay.

Could we ever sleep through that?

Its clangor was smitten into by another, hard by; then another, slightly more aloof, and sweeter; then suddenly everything in the town began to ring, to pound, to beat, to jangle! adding to the reverberations that already filled our room to bursting; we almost felt we were being shoved into the street. . . . No room for us and that too! Babs, in the act of brushing her hair at the bureau, dropped the brush, clapped both hands over her ears and, raising both eyebrows, stared whimsically at me by the wash-stand—who, in an even worse case with a face dripping wet, had taken refuge in a towel and was giggling over the top of it. . . . Wow! the bells of Siena. We had heard of them: had heard that there were more bells to the acre, here, as it were, than in any other Tuscan town; but we had not expected to sleep right under them. For when we reached this street, I had not thought to search the air for belfries; that was not one of our usual preoccupations, when engaging a room.

And in stony Siena, how they echoed. Each deep little lane clutched at the sounds, old palace throwing them back to old palace, church walls catching and prolonging the multifarious din, till not only the hills of Siena but all the seven hills of Rome, it seemed, might have been joining in the clamor.

It ceased at last; but the town still hummed—like a great tuning-fork. Vibrations, driven here and there upon its air, ricochetted amusingly about. . . . Sweet Siena! We really loved those bells; and from our window we now saw that a priest with a lace cape over his cassock was moving about in the robing-room opposite, which was lighted by a solitary candle. Intriguing, that was; though I didn't see him look once at his vase of flowers that the person in black had arranged for him with such care. . . . Perhaps he didn't like to have flowers arranged for him.

A gong sounded; putting an end to this gossiping, we wandered down the long, straight hall, bare and somehow sculptural as Italian halls pleasantly are, to dinner.

A smallish *sala,* with tables for four; two New England spinsters were to be our companions.

The elder was an excellent *raconteuse;* their idea of dinner entertainment in fact was one story after another, a procedure we usually find wearing; but the sisters, though a trifle bitter in their outlook on life, had a conspicuous sense of humor; their stories were fresh and good. They were civilly, if as yet distantly, interested in Nicolette, they meticulously passed us the butter; we strolled affably to the drawing-room together, for polite coffee, and Babs' one smile to me, in the rear of the spinsters, was as satisfying as a two-hours' talk.

For although we had had no chance of conveying to each other these reassurances, they were already conveyed.

I woke with a start. Where was I? Ah, the bells of Siena. Bells, *bells!* No sunlight yet on the church wall; I reached for my watch. Six o'clock; yes, the signora said they began at six. . . . I lay there, wincing at the enormous clamor. It would wake Babs up, of course, and the lamb was so tired last night; everlastingly dash those bells!

I raised myself on an elbow, and looked across. Motionless dark hair, yellow satin quilt rising slowly, evenly; how gorgeous to sleep that way. But the stone echo-chamber outside was doing its finest; I rose and softly closed the window. . . Ah, one could live now. I sat up and wrote notes.

Seven o'clock struck—merely seven enormously multiplied strokes; but there was a stir from the other bed. A turn, a sigh; a dark eye that lifted itself at least a quarter of an inch above the satin quilt.

" 'llo!" I said, unfeignedly rejoiced to see it.

"Mm," remarked the eye; and, like a Florida fish, disappeared again. For a moment I stared hopefully at the quilt-edge; then went on writing. The bells had long since ceased; we must have that window open again. I stole forth. On my stealthy return, again the eye, this time much illumined by a growing smile.

"Howdy, A.B. . . . Wottimesit?" muttered something that would be a voice presently; and a lavender-and-white striped arm reached out for Minnie, in a chair. "Uh! Slept, didn't I. S'pose we'd better—ahooo-oo!—have breakfast!"

Siena's rolls are plain and watery; the sort that chill you with a sort of everlasting, rock-like look and one specious fold down the middle. They are pale rolls too, and pallor never adds to a roll's charm; this morning we spoke with regret of the rolls of France. . . . Luisa, dimpling, had hurried them to us with the greatest good-will—we had heard her busy felt slippers running along the halls; Siena *would* run with your breakfast. She ran with our jug of hot water, she ran for honey that the cook forgot; it seemed but a short time before we were out on the pavement in a strip of sunshine, climbing the hill for Nicolette.

We were going to Arezzo. It seemed strange to be driving away when we had just arrived, but we had done a lot of stony things lately, not much country—and Babs was feeling languid and queer; like sitting in the soft sunshine, and distinctly *not* like cold cathedrals or tiring galleries.

Arezzo, like San Gimignano, was very much in our hearts; though our vision of it was not in the least scenic, but mental and romantic—and due entirely to Browning. Both of us had been brought up on "The Ring and the Book": the beauty and simplicity of Pompilia, her rescuer's self-abandoning love; for Caponsacchi with his high-mindedness, his psychic resilience, his wit and gaiety, is a Hamlet turned satisfactory . . . without, perhaps, some of the wistfulness of Hamlet's appeal. Caponsacchi was by nature a man of action, yet even he had the long struggle with himself, the first stunned incredulity, the weeks of agonized doubt and self-probing, which makes the development of Hamlet's tragedy so pitiful and so enthralling.

Well, Arezzo was the scene of their drama. Guido's house must be somewhere there, and that remote seat in the Pieve where Caponsacchi first saw

> . . . enter, stand, and seat herself
> A lady, young, tall, beautiful, strange and sad.

"THE GOOD OLD WOMAN POSED FOR ME WITH HER KEY"
Caponsacchi's Church, Arezzo

Then the window from which Pompilia, unafraid in the quietness of her despair, spoke to the young priest and implored him for rescue:

> I have more life to save than mine.

The road to Rome too; the gate where on that black night they attempted escape, and he awaited her,

> With a tune in the ears, low leading up to loud,
> A light in the eyes, faint that would soon be flare,
> Ever some spiritual witness new and new
> In faster frequence, crowding solitude
> To watch the way o' the warfare—

till at last

> . . . there did Pompilia come:
> The white I saw shine through her was her soul's,
> Certainly, for the body was one black,
> Black from head down to foot. She did not speak,
> Glided into the carriage,—so a cloud
> Gathers the moon up.

In London my child had been re-reading the poem as a mere contrast to the tremendous tomes in which historians and archæologists express themselves, and which, at other times, she steadily devoured.

"I used to think 'The Ring and the Book' was hard reading," she confided one day, coming out of her room with it in her hand, and sitting luxuriously down before my fire; "but now—good gosh, it isn't anything. I read it right along; like any sort of mush!"

"Do you?" I said, pleased. "All that Law, and the Other Half Rome, and all that? That's grand. *I* don't. I skip it!"

"No, I read it all," said she, with a half-humorous glance at me. "I like it. It's *such* a relief from Gibbon."

So Arezzo it was for first choice, if we were to motor anywhere today . . . and then we could see Siena next day, we told each other comfortably, as we toiled up the hill. And if we wanted to stay on longer at the signora's—why, we could.

"I like her," observed Babs, squinting upward at a delicious gargoyle, green with age, that hung over our heads. "I like her very much, somehow. And I like the cute maids. . . . Once we get a room on the view, it will be grand."

For this morning from a hall window we had looked out over the Duke's garden, and realized what we were missing . . . by looking out on any street, however interesting, or any church rear, however fruitful of gossip.

The kind little signora had told us which *porta* to take, so down through Siena's windings we cautiously went. The view burst very suddenly upon us, as it does outside any Sienese gate; down and down a swinging white road we glided, with the pink and green country before us and the Apennines blue and bumpy in the north. . . . Across the plain at a fork, two stately old gateposts of pink stone, one on each side of the road, said *"Per Arezzo."* How reassuring! You couldn't disbelieve anything as stately as they were. A fountain was near by, and two lovely children coming to it with copper water-jugs; a new blue flower bloomed beside the road, and along it came a big cream-colored horse with a little brown donkey on each side of him—the donkeys leaning forward and pulling hard, the horse looking benignant and immense between them.

And then to our amazement, the clay country began; fields of clay, mounds and steep little hills of it like inverted bowls, mud-colored and unprepossessing; but a jubilant bird sat on one of them, undismayed by his surroundings and singing loudly. It was April, if one did live in a clay desert.

And when Babs advanced the idea that these might be some of the clay burial mounds 8,000 years old or more, which exist in Italy, the mounds at once became thrilling. "Bones and pottery! Oats growing on them!" Only it was really wheat.

But it was hard on the peasants, this clay. Endless white oxen were here ploughing the stiff slopes, four or six of them to a plough; moving imperceptibly along, pausing almost every other minute to rest. The whole region was dotted with them, posed at uncomfortable angles on the steep pitches—a fine suggestion for a cubist picture, we told each other; strong, muddy, dismal, well-patterned, and with an unreasoning use of white.

In nature it was not so dreary. The sun shone, and peasants were spots of color; a few fields showed greenishness as the blades of young wheat struggled through. But those chunks of clay the oxen had turned up! We looked closely at them as they lay by the road; some were already dried as hard as bricks. . . . The labor must have been heart-rending; yet there seemed to be plenty of peasants. If you are born in a clay desert, I suppose, you stay in it; you live and work, endure the heat and glare, shrivel and die there. . . . At least the patient Tuscan peasant does.

But along the valley came an ardent creature; a hustling goods-train, its two engines, back to back, working very hard. "Ziz-ziz—*bum*-bum-bum-bum!" It hurried past us, its pistons whirling and thumping with the greatest energy; Babs laughed.

"New potatoes for Paris!" said she.

And the new potatoes, whistling violently, soon grew small in the distance.

We climbed higher among the strange clay hills, which now looped themselves ambitiously upon the sky; and grass began. All along the way, peasant girls were tending high-legged pigs; pigs eating the thin grass as fast as possible, and not rooting at all. We watched the complacent, half-surly saunter of an enormous mother pig, blue-and-white and extremely muddy, coming grunting toward us across a field, very conscious of the fine litter also grunting behind her. Among pig families, I suppose, it is only decent to answer one's mother when she grunts; at any rate all little pigs do it, and it is one of the touching things about them. I am always melted by little pigs.

Further up the hill a fair-haired girl of eleven or twelve was sitting on an upturned donkey-cart, from which the donkey had been removed, knitting with a wise and pursed-up expression and at the same time tending a cluster of sheep. Near her an older girl, pretty and dark-eyed, in a blue dress and primrose-colored kerchief, was rather sullenly chaperoning six large pigs who were gobbling grass in the ditch. She looked almost malevolently at us, one thought—with a pang of sympathy for her: "*I* tethered here—and you, free to wander!"

At least that was how one could but interpret the look. We often wondered how these peasant children endured their monotonous days; with animals they knew—doubtless to weariness, with so little background for their minds, and here, as foreground, the terrible clay sameness. The younger ones looked cheerful—or more often vacuous and nothing-in-particular; but this girl with the lovely dark head in the primrose kerchief was old enough for bitter thoughts . . .

Heretofore (as often in Italy) the landscape had been treeless, but as we descended from the ridge of mounds to a slightly greener valley, a stream appeared.

"Somebody got up their nerve to plant a few poplars!" murmured Babs.

A double row of them, along by the water. . . . Never had we so appreciated the mere fact of trees; and these had silver-backed leaves that shivered, and pretty, pale trunks. We stopped on an old arched bridge of pinkish brick and looked down a charming perspective; the winding stream, of a lovely, chalky turquoise, its grassy, sunny banks striped with the systematic shadows of the two tall rows of poplars—shadows that swayed as the trees moved, their lacy, golden tops spiring into soft blue sky. On each side of the stream curved a pink path, as perfect a design as if Boutet de Monvel had drawn it; and iris bloomed beside the water.

"Why can't *we* do that?" said a wistful voice beside me.

For we somehow don't. Was it entirely age or Italian color in that scene that made us loiter there, and go reluctantly away? I think not. One loved the sense of design that in these older countries every peasant seems to possess; the care for line, the training and tending of every inch till perfection is reached. . . . For here was a flat bit of landscape that might easily have been meaningless, made as significant as a master's drawing.

After this the soil grew pink and the country pretty.

"Uphill into wild untended landscape," say my notes, "with gnarled oaks in young foliage, and broom in blossom underneath. Somebody was redeeming this ragged oak-region; a wall held up the rough land beside us, olives had been ventured on, and young vines." A flagged path, most delightfully bordered with groups of purple and white iris, wandered charmingly away among the olives; and in their sun and shadow a very brown, gnarled old Italian, in a wide black hat, was working with a mattock. He glanced down at us rather crossly, yet quite casually . . . as befitted a dignified old hill-peasant laboring with stones.

Circular *chilometri,* these! climbing and winding, with the blue of the mountains leaping at us, and Nicolette flying. After the delaying mud of previous days, it was fine to fly. "More oaks and broom. Great blue view. Hayricks of brown furze; for fuel? High and early here; little locusts scarcely in leaf. (Blooming, in Cascine Gardens.) Little lavender rock-flower, on banks. Houses Alpine, low, of stone; stone-slab roofs almost flat, and weighted with stones. Only few of them. Great big one, walls, cypress, on hill. Great gorges around."

Across a valley a lovely pudding-bowl of a village, just neatly fitting the top of its hill, was a graphic illustration of medieval fright, huddled within its round and perfect wall; not a shed, or a stone, had dared to be outside. We took a picture of this village, which might be Gargonza—or Liggiano; or maybe Palazzuolo Alto? Our map seemed a little dim on villages. At any rate, it was too far away; but we put the camera on a wall and did our best.

"It'll be tiny, of course," said Babs, winding up the film. "But you can always take out the village and enlarge it, if it's clear!"

I knew exactly what she meant. And in that sunshine how could it help being clear?

"Wonderful descent to San Savino," continue my notes. We floated down and down a smooth gravel road, still nicely pink; how lovely, in this soft sun and mountain air, with lovely things all about, to float and float into an Italian view.

" 'Ringed with an azure world,' " I thought; for indeed the entertainingly peaked and bumpy Apennines *were* that tint.

Near us, the gray-green slopes alternated with a sweet pink crop like clover—only it was really crimson—blossoming incredibly against the mountains . . . with strips of golden broom, wild purple valleys, wild blues and browns—a whole palette of color; and all the time that fine sense of easy descent, with the wind blowing to us the good, wild, heathy smells of the April hills. Only it was nearly May now, we told each other.

"Look!" said Babs . . . and far below us were some old brown towers. We thought it must be San Savino. I dove for the guide-book.

"Yes, it's the right spot for it. 'Monte San Savino, 330'—that's meters, isn't it. . . . Well, we'll still be a thousand feet up, nearly, when we get down there!" And we gazed at the brown walls, coming rapidly nearer.

"Air's been smelling high all along," said Babs, turning her head to me with the sort of smile that always meant . . . home. "Made me think of Mt. Moses—didn't it you?"

Thin, high air always did. We looked at each other. After all, our own hills. . . .

But on the last swingings of the descent we overtook some great wagon-loads of brown furze drawn by immense and glorious white oxen, with the usual scarlet yokes; they were resting, just below a sharp turn. We gestured across to them, and waved the camera; the drivers laughed and gesticulated back, and posed, proudly smiling, beside their beasts.

Again too far away, but the best we could do; sliding by, we called out *"Grazie, signori!"* to them, and the pleasant creatures laughed delightedly again, shouting back quantities of nice colloquial things, of which I could only understand enough to know they *were* nice.

We passed an olive orchard lifted upon a bit of high land upheld by a wonderful old wall—how one enjoys these walls, abroad!—and then came the lovely *porta* of the old town. A very beautiful, olive-skinned young Italian, beautiful enough for sculpture, gave Nicolette her *due litri* from a bright red pump—always a strange sight in Italy's ancientness; then around a corner of perfectly immense masonry our road squeezed along the hillside, just skirting the tight heap that is San Savino.

On our right, vineyards fell precipitously away to the valley; it was delightful, thus circumventing the sunny roofs of the old town. Italian hill-villages mostly manage this way; and it would have been inconvenient both for us and the village if we had had to drive through the inner gates and up the picturesque cobbled way, where so much living is being done, and so many are the chairs and babies and salads and industries. Regretting what one misses, yet very thankful for the omission, one navigates the outer wall. Belfries and dormers protrude, the wall bends and swings; we felt most familiar with San Savino even without entering it. The road gave us a taste of it: old houses built on a steep downhill, a wide doorway where peasant women sat in the sunlight making the brown brooms, with darkness and a red fire behind them, and half-hidden in the duskiness, great piles of furze waiting. This, then, was where the cheerful peasants were bound with their brown loads. Quantities of brooms, those women must be expecting to make. . . . A nice town, San Savino; every one looked with great benevolence at us and Nicolette as we slid closely past their doors.

Down we plunged, to a rich plain. Rye was six feet high here, the oat-crop fabulous, the crimson clover an amazing blaze.

But twelve-fifteen, and the peasants still working? Their clocks must have been slow; noon-hour is usually such an accurate thing. Yet this was the time of lengthening days. A leisurely sun shone on the leisurely plain, had shone for many hours, and would shine on; why hurry when, after the long nooning, you work comfortably on till dark?

A sudden village surprised us; just a tumble of cottages curling down around a turn, color and life abounding. Graceful girls in peasant dress were bringing water to the cottage doors; in one yard, where brown stacks of faggots were piled, a donkey with great cheerful ears was being unhitched from a blue cart before a little, stained, rose-pink house. A grapevine, mounting on a very thick stem, had a single strand along under the eaves; the rest of it was trained across the gables in a sweet yet simple pattern, and wherever the vine went, an echo of its pattern in turquoise-blue (from the spray) was on the old rose-pink stucco behind it. . . . In Italy these incredible things really do happen; yet the little house was only a fit habitation for the two peasants who were unhitching the donkey, and laughing splendidly with each other meanwhile: a man in dark blue, a woman in an orange kerchief and bright violet apron—how did she know how to do that? An impression of extraordinary vitality came from them, and of powerful, vital good-humor; he was tall and strong-looking, she was stout and jolly and strong-looking—meltingly kind and good too, one was sure—and they both smiled at us out of such honest, sunburnt faces.

Their beast, not to be outdone in these matters, had an importantly happy face; was fairly chuckling to himself while he thought about his coming supper, and staring straight ahead of him (as equines do when they have triumphant thoughts) with those fearsome ears at full height. An inspired donkey.

On, through a crack in the hills, to Arezzo; the sun suddenly very hot on Arezzo's white and stony beginnings—and too much for my child.

We went quickly up through the town's agedness—very old, it is; Mæcenas the patron of Horace was one of its eminent citizens, and *he* died in 8 B. C.—found a decent *albergo* on the cool side of a little square, and lunched upstairs in a long, shady *ristorante* intelligently arranged for hot siesta-time, with plants in its long windows and a stylish menu.

That, with the shade and greenery and the discreet kindness of everybody, proved reviving; we descended to the little stony square to find Nicolette completely covered with nice though excited little boys, well-dressed and white-collared, whose one object in life at the moment was to point out, at the top of their young voices, that we—that the *macchina*—had a flat tire. "*Eccolo,* signora!"

It was too true . . . I found myself looking darkly at the little boys. But they were all innocence, all eagerness to help; their white collars so appealing! Babs, having rejected my aid, philosophically inserted the jack, when—as if this had been a fairy-story—out from the hotel door bounded a young man.

Literally bounded. One instant he was in the doorway, the next he was taking the jack from Babs' astonished hands; a young Italian, dressed as if just out of a band-box. (I particularly remember his cuffs—of a pale and refined gray-blue; and the cuff-links, of antique silver, were worthy of them.) But how swiftly he banished the little boys, whirled the tools and inserted one of the spares; all the time murmuring sympathy and concern, and counseling Babs like a brother.

Charming young Aretine! Dusting himself very slightly—for he had managed with marvelous neatness—he bowed and hurried away. This rescue was reviving too; Babs felt better, but not like stirring about, so she and Nicolette sat in the shade before Caponsacchi's church (which was closed) while I and the camera toiled up the sunny hill to the top of Arezzo.

The paving-stones were hot, the walls very high; it seemed a long way up that hill, though towers and walls were exciting. Arezzo seemed somehow small; very simple, and basking in quietness, it suggested neither priestly intrigue, nor villainy, nor any lady, "young, tall, beautiful, strange and sad." Whether it was the heat, or the hour, or the silence I do not know, but the farther I climbed that hill, the less I could seem to make Pompilia belong there—or any of the romantic tenseness of "The Ring and the Book." Where was the Torrione? the "low, dilapidated wall," and San Clemente?

> . . . there's no other gate
> Unguarded at the hour; some paces thence
> An inn stands; cross to it; I shall be there.

I did not know. What was worse, I did not seem particularly to care. And I met no one to inquire of. Desperate need, heroic midnight romance—a romance the more nobly put aside, smothered, foregone; could those ever have inhabited this bare and placid stoniness, these walls, not particularly anything, but sloping from very age?

Siena, now, could suggest anything; Florence breathes intrigue to the last crack of her, Venice simply *is* medieval craft and charm and gliding romance; compared to these Arezzo's voice seemed not only smaller, but uncertain of accent; a little—must it be confessed?—dull. She didn't even look as if she could make "red earthenware vases of superior quality" —though we are told she once did. A little of this, a little of that, there might have been, here or there . . . behind the barred windows of that old *torre,* perhaps.

I hurried on past an old palace or two, stern and bare and original-looking; past a sweet mossy fountain, and moss and little plants in a high wall, to a wide piazza where, with its back to an enormous view, sat a tan-colored church with a fine portal, a fresco with a delightful lot of blue in it (which the church needed), and a mile of very hot steps. "Crude work in its upper part," say my notes; "holes here and there; the under-bricks were showing. This was the *duomo,* begun in 1277, not completed till the sixteenth century; even so it did not look quite finished." Or was it medieval artillery that had made those gaps?

But the whole hilltop was charming with sunshine and shadow; horse-chestnut trees in white bloom, thick green turf, and bright blue Apennines beyond; a tiny silver Arno winding far away to the north in the great valley of the Cassentino. And there were little daisies in the turf

The church being shut for siesta, I stole a glimpse down the Via del Orto where Petrarch was born (in 1304; the brass plate on his house shone wonderfully); didn't stop to translate the very long Latin inscription, but hastened back down the stony hill. *Oh,* that old torre! I took a distracted picture of it, with the tower wildly askew; but I got Nicolette in it, and my unconscious child, dreaming in the shadow.

By an arcade, the loveliest young girl I had seen in Italy was playing an accordion; a delicate, grave-eyed child with a sort of innocent bloom about her as she moved her arms in playing, there in the sunny street. Softly-streaming, golden-brown hair she had—it fell waving over her shoulders; poetic lips, and a cheek and chin worthy of Botticelli. She was dressed, as an artist would have her, in clear soft old faded colors such as one sees in pictures of the saints; and two smaller children were with her—a memorable group, on the antiquity of Arezzo's pavement and wall. The young girl glanced once at me, a delicate and most unwishing glance; I absolutely didn't know what to do with it. Anything one could think of on the spur of the moment was too ridiculously impermanent; beyond transplanting her at once to the society of poets, to everything exquisite in life forever and forever, there seemed nothing one could do for her. . . .

I took a hasty step along the arcade, perceiving an open space, and a statue, white in the sun; ah, Babs must see this. We could drive here.

By the Pieve an old woman was crossing the street, a huge key in one hand, a wicker-covered *fiasca* in the other; would the signora like to see the church? She unlocked the low door. Cool, gray, shadowy, with a few immense columns, and bits of gem-like color in the shadowiness, the interior surprised one with its beauty; there were dark wood-carvings, and an aged altar-piece of saints, very primitive and strangely drawn—tiers and tiers of little lantern-jawed saints, all in richest colors, their haloes crowded on a gold background.

Yet it somehow did not suggest . . . the light didn't come right . . . it was too perfect, too *soigné:* it was *not* Caponsacchi's church! For when you have had a thing in your mind for years and years, just how it was, choir-stalls on the left and lovely mists of incense rising to the sun, and then find it's all different and there aren't any . . . why, it isn't what you came to find, that's all. The façade, outside, was amazing; very tall, and all covered with little columns—though we hadn't come here to see façades; so on the Pieve's heavy-lidded porch the good old woman posed for me with her key.

At first she sought about for a place to set down, or hide, the *fiasca,* but I begged her to hold it. Embarrassed, she did; and then I tried to find out if she (being thus ecclesiastically connected) had ever heard of Caponsacchi, or Canon Conti or Guido—in short, of any of the characters in the great poem which has once more, as we say, "put Arezzo on the map."

She had not. She was an intelligent old thing, if rather silent and self-contained; too intelligent perhaps to waste good Arezzoan (or Aretinian?) on mere *forestieri*—a romantic-sounding word, by the way, which means strangers. . . . She had known all about the works of art, paddling industriously about in her felt slippers and showing them; unlocking a sacred door or lifting a curtain over some special treasure, pointing to this or that. *"Molto anticho!"* she had once piously murmured before a wood-carving, as if overcome by its possession of that quality; but for the most part she was silent.

But it seemed as if she must have heard of Caponsacchi, the hero-priest; or at least of the poem.

"Non il poeta Inglesi—Roberto Browning?" I pursued, conscious of taking liberties with a famous name, but still hopeful: they *must* know Browning in Arezzo. *"Un libro, signora"* (ah, this was simple, we'd had book in our first lesson) *"—si, un libro di poesia, appellato 'Il Anello e il Libro'?"*

I made appellato up and it was probably wrong, but remembering the word for ring was easy. We had had a great deal about jewelry—travelers in Italy are supposed to aim straight for a *gioiellière*—also about smells, and sunsets, and touching the ceiling (*toccato il suffitta*) and the wind blowing one's hat off: all sorts of things you wouldn't think you'd have, but you do.

The old woman listened, patiently.

"Roberto Browning?" She looked up at me, as I waited in expectation, but with no answering gleam; she shook her head. A solid head, under the tight kerchief; a solid little shake. It was conclusive. *Poesia* did not come within her province; nor, to my surprise and disappointment, within that of a hurrying, red-nosed priest whom I followed inside and interrogated; a horrid green-eyed creature who was slinking up a side-aisle and wishing to dive in at a little brown door. ("Beware of a dog with gooseberry eyes!' one of my father's dog-books used to say.)

At first, a flash of interest lighted his little eyes. This female, inquiring after one of his fellows? Chance for scandal, here?

But as he heard the name, interest died. He looked loathingly at me. (One hoped, again, it was anti-Protestant loathing.)

"Come?" he grunted harshly. "Caponsacchi—*un padre? Non vi è!"*

And the door received him. Almost banged in my face, if such an ecclesiastical little old thing could bang. . . .

He had not even taken it in, that I was asking about some one in a book . . . let alone in a poem . . . let alone our beloved "Ring and the Book." (I did think a priest would know about poetry.) Feeling suddenly desolate and bereaved, as if something precious had been wrenched from me, I went rather blindly out.

Ah, nice sunshine! Nice little boy going along the street with a jug. Nice old peasant woman, with her key and her comfortable kind face. . . . Arezzo was not all horrid. This warmth was healing, after churchly chill; and Babs smiled at me once more, a sleepy smile, as I climbed back into Nicolette.

At that, poetry existed . . . Caponsacchi existed; if Arezzo's people had forgotten, it was their loss.

Florence had *not* forgotten.

Nicolette, as if sympathizing, took us very gently along the short, shady distance by the palace; its loggie are useful and shady, but very bad. . . . Vasari did them, that Giorgio Vasari who did so many things, architecture, painting, and biography; and none of them very well, except the writing. At the entrance to the arcade, very high up, hangs a bas-relief of him; sun and shadow, at the moment, divided his face lengthwise, but one could see that he had a beard and a long face and looked serious rather than spicy. Spicy biographers do not always look as they write—witness the long and solemn countenance of Mr. Strachey; but if Italy's lyricist was Arezzo's first citizen, then this lively Renaissance writer of the lives of artists was its second in renown . . . and Arezzo, strange to say, is aware of it. There may be a Teatro Petrarca or an Accademia Petrarca, on the Via Garibaldi—or was it the Corso; near by, there was also a Piazza Vasari.

It was the space I had seen; an interesting, downhill piazza with a fountain in its lower corner. Beyond, springs a campanile with tiers and tiers of exquisite little columns; there is also the beautiful apse of the Pieve. The tall young Caponsacchi, as he strode across to matins, must often have looked at that apse and loved it—one of the most beautiful anywhere, it seemed to us; the most original; but Caponsacchi probably did not compare it. It was his.

> . . . the pillared front o' the Pieve—mine,
> My church. . . .

Only this was the back we were looking at . . . even lovelier than the front.

But in the bright sun before the loggia was the white marble back of Ferdinand of Austria; much elevated on his pedestal. *"Erected by the loving cizens of Aretium"*—oh yes, said we. These Tuscan towns had suffered horribly from what Sedgwick gaily calls "the Spanification and Austrification of Italy," and conquerors had a way of forcing their monuments upon a reluctant people. . . . So had lesser tyrants; the Aretines once lost their tempers and put a rope round the neck of a Medici statue, threatening to drag it from its pedestal, in return for which outburst another Medici pleasantly doomed the city to be razed, ploughed, and sowed with salt; a sentence which, luckily, was not carried out.

We crept thoughtfully around the town, through the brown shadows of one stony via after another; very glad we had come. We should have stopped at San Francesco, in whose choir are the beautiful frescoes by Piero della Francesca, "master of Luca Signorelli (best light in the evening)," as Baddy kindly says; but the shadows in the lanes seemed chill, so we crept on, not especially searching for the Torrione, or the Road to Rome.

"Gubbio's over *there,*" remarked Babs, looking in affection, if rather faintly, at the eastern-most hills. "But I remember it awfully well—don't you?"

"Perfectly. I can just *see* that little old faded Madonna behind the church door. How's your head now, Babbits?"

"Bum!" said she cheerfully.

I did feel a pang of regret over the Casentino, which we might cross fleetingly but otherwise should not see; a beautiful spot—though Dante, when it was his lot to follow the course of the Arno, accompanied it "from its source to its mouth," Gardner says, "with bitter complaints of the swine of the Casentino, the dogs of Arezzo, the wolves of Florence, and the foxes of Pisa. . . ." A charitable list; but if the poet—perhaps one of the first authors to follow a river and write it up afterwards—had to make his way through all that, it must have been a worried trip.

The adorable hill-village was clearer in this light. Was it Vignale; or San Zeno? We could not tell; suddenly remembering the Florentine field-glasses, we took them out—stopped the engine, and stared. . . . Ah, it was worth these preliminaries. The village had a fortress, an ivied wall, and the loveliest rabbit-warrens all huddling on each other; we could see pink and blue washings hung out on a terrace above the wall, and peasants walking about. At that distance!

"These glasses are certainly grand for villages," murmured

Babs, busily gazing. "Glad we went into that shop, aren't you. . . . Turn 'em down—or up a bit, probably, A.B."

Yes, all the old colors were before one; almost every leaf on the ivy. From far down in the valley, vineyards and olives ran uphill to the wall and stopped neatly there; a complete Tuscan sight.

"We can climb all the mule-tracks now—without going up 'em!" observed Babs, turning a pleased eye of security upon me.

For in France mule-tracks had been one of our griefs. They wound up to inaccessible villages, they turned so pink in the late light . . . and we could never take Nicolette up one of them. Blessed be extravagance. We felt, as I have said, frightfully splurgey coming out of that lane in Florence with the glasses, but they had scraped many a fresco from obscurity and tucked it among our possessions; the sort that moth and rust do not—etc., etc. I put them, with regard, in the door-pocket.

"Maybe we'll remember we have them, now!" I said.

For if you've not had a thing for years and years, it is easy to forget that you have it; and in this case, as with evening clothes, new saddles, hired men, and other minutiæ—Babs and I were used to saying to each other, "Get on *perfectly* well without 'em!" Which we did.

But it still seemed funny to have an evening frock in one's bag.

And then to make up for stopping, we drove rapidly along.

"Petrol village again; San S.," say my notes. "Missed adorable, swan-like white oxen and red cart, with load of broom, but got snap of old *porta:* pink-purple wall of *trattoria,* yellow-green branches of tree, two pairs of white and gray oxen resting in shade, red cart, shafts up."

Some painter should sit before Monte San Savino and get the beauty of that entering bit. More oxen were being shod, and all sorts of properties lying about; the white of the animals took the eye down, and the brilliance of the tree took it up; it tumbled over the pink-purple of the wall, was seized

THE VIEW FROM OUR WINDOW IN SIENA

in a fatal hold by the sculpturing of the old gate—altogether didn't know where to lodge next.

A sculptor, indeed, was born in this place, Andrea Sansovino, master of that Jacopo Sansovino who did so much in Venice. Andrea's real name was Contucci, but like most artists of the period he was renamed after his village . . . and why they changed the *a* into *o* I don't know, unless it looked more masculine or something; the Italian tongue is always taking liberties with its vowels.

So the village church has a "group by Sansovino" as well as a most unexpected terra-cotta by one of the della Robbias —who had a miraculous way of scattering themselves about in mountain villages; one reason why driving among these hill-towns is so amazing. . . . The smallest one may be very important; *its* church had to have Ghirlandaio or della Francesca or somebody come and do a fresco in it, or an altar-piece —or he was born there, as was Andrea Contucci in this unregarded spot, and came back to honor his native village with a bit of his work.

Though I don't wonder that somebody born in San Savino grew up to be a sculptor; design lingers in the very stone of it. The straggle of its wall is an inspiration. Few great Renaissance artists, we discovered, were brought up in cities; the hill-towns were stimulating enough. . . .

At almost any peasant's house one sees something exquisite; beyond San Savino, one tall old *casa* displayed layers of charms. Against its stuccoed wall was a border of blue iris; over this, a great jar of soft orange pottery; above that again, the lovely head of an Italian girl looking out from the dusk—and directly over her, on another window-still, a fawn-colored hen. A nice, red-combed hen, very happy and contemplative; standing there with her tail to the view. (An Italian touch, that.) She made a pleasing Japanesque composition there, but her contribution was chiefly comic; how did a hen get to a fourth-story window? For by her pose of leisure and habitude, we thought she lived there.

Very probably she did. Probably there were at least a dozen

families in that tall old *casa,* and each with its adjuncts; one finds out only gradually what old houses in Italy can contain.

"Drove up hill," pursue my notes. "Gorgeous scenery. Loafed in lovely pine grove. Cuckoo sang; also thrush. Also pines."

That pine grove was at a high corner above the road; the world of southern Tuscany before it.

The light grew lovelier, the thrush sang and sang. . . .

We strolled about, looked here and there; at last ran down that piney bank hand in hand, hating to leave it, yet lured by the beauty before us. . . . There is something angelical about Tuscany in afternoon light—an indescribable sweetness. Birds still sang in the oaks, the world was golden, the hills blue. As we drove, the towers of Siena were upon the sunset, tiny at first, then growing larger; a glorious sight, now hidden, now flashing from behind a rough little hilltop or a group of oaks. Even the clay desert was glorified—its monotone that "so reflects the mood of the sky"—and as we drew near, the city's wall brightened to golden-rose. Lovely old wall! We climbed past the gardens and blossoming peach trees, and (with a few sputterings on Nicolette's part) were soon inside the great gates. Glad to be there once more. It all seemed like home now. We knew our way, we knew where to find tea, we knew everything. . . .

CHAPTER XII

SIENA THE INTRIGUING

"WET Saturday. Errands. Awful hunt for *tabacchi.* Found it when I had given it up in favor of staring at a façade!"

For my child, though very sleepy still, desired cigarettes. I tramped past little old San Cristoforo, its yellow-gray columns seductive in the rain, and down the Via Trieste, for there were shops there—shops and shops, but no *tabacchi;* past the Mercato and into side streets, most of them violently downhill and blank of wall. Beautiful ironwork over my head, beautiful clear puddles on the pavement, but no *tabacchi;* and soon I should either have to start climbing a hill into unknown regions, the Via di Citta and enormous palaces (I saw their battlements upon the sky), or dive into indefinite lanes.

I chose the lanes. My-mother-told-me—! I went to the right. It was a nice lane, short, with pleasant things over one's head, and a *piazzetta* at the end; an odd, triangular-shaped one with nearly every corner cut off. In one corner was a sort of loggia with very high steps; the rain was coming down hard, there was no *tabacchi* visible—I climbed the steps and tried to read the Latin under three bronze busts, nicely greened with weather. Somebody the Magnanimous, with a gentle and drooping look and a drooping mustache; on each side, as if to support him, a very fierce one: Victor Emmanuel I and Umberto, with those unexcelled mustaches peculiar to Italian royalty in the nineteenth century.

There was a cool damp smell even in that loggia, for the rain did not stop; streams of it were dancing beautifully on the large clean stones of the *piazzetta* as I and the Florentine umbrella, its border looking so cheerful in the grayness, descended into it. For I wanted to get back to the Via Sallustio

Bandini. . . . We rounded another queer little corner, and there was *tabacchi,* fairly jumping at me.

With much relief I secured those *pacchita-Macedonias* and hurried off. How lovely the Mercato, in the rain; how intriguing the Sienese signs—the mouths of lanes. Shop-windows showed reproductions of things in galleries, as yet unseen by us; it was hard to make progress, but I steamed along, soon passing another she-wolf on a column with two tiny and very alert babies sitting beneath her; the founders, again. Mamma more primitive than ever.

"That's two of her," I reflected; and went on down the Via del Re, where I had a message to deliver. Babs and the signora had devised it, and the signora had written it out for me; a subtle message, it referred back to Florence. . . .

He listened, the broad-shouldered little man, with sparkling eyes—everybody's eyes do shine and sparkle so, in Siena; then he and his cohorts plunged at Nicolette. I dropped a worried word or two, was valiantly reassured, and fled.

I found my way home by a new lane, the Via del Moro, with a brook in its stone center. Dodging it, I discovered a Dante quotation set high in its gray wall, under the thing like a black and white egg that is Siena's device; the *balzana.* (She puts it over any nice thing she has done, like this quotation.) How charming to find poetry in the streets! It was a remark about Salvini, and in the nick of time I met the older spinster, who reads books in Italian and knows a great deal, and was also sagely dodging the little brook; she informed me, gravely, about Salvini. That is, about Dante's putting him only in Purgatory, not in the Inferno, because he (Salvini) had done "an act of humility" in the Campo, standing there in beggar's guise till he had collected enough money to ransom a friend from prison.

Heroic, I expect; a beggar, in those vigorous days, might not have had too nice a time in that Campo.

One more tale the spinster told me, apropos of a palace we were passing—I, wishing to hasten, yet harvesting all this for my waiting child; about Dante's thunderings against the criminal extravagance of a club of young nobles who used to meet in this palace, and persisted in having cloves with their food. It was nothing, said he, that they should eat from gold-plate, they were expected to do that; but cloves—anathema! These spices had just been brought in from the East, it seems, and were worth their weight in princely gold.

Babs was up for lunch, and delighted to hear about the search for Macedonias. The signora had provided a special dish, and came cherishingly round to inquire if it was *buono,* and my child, who cares so little what she eats, turned up a gay young smile and assured her it was.

Babs felt almost enterprising after this, so we went off to see the *duomo,* whose minarets I had perceived that morning on a hill above the *piazzetta.* Guided by the Mangia Tower, I had marked out a short way from our street, down some side-lanes, to the Campo ("the heart of Siena, where its three hills meet"), and upward to the heights; so that we could walk if we wanted to. . . . We did; and were surprised at the emptiness of the great Campo. Just a peasant or two lingered by the fountain, a solitary citizen was passing under the porch of the Palazzo Pubblico; this ample piazza was not the gossiping-place it looked like.

Too ample, perhaps. The sun had too much scope. Siena's people have a habit of gathering in deep shadow. But the Campo's posts were good to lean on; pink marble ones, with rounding tops.

A simply delicious piazza; Babs slipped her arm unconsciously in mine as her eyes strayed round its grace. (Anything looks so wonderful, when one is just out of bed.) The sun came out—how kind of it—for a flitting gleam; even after it went in, one could feel it plunging about up there, and ghosts of its gleams scudded across the pavement. . . . A delicious day, too. They were warm, those shadowy scuddings; we could feel them go. Ra, under even the dimmest circumstances, is a very real person in Italy—yet we were comfortable in our tweeds; extremely comfortable, we told each other, leaning against those posts. They felt so soft.

Blashfield, in one of his chapters on Italy, says that Siena is "brown and truculent"; it is only in the Campo, one comes to feel, that this truculence lets up. The famous oyster-shell is almost pretty with its gay color and down-drooping shape; flattish along the lower edge, attractively curving elsewhere.

The old curving palaces are reddish, too . . . yellowish and pinkish, with the sun on them; the Palazzo Pubblico and its tower are brighter red, with giddy, cream-white tops. For all these structures have battlements; and the hardware hanging from little shops at the northwestern end, when it isn't ironmongery and mops and pails, is mostly copper, with brilliant brass edges; sunsets of copper, whose gleaming pink just goes with the Campo's general frivolity.

Leaving this mellowness we entered humble back-streets, but soon found ourselves facing a wide, twisting flight of steps which ended, far above, in the most surpassing bit of Gothic —a gateway the color of primroses. Babs undid the camera with one jerk; then backed and backed, stood here and there.

"Can't get it all *in!*" said she.

That is the trouble; one usually can't. In Spain, one is told, cathedrals are so jammed in with everything else that they can hardly be seen, let alone photographed; artists, breaking their necks from below, or borrowing a roof, must etch or sketch . . . and that was what should be done here.

So we climbed—to the highest hilltop of the town, "where soars the dazzling cathedral."

At least most writers say "soars"; to us it seemed more a long-lying thing, with most of its glory in front. It is only the nave of what the Sienese once intended for their *duomo,* yet it lies there in its roomy golden piazza as if the ages could have thought of no other thing. The sun broke through the clouds, great spaces of blue came behind the lacy, snowy marble of the façade, and we shut our eyes. Intolerable glory, indeed; it is whiter than anything I know. Milan has grown quite gray, except for some of its "upper works" that get rained on the hardest; but Blashfield speaks of this façade as being "suggestive, with its white marble ornaments upon a pink marble ground, of a huge sugared cake. It is impossible," he adds, "to look upon this restored whiteness with the sun upon it."

From across the piazza, it was like a forest in an ice-storm; we adored it, and almost ran to be nearer; climbed the shallow steps, and recoiled. Siena, ancient and brown—and *this* confectionery?

For the restoring is the sore point. It all looked as new as yesterday. Spic and span, bright and fresh, every nose and wing-tip perfect, the pink and blue of youthful mosaic staring offensively down at you from backgrounds of glittering gold; and the extraordinary frilling of the marble like fresh foam. (It is frilled, to the very tips of its minarets.) We went mournfully into the little Museo and saw, lying about on its floor, the fragments that have been saved: soft and delicate old coloring of fresco or mosaic, gnawed old sculptures that looked like the age they were done in.

Going out, we tried to console ourselves.

"I suppose it's better to have raw copies than nothing. And some day these things will look decent . . . a few hundred *years* from now!" observed Babs, with a bitter glance at a particularly glistening bit we were passing.

And inside was different. Inside shook one. Massive, gloomy-golden, rich; solid as a vast elephant on its pavement—with the heaviness of its arches, the down-looming of its sculptured roof—yet uplifting to the heart; for on that solidness what threefold aspiration is inwrought. . . . This is Italian Gothic; and "Gothic austerity," Gardner says, "is tempered here with the grace and fascination of the early Renaissance."

It is certainly tempered. Everything is tempered and toned, as things in a cathedral should be; the great interior almost succeeds in swallowing its own stripes—which most people don't like. Even Blashfield, who loves and understands Siena, is worried by the markings of this "tiger-striped" *duomo*. "The Northerner," he says, "is painfully impressed by the black and white horizontal stripes which . . . seem to confuse the vision, and the closely-set bars of the piers are positively irritating."

They would be, if they looked quite as that sounds; but the stripes are not black and white. To begin with, they are of inset *marble,* which changes the effect completely, giving the layers a more compliant air; and then the white layer is either toned with age or originally never was white, being now a shadowed grayish-yellow like the stone often used for fonts, almost taking color from its surroundings and melting, therefore, as well as a stripe can melt, into its neighboring tint—which is also very far from black; just a sort of warm dark, indescribable and attractive, and somehow akin to the transparent warmth of the other.

I mention this matter of striping in some detail, because it was rather a shock at first. We loathed it! But the more we walked about in it, and saw bays and shadows, lights coming and going, and the marvelous glooming or brightening of windows as the sun went in and out—blue and crimson and gold picking out a fresco here, an altar or a bit of grille there . . . the more we grew used to it, and began to feel it sublimely beautiful.

For in any aberration of art as singular as this, one must feel one's way to it with gradualness and care. This cathedral is an overpowering thing. One has to get a sort of striped feeling in one's soul, an acquiescence to an architectural idea which conceived that tiger-striping was the thing to do in this *duomo,* and nothing else; a sort of running-together, in one's mind, of gold and dark, of one thing on another, of richness surmounting richness and color and gorgeousness everywhere—and then you are all right. You are striped, from the heart outward; and you stay so. . . . I naturally dislike stripes, in architecture or dry goods, in ginghams or in Genoa . . . especially Genoa, where there are so many of them; but after an hour or so began feeling that these *were* the cathedral, and upheld the cathedral's beauty. That was nice. We strolled about, growing steadily happier.

Even Babs, almost fanatically opposed to any such meddling with a plain surface, had succumbed to the inevitableness of the place; a victory indeed. We gazed about us with scarcely a wince. . . . The brass-inlaid design of the flooring, that *pavimento* which critics admit is "so bad in principle, so splendid in reality," was concealed today by a worn wooden covering, so that we had at least simplicity under our feet . . . which may have been as well for a first visit.

"More than 40 artists, most of them Sienese, worked on that pavement," said the guide-book. Fancy the chattering, the clinking!

We came out, blinking in the piazza's radiance; but it was later, the sun was richer on the pinnacles; a shadow, even, was sliding up the lacy front.

It didn't seem so bad now. We perched on the pink marble bench that runs along the bare old *palazzo* opposite, its marble still warm from the sun, and positively liked that façade. . . . Was this decadence, one wondered? Taste growing worse by the hour and minute? We seemed to be getting accustomed to so many things.

Perhaps it was because that bench is such a genial place. It is a little high, and one's feet dangle, but one is weary enough to be grateful to it. One feels forgiving. The pigeons of the piazza strut before you, a cab-horse restfully clinks his bits; Franciscans go by with their long limber strides, their sandals noiseless, the knotted ropes of their girdles freely swinging; an old woman comes along selling candles to burn before the *duomo's* altars. Cabbies sit there, and women with babies; American girls with shrieks and cameras help each other upon the end of it—a high step, facing that long nave and delusively lofty campanile—"to see if I can get it all in!"

A difficult thing to do. We did not even try. That bench was too delightful. We would come back another day, and do details we had been too dazzled to perceive. The Libreria! we had not even seen that.

Just now it was nice to sit idly here and look about us; idly open a book we had with us—written by a professor with whom Babs had studied Italian literature, so we felt a proprietary interest in it—and read about the ladies of Siena. Siena's history seemed to us worse than San Gimignano's, because of the siege; mercenary soldiers had "swarmed on Italy like locusts"—not neglecting Siena; in one year 80,000 of her people died from the plague—but the siege was worse.

Things led to it, of course. The town was a republic, happy and glorious except that her affairs were always in tumult: so torn by mad factions that she finally appealed to Charles of Spain for protection—against herself; the first step, it seemed, toward the end of government by the people. . . . All went well for a year. Charles visited the city, and was greeted with jubilation—babies, on every hand, were named after him; then he tactlessly announced that he was going to build a fortress just outside the walls—and Siena was to furnish everything. Enslavement had begun. The Medici in Florence chimed in gladly with their Spanish relative, while poor Siena sent useless petitions to the Emperor, and made a vow to the Madonna . . . "that 'so long as, by thy intercession, our sweet and dear liberty shall last, fifty poor little maidens shall every year be married at the public expense, with a dowry for each of twenty-five florins, to thy greater glory and honour.' "

Plots were soon laid at Rome, or in France, to liberate Siena; at last an actual French army arrived outside the walls, and "when evening came, the people rose in mass, shouting for France and liberty. . . . Such was the flaming of torches and the glow of lights in the windows, that 'through all the city one walked as though the sun had risen.' "

The Spaniards and Florentines had to march out.

But the Medici were not downed so easily. Cosimo and Charles joined forces; on January 26, 1555, their armies arrived and the frightful siege was begun. "For ten miles around, the once-smiling country became a desolate, fire-stained and blood-soaked wilderness. . . ."

In June, Blaise de Montluc came from France with reinforcements . . . it seems to have been the pleasant habit of France, even then, to come to the rescue of republics. There had been some question, Gardner says, "as to the safety of sending this dashing Gascon to Siena. . . . As it turned out, his dauntless heroism, his never-failing high spirits . . . his amazing harangues (for he prided himself upon his Italian, and had got up some Sienese history to serve his need) chimed precisely with the temper of the people. . . ."

The industrious general wrote a book, too; the *Book of Montluc,* he called it. "He found, he tells us," Gardner said, "that 'the Sienese were stark mad of fighting, and I do believe, fighting for their liberty, would have played the devil.' The heroic devotion of the ladies of the city especially moved his enthusiasm"—and this is what I wanted to quote:

> It shall never be, you Ladies of Siena, that I will not immortalize your names so long as the Book of Montluc shall live; for in truth you are worthy of praise, if ever women were. At the beginning . . . all ladies of Siena divided themselves into three squadrons; the first led by Signora Forteguerra, who was herself clad in violet, as also those of her train, her attire being cut in the fashion of a Nymph, short, and discovering her buskins; the second was the Signora Piccolomini, attired in carnation satin, and her troop in the same livery; the third was the Signora Livia Fausta, apparelled all in white, as also her train, with her white ensign. . . . These three squadrons consisted of three thousand ladies, gentlewomen, and citizens; their arms were picks, shovels, baskets, and bavins; and in this equipage they made their muster, and went to begin the fortifications. Monsieur de Termes . . . has assured me that in his life he never saw so fine a sight. I have since seen their ensigns, and they had composed a song to the honour of France, for which I wish I had given the best horse I have, that I might insert it here.

This of course was during the early part of the conflict when ladies had heart, and strength, to trifle with fancies in costume; but horrors and starvation soon arrived. "The ladies of Siena—now laying aside the sportive spirit and gay dresses in which they had first worked—laboured again on the fortifications . . ." but even their courage could not avail. After thirteen months of heroism, gaiety, and fearful misery—citizens were falling dead in the streets, thousands of "useless mouths," the *bocce inutile,* had been thrown, with weeping and lamentation, outside the walls—the Sienese surrendered.

At the *duomo* the Spanish Marchese di Marigno "had the Mass of the Holy spirit solemnly sung, but the choristers broke down in sobs and tears, and the lamentations of the people drowned the music."

Sunset was now of rosy, fluffy clouds, floating on blue; the piazza was in delicate shadow. . . . The cabs had every one gone; and when we went out, an old beggar-woman growled at us! She was a flossy old woman, very clean, all in gala peasant rig and with a fine, red-and-yellow chair to sit on; she had established herself by the beautiful primrose marble of the gateway and rose, holding out a tin cup and glaring . . . We didn't like her, she looked so well-off, and so cross; she was evidently a pampered old creature, with a monopoly of these precincts for begging. . . . All against modern Italy's ideas, said we. Curse away, dearie! and walked off, followed by louder growls.

It will take more than Mussolini to subdue that old woman. Centuries of defiance lay behind her, and those frowning brows are legitimate. . . .

We walked on homeward, looking with respect in the faces of citizens whom we met. The ladies of the nobility can still be seen, the spinsters told us, in their boxes at Siena's theater, elegantly gowned and staring very haughtily at each other—a remnant of the old hostility, perhaps. . . . Well! I thought, ladies of Siena, if you are descended from heroines like those of the siege, you can be haughty forevermore; you have a right to be . . . and as for the dash and spirit of Siena's crowd, Babs and I were experiencing that every day.

No one, however, was in the center of town; and at the Via Sallustio Bandini we found that an angelic signora had already moved us to the other room . . . whence magics went on; where vineyards sloped to the city's wall, and the countryside in its spring colors stretched away; where cloud-shadows forever flitted over the Monte del Chianti and the Apennines. . . .

And now sunset was upon it all. We looked down at Count's terrace, with its loggia at each end; of lichened gray stone, those *loggie,* with slender columns and arches. By the old balustrade were potted carnations, round the fountain a circle of marguerites; chrysanthemums by one loggia, rhododendrons by the other. Crimson ones. Late sunlight was on the city's wall, on the tops of the greenery, on San Francesco's tower, gold against that sky; by leaning far out we could catch a glimpse of aged Siena, conducted safely out of sight by her wall but giving us just one more belfry upon the mountains; then one's gaze came back to the flowers and the *loggie.*

How the light Italian shadow had stolen upon them, was stealing upon the gardens; even beginning on the battlemented wall. The sky grew lovelier every instant, the hills a darker violet—or a more golden mauve, a paler forget-me-not blue; but along the hall went steps and voices. . . . We frowned, but we went: *zuppa* had a way of getting cold so soon. The spinsters outdid themselves in stories that night, but as soon as was decent we returned to our window—where the stars were telling stories to the hills.

Immense and glittering Italian stars!

How lovely Siena was. Surely, we need not hurry away.

CHAPTER XIII

A ROOM ON THE VIEW

THE fourth Sunday after Easter. The belfries, from this side of the pension, sounded quite far away; melodious and nice. . . . The too-brilliant stars had brought unexpected showers and misted our view, but the sun came out so gloriously after lunch that we captured a good-natured cabby and had a *giro,* all the way round Siena's walls and indigestible windings. (It was a grand *giro,* and led to a streak of luck.) Our horse was relievingly good, our driver fervid but kind; he flourished his whip over alleyways and bade us admire—and saw to it that we did admire; pointing out an entrance, a banner-holder, a vista of arches, and looking down at us till we produced the proper exclamations. The Via Galluzza is excessive with arches; falls downhill enchantingly, with ironwork and lanterns; our horse wished to stand for some minutes at the head of the Via Galluzza. . . . Very much of an egotist, this big bay horse, who wore scarlet bandages, white knee-caps, and a feather a yard long trembling between his ears; if a fly attacked him there was no rest till that fly was disposed of, at corners he wished to turn this way or that and had to be loudly remonstrated with.

"I don't *like* my water-cap to have so much psychology!" whimsically remarked Babs; for we were used to Nicolette's wordless docility.

But the beauty of Siena's old walls, and what was beyond them, was past all thinking. Sun and shadow, pale greens and pinks and gentle blues; cypresses on a monastery hill, gardens and gardens.

We looked out of one town gate after another, saw Siena's fountains, and the heavenly view beyond; entered the town again up some twisting street with a shrine in it, or a fresco in blue and crimson over a church doorway—even entered some of the churches, the cabby telling us that he wanted to rest his horse now and then, *"non sempre avanzare, avanzare!"* At last we thought we were going home, but ended at the tea-place—the cabby having persuaded us that something was going on up there; and when we arrived we found there was indeed. Streets were frantically trimmed with bunting. . . . Good heavens, this was Siena's great day when St. Catherine's head is carried in procession round the city—and we hadn't known anything about it.

Grave-faced priests were making more than the usual splotches of black in the color, as we started toward San Domenico; and here were still more frantic decorations, for this is St. Catherine's own *contrada.* Did not we hear symptoms of the procession approaching? We felt very grateful to the cabby, kind soul, for bringing us here.

San Domenico is the great red-brown thing, as big as a cathedral, out on an abrupt edge of Siena—one looks far out over the beautiful country to the Apennines, or down to the ravine and huddled roofs of the Fontebranda; from there the town climbs the hill to the *duomo.* In any light this is the loveliest view in Siena; at twilight it is a vision of mounting purples, vanishing walls, lights scattered about—and tonight a great glow in the windows of the cathedral. . . . We walked under the young chestnut trees that grow in the hard red soil, looking up at the big red campanile; its two bronze bells were wagging back and forth, their great tongues in full action.

"Whong—*bong!* Gl-wong bb-*dong*-gg-g!" The notes shook the ground under our feet.

Inside, across red-brown spaces, we were enthralled by the blaze of candle-light in front of an altar; the side of the church was illuminated by it, the great bare floor a miracle of increasing light; the altar itself glittering and aflame. Worshippers were thronging up and down the steps—all Siena was afoot and worshipping today; the light came from little squat candles—thousands of them, a flower bed of little golden flames; silver lamps, that burned scarlet, swung from the altar, flowers in an enormous mass sent up their perfume, and across the vast duskiness of the church—a space unthinkably empty, uncolumned, unadorned—another flood of candle-light showed the sculptured doorway of St. Catherine's chapel.

Not light enough to see Bazzi's frescoes now. We wandered and absorbed beauty. In remote chapels a fresco or two floated out at us; pale robes, lovely faces of saints, a glint of haloes. . . . Something else we must see in San Domenico.

But did we not hear music outside? Sunlight was still on the chestnut trees, and here came part of the procession winding along: little children, two by two, dressed as saints and angels and carrying candles. How delightful! They cast demure glances at us as they stepped past, the sweet little things, crowns and haloes on their little heads, and tinsel decorations of all kinds upon their richly-colored robes.

And this was only a fragment. Monks and friars followed; the Madonna; the parish priest in violet and gold . . . costumed youths tossing banners. . . . Purple and silver of the procession, black and white and gold, scarlet and yellow, all went winding away into Siena's stoniness, down the steep crowded Via Benicasa. We listened to the sweet floating-backward of song—the general descending hum on its way to join a deeper hum somewhere below; and a gray horse whirled up. An ingratiating cabby was raising his whip; there was just time, if the signore would jump in. . . .

"Un buon' cavallo—si si!" (A good horse, who would get us there.) *"Permess'!"* and he nimbly helped us in. *"Ec-co!"* and off we went, downhill to a narrow piazza; with the thrilling, sonorous music of the procession just turning the corner. . . . They were playing Chopin and all sorts of things. Color and richness, here it came . . . every moment another band, playing deeply and magnificently; at last, with a new, high chanting, St. Catherine's shrine borne high, with its golden canopy; escorting prelates, a resplendent goldenness, and— Somebody

"THE FRILLING OF THE MARBLE, LIKE FRESH FOAM"
The Duomo, Siena

walking, in robes massed and weighty with gold. The cabby bent over us.

"Vescovo!" he whispered.

Surely, the Archbishop's golden mitre; under it a sensitive face, already pale. . . . Steadfastly, with gentle dignity, he walked, looking slightly above and before him, or here and there to bless his people; holding up one slender hand. One's heart went out to the cabby's *Vescovo*.

Music fading, only to be replaced by new, a cold shadow settling in that stony dip; our cabby, with a wise nod at me, tweaked the blanket off, the gray horse almost galloped up the Via di Citta, raced in to the Piazza del Duomo, and there we were, settled in a perfect place . . . and sun was on the pinnacles. Color and music, oozing from the dark mouth of a downhill street: the whole thing over again—stretching brilliantly across to the duomo's steps. . . .

Incense bulged out of the great doors; then they closed—somehow solemnly.

The great piazza was alive with booths and color, also with whatever of Siena was not jammed inside, holding tapers and listening to the Mass; belated youths went leaping up the steps with their banners, music came out to us; a little dog wandered about, being friendly with all; our horse slept.

All at once, in a new strength of song, the procession magnificently reappeared, brightening the great doors. It was at its finest there. We sat up, transfixed. St. Catherine's empty shrine was borne, rather sidling, down the steps . . . and the cabby had an idea. He whispered, I nodded; we wheeled and escaped.

Down a long narrow lane, the gray horse melting freely along— "Well, we were never *here* before!" we said. "This is fine. We're seeing lots more town!" But our lane opened suddenly on the Campo; a southern corner.

Boom, boom! there it came, out of shadow, into the light, in the soft quivering way a procession has; utterly of another age, rich, medieval, melting downward into purple, pointing into brilliance. Light, dim but gorgeous, was on the lance-headed banners; on the tips of palaces, on golden pinnacles of the *duomo's* hill; blue and purple settling in the nooks of everything, softly, softly dimming the spaces.

We watched till the Bishop came up the little hill—fingers still raised, blessing his people; passed us, and was gone.

The last sunbeam flicked off the pinnacles. Siena was full of distant music still; very sweet, it sounded. . . .

St. Catherine of the clear brain, what would she think of her procession, I wondered. . . . Marble, lace, the golden glory of Maria Assunta; months later, back to the frowning red-brown basilica above the gulf of Fontebranda. No nonsense about Catherine, or she wouldn't have been the internationally-known person she was: championing lost causes, rescuing eminent men from prison, helping them die if she couldn't rescue them; writing famous letters to kings and tyrants, persuading the Popes to go back to Rome.

I don't care if she saw visions; I am all for St. Catherine.

Every one in the pension was worn out that evening, yet conversation for a while rose to a feverish pitch. We all related where we had sat or stood, and just how remarkable our view of everything had been; then, freshly exhausted by this spurt of enthusiasm, allowed local topics to fade and vanish, whereat one of the Englishwomen, a tall, placid, colorless person, came over and consulted us as to the hill-towns—the very cream of which she proposed to visit. At this our weary minds lighted. and we were proceeding to speak, with all the eloquence at our command, of San Gimignano and the wonder and beauty of its view from the Rocca, when she said, so very amiably and blandly,

"What is a *rocca?* A rock, I suppose."

Breakfast next morning was a translated thing, in our room looking out on gardens and Apennines. San Francesco was a golden pearl in the early light, the wall, a thing of dreams; and a thunder-storm just clearing off Siena's country-side. The signora's rolls might be a trifle thin, the *marmalatta* a hint bitterer than even an orange of Seville necessitates; but who minded? Colors of the outside world were sweeter than any fresco, the glories of yesterday fresh in our minds. My child still felt dream-like in the morning, a bit languid and not averse to bed ("loafed A. M." says the diary); but we had an industrious afternoon.

"P.M. Saw *duomo,* Library, Pal. Pubblico," it continues, "tea St. Catherine's house Fontebranda"—these last with no dividing commas, a fact in itself eloquent of fatigue; for in a corner, in small and almost abashed writing, she adds, "Done in!"

But we had a lovely time. After a hot stroll through town, we stood ourselves in the cool Libreria and began unraveling its frescoes. They take a good deal. Like so much of the mural painting of that day they are sequent, and tell a story—that of Enea Silvio of the Piccolomini family, who became Pope.

We had passed the huge Piccolomini palace on our way up—passed it almost every day, in fact. Wonderful cut blocks of masonry, it has, grand banner-holders, and a courtyard with palms,—the guide-book said it has "admirable suspended capitals" too, whatever those are; for the Piccolomini, except perhaps for their enemies the Malavolti—or the Tolomei and the latter's terrible enemies the Salembini—or again the Saracini and Scotti, two other ancient and embroiled houses—were the most prominent of Siena's noble families, terrifically identified with the most passionate moments of Siena's vivid and impassioned history. In fact they seem to have been quite desperately "in" everything that went on in their beloved town.

Their relative's becoming Pope of course influenced their fortunes; Piccolomini became Archbishops, the great palace we so often passed was built for two of his nephews, Giacomo and Andrea; his sister began a little palace of her own, called "delle Papesse," but work on it was ultimately halted "owing to Madonna Caterina's lack of means—" though she had asked the Signoria to exempt her from paying duty on materials, since "the said Madonna Caterina . . . wished to make the said house in the most noble fashion and with great cost, to the honour of this magnificent city and of your Magnificencies and Lofty Lordships."

Enea in his student-days was a gay young soul, much given to poetry and wild living, but the first fresco—a very delightful one—shows him in spendid costume riding off on a white horse (also wonderfully arrayed) upon a journey to Switzerland as secretary to a Cardinal; ah yes, it's been done, this putting the hero on a white horse! And Pinturicchio doubtless got the idea from something Persian he'd seen, or early Chinese—only they weren't seeing very much that was Chinese in those days. . . .

The young man prospered along the paths of diplomacy, but decided at last to enter the church. He had been sent several times to Rome, and seemed to find his goal there—as Browning's hero was urged to:

> Rome's the eventual harbour,—make for port,
> Crowd sail, crack cordage! And your cargo be
> A polished presence, a genteel manner, wit
> At will, and tact at every pore of you!

Incidentally, on one of these visits, he had been crowned poet-laureate by the Emperor—it was a new thought to us that poet-laureates existed in those days—though this honor almost counted against him when he was about to be elected to the Papacy; a nominee, we should say, and exposed to mud-slinging of a churchly sort.

" 'Shall we raise a poet to the Chair of St. Peter?' asked a rival Cardinal, 'and let the church be governed on pagan principles?' "—which struck us as an amusing comment on the estimation in which poets were then held.

But Enea seems to have filled his great office with dignity and energy. He promptly canonized St. Catherine, did his best, though vainly, to arouse all Europe to embark with him upon a crusade; and ranked high among those ten Renaissance popes who contributed, Sedgwick says, to make Rome "more artistic, more intellectual." One doesn't hear much about his poems, that his enemies were so disturbed by; they seem to have faded away with time. Perhaps no one who is a successful diplomat can be a poet too; but with his historical writings Enea Silvio won the repute of being "the most eminent man of letters of his age."

The frescoes, planned by a nephew of his, were ordered, we are told, with special regard to the "gold, azure, ultramarine, enamel blue, azure-greens and other pleasing colors" that were to be used in them. No expense was to be spared. "Pinturicchio's frescoes," my notes say, "remind one a little of Boutet de Monvel; or rather, de Monvel must have studied Pinturicchio. Clear line—nothing melting into anything else—and fresh, clear, water color coloring. Done as decoration. Art with an object is always splendid." After the charming first one we loved the fifth, where Enea, as Bishop, is presiding at the meeting of the Emperor of his bride outside the Porta Camollia.

We stood before this fresco for some time, joyfully pointing out things we knew. The wall of Siena goes jiggling up the hill, with the dear familiar tops of things looking over it and groups of trees being charming before it; it was endearing to see the Porta Camollia, where we—in Nicolette, and dust, and *no* trees, had come in—as it was when the Bishop and the Emperor really stood there (there is a pillar to mark the spot), and the costumes matched the wall and the old gate.

That is the way to get history, we said; have it painted by somebody on the spot. This wasn't quite on the spot, having been done some fifty years later; but what was fifty years in days when fashions in dress or architecture changed so little, and so slowly? Pinturicchio was in his ambitious boyhood while Pius II was still Pope; I do not know how soon he began studying with his master Perugino, but these lads in Tuscany were apprenticed early—Cellini speaks of one of his who was only twelve years old; and it is not far from Perugia, on its lofty hill, to Siena, arrogant on hers. Considering the difficulty of it, those Old Masters traveled surprisingly about; we agreed that very probably Pinturicchio, or Bernardino di Betti, as his name then was, had visited Siena in his young manhood and knew her gates and walls as they then were. Things *must* have looked like that, said we, gazing affectionately at the fresco and a beautiful creature at one side of it, caracoling on a curly horse with marvelous trappings; we wanted to think of the Porta Camollia like that.

It's a bit bleak, now. Not all of them are; but Camollia has a good deal of commerce going in and out of it, and all the motoring from Florence; and they won't let the white oxen come in with their romantic pacings, any more. It crams up the town, they say.

The oxen still go into San Gimignano, thank goodness, lighting the old *vicoli* with their whiteness, keeping them safely medieval with their slowness, for though a cattle market is sometimes held outside Siena's gates, that does not give the charm of their individual progress with cart and wine-barrel, or load of broom, mere thought of which rests one in these rapid days. . . . We moved on among the frescoes; had a thoroughly happy and rewarded time in that beautiful and consistent place, and went out. . . . Pinnacles were again in sunshine, and we had to stop and stare; that gold and snow-white on the blue of an Italian sky is not to be lightly passed over, even if the whiteness might be older. The more one sees of this cathedral, the fonder one gets of it; it's beautiful, if the real façade is in bits in the *museo.*

The sun shone and the wind blew, great white clouds rolled up, and we ran down the steps in great happiness. Lovely shallow steps, and no beggar-woman there today; lovely downhill lanes with their clean flat pavement. (Siena is really very clean.) On the steps by the Mercato there was such a nice little flower-shop, too, full of roses and freesias; one turned and saw them, suddenly, with the carvings of the loggia still in one's eyes; old stone and roses. . . . From here the Campo's battlements were very jiggly on the sky; we went down to them.

For there was art here too. Outside they might fortify it—that great palazzo; inside they took the greatest pains to beautify it . . . with Siena's idea of beautification, which was to be plain and stony and then burst into frescoes. The rooms in the palazzo are chill and dark, but Siena would have them decorated. Civic pride was tremendous, in this fiery little walled city, and Gardner quotes from a report of the Council of the People:

> In every good city, provision is made for the adornment and improvement of the city. And you have this your piazza of the Campo which is the most beautiful that exists, and you *had* that ornament of the Strada de Banchi which began at the piazza of the Tolomei . . . such that, neither in Venice nor in Florence nor in any other town in this country, was there a more beautiful street. Now it is spoilt; for the shoemakers and tailors have returned to it, and it is spoilt. Let therefore our Signori choose four citizens, who shall have to embellish it, so that the bankers shall be in one part of it, the drapers and goldsmiths in another, the furriers and armourers in another, and that within these limits no other trade can be exercised save those that shall be ordained by those four.

That sounded to us like zoning; in 1398.

The murals in the palace are of battles and madonnas, of ideals in government and of holy visions; some of them stiff, some dusky, but all sumptuous; one remembers the lovely spirituality in the faces of madonnas and saints. . . . We loved the brave little warrior Guidoriccio, too, with the little humpy tents of the Sienese camp behind him, riding proudly alone over what look like waves of the clay-colored country, to demand the surrender of the little walled town with fantastic castles, which rises in front of him. An inspiring sight, that little man. And his townspeople seem to have appreciated him; after being Captain of War for a few months, he was reëlected for the next seven years—a long time for the turbulent Sienese to be satisfied with anything.

I wanted that bit of indomitableness to take home with me; bought a colored strip of him—rather tepid, not too bad—and above my bed, in these latter days, it faintly revivifies the morning. It's odd; neither Babs nor I, by the slightest tinge, are military in our leanings, yet at the foot of *her* bed my child once tacked up a print of some Scottish charge—gray horses coming gallantly at you, ears pricked, manes flying, beautiful heads stretched out in a fervor of galloping; a rider falling, a comrade reaching to support him—all the pitiful, heart-rending bravery of such a charge. . . .

The picture, curling slightly round its pushpins, is still there; it gives one a sense of "valor unto death."

We stood about till we could stand no more, then crossed the Campo on our way to tea. A very bright warm Campo it seemed; we leaned against its hospitable posts, marveling that the *palio* should be held here. (All about the rim of the oyster-shell goes a sort of paved corridor, and it is round this impossible thing with its stony, downhill corners that the local lads and their horses race, for the prize of a banner.)

The more we saw of the Campo, the more we felt that nothing would induce us to see a *palio* there. Some of the horses always fall, but nobody minds; Siena knows how to fling priceless brocades from her palace balconies, and the color, crowds, and shouting, I hear, are unparalleled. Friends have told us about it! though it seems more a spectacle for people like those in *The Sun Also Rises;* the sun also rose, in Rome, on much that sort of thing. . . . And "so clearly and simply told!" Mr. Hemingway's fannish fans do say.

Yes; dip your pen in degeneracy and then be very simple about it . . . which makes it about six shades worse. Though if it didn't involve cruelty, one wouldn't mind so much.

"It seems to be rather a matter of growing up, doesn't it?" I said, as we climbed the Campo's worn and beautiful old steps; "psychologists say that children, you know, always laugh at some one else's pain. . . . Odd, isn't it?"

"Sickening!" said Babs with great cheer. We smiled at each other, and strove on up the hill.

What a mob! One would think that Siena would get over being so thrilled with itself every afternoon from four to six, but it doesn't. Every day there is the same animation. . . . Divine heritage; "Enthusiasm, the only virtue; the only vice, inertia!"

OUR FRIENDS, THE DISCURSIVE CABBIES

Siena

We grew to recognize many of those we met, but they apparently did not know us; to them we were forever new, and when Babs drove through them in Nicolette, the spectacle of a young woman doing that was a thing to bless the saints for. . . . I was glad she did not seem to mind this rapture of inspection; but who could? It was just the glee of a great, happy, careless, giggling family . . . though on foot, as we were today, we were a little glad to reach the shelter of the loggia and drop into homelike seats.

Art may be tiring, but the zeal of discovery was upon us. We could not resist St. Catherine's house, close by us, and that was on the way to the Fontebranda, so we scrambled on down there; loved the old arches and the clear water (where it wasn't bright blue with soap), loathed the tannery smell (skins in the sun—ugh!), and climbed back again. . . . Even up by San Domenico we got that faint smell; and decided that though we loved it, we wouldn't stay in that part of town for anything. Our side was *much* nicer. We took a cab back to it.

Again the sunset was on the mountains, and on Siena's wall; on the graveled terrace below us, the old gardener was wandering. We leaned on the sill and watched.

End of afternoon; the Count's garden. Light on some hills; the pale colors, the greens and pinks that Sienese painters are so found of—they get them from a Tuscan landscape in spring. Especially the country about Siena. It takes the light just right. . . . Then a thunder-storm is dark on other hills; a tiny rumbling, a bit of lightning forks itself right down at Arezzo.

The gardener stops to look at it. Does not like it. His marguerites round the fountain were all beaten down this morning; they have just straightened up again. Even a Count's garden suffers from a thunder-storm. He shakes his head a little; goes on.

It is his hour to browse. The gardener's perfect hour when work is done and the last sunlight is on the flowers. The terrace is almost in shadow now; the light Italian shadow, so full of color from a sky still brilliant. . . . The gardener wears a dark-blue apron and old felt hat; his legs are bowed, his pipe has a very long fine stem and a square bowl. He looks at his row of chrysanthemum plants; walks on. Looks again. He picks one leaf; moves on a little—to the row of potted pinks; takes the head of one between his fingers.

He goes down the row. Four more blossoms he holds in his fingers—lingeringly; then paddles on through the old brick gateposts, under the white banksia roses he has trained across them to his other domain, the vegetable garden. Very good-looking little angle of vegetables, bounded by a down-dropping wall, two neat young magnolias and a rather sprangly fig tree (fig trees always do sprangle), and ten feet of grape-vine; the distinction of the ancient loggia on one edge, a descent of old steps on the other. The gardener disappears; comes back lugging a heavy terra-cotta bowl in which seedlings have sprung up. They are interesting enough, he thinks, to go on the post of the stairway; nothing in this garden, no advantageous bit of old masonry, must be empty. He heaves the bowl upon it; adjusts. Leans far over to squint at it; sees a lawless plant growing in the wall, and picks it irately out. (Some few permitted rock-plants he has, in crevices below; this one *not* permitted.)

Jar is right at last. He goes into v. garden; stares a long time. Cuts one shoot from young pear tree and walks off with it; returns. Balances on wall, holding to fig tree; looks for bug. . . . Goes to the upper terrace, takes one chrysanthemum plant into the house; after long inspection, another. Goes down terrace to rhododendrons. Admires. Has an idea. Toddles length of terrace; reappears with stick. (Something needed propping.) He bends over, works and fusses.

Goes back into the house; is gone some time. Comes out with his coat hung over his shoulder, his pipe in his mouth, a sieve with a little green *insalata* in one old brown hand. Slowly he goes through the gate of the loggia, yet even there has to stop and putter. There are tubs of crimson rhododendrons by that loggia; he must pick a leaf or two, take a blossom in his fingers, then really close the beautiful iron gate behind him—iron work like black lace—and go.

We saw him slowly mount some steps; then disappear behind a wall.

What was sunset to him, but something to light up his flowers; or evening, but a thing that veiled them from him—

sent him, reluctant, to his home and his charcoal fire? We hoped he had a nice comfortable fat wife, as old as he but just as faithful, who would have their kitchen very neat, the spaghetti hot and oily and simply wonderful. . . .

CHAPTER XIV

MONTE OLIVETO

May 4th. Took a newly new and awfully fit woman to Monte Oliveto," says Babs' diary. "Lovely day."

Siena at that hour was almost quiet, and Nicolette indeed very fit—to my joy, the message had worked—so out of a new and splendid gate we sailed, southward and rejoicing.

Lovely sun and shadow flitted over the valley—uneventful at first; then we passed Malamerenda, "where the Salembini slew the Tolomei in 1339," and drifted along the miles, watching the peasants at their work; so happy they seemed, in the snatches of sunshine. . . . The signora had put up a lunch for us today, so we felt competent and well-provided for as we hummed along; she had brought it to us in a great hurry at the very last minute, hazel eyes benevolent, her curls distracted.

"Boiled egg!" she panted, "sheese, small bottiglia that white birr English ladies in next room say is good—!"

We smiled our heartfelt thanks. No more risks at little roadside restaurants, that day; and earlier as we had leaned out of a hall window together, discussing the day's program and gazing at landscape, she had told us about the peasants' doing profit-sharing in Tuscany ("where," one writer remarks, "there is no brutalized lower class"). The system here is not like that of Sardinia or Sicily.

"That," she said with a displeased shake of the red-brown curls, "is ver' bad for them. Here they pay no rent; they gif padrone half—only it is always less! Half of corn, oil, wine, potatoes—but *not* fruit. They carry lil' basket of fruit up for him maybe once a week."

"And the extra crops they sell . . . they work with more

playsure so!" she added, with her nice socialistic smile; it struck us very pleasantly that a person like our signora should care so much for the welfare of the peasants. The two classes are not always sympathetic—but then she was an unusual signora; she gave you Italian lessons if you wanted them.

And profit-sharing surely seems to work well here; the fields are marvelously kept. The peasants work till dark, but they dictate their own hours, their own procedure; can sit in the sun if they want to—be free and happy. (They and their forbears were born on the land, so who should know better what is good for it?) We had wondered who looked after all this valuable agriculture, since we had seen no one going about supervising it—just automatic peasants starting out from their cottages as if they owned things. . . .

And doubtless they feel they do.

The worst of spring's work was now over, one perceived, and the era of spray setting in. Men and donkey-carts were everywhere among the fluffy vines, and here, as on the road to Arezzo, patterns on the cottage walls. (A pink house with an old outside stairway and balustrade, usually; a flush of lovely blue behind its vine-leaves.) Even the spray-carts were picturesque; their tubs charmingly shaped. . . . One old rose-colored house had a large white pigeon sitting on the wall of its *scala,* above the cavern in which the tub was kept; it sat there, quiet in the sun, its head and round white breast clear-cut as in marble. "Perfect grace and beauty of the whole; dark arch, sunny *scala,* white bird, the great pale-green spray-tub."

The sky was magnificent today, the air just warm enough; and by a stream a woman in blue was spreading yards and yards of linen to dry—or bleach.

Had she spun the linen, too? Great clouds were hurtling overhead, those home-spun yards might get wet. But she seemed quite carefree about it, spread and pulled and patted, and smiled brightly at us. We glanced back—not at her but at the brook, which had lovely natural banks and flowering bushes—and the sweet soul waved to us.

Buonconvento, where we were to turn off, was not difficult to find, as it was in the open valley; a round, brown, fortified thing with surprisingly high walls, which had a frill of fat little trees all around them. There was a gate at this end; should we have to drive through? No; our little road turned in beneath the trees, then up and along a lovely wild hillside with a great view at our left, and a steep, pasturey climb with oaks and wild flowers on the right. Careless trees with branches growing as heaven intended—a little road with careless edges; it all seemed as fresh and new to us as if we had never been out of a city, and after days of stony Siena, one needed it. We were sure it was extremely crude of us to feel so—and then read Blashfield and were consoled; "after such an orgy," he says, ". . . one longs for the blue of the sky and the green of the meadows."

Meadows? Tuscany doesn't have meadows, exactly; but there are crops and vineyards, to make up.

And here, as we climbed away from the valley, was a land of innocence. Nothing knew what to make of us. "White oxen all scared, tan-colored goat blinked timid eyes, finally got up courage to go past. Lovely uphill; solitude; respectful peasant smiled and bowed. Oaks in sunlight, quivering view. Lunch. Birds. Delightful rest."

It was. The signora's eggs seemed perfection. We took Nicolette's rug under a young oak tree; so golden, over our heads! Birds sang in it, and in the other oaks, as we had not heard them sing in Italy; like ourselves, they liked the wildness. . . . Oh, the beauty of dark-blue cloud-shadows sailing over the landscape, blotting out a hill-town, then leaving it to gleam out once more—and traveling on with their floating blue. We had the sweetest and most basking noon-hour with all this before us; flowers swaying in the wind, bright leaves murmuring, a scent of loam and grasses on the air, and birds—those birds!—singing and singing.

And it was all so just—Italy. These hills did not remind us of hills in Devon, this singing was not like anything we knew—it was all just a respite in classicism, with bits of classicism still there. . . . On that sunny peak a tiny, delicate pinkness that must be a hill-town, on that cobalt-blue one, a gray hint of a castle; clinging to the side of that shadowed range a tiny, ordered spot very much made with hands—perhaps a monastery.

But the sun clouded often; we must go on . . . Monte Oliveto, somewhere beyond in these wild hills, was very much a monastery; old and Benedictine, distinguished for piety and simplicity, art and revelry; always for beauty and loneliness. Sodoma, or Bazzi, the great Sienese painter and practical joker, had worked on the frescoes in its cloister, as legend goes, by bringing up dancing-girls from Siena to act as models—he was aided in this by an iniquitous *frate,* afterwards banished; on the other hand its founder, Bernardo Tolomei, left the safety of the hills, took his brethren down to Siena during a fearful visitation of the plague, and died there, helping the stricken and afflicted. . . .

Yes, a navy-blue Italian thunder-storm was racing up over the bright sky; glorious to see, bracing to smell, but just as well to avoid. Would it keep its course—it was apparently flying up the valley below us—or would it whisk around our way? I don't like driving in a thunder-storm.

But such views. Confusion of hills upon hills, spots of dark cypress, the far-off reddishness of some walled town; "terrific ridges and ravines," say my notes. For we had come to an amazing wilderness of mud-colored cañons, crossing and criss-crossing each other, riven in pure clay; our little road went twisting along on top of this strange world. It was the clay desert made into dramatic ridges—and a skyful of drama overhead. Brilliant masses of snowy cloud, on clear blue, were fleeing before diabolical black ones; beneath these a strip of green horizon, then sulphurous, yellowish gloom.

Magnificent; and it *was* going the other way.

"On to monastery; more scared oxen. Woman with back-load of grass, and scared goat."

But I shall not forget our first sight of Monte Oliveto; the old red of its flying-buttresses through black candle-flames of cypresses, its long fortified bulk lying along a ridge, above a cañon also thick with cypresses. (San Bernardo and his monks must have planted them.) The sun had been warmly upon us, but now a cold shadow fell; the cañons below us were half-lighted, half in dusk. . . . Ah, another storm was hurtling across the valleys. Which way would this one go? It looked as if it were coming straight at us. Should we stop at the monastery, or fly?

Nicolette swung a corner into a lane of immense cypresses; a fit prelude to Monte Oliveto's fortified gate, its low stone bridge, the exquisite blue-and-white of the della Robbia over the gateway.

The sky still menaced, but a sudden sun came out; and down a far vista of cypresses and bright-green turf, framed by the old gateway, some brothers in white stopped to look up at the sky. Our emotions can be imagined; though my notes are brief over the episode.

"Took picture; brothers in white posed beautifully. Threw back their cowls. We backed away—no hankering for monasteries!"

Which at the moment was true. The skies were too frightful—therefore gorgeous beyond speech or description. Thunder was growling now from the darkened hills of Montepulciano; we would do frescoes "some other time"—a pet phrase of ours; for what about Tuscany's evanescent frescoing of the hills? Why miss the divineness of this particular day?

But we had seen nothing more satisfying than the picture through that gate; the brothers in those heavy woolen robes, unaltered since the *cinque-cento,* throwing back their sheltering cowls and looking up at the sun. We were delighted with that rather symbolic touch . . . it was like a bit in an illuminated manuscript.

But they saw us, we felt. Were they coming out to welcome us? Lone monasteries are usually quite welcoming.

We turned hastily away.

Ah, the glorious cypresses! the mud cañons once more, the wild flying color, the gleams. . . . We hadn't the heart to go directly back, but swung along to the right. The road was level a short way, tracking along the spines of extraordinary cañons or bridging their ribs and ravines—of which we snapped a cloudy and uncertain picture; and somewhere, over in their wilderness, ran the railway to Ascanio. We could dimly see Siena; Monte Amiata to the south, rising high and pale-blue, and more to westward, "that loftily placed last home and refuge of the battered Republic, heroic Montalcino with its towers."

But here was a place to turn round; would there ever be another? We yielded to prudence and the divine wet smell in the air, and turned.

A last glimpse of flying-buttresses, through the black candle-flames, and here were oaks and prettiness again; birds rapturous as they are about a rain, either coming or going—we hoped it was going; then the valley, and the great brown walls of Buonconvento.

But we were meditating more hills—a back route to Siena: so prowled on, about the town.

"Round B. Convento (four holes into adorable crooked old town—fine lofty gate; charming loggias and tower, curving street)." For Buonconvento deserved a little attention. Magnificently walled, otherwise defenceless in its open valley, this small place had seen the march of emperors; Pius II had been within its gates, Henry VII, after his descent upon Florence, had died here, and here Boccaccio had laid the scene of one of his *novelli*. Siena's lion and *balzana* are now over the old gates—decorative, but once very enslaving; we drove slowly away, gazing back at it, and took the road to Murlo.

Up and up [say the notes], wild country, fine purple road, wild olives, far-off view. Storm over Siena! Road soaking, every twig glistening. Wild hills, towers under the storm; dark-blue and cream color, flying silver in the sky. Oak-greenery in sunlight, with thickets of broom. Radiance—the soul of spring! The oaks were so golden, one almost thought they were broom, too. . . . Purple road keeps on—still wet, sparkling in the sun. Old ruin on wooded peak ahead; brook dashing below. . . . Wonderful to see something as natural as a storm over anything so contrived as Italy; so used and scraped and gardened and untwigged!

Nicolette going wonderfully up Alpine climbs. Wild and wilder hills. Sky doing all possible things. Five or six storms careering about. Wild little villages, to match the hills; everything we met was petrified at Nicolette. Four reliable old hens ran to the cock; grouped anxiously round him: "Oh dear, this strange noise! Does *he* think it is all right?" They stared hard at us, but did not move. Good for them.

We were sorry to petrify so many animals. Oxen shied quite wildly at us; sometimes we met a convoy of donkey-loads and then the tall peasants, walking beside them, would flash into fierce activity, pushing and shouting, grasping rude shafts, hauling at wheels, till the last trembling beast was shoved into a hedge.

I never thought donkeys could behave that way. . . . These drivers were handsome, cross-looking creatures, and glared at us with justifiable distaste; what were we doing there on the lone hills of Frontignana—in their own little back-road? A dragon's nose was our Nicolette's, coming round a hedge-corner at them; and more than a dragon's noise she was making, I told her, as she struggled in Frontignana's greasy mud.

But *we* felt intensely brilliant to be doing back-roads in Italy all ourselves—with rain-drops on everything, and sun on the broom; and at the summit of the ridge came to the reward of a fine old castle, inhabited, beautifully kept. (One was sure there were embroidered pin-cushions in *its* guest-rooms.) Battlements and griffons, gorgeous iris edging everything; it even looked as if it had a moat. Its view stretched infinitely northward—Volterra, perhaps, its highest tower could see, or old Montagnola.

"Swell *castello*," say my notes. "Real thing. Reverent peasant, bowed almost to the ground. We'd been lunch-guests of the Count, of course. 4 teams scared oxen, 2 scared donkeys, in bully village with tower."

Back-hills are wonderful for arrogance. After that peasant

—so happy to obliterate himself, to brush his boots with his hat—we drove on feeling lofty. One quite sees how counts occur. In the village we accepted the rearings of its horrified procession quite calmly, and let them do the turning out. (Nicolette had nearly got herself stuck in a ditch, being too accommodating.) They went lunging and shying by, shouted at by more of the beautiful, brown-faced drivers with those hawkish profiles that seemed to go with the mountains; behind them, the squat tower of the village was ancient and grim against smiling Tuscany.

Was the village Bugnana?

At the moment we didn't quite know where we were, though we had gone to the pains to join the Touring Club, in Florence, so as to have its detail-maps for these hill-roads. They were nice, intricate little maps, white for valleys and blue for rivers, really valuable if you want to go off the beaten track; but so brown and furry with altitude and mountains, so blackened with countless small names (or large names for small places) that they were extremely hard to make out. . . . But we could see Siena almost all the time now, and if that village had been Bugnana, so much the better. Bugnana was a nice name.

It was glorious all the way back. One rain pelted us, but Siena was getting it too, so we didn't mind; then Siena leaped out again—and so did we, to put the top down—and the rain went hissing beautifully away up the valley.

Lightning was forking here and there, the magnificent hills kept on—also the exquisite sight of the city's creamy towers in sunshine against a lurid dark-blue, with all the exquisite valleys between us: every fabulous tint of emerald and turquoise, of flitting sapphire and fairy pink, with patches of bright yellow kale—brighter than buttercups; strips and patches of crimson clover. Oh, those colors! We could hardly sit in our seats. We had seen France from the Montagne Noire and gasped at Languedoc from the top of a rearing Cordes, but Siena, and the country south of Siena, won.

And soon we should be leaving it; we had already stayed

five days instead of the two we had lightly planned. But that was Nicolette—you could spend your time unplanning; she was perfectly pleased with us, whatever we did. So now she dipped us downhill, and flew along faster; went whirring up the slopes of Siena and back to the Via del Re.

"Of course," said she, "my garage *would* be on the Street of Kings. . . ."

Inside, however, a huge Italian limousine was blocking the way, and as we were extolling Nicolette's performance, to the enthusiastic response of the little padrone, its magnificent chauffeur standing by in purple livery said, with a scornful wave at our treasure,

"Zose lil' cars—no good, on zese roads. Shakk to peezes!"

Now that was an insult. She had been doing some "shakking" since she entered Italy, we couldn't deny that; but—shakk to peezes! Bet his old limousine would have got stuck, some of the places we'd been today . . . and Nicolette taking us through like a bird. Rough roads probably weren't good for her, they weren't good for any car; but—wait till we passed *him* sometime, on a hill! And we laughed at our own wrath.

The spinsters, that evening, were extremely indignant about the affront offered to Nicolette; they agreed with us as to foreign chauffeurs, told witty stories very much to the point and were in all ways most consoling. For they were beginning to feel entire confidence in Babs, and stood ready to take her part in any situation. We were getting much attached to the spinsters; there was a doughty something about them that you could depend on. New England, ha! Rock-ribbed hills, and all that. Nothing like it, said we!

And rain danced on the pavement that night, and fell softly on the gardens; the scent of wet flowers came to us, drowning the scent of Siena. One grows tired of a hint of tanning forever in the air; tonight it was all marguerites and pinks, and the clean smell of wet stone.

CHAPTER XV

ONE MORE DAY IN SIENA

IN the morning, rain still danced on the pavement; the marguerites on the terrace were sadly bowed with it. But we went to the Accademia and in spite of the gray light had a beautiful time with the grave, sweet-faced madonnas —*les madones au longs regards.*

A few critics say that the Sienese painters depended on ornament and color "to conceal their mediocrity"; but there was nothing mediocre in the effect those long, pale beautiful faces had on us. One of those heads was like—any single exquisite thing: a lily, alone in a swamp; a wild white Cherokee rose, as I have seen it in the South, high and solitary upon a live-oak trunk; shining there, the one potent thing in all the gray monotone of a river-bordering woods.

"Afternoon, lovely drive to Chiusdino and back; good deal of rain. Very wonderful country. Steering-gear wanky." For we saw a castle, dark against a flaming sunset, and then Nicolette refused to turn to the right; so we had a wonderful time getting home again. I did the warning and gesticulating, Babs sat alert and straight, doing her best with the crippled car; but it was a taxing drive. The steering-gear was bent so that it would have to be reforged, the garage told us. . . .

"Well, these hills are enough to make her," defended Babs, striding stoutly beside me. "You know how it was yesterday; I had to keep wrenching at her every minute."

"Yes. . . . And when we go to Spain it will be worse," I said feeling about for a consolatory topic but only coming on something even more woeful. "Remember what we read in some motor magazine—about how a Humber, I think it was, was the only English car that would stand the roads there? And they're fearfully well-built and strong. English cars, I mean."

"Yes," said Babs slipping an arm in mine; "poor Nicolette. . . . Do you think Nicolette could go to Spain?"

"I wonder," I said—not, at the moment, feeling too sure; and we turned in at our aged entrance. Poof! cats. How could they allow it?

On the other hand, how could they help it? It was almost like a bit of loggia, that portal, and you wouldn't close up a medieval loggia because of cats . . . though it wasn't the best introduction to home-coming.

And we had so hoped to go on tomorrow.

"Oh well!" we both said as we opened the door; then laughed, pleased at this mutualness. "Oh well" would do, for a frame of mind; would get us through tomorrow. . . .

For we wanted very much to leave Siena, and yet we didn't. Siena was abominably interesting, and our nostril for history never keener than at this moment . . . yet delay here meant pinching off days somewhere else.

But we refused to feel torn any more—really grievously torn, that is, for many were the small decisions of a sad nature we had to make every day. Tomorrow, I remarked, we could go to San Domenico again—that angelical fresco; and we walked till tea-time, discovering treasures.

But as we returned to the fresco for a farewell look, we felt once more the marvel of finding this touch of unearthly beauty in the great bare church. Coming out of its cold dusk, a dusk glowing with rich color however, we wandered rearwards by its convent wall, and through a little thick door had a glimpse of a friar, in a short black robe, bending over a bed of vegetables. The neatest little three-cornered garden was tucked in under San Domenico's high walls—we had never known it was there; rows of every bright promising thing, hectically green, meticulously tended. It seemed to be a very special garden, in fact, and the good friar—no he wasn't a friar, he had thick brown hair; he must have been some sort of lay-brother—bent and worked devotedly, humming to himself in a robust yet pleasant singsong. His face was red from bending, we expected every instant he would straighten and see us peering at him—but we just had to look. If those two huge bells began to ring, we *knew* we should jump.

We adore monastery gardens, and benevolent robes flicking about; silence, a bird singing, old stone walls, and peace. . . .

Then we walked on and bought books in a nice big bookshop in the Via Vallerozzi—or was it the Via Magenta?—and walked stumblingly along the pavement reading them; and it would have been sad to go away without a farewell tea at our *pasticherria.* . . . There was sunset from the *Lizza;* we had grown very fond of its old fortifications, its pretty flowers, and statue of Garibaldi—lively soul, in a beautifully wind-blown shirt, leaning one hand on his horse's hips and staring keenly backward; the chestnut blossoms were falling in a light breeze, the mountains were very blue beyond; and we listened to the dim something, a sort of buzzing hum, that was Siena changing for dinner. . . .

Serious packing went on that night—we had worn entirely too many clothes in Siena; but it would be one-night stands until Ravenna, now, unless we stayed over at Perugia . . . so with a lovely sense of permanence we packed dresses away. Babs was looking forward tremendously to Ravenna. Things almost began to be old there, said she; this medievalism was too new for anything.

The signora seemed grieved to lose us. She had worried over Babs, urged on my Italian, explained the country-side and suggested drives; we felt attached to that red-brown head of curls with eyes to match. Ardent were the farewells therefore; Luisa and her mistress waving frantically till we swung the corner.

Nicolette had been only just finished, when we went for her. Three youths crawled out from her undersides and, dusting bits of floor off themselves, pronounced her perfect. There was relief in their tones. Babs tried her at every angle, the padrone illustrated and expounded, and downhill we took her (with *such* a sense of farewell) by San Cristoforo's small, dark, incense-breathing door, the clean, flat stones of our via. How well we knew it now, how fond we were of it; how relieved to be going on!

Good-by, Porta Romana, splendid in tan-color and blue; we hope our picture of you will come out. The skies were tumultuous, as they had been for days; Nicolette dove gaily off the hill and into the day's fortunes.

They were various; but as Babs wrote to a friend, "You ought to take that drive from Siena to Orvieto, it stands out in my mind as one of the most superb of many that were so gorgeous you wouldn't think they could exist in this mundane world."

Across the Ponte d'Arbia, therefore, we came gently down to Buonconvento; gently, because we saw a vast whiteness shining in the sun, before its walls and its fat green trees. That whiteness was cattle—with dots of color in it; peasants, in charge of them. . . . Young oxen, a quarter of an acre of those; older ones farther on; cows and calves fringing the edge of this multitude—oh, those snow-white calves, with dark, liquid eyes and long silver eyelashes. . . . With Buonconvento's agedness behind it, it was a rare sight; but our road disappeared under the middle of it. The peasants looked aggrieved, even insolent, when forced to stir; and during all the time we hooted and shoved and pleaded and apologized our way through, everything within me screamed for a camera.

Yet—stop? In this? If we survived, it would be something. I alternately yearned to get out and beat these people, or prayed for this little calf and that: for this pair of yoked, placid beasts, this vision of a smooth snowy cow that no one would move an inch; for this peasant's back, that woman's arm—that child with the long brown curls, scarlet frock and Michelangelo legs . . . who was snatched up just in time.

Cowy smells, moos, horns, hoofs, swishing tails; it was like motoring through a jammed barnyard. And Nicolette so low down in it all, so admirably French and near the ground!

Wincing, frowning, admiring, we came at last to the outer edge of this obstruction—I don't see now how we got through it; looked back not even once at medieval Buonconvento but crossed the little Ombrone with a bump and a bounce, and fled along the valley. . . . At least we fled for a time; then mountains drew near. All the while they had been rearing up beside us, high and rough and thrilling; now they tilted sociably toward us, and Nicolette heaved a sigh and said, "I'm rather tired this morning!" She would run along a little way, then suddenly "go limp in our arms," as novelists say of a fainting damsel.

CHAPTER XVI

ADVENTURE BY MONTE AMIATA

SHE spent so long doing this that it was noon before we got anywhere; we had a concerned lunch by a brook. I have no memory of how that lunch tasted; I don't think it did taste. I remember that the valley was very green, that the sky looked like rain; and here we were in the uninhabited middle of everything, and Nicolette doing this. . . .

A queer feeling arrived under my breast-bone; almost like stage-fright. My child could clean spark-plugs—she was doing it at the moment; but after all, as we held the bonnet up and looked at the metal intricacy inside—and Nicolette had "such a simple engine," everyone said!—we realized, as we had done with qualms in England before starting, how little we knew about that mysterious thing and its possibilities; its complaints, its needs, its fleeting sicknesses.

We climbed in again, and a fine rain began to fall. Also the valley thought it was time for the hills. One slid down and confronted us; a steep, pale-gray thing shining prettily with wet. We knew what that meant.

". . . Try it!" murmured Babs; and at it we went. No flying start, for Nicolette was not flying just then; she approached in little jerks, ascended three yards, and ceased trying. Up went my child's eyebrow; out piled I . . . old story, this! rather fun than otherwise; Devonshire roads had been steep and slippery too. Where was a stone? Ah, a good one; big enough so that wheels wouldn't back down over it.

"Sorry, darling," said a voice from inside; "wish *I* could do that. . . . Ready?"

"Right!" and I seized the rock as it was spewed back at

me. Nicolette's rear left me for a yard or two, then began to slide back. I hove in the stone.

"All right—!" I cried.

On she went; back she came.

"Chuck it!"

"Did!"

Time after time, with the stone in one arm, I panted after Nicolette in her short rushes; but they were getting shorter. The steepest swell of the hill was in front of us—the crucial bit; as Nicolette started, I lay out flat and pushed with all my might. Oo! that was hard work. I felt myself turning a bright shade of purple—and she went no farther than before; still if we could just keep going along like that. . . . But Babs looked out, and her face changed.

"A.B.! You've been pushing. You *mustn't,* darling; I simply won't have it. . . . Tell you what—I'll go down and run her up backwards. You know that works sometimes. Gangway!" and Nicolette was slipping past me.

Down and down—how easy it looked; Babs glancing back and steering carelessly with one hand. They turned and came on, quite rushing; went just past me; slowed, and swung round. I rushed with my stone; Babs' voice came back to me—cool, a little weary.

"Well; I wonder."

"So do I!" And just then we saw something. Against the sky and down the rolling field above us came a peasant boy with a green umbrella; his teeth flashed, his sunny hazel eyes smiled as he strode toward us with that graceful, loping walk these peasants have. With a stream of smiling Italian, he gestured toward the car.

"Si si!" I told him. *"Volere—*? He's going to push, Babs."

"Good for him," said she with calm cheer.

I flung myself beside him. If only we could get her round this twist, maybe she'd go; it would be fatal if she stopped, here. . . . Hurray, she was going; we were doing it—push, push! Her wheels buzzed wildly in the gray slime—hah! we were up, and some level yards were ahead of us.

"Go on!" I shouted, "I'll catch up!"

But beyond a little rise Babs slowed and looked out. The boy and I panted up.

"I think she'll go now," said she. "Come on in, darling!"

The boy beamed as I tipped him, his brown face lighting. Such a nice, friendly smile; indeed, he had smiled all the time he pushed. His green umbrella retreated over the hill; Nicolette started slowly along.

"I don't know . . . dash her!" muttered her owner, doing all the things one does to stimulate a lagging energy.

For the tune was sinking; Nicolette's usual brave "ra-ra-ra" on hills. Oh, why had we let that boy go? I climbed out . . . and there he was running to us, from nowhere as usual; his face one smile.

"Non—parte, signora?" he cried cheerfully in his rich soft Italian. *"Allora—!"* and he applied his shoulder. Ah, that peasant muscle! *Allora* indeed: Nicolette, with a return of energy, kicked out her stone, sailed off and left us. Feeling light and inconsequent without her weight upon us, the boy and I beamed at each other.

"Bene!" said I.

"Benissimo!" said he, backing radiantly away and refusing a further tip. Astonishing boy.

I hurried after my disappearing child. . . . I hoped she would go and go and never stop till the top; but round a turn there she was, waiting for me.

"Didn't want to leave you *too* far behind!" said a cordial voice, from inside.

For indeed the world was getting wild and vast; the views magnificent. It was level just here; Nicolette resumed the way. Her tune was fainter than it should be, still she proceeded, and on a drier bit of road had a real burst of enthusiasm. Happiness; we actually began to look about us, instead of concentrating every second on her. . . . What a sky! What grand wild country; not a house in sight since before lunch. We still wondered where that boy had come from.

"Perhaps he stays there on wet days, to push people up that pitch," I suggested; and we laughed, remembering the prudent green umbrella.

"Pretty good job," said Babs, "if it's always as slippery as that!"

The little road curved gently along; our hopes were high. This surely seemed like the top of everything, with that tremendous valley below; but still the smooth green country rose and rose in front of us. Where were all the peasants that must cultivate this land? At home, we supposed, out of the rain—though the storm had left us and rushed dramatically away over the mountains; we could see it, a gray swirl, half-way back to Siena by now. . . . Wasn't that Siena, that pale bit on a hill? Nothing else would stick up like that.

" 'By, Siena," said Babs. "Gosh, I'm glad to be going on, though."

But were we? Nicolette had grown feeble again; and dismay seized us. Was she going to bother like this all the rest of the trip—and we wanting to climb Apennines? Ought we to have bought a new car, in that persuasive courtyard off Piccadilly? She was only six months old when we got her; had been beautifully taken care of, and her speedometer said only 7,000 miles. . . . Had that young insurance man "done" us too badly? She had behaved so nobly up to now.

But new wet hills had begun, and once more the old process; the rock, the rush, the halt. After a few unavailing pushes, Babs steered to one side of the road.

"No use, A.B.," said she. "I'm going to look at the engine again. Maybe I can see something to do. If not, we've got to ask for help."

My child, willing to do that? My heart sank. Things must be pretty bad then; and I stared down the road. We had met no one all the way from Buonconvento; suppose nobody, on this lone height, came along?

"Wish I could take out that carburetor," came Babs' voice, from somewhere inside the bonnet. "But dash it all, it's just been taken out! She ought to be absolutely all right.

She was *grand* on hills, you know—day before yesterday."

We hung over her, perplexed; but everything seemed to be functioning.

All we could do was wait. Lovely mountainous Italy was about us, the sun still doing marvels with flying gleams; Nicolette had chosen a charming place to break down in, if it hadn't been quite so vast and far from everything. . . . A bird sang; otherwise there was silence. Well! it was a good time to study maps. We had come just below the edge of our larger, linen-mounted one, and were using the Perugia section of the Carta d'Italia, pleasingly dark with altitude. Tuscany and Umbria were nearly all dark-brown.

We sat down on a bit of bank and pored over it. There were streaks of valley, one further east, following the Fiume Tevere—which we had never heard of, but which seemed to be an immense, exciting and persistent river. Its valley began at Sansepolcro in the north and went on down to Todi, where it took a great swing to the south-east; there, a fold in the map prevented our following it any further. We weren't going down that way, anyhow. . . . Todi looked rather nice, stuck up on a furry hill with red wiggles of road leading to it; red wiggles meant a four to seven grade, and brown ones, more than seven.

"'Bet it was more than seven where we got stuck," said Babs. "Look! No wonder. And it was slimy too."

"And look what's coming—that brown bit! Or perhaps this is the brown bit right here."

"Don't think so," said my child gravely. "We haven't been through that town yet, you know. . . . San Whatever."

"So we haven't," I said, and we sat in contemplative silence a moment.

"Looks a long way to Orvieto, doesn't it," remarked Babs. "We'll be lucky if we get there, with Nicolette like this. . . . Do you *think,* darling, we'd better go on to Rome?"

Again a pause.

"Hark!" I said. "Do I hear—"

"Car, by jinks!" and Babs jumped up. "Coming like mad

too. Now we'll see. Don't let's stop them unless they look as if–"

They didn't. Her words were drowned in the roar of them. They were traveling with a great many trunks, and they simply flew by.

"People like that never know anything," said my child philosophically. "Ah, here's something else. We're in luck. This looks better!"

It was a landaulet, climbing rather slowly toward us; the chauffeur, out in the open, looked not only accessible but pleasant–a thin-faced, hazel-eyed little Italian with a thin, high profile and a cap pushed back on his head; as they came by, he raised an inquiring eyebrow at us, and turned a thumb toward Nicolette. We nodded; and a great ease fell upon us. . . . He steered beyond us and stopped.

"Huh! Roman license," said Babs.

I had noticed, with dismay, a white-frilled pillow inside the rear window, and a flushed face on it, but the chauffeur had no compunctions; he rapped smartly on the window-pane; shouted something in vigorous Italian. A dark head raised itself and a tall, rather stout young Italian clambered out; he bowed to us, blinked an instant, became less flushed with sleep, and came toward us, talking to the chauffeur. A delightful voice he had, soft and sweet–a friendly voice; he and his servant were evidently on the best and easiest of terms.

"You are in some trobble, madame?" inquired the young Roman in soft and pleasant English. "What iss the matter?"

Enormously relieved at hearing our own tongue, we told him; he translated rapidly to the chauffeur, who nodded, somewhat wearily, and raised Nicolette's bonnet, then ran back to put their car nearer the road-edge. His master dove expertly here and there inside the bonnet; he unscrewed, he inspected, he listened to whirrings.

"Your carburetor is quite right, mademoiselle," said he, turning his nice dark face seriously to Babs, who still sat at the wheel. "These hills of course are very bad, and she is a small car; but I think she will go—with a little help. . . . Nel-lo!" he called, in his sweet high tenor.

Nello ran back, and was obviously not too pleased to be instructed to push. His eyebrows went up. Efficient as far as need be, that little man, and kind—but no extra deeds for him; not without significance was the touch of laissez-faire, of semi-insolence, in those narrow-lidded hazel eyes. Had he been an American of similar status he would have chewed gum violently, noticed everything without seeming to, and never raised his voice. Yet it was he, with a sleeping master, who had seen us and drawn up; his eyebrow, now, was no wearier than then . . . and he was being told to push!

"If mademoiselle will permit me, I will drive," said the young Roman—we were sure he was a count, by now. "Perhaps I can—" and he climbed nimbly in, ducking his dark head to dodge Nicolette's top. We almost blushed; she didn't look her best with her top up. Not right for a count to clamber under; but this was a democratic soul. He gave one flashing glance at her levers and gears (he'd probably never driven a Cit before) and started her very nicely; Babs, who had been looking anxious, gave me a little nod as if to say, "*He* knows how!" and we three in a communistic row (though Nello tried to wave us off), flattened out.

"Don't, A.B.," said Babs; "You'll hurt yourself."

But Nicolette was sticking—and didn't I know how heavy she was? It did feel a trifle funny; I hadn't in the least minded pushing with the peasant boy, that seemed natural and jolly; but—stretched out in a row with a chauffeur? . . . That nonchalant creature could work like a little fury, however; Nicolette gained speed, we two dropped off, Nello still ran and pushed, and she sailed off.

Well over the hill the young Roman was waiting for us, his cheerful face alight with success, Nicolette's engine still whirring vigorously.

"I think—she will go. I think—there is nossing the matter with her!" he said simply. "If you wish, I will drive her over the next hill for you. Beyond that, it is not bad."

We expressed entire willingness. By all means let the magic continue! and this time she started with scarcely a shove. We walked on, with Nello following a little way behind us; nonchalant as ever, his eye slightly fleering. We must tip him, of course; what did you tip a count's chauffeur?

"I'm going to give him *this!*" I murmured, showing a ten-lire note; a terrific sum in Italy. Babs lifted an approving eyebrow, I dropped back a little and held out a hand and a smile to Nello; to my surprise he did violent things with eyebrows, waved hands, dropped renunciatory eyelids—in short, declined to be rewarded. . . . Noble Nello. No Neapolitan he, at any rate; I never met a south Italian who could withstand a tip. (Indeed, those hazel eyes did not belong farther south than Rome.)

We had now caught up with our benefactor, who was leaning over Nicolette to do some last trifle. He and the chauffeur had one final conference, then Nello, with his weary trace of a thin smile, but a highly benevolent eyebrow, held the door open for us.

"I think you will have no trobble now," said his master, leaning in to us with his expression of a good and serious child, so amusing on the rather self-indulgent plumpness of that dark face. "It was not—she had not—I think there was nossing the matter!" he concluded, wrinkling his forehead as he tried to express something subtle and technical. "She is leetle—the hills are bad; it was jus' too much for her!"

We hoped he was wrong—in fact we knew he was; but everybody smiled tremendously, Nello ran for the landaulet, and the young noble waved his hat with a boyish farewell.

Whizz! Nicolette dug into that grade with the beginnings of a small zeal. Cheers! What had the count been doing to her? He could not explain, and we never found out. Some sort of Italian miracle it was; and after a week in Siena, surrounded by St. Catherine, one is ready to believe anything. . . .

He and Nello were now driving slowly along behind us, to be sure we were all right. (Angels!)

"I hate to keep them back like this," muttered Babs. "This *must* be nearly the top!" and she waved vigorously. They came by, both sitting in front and staring intently at Nicolette's bonnet.

"All ri-ight!" called the young Italian, in his sweet voice. "You are nearly up now. She will go!" and they sailed on. On a hill against the sky they stopped and looked back, however; we waved, the brown hat waved; they disappeared.

One more glimpse we had of them, a speck in a valley far below; then they were really gone—and our blessings with them.

We toured along an immense plateau, gazing at sun-streaks on wild velvety mountains to our right and a thunder-storm on others; spring and Maytime were everywhere. We could look at them now, for Nicolette was forging determinedly along—our faith in her recovering fast, though it had had a severe strain. We came to a field of hayricks and could give them all our attention—dark-brown shapes, carved till they looked like chicken-bones on end; most pictorial against the hills and above a gorge-like valley in which reposed little pink towns . . . upon whose brightness fled the vivifying gleams of Ra, and above which swirled and reared and snatched the most memorable of skies. (We had been having a belt of days with skies, lately; or did Tuscany always have them?)

And in the foreground Italy was going to wheat. Mussolini had decreed it, hilltops are good for it; there it was, young but doing well; Monte Amiata, very conscious of her chestnut forests, looking benignly on. . . . We had time, now, to digest Monte Amiata.

San Quirico was a knot of nothing on bald hills; we dove down them and saw a seductive little side-road, crossed the F. Orcia, and went on by another little river. Pienza (once Corsignana) was on our left, the village whose name Enea Silvio changed, because it had been his birthplace; he then instructed Rossellino, the Florentine sculptor, to "make it a center of art"; so that little Pienza, sitting in its wild, clay-desert surroundings, has "a more compact survey of early Renaissance architecture than is to be obtained in most Italian towns."

We should have very much liked to detour there, but still had a little feeling that we had better keep on to our night's stop while Nicolette was in the mood. Attractions leaped on every side of us, as they do at such times; to westward, over especially wild hills, was the walled town of Montalcino, which during the siege of Siena had been besieged for two months by the army of Cosimo, Giordana Orsino defending it "with the utmost valor, and heroically supported by the inhabitants." The French and Italian fleets at last appeared off southern Italy, however, and "the Spanish commander was forced to raise the siege; he burned his lodgings and started south to defend Naples.

From Monte Oliveto we had seen the "heroic towers" rising; they were hidden by mountains, now.

Our road twisted and climbed, till we were nearly 3,000 feet up; Monte Amiata just opposite, clear and blue and beautiful, with its forests and little towns. Being the highest peak in Tuscany, it gives "an admirable survey of the whole country between the Tyrrhenian Sea, the Apennines and the Ciminian Forest." Now we had never heard of any Ciminian Forest, though it sounded frightfully pleasant (as forests are all too few in Italy); we were enlightened to find that it lay about 50 miles south of us on the slopes of Monte Cimino. Near Monte Amiata, too, there are beautiful woods on the way to Vivo, "a suppressed Camaldulensian monastery, now the property of Count Cerrini."

Oh, these Italian names! we could never have enough of them. They are a romance in themselves. We stopped at a high place near Radicofani to let Nicolette cool a minute, and to look at maps, and were enchanted with our environment, linguistic as well as actual. . . . Camaldulensian, we agreed, is a lovely word, though we did not know its monastery; there was one somewhat of that sound at Camoldi, to the north of Rome in the Albanian hills, but we soon discovered that one more syllable belonged in the name (which made a difference of some hundreds of miles in its location), and that this retreat was at Camaldoli, north of Arezzo, having been "founded in 1018 by St. Romnald of Ravenna, for hermits living in entire silence and isolation."

Mountains up there seemed favorable to retirement, for near by are also the "noble sanctuaries" of Vallombrosa and St. Francis's monastery, La Verna; "that harsh rock between Tiber and Arno," as Dante calls it.

I had found a book about this Monte Amiata region, a beautifully gasping book called *In Unknown Tuscany;* we took it out now, and gurgled at its descriptions. The author begins by being very pensive, in Siena; stone has been worrying him, and the ways of a city. It is a hot evening; he wants to go somewhere and doesn't know where, so he sits on a hill by "the great half-forsaken church of the Servi di Maria."

It was the hour before sunset. Behind me, on her hills, the beautiful pale city of the Virgin rose, as ever, with a little strangeness in her beauty . . . a little hysterical maybe, as in that vast swooning Tower, that curiously over-expressive Palazzo Pubblico, that visionary Cathedral [Dear man, it's as solid as rocks]. Before me stretched the *contado,* a restless country of up-tossed, tawny hills as in a picture by Piero della Francesco. And over that strange, arid world, where little cities burned like precious stones, hovered Mont' Amiata, that beautiful mysterious mountain, not too near, not too far, very faint in the heat, the last outpost of Siena, looking toward Rome and the sea. . . .

The sun had set. . . . Again I looked out across that world . . . to Mont' Amiata, that in the failing light seemed infinitely far away, like a mountain in a dream. Ah, if I could but reach her! There, why, there, if anywhere in the world, was all that I could desire, coolness and silence [just what you need, dear, said we] the wind among the trees, and laughing streams bordered with forget-me-nots. . . .

So he decides to go—"at dawn out of Porta Romana . . . reaching by nine in the morning Buonconvento . . . where —is it not so?—it is convenient to hear Mass."

Farther on, he says (about where we were now, on the road to Rome), "the cities begin to glitter about you—Castiglione d'Orcia, like a ruined fortress, on your right; Pienza, that lovely vanity; Montepulciana, like a rose on its hill, to your left; and before you, between the mountains, the scarped ruin of Radicofani soars like an eagle over the valley. . . ."

Well, Radicofani does soar, though it is rather a solid eagle; and from there the author-pilgrim found his way to Mont' Amiata, "to Abbadia di S. Salvatore on the verge of the woods . . . whose prospect is of a thousand hills and valleys . . . but in spite of their beauty, it is southward one looks oftenest, across the vast restless plain of the Patrimony, where, like a vision, like I know not what passionate and lovely thing, Monte Cimino and Monte Venere, joined indissolubly by the marvelous blue line of hills like a bow, which marries them, rise on the farthest horizon in a gesture of profound and exquisite beauty over the Lake of Bolsena . . . and Viterbo shines at evening like a white rose fallen on the skirts of Monte Venere."

Now that is the way to write about Italy, if one can. A critic recently remarked how writing has changed since the war, so that it is "more like a skin than a garment"; in which case the above paragraphs have surely donned flowing robes. I admit that there are moments in Italy when one feels like that, but to have one's town *always* resemble roses . . . and we really resented having the Mangia tower called swooning, when for centuries its bells have rung Siena to arms.

There is very little in Italy that swoons. In fact I can't think of anything. Here and there in her palaces she may have held languid folk—*The Valley of Decision* tells you about some of them; but they mostly lived near marshes and had malaria. On the whole Italy is a rugged, mountain-challenged country, impetuous and vital; and the farther south in her you go the more vital she becomes. Could there be a more jabbing energy, for instance, than inhabits the lean, barefoot, shrill-voiced, wasp-like people of the shores just south of Naples, and their merciless hot hills?

(But it needs energy to skin a living from those shelves of earth and rock; or for that matter from the shallow, uncertain cruelties of that siren, the lovely Mediterranean.)

We had a pleasantly ironic time with our book and its I-know-not-whats; the main trouble with an emotional volume like this seemed to be that it was all "perhaps," and we dislike a book about real places and people, founded on perhaps. We even felt like quarreling with the title; Tuscany, that desperate and unknown region. *Et ergo*—Babs and I were now exploring Tuscany . . . feeling most familiar with it, with its mud upon our boots; and Monte Amiata, on this day of dramatic clarity and blue velvet, looked anything but unknown or remote. How easily would Nicolette, in her recovered humor, wind us about those clinging spots that were towns, or take us for picnics in those chestnut forests. . . .

Nowadays, in the summertime, everybody probably climbed up to Abbadia San Salvatore (beautiful name) and went on, and around the mountain, and saw the castles, and the little tucked-away churches and monasteries with della Robbias in them, and the little gardens, and his precious Maremma and all; even the farthermost village, where the peasants' saint, David of Arcidosso, was shot for disturbing the peace. David himself was a peasant, it seems, a particularly rough and blasphemous *barrocciaio* who heard "voices" and was converted. For a time he walked the mountains and did good, then grew proud (as leaders will) and founded a sect with fantastic costumes—proposing to lead his flock over the mountain to a new kingdom "where, so he had seemed to say, they would have a larger share of their crops and harvests than their masters."

This migration was to take place on August 14th, the Vigil of the Assumption, when in ordinary years all the mountain and plain are alight with bonfires in honor of Santa Maria Assunta.

But on the night when David, the New Messiah, would have led his people into a promised land, "there were no bonfires on the Mountain or in Maremma; Madonna was forgotten, the Kingdom was at hand." He led them over the other side of Monte Amiata, but Arcidosso became alarmed at "a crowd so great that all the Mountain seemed to be alive with men," and sent out *carabinieri* to meet them. That was the end. "David's followers had no thought of revenge. . . . They thought all had befallen to try their faith; and even if David were dead, would he not rise again on the third day?"

We loved these peasants. Religion grows a simple thing when one is among simple people who believe it all; it is one of the things about being in Italy. . . . George Sand was devoted to her peasants of Crozant, on the Creuse; if she had known these of Tuscany, I think she would have cared for them as much.

But now we were under Radicofani. Beneath the fragments of its *rocca,* the village clings almost invisibly to its cliff; we went by, scarcely realizing it was a village. I am sorry, now, we did not stop to see the della Robbias in the little churches of S. Agata and S. Pietro. "Guide-books," says Mr. Hutton, "have ignored Radicofani as they have ignored Mont' Amiata . . . one expects to find nothing there, whereas both Radicofani and Santa Fiora are as rich in della Robbia ware as any city in Tuscany, save Florence." He thinks that the Sforza Lords, who then held Radicofani, induced Andrea and his pupils to take the (then) long journey from Florence to this wild place, "where in the small and beautiful churches even today, their work, so full of coolness in the summer heats, shines with the country flowers upon the altars, not less in place than they."

That sounds pleasant; one can quite see those terra-cottas.

We stared up at the ruin, once a robber's stronghold, built by Ghino di Tacco—who, with his father and brother, "disgusted with the Republic," had been banished from Siena and lived high up in their Rocca here with a company of brigands and swift horses; but Boccaccio tells of their generous treatment of a captured Abbot which led to Ghino's receiving a free pardon from the Pope. Boccaccio finishes the story there, but Ghino really had a violent end; after he had retired in peace to a castle near Siena and his son Dino had become an Archbishop (suitable reward) he was one day set upon by armed men and fell, as our book says, "under the daggers perhaps of the Counts of Santa Fiora, who hated him and whom he hated."

Daggers perhaps! said we . . . and drove on, grinning at Monte Amiata, now very blue under a cloud-shadow.

Someday, lovely thing, we'll see you and your forests, we said, looking invidiously at the world of hills rioting about us. It would be nice to see a storm on these mountains; for our book added that "In Monte Amiata, as elsewhere in Tuscany and Umbria . . . bells are rung to avert lightnings, winds and hail, which are attributed by the peasantry to diabolic influences. . . . Satan is the 'prince of the power of the air' and it is believed that bells, especially church-bells, may prevail against him."

(Angels ringing bells in San Gimignano, and causing whirlwinds to cease?)

But Satan's whirlings just now were merely scenic; clouds fled and hurtled, while sunbeams pursued them. Brilliant were the valleys, now in gleams of sun, or engulfed in purple gloom. What a day for this drive! And we were in Umbria now; below Radicofani, one enters it. Weren't the roads already a little smoother? Umbria's roads are supposed to be.

Nicolette liked Umbria, we were sure; she was now so cheerful and altogether herself that after crossing the unnoticeable Paglia (which we were to meet again), we grew very bold, took a chance on her good behavior, and sped on past our Orvieto road for a glimpse of the Lago di Bolsena.

As soon as it came in sight, we turned and scurried nervously toward the Orvieto fork . . . as much as one can scurry in this land, with donkey-carts appearing around turns; but even so, we stopped once on a high place, and stared back toward Rome. . . . Ever since Siena, it had been a fine feeling to know that we were on the road to Rome; and we had just discovered that the F. Tevere was the Tiber! Stupid, not to have unfolded that map to its last crease, but

MONTE OLIVETO'S FORTIFIED GATE

with the wind blowing and whirling as it was by San Quirico, that was what one didn't do; so we just hadn't seen where that long blue streak was bound. . . . We traced its course again; and pangs assailed us.

Should we go on—to Rome? We had decided, long before we left London, not to go further south than Orvieto; but the road took a much straighter line than the river—and think of motoring ourselves magnificently into Rome. . . . All across the sheep-dotted *campagna* (with shepherds in long cloaks), and straight at St. Peter's dome. We knew so well how it would look; that was the worst of it.

"Better not, this time!" said my daughter heroically, and with that inconvenient wisdom of hers. She was right. We folded the map.

And then we were glad—oh, how glad we were—that we had not dallied another instant. We had been prowling along past hedges and under trees, with a green hill blotting out prospects and a rose-colored sunset setting in, and wondering when we should see Orvieto—which we knew was on a peak of its own in a valley; of a sudden the hedges ran downhill, everything dropped away, and there it was, below us. The valley was one lake of mist, and from it protruded Orvieto, a rosy island; an island in that mystery of fog, its towers and walls rosy-golden—drifting, disembodied, above a great bowl of hidden valley.

Somewhere in that fog was the Tiber, and above its shroudings were dim peaks, Monte Peglia, Monte Citernella; but we had happened upon Orvieto, as upon Avignon, in a moment of supreme beauty. Belfries rose from it, and the *duomo's* Gothic façade, shining with gold; our book would have let loose upon it all the roses in its vocabulary.

Long windings led to the valley, giving us a chance to stare at it; we drifted past cosy cottages, their pretty gardens and mulberry orchards, then halted. Babs climbed out, put the camera on a wall and focussed long and devoutly; came back to me with happy eyes, but shaking her head a little; climbed dreamily in.

"I don't know—!" she said.

For even sunset was dimming, now.

We felt our way through the valley fog, wondering about getting up to something "perched on a bold brown rock 600 feet above the valley."

It was quite simple. One straight climb went up to an ancient gate at the top—from which the view was now all twilight fog—and there we were. The town was close-built and twisting, with an air of poverty and neglect—only an occasional pot of flowers on a window-sill, yet somehow the more interesting for that; also uncommonly full, it seemed to us, of lean old women gabbling together at bare corners, and on door-steps. We passed one rather self-conscious looking hostelry with orange trees in tubs and concierge in livery but went on through another gate and into a longish piazza—did Orvieto have to be fortified against itself then?—inquiring the way to a little *albergo* we had been told about, down a lane near the cathedral.

Down a lane indeed; steep and dusky. The inn, or rather house, was distinguished from others by a flight of outside steps and a pansy-bed beneath them—dark-purple pansies—and came hospitably out, very glad though much astonished to see us: *due signore,* finding their way about Italy alone! *"Mirabile!"* said they kindly; if they could have seen us pushing ourselves uphill by Monte Amiata, I thought, it would have been *mirabile* even more. . . .

Dropping our things in our room, which had a fine jumble of old roofs outside its windows and a look-off on mountain and plain, we drove hastily up the steep lane again. Our *albergo's* dining-room was a *ristorante* in the street above.

Lights were coming out, and lanes were already dark, though overhead a star or two was hurrying, in clouds still colored from the afterglow; hoping for a fair day tomorrow, we entered the warmth and light of Orvieto's restaurant. Particularly cosy it seemed, with potted plants about, and red cushions on the benches along its walls . . . officers and their families were dining here, beaming and chattering as only Italian families do at such moments, the padrone was grave and cherishing, our waiter smart and solicitous, and the fame of Orvieto's vintage having reached even us, we ordered a *mezzo bottiglia.*

Cobwebby and dusty outside, within the wine was as poetically yellow and fragrant as it had been said to be; it lent luster to the *frittura mista* which the waiter soon set, smoking hot, before us—we owed that *frittura* to little Fucecchio. The nice Italians at tables near us, though sparkling with vitality and evening spirits, also with a wine redder than that of Orvieto, were polite and scarcely stared. And we had come tramping in in our tweeds! Orvieto was very cosmopolitan . . . or else just small enough to be sweet; we said as much to a gratified padrone, then wandered out into the cool romantic lanes.

It was nearly ten already; we took one look at the vanishing façade of the cathedral, the gold of its mosaics gleaming a little in the street's dim light, gave one last glance at Nicolette, and paced contentedly down our little lane. The pansy-garden was a velvet blot in its shadow, scarcely a fragrance now; but it was nice to feel it was there, as we climbed upward to our door, our frescoed ceilings, and our Italian beds.

Iris in a nice faded way bloomed on those ceilings, a breeze from the mountains was blowing our curtains, more and glittering stars had come out . . . and a strange but real silence lay without, on the old roofs.

This was the quietest room we had had in all Italy.

CHAPTER XVII

GOOD ROADS IN UMBRIA

ORVIETO is blessedly quiet. No studying of maps that night, no poring over Tauchnitzes; such abandoned sleep did the Umbrian air vouchsafe us that it was late breakfast-time when I woke and called the pretty little *cameriera,* who came in, sweetly inquiring about *caffè latte.*

Not a note had I written; but as I said to Babs, looking guiltily from my pillow and my tray out to the sweet Umbrian sky and the mountains,

"Don't need any notes! Shan't forget *that* day. . . ."

"Rather not," said she.

And it seemed strange, all at once, to have it Umbria. Every single thing had been Tuscan for so long, every bird and breeze and bump in the road; it was nice to have something new to call mountains.

And we had always thought Umbrian a beautiful word. Is it . . . or was it because Umbria itself is beautiful, and we had so loved Perugia, two springs ago?

"Maybe!" said Babs, folding one of her blouses and laying it beautifully in the bag. "Yours ready, A.B.?"

"All done," I said, presenting a flattened garment and the sponge-bag—I always do up the sponge-bag; but Babs was laboring with a humped lid that wouldn't shut.

"Darling," said she, "we mustn't buy one thing more. Stand on it, will you?"

"Not even a post-card?" I asked, smiling down at her.

"Not one!" said she, straightening up and defiantly tossing back a lock of hair—the cowlicky one that will fall over her forehead. "Nicolette wouldn't hold it!"

"Glad these are tough hinges," I remarked, stepping off

ON THEIR WAY UP FROM THE VALLEY

One of Orvieto's Old Gates

the bag; and we restored the poor thing to a normal pose. It didn't seem to mind being stood on; it was of thick cowhide and terribly heavy—Babs' own, and her love and pride; the little one was a frail flower and held lighter things only, whereas all the boots and knobbly things went in this one: a nice, leather-smelling, man-like bag.

"Orvieto, saw it," remarks the three-line diary.

That was about it. We liked Orvieto, we gasped and were amazed at it, yet any desire to stay on this elevated rock seemed to be lacking. We had been obliged to dally in Siena, and nothing was holding us here; Nicolette had her ears pricked for the road (we hoped), and Umbria was before us. *Avanti!*

We could see it all about us, that was probably one reason for our wish to flit; Umbria very green in the plain, very white and shining as to river, very alluring as to wild hills about; with ribbony roads, whiter even than the rivers, winding everywhere one could wish a road to go. We leaned on Orvieto's wall and looked at them, walked her lanes and were aware of them—threads of invitation, twisting into the sun-dappled blue and green and violet of the hills; towns that wished to be stayed in shouldn't put themselves on lone rocks so high in air.

So we put our things in Nicolette, and drove up the lane to the cathedral. I remember a glitter of gold—the lavish pink and blue of mosaics upon the gold; and backing exasperatedly down a side-lane with the camera. The piazza is long sidewise; you forever approach a profile, but the front is what you want. (The sides of basilicas are not their strong point.)

So of all the stiff and unrepresentative pictures we got the worst, and knew we were getting it; in spite of ironic eyebrows from my child, I overloaded Nicolette with two post-cards from a shop on the corner. Fabulous post-cards.

"They'll go in the door-pocket!" I said quite crossly—for I knew she was right; and inside the beautiful little cathedral we hastened.

We were used to stripes now and these were gentle ones; gray stripes, and grayish-yellow, even with the sunshine flooding in at windows above, and being as gay and golden as possible.

The columns of Orvieto march straight and impressively to its choir. There is no open-hearted break in the line of them, and it is by accident almost that one finds the dusky "south transept" where the great frescoes are—Fra Angelico's, and Signorelli's; frescoes one studies a long time and, in spite of the dim light, goes back to again. (Signorelli's medallion of Dante, with its decisive dark-red and gold, reproduces well, and was conspicuous in the window of the little art-shop by the piazza.)

It is fortunate that the striping of the *duomo* is gentle, for because of its plain glass windows, everything is fearfully visible (except in the chapel where you want to see frescoes). That is the trouble with most Italian churches, even St. Peter's in Rome; things leap at you without atmosphere. By their virtues alone, and perhaps a little by their oddnesses, do the basilicas of Italy exist—not by illusion; or if they have little beauty, then by sheer force of columns and architectural vastness; by their collections of well-lighted treasures. A friend had said of Orvieto, "It is a jewel-box;" and it is. Everything in it is charming; little insets in its walls, the candlesticks, fonts, enameled reliquaries; a hundred details. "The guardians of the building," one reads, "were unwearied in providing for its ornamentation."

It was quite empty as we wandered through it, and we had a beautiful time climbing about in the chancel; finally walking impudently up the very middle of the altar steps and taking a time-exposure of the nave with a bronze Easter candlestick, higher than our heads, as foreground. . . . The cathedral obligingly stood still, Babs counted off the seconds: Done! And nobody saw us.

Just then two tourists walked in, and the sacristan after them. What luck! Another minute, and it would have been too late. He looked at us in a worried way, but we joyfully retreated and drove off for the *fortezza.* Cobbled, downhill streets; then an opening-out, with pear trees showing over stuccoed walls: the *fortezza's* gate and its gardens, whence is the famous view of the valley, and ring upon ring of mountains. Umbria, near and beautiful, is just below you; far and beautiful, it fades into heavenly color.

The garden has flowers and trees, but we made for its dizzy edge, where are square bastions you can walk into, and, over a width of wall, peer at the terrific drop-down. Orvieto in the Middle Ages was a Guelph stronghold, and this *fortezza* often received the Popes when they fled from revolts in Rome; now, like those of Santa Barbara, its great walls hold up a lounging-place. . . . Wallflowers wave from their smooth, sheer stones against the purpling color of the plain; it is a lovely spot.

And a lovely valley the Tiber had; though we felt it should be called the valley of the Paglia, because the shining river *is* the Paglia just here. One stream is quite as big as the other; indeed it looked to us as if the Tiber, from the north, ran at a right-angle into the other stream, and was lost in it . . . and that it was the unnoted Paglia, poor thing, which continued on its way, made the momentous swing to the southwest, and should have had great Rome upon its banks. Alack! If so, what a geographical injustice.

Tiber is a nicer name, however, with more bite to it for purposes of heroic poetry—Horatius' outburst, as O Paglia, Father Paglia, would have sounded strange. In fact I think it might never have been written, and that would have been a loss . . . just that linking, between nations, of the heart-beat of the day's gallantry, and some sharp necessity of this.

We went through a beautiful gate with Gothic arches, then skimmed down to the "picturesque and varied plain," meeting peasants and donkeys on the way. One donkey, with a woman driving him, had a load of little pigs in its panniers. I don't remember crossing any river, though we must have (Orvieto was wonderful to look back upon in the clear morning air); but I remember very well, as we turned northward and began to climb hills, how pleased we were to find the Umbrian roads really so good. White and marble-smooth. We were on a ridge, the world was of freshest spring; the sun shone, the air was clear, we saw almost to Rome. Good-by, Rome; *au revoir,* Tiber! We'll see you farther north.

A great wind came out of the flying sky, but Nicolette was merely stimulated, and went flying along. We sat up and were stimulated too. No halts today; our wish was to fly. There were some steep pitches—*più del 7*—and an ox-cart blocking one of them at the very steepest bit of the worst white pitch . . . white like sunny snow; I remember how it bit into one's eyes, and how deeply blue, across it, was the shadow of a roadside shrine. Lovely white oxen, and their driver asleep over his load; waking, he pulled frantically on the cord that ran to their noses, Nicolette bumped over a block of marble and (with all her start spoiled) went hooting and ra-raing up over that grade like six Rolls-Royces in one. . . . Except for the ox-cart there was no traffic on our ridge—there isn't, in Umbria; one could look for miles, if need be, anywhere but at the road—so now we stared at each other.

"Not much the matter with her today!" said Babs, in a tone half pleased, half disgusted.

"Should say not," I muttered. (My shoulders were lame that morning.) "What do you suppose struck her yesterday?"

"Give it up!"

And we smiled brilliantly at each other; from pleasure in our agreeable pace, the smoothness and ease of everything. Monte Nibbio was close beside us; we whirled up toward a walled hill-town (Ficulle, or Santa Christina), rosy-brown, plain, and close built, as Umbrian towns seem to be; then down to the level of the *chianetta,* a river-valley; up again to the high hills.

"No rain, but a very vile wind," says the diary.

The wind indeed was getting rather blinding, it was hard to see scenery through it; we pounded down our hats and flew on. Monte Leone was now on one side of us, Monte

Gabbione on the other; we decided that instead of swinging off to Perugia the short way, we'd keep on and see Città della Pieve. There was time, in fact there was all day; and we wanted to see as much of Umbria as possible. Perhaps we could even go on and see Chiusi; though that was twenty *chilometri* away.

"Why not?" said Babs, composedly. "I'd like to, wouldn't you?"

Wonderful, to be able to consult one's preferences like this; but we were no longer nervous about Nicolette. High and high it still was, with green fields and glorious views; with dives and dips, and bits of ruins and loveliness—and Città della Pieve on the other side of a triangle of road, across a pretty green.

It is a striking sight, bunched there upon itself: rosy-brown, very clean and bare as to walls, somehow with an air of leaning toward, or into, itself; away from the inquiring world. There is a belfry, and a jumble of old roofs; things protrude, in a stark, stylish way; but all upward. Nothing spills or drizzles from Città della Pieve. It simply grew upward from the plain short grass in a plain, tall, pink-brown way; began at once and ended at once, and that was all there was to it. . . . We were struck by its ways; glad we had come. Its sole fame, of course, is as the birthplace of one "Pietro Vannucci, called Il Perugino (1446–1524)," though it holds a few paintings by him and his pupils. . . . Mostly by the pupils, doubtless, said we; and did not stir from Nicolette.

For was not Perugia before us, simply dripping with Peruginos? Why should they have left any in little Città? . . . And we found an illuminating sentence in Baddy: "The town possesses several of his pictures, but they are works of his later period, hastily painted and chiefly done by his pupils, as the master apparently deemed his native place not capable of appreciating works of a more elaborate kind."

Città did not suggest art, somehow. It looked too aloof and cool—or perhaps the wind was blowing too hard for art to seem real to us; at any rate we wondered a little why Vannucci, from that bleak beginning, should have become Il Perugino; and coursed on. His talent must have been conspicuous or Città would never have noticed it; and then his calm, soft faces of angels and madonnas—almost vacuous in their calm; did those troubled times beget such? Could he in the midst of Perugia's frightful history have found models who looked like that?

But here were his backgrounds; his poplars, small and slim, his dipping hills, and varied greens, and soft blue sky—only today it was full of rushing clouds. Perugino was quite the first to naturalize landscape at all, and it was sweet to see his sort around us . . . to drive, in these days when realistic art is being threatened, so placidly along through the country of its origin.

We had merely a glance at Chiusi. It is marvelously Etruscan and old, having been in full flower in the sixth century (B. C.), when its king, Lars Porsena, made the attack on Rome so famously foiled by Horatius at his bridge . . . which shows, after all, the use and effect of poetry; would many people even have heard of Horatius (and Babs and I named a rooster after him, once) had it not been for Macaulay?

And this was not all levity on our part. We had a great admiration for Horatius, who was a dignified and splendid rooster; he used to walk up the hatchway to a back living-room window and tap on it for cake-crumbs—we had given him some out of that window once, and he never forgot it. Beaks are grand to tap with. So it was Horatius at the hatchway; and we tried to eat him for Thanksgiving and couldn't. . . .

Chiusi had an inn "hardly to be recommended to ladies," where the padrone sold, at large prices, Etruscan antiques that were "largely manufactured in the town." Without stopping to burrow in its labyrinths of Etruscan galleries (some of them have to be entered on all fours), and feeling, on this wind-blown day, a sudden desire for sheets of water, we drove on for a glimpse of the Lago di Chiusi. A remarkably insignificant and flat-shored lake with marshy edges, and rushes growing in them; we backed quickly around, with some amusement at ourselves for having come, and struck off for Perugia by a new *bivio*.

Another hilltop road, it proved to be, just as white and good and winding as our other one and full of immense prospects. Umbria was so green—*GREEN!* so emerald with grass and young wheat, golden-green with mulberries and vines; so bright, as to roadsides, with poppies and daisies, blue speedwell and buttercups . . . and Nicolette still flying smoothly along.

Indeed it was a sailing sort of day, with plenty of signs and no inquiries necessary; altogether we felt singularly self-sufficient and on top of things, except that we began to wish we had brought lunch with us from Orvieto. Villages, besides being few, looked more and more incommunicative; food not having occurred to us in Chiusi, where there was doubtless plenty of it. But we had breakfasted that morning for the first time in Italy on poached eggs—*uova affogati;* besides this *was* Italy, and everything was everywhere. Lunch? Pooh. There'd be a *trattoria* somewhere, or a little *pasticceria;* much nicer to get it in some tiny place . . . and we flew scornfully on.

At last a road branched across a level green, like the one at Città, to a scrap of an old village; just a cul-de-sac of a close-built street, lined with little fat trees. We swung gladly into it—Piegaro, or Tavernelle; or perhaps San Martino? We were mixed in our villages. The cottages ran together in an unusually uneventful stream, with one window and door each; across one doorway was a swinging leather curtain, which, as a rule, meant "vino."

It did, even in this case. (The hamlet did not believe in other sorts of signs.) Pushing aside the heavy curtain—though with a feeling of some hesitation—I entered a clean, bare room with a bit of counter. The stout, white-kerchiefed woman behind it regarded me with astonishment, though pleasantly; I secured a small bottiglia of native wine and learned that, besides this, only *pane* could be obtained in that village.

"Non il formaggio?" I asked incredulously. "No cheese, signora?"

"Non qui!" said she. *"Solamente il pane."*

"Dov' è?" said I—my vocabulary as unadorned as the village; and looked questioningly out the door.

"Là, signora. Ec-co!" and she pointed across the way.

What a limited village! Where did it go then for its cheese and its macaroni and other necessities; all the way to Perugia? Raising a foiled eyebrow at Babs, who had driven up very close, with a worried eye on my proceedings, and who now swung Nicolette promptly around, I ducked in at another dark little door. A great loaf, rough and freckled and interesting-looking, was shown me, and another stout and astonished peasant-woman, with a white kerchief on her dark head, carved off a third of it for me; at which a very sour and potent smell arose. Peasant bread! We thought we had had some in France, but this was the real thing; I hurried out to Nicolette, pleased with my find. . . . At last we should fare as these people did.

By this time many heads were peering out of the little dark doors. The village quite blossomed with kerchiefs; and a soft gabbling arose. Smiling at them, Babs and I drove gently away.

We hadn't a thing left in the car, not a remnant of cheese or chocolate or fruit; Nicolette's usually resourceful larder was empty. Well—bread and wine? A classic meal, but not worth stopping for; we ate as we drove. I hewed the bread open—it was powerful stuff; and while Babs took a sip of wine, I reached over and steered. We had done the same thing on horseback more than once, when in a hurry—with a saucepan of coffee too, which was a trick to handle; we were in no haste now, but driving along seemed to illuminate the menu. . . . We took an immense long time over each hunk of bread—it smelled more than ever like elderberry blossoms, and had a fine resistance; occasionally one of us choked a little over the sour thin peasant wine. It was nice to drive and choke. We giggled a great deal during that meal, and had an imbecile time with crumbs; you took a bite out of that bread, and half the rest of it dissolved and fell in showers upon your lap.

But it was all exhilarating; we quoted *The Rubáiyát,* and felt pleased with everything; stopped by a stone-walled brook and brushed Nicolette out—she was floored with bread-crumbs—and put the rest of the bread on a clean rock by the water. Invitation to a temperate meal! for we poured the wine out in an unregretted pool. It was simply too terrible. Peasants, we had heard, like their wine dry; but dry does not express it; this made one's hair crinkle. . . . Hurray for the sporting and the disagreeable, however. They do one all kinds of good; and the next town we came to, we agreed, we'd lay in some permanent chocolate for Nicolette's door-pocket.

"Would it be too warm by the door? Would it melt it?" I said.

"Couldn't tell you," said Babs, laughing; and we ran merrily along again.

For all the wind and the hills, my daughter declared she was "simply having a vacation on driving"; Nicolette careered as if on her native heath. . . . Umbrian engineering is good, she informed us; almost as good as French . . . and from here on (except once) she had no complaint to make of Italian roads.

Across a somewhat too-inhabited plain, and beside vegetable-gardens, we approached Perugia; seeing her towers and walls above and beyond us, on a fathomless blue sky. A thousand feet up, they are; an inspiring sight. Nicolette hastened quite riotously along; then—bumpetty-bump! she did a surprised hand-gallop for a moment. "Not quite so smooth, here. Ee-easy!" said Babs. For these were our first Umbrian potholes; we moderated, and approached with discretion.

This plain was a trifle hot, but mountains were about us; soon we should be where we could see them; feel their cooler air. Would there be a snow-peak or two? There were, when we were in Perugia before; and with those walls goalfully above us, we attacked the long curves of Perugia's hill. Especially long curves, they are.

"Remember coming up here in the bus that night?" said Babs. "It seemed forever."

"Heavens, yes! How lost we did feel. You were sure we were going to goodness knows where, and would never get to a town at all!"

"I was," confessed Babs with one of her frank grins. "I'd been asleep most of the way from Rome. . . . Goodness, it was dark, that night!"

"And we, furious because we couldn't see the view—"

But we could now; Nicolette had us almost to the top. There was Umbria again, shining with streams, dotted with little towns; and there *were* snow-peaks! almost more beautiful than before.

And here, under our wheels, was Perugia; very white as to pavement, very waving as to palms, in its piazza with the splashing fountain—and a view, over one's shoulder, back to the mountains. How homelike it all seemed; how well we remembered it. And here was the same concierge, bustling out to greet us; goodness, we remembered him too. He didn't know us, we hadn't had Nicolette before; but grandiloquent was his welcome, glorious his seizing of bags and showering of orders upon inferiors that clustered about him, gathering up our books, umbrella, tea-basket, and other encumbrances as sacredly as if they had been treasures of Golconda.

"A room with a view?"

"Yes, yes!" said the Palace Hotel; *"Sisignora!"* All in one word, such was its willingness; and the lift took us up.

A lift; we had not met lifts, lately. There were wide and palatial stairs in this hotel—of carpeted stone, with palms at the landings, and we really liked climbing them; but just for expedition's sake, we would be lifted. . . . Top floor; the view would be that much better. I had protested a little about the price—just as much for a room under the eaves as for a magnificent and brocaded one on a lower floor; but the suave little padrone made short work of me.

"Of course I *have* always others that look upon the court, or the town," said he calmly. "The Italians choose those; they do not care. The others—they are not many—I save for the English and the Americans. They *will* have the view; and of course it is more expensive, signora!"

Of course. And eaves were quite magnificent, here. Also it was the only one left, toward the view; we went straight across to our windows, opening the casements and leaning out. Yes, there it was; there were the snow-peaks. And just wait till tonight, when there would be a moon! It would come up right over them; it did before, remember? And the sky like velvet. . . . Was that Assisi on the hills there? That was the direction. And wasn't it *grand* this was Saturday night again? It had been, when we were here the other time. Just the place to be, for Sunday . . . and then we remembered to take our heads in and dismiss the porter.

We were fond of this room already. Its ceiling gave us a noble mixture of frescoed flowers, impossible ones, but full of cheery color; the carpet was soft and fresh, and gay with flowers, Italian beds are always perfect, and our two casements looked out, we were sure, on the finest view in Perugia. The only view, for this had foreground; old roofs, a belfry, church-steps, and a dark lane disappearing under arches. We wouldn't be on a bald edge like that other place that thought it was so grand—for anything.

And the *sala à pranzo* was a mass of flowers, at dinner. We enjoyed comparing notes, afterwards, with some friendly Americans who were likewise "doing" Italy; such a nice easy-going family with five children, all apparently having a wonderful time, and engaging huge suites at hotels wherever they went.

"Private bathrooms—for the children especially," the young mother confided to me; "so necessary, you know!"

After they had disappeared upstairs—gradually, sensibly,

and humorously, smallest children first—we read, in the glass-roofed court, by charming, insufficient, pink-shaded light, an English magazine or two (a luxury to have magazines about once more), and departed sleepily up the staircase to look out on Umbria.

It woke us up. Nobody could be sleepy with that before one. A silver moon was sailing over the mountains, the air was fresh and sweet; and we could hear the fountain splashing, below us. Down there the shadows were inky black; the moon's light was on the belfry opposite, and on the waves of tiles; it shone dimly on the snow-peaks, on winding streams, on the tops of dark hills, above their little twinkling jewels that were towns . . . and over Assisi, above Monte Subasio and the faraway valley, with its vanishing twinkles, was the soft purple-blue of Italy's night sky.

Never was such a blue. Violet, really. It held us breathless. The silver moon swam in it; and there the mountains lay, along the valley of the Tiber.

CHAPTER XVIII

A SUNDAY IN ASSISI

ROGATION Sunday. Up late," says the diary.

Sunday morning sleep seemed good to both of us, but I rose at last, and went out into the brightness of a boiling Sunday morning in Perugia. Nothing can be brighter than that; either Perugia's pavement is whiter than most, or her hilltop nearer the abiding-place of Ra. I stepped into the piazza, where the coolness of fountain and greenery seemed miraculous; then, via a bit of biting sun, into the Corso Vannucci—divided in accurate halves of black and white.

It was empty except for a few church-goers, and I wondered if any shops would be open; I was going to buy a hooter for Nicolette. Not another day would we wait, after that episode of the sleeping driver and the oxen; our horn was a soft contralto one, no one paid any attention to it . . . and here, opposite Perugia's fountain and the door of the *duomo,* was my shop; open!

It was just on the verge of closing, the young padrone was putting on his hat to go home, but he took it off again and smiled a welcome. Hooters of every style were laid before me, others were pulled from boxes, and the padrone laughingly exhibited their powers. He loved doing it; the shop resounded with hoots. Selecting the most piercing one—it had a long silver trumpet and looked as if it could hoot—I came joyfully out into the piazza with my treasure. Not many lire it had cost; would those buy peace? Beware, donkeys; here is something that will make you jump out of your long-enduring skins and fly for the gutter.

I hoped it would, at least; and loitered a moment by the

fountain. The cool sound was lovely. . . . It, too, is lovely, this Fontana Maggiore, with its three basins, and three nymphs by Arnolfo, and a border of reliefs by the Pisani. . . . These two had done many things for their own city, but here they were again, father and son, doing a fountain for Perugia. Artists were in demand, in those days; Niccolo was a sculptor and painter both, Giovanni a sculptor, and a delightful life they must have had working together over beautiful things. It was enviably early in the history of Italian art; the field was before them, their way unhampered, even by wars and sieges. The period of Niccolo's activity was that of Pisa's greatest success "as a maritime republic," yet art was encouraged and protected; even here in Perugia it went placidly on, that fiery town being, Muirhead says, "the chief center of Umbrian painting, which flowered in sweet calm through the storms of civic history."

I could not help thinking, as I leaned over the fountain's rail, that it was a long way from Pisa to Perugia. For the Pisani, traveling on horseback, a momentous journey; but they accomplished it: all along the Arno, then over wild prefatory hills, stopping just short of the main range of the Apennines at this ancient hill-town. One could imagine them glad to reach it; welcomed by the *podestà* and the people, and given every facility for their work. . . . I was glad the Perugians had wanted a fountain here and that the Pisani had done it; the three basins are so pleasant, the water sweet-falling and clear.

Added to bas-reliefs, it was worth lingering by; and, thinking of the Baptistry in Pisa, I could almost see delicate little pillars reflected in its shining circles.

For pulpits ran in the Pisano family—the beautiful one at Siena is theirs, too; one detects a hint of pulpit-style even about the base of this fountain. I think bas-reliefs belong more on pulpits than on a fountain. They tell stories, and inculcate morals; one had a sudden feeling that sermons should be issuing from the lips of the charming nymphs, instead of sprays of water. . . .

For many months the two Pisani were engaged on this fountain, but the old father was in failing health and died while the bas-reliefs were being executed; so Giovanni carried out the last of their mutual work alone. I wished I knew which of the reliefs the old man had done; seventy and over, and still modeling—working away at these delightful little figures; but no one seems to say which are his. . . . A sad journey home for Giovanni, riding away down the hill-paths of Perugia in his cloak and velvet cap, an apprentice or two behind him; a great ache and blankness in his heart when he thought of the years of lonely work ahead.

This loss must have been almost a paralyzing one to him, I have felt, for it was not till long afterward—nearly twenty years, that his chief works were conceived. Young Italians of that day seem to have been fond of their fathers; of the patient, hard-working *madre,* somewhere behind the scenes, there is rarely a word, but even the stormy Benvenuto speaks often of his feeling for the elder Cellini, and of keeping up the music he detested, just to please that good old man. A pretty story it is, of mutual devotion and concession; even after Benvenuto had achieved his ambition—that of being a sculptor and goldsmith, "I did not," he affectionately adds, "neglect to gratify my good father from time to time by playing on the flute or cornet. Each time he heard me, I used to make his tears fall, accompanied by deep-drawn sighs of satisfaction. My filial piety often made me give him that contentment, and induced me to pretend that I enjoyed the music too."

And this from that murderous, though honest, swaggerer—the *bragadoccio,* wayward friend and violent lover; but his father's letters were enough to make anybody devoted.

Feeling suddenly that my own child was awake, I hastened back to her. I did hope she'd like the hooter; for I didn't know much about such things.

Church-goers were frequent now, the Corso was sprinkled with black figures, and with voices; dodging the streaks of sunshine I regained our shady piazza, then the hot and sunny steps of the hotel. Its halls seemed a luxury of coolness; and Babs, who was putting on her hat to come and look for me, pounced with joy upon the hooter.

"*Just* what I wanted, A.B.! Where did you find it?"

We refrained with difficulty from sounding it in the bedroom, and trotted gaily downstairs. In fact, oblivious of amazed chambermaids who appeared along corridors, on the various floors, we had a little race down those irresistible flights. Their steps were so wide and shallow—why aren't all stairs made that way?—had such a soft thick crimson carpet, and nice stone border; fine for speed and hilarity.

But we went, before we did anything else, straight along the Corso to Perugia's museum. It is housed in that finest of fifteenth-century buildings, the Palazzo Communale, overlooking the Pisani's fountain; we were soon upstairs, adoring everything. The entrance room is like the noble hall of a castle, lofty and stone-floored, stone-colored, with immense deep-set stone window sills some four or five feet thick. Armor and clusters of painted battle-flags—for this part of Umbria excelled in banner painting—carry on the castle idea; with a few pictures to lead one, in Perugia's own fashion, toward the sweetness and clarity of her art.

There seemed more things in this room than there were two years before, we missed a little of its rarity, the almost cloistral simplicity that had so enchanted us; but there was still space enough for one's thoughts to have room—a strange quality, in any gallery. We wandered on; slim rooms, paintings on wood, lovely primitives with much gold and color, sweet faces of clustering saints and presiding madonnas; rapt was the atmosphere of these little rooms. There were views out of the windows, too . . . an asset to any gallery, these slits of sunlit Umbria; hills and olive trees and sweet fresh sky.

"I never feel tired in this place," confided Babs, as we stood at last in the room of the Peruginos; a well-lighted, confident room.

"Not a bit!" I said, pausing with her, under one of our

favorite faces—oh, that clarity of look! "I think I'm rested, in fact. . . ."

For that is how the gallery at Perugia affects one. It is never crowded with people—never at least had we found it so; we had a real love for the place itself and its soothing quality, not only for its Bonfiglis, and Pieros, and Mariettos. A place where emotion could be fitly housed, where one could wander affectionately and at will, and where "the characteristic Umbrian gentleness is felt pervading the whole gallery."

"Yes," said a scornful friend who likes 'strong' things; "you would like Peruginos!"

"Uh huh," I replied, with much the mental technique of the prize-fighter who begins to dance, busily, before his opponent: "I Do Like Peruginos!"—and there's something the matter with you if you don't! I wished to add, but did not. For that is one's instinctive (indeed prehistoric) reaction when others don't like what one is fond of, and I object to being instinctive; yet this affection for the Peruginos has come to be almost a tender point with me—perhaps because I have seen, in innocent moments of gazing upward at a sunset, my ironic child look rather like one, and it is very melting when ironic people do that. . . . And what a name it is anyway; honey on the tongue; grape-tendrils in a morning breeze; one could draw a cherub with the flying curls of that word.

Almost any one of the Peruginos, indeed, comes upon one like a breath of spring air, with fresh leaves dancing and shadows moving on the ground; some of the drawing may be "unscholarly," but Perugino was a revelation in his time and still gives one something to carry away; the sort of thing which one likes to carry away with one, and which, from galleries, one so rarely does. We had done it out of a monastery or two—from San Marco in Florence, for example; but a collection of primitives in a hill-town has a great and unfair advantage over one in a city. The things belong there—belong with old tiles and hillsides of olive trees—some of them had been done there; and what *is* there, in this world of visual things, that is not the better for its own setting? . . .

The Venetians are best in Venice, and reached by gondola—it is essential to splash a little, on the way; just so the Umbrian saints should be seen in their own country, Perugino in his very own hill-town: a town calmed somewhat from its medieval turbulence, to be sure . . . but then we hadn't known the turbulence.

Besides it had had calm epochs; and outwardly Perugia is little changed. Her palaces are there, her aged gates and down-dipping streets, her stairways and hidden gardens. Scarcely could she be altered without vital inner disruption, so tenacious is her hold upon the hilltop, so closely is she fortified and built; so buttressed and upheld, where she begins to slide over the edge. . . . Walking along some shadowy lower lane, with stone forever shutting out the sun, one glances up and up at this enormous masonry, wondering when one's eye will reach the top. It slopes inward a little—Etruscan in foundation, purple-brown in color, cold and damp to the touch; sometimes a flight of steps winds damply up through it, twisting to include an inconceivably tucked-in old house-front (just one window with a plant in it), then, with a resigned stolidness peculiar to ancient steps, and possibly to the mood of those who climb them, winding on upward again.

And the plant blossoming in that dank shadow was a red geranium! Was this purely Latin fervor—or idiocy on the part of the geranium?

But this is a hill-town that it is particularly fascinating to ramble about in. The churches are not wildly interesting, it is just Perugia one grows fond of; her bastions looming over the valley, her heavy arches holding a mountain view; even the byways, dark and diving, where her inhabitants cheerfully carry on their (sometimes gruesome) occupations (we collided with a butchering, in one of them), but where are glorious glimpses out to the radiant country-side beyond. . . . If forced for any reason to stay in a town, I should far rather spend a summer here than in Siena. Perugia is higher and smaller, built along one ridge instead of on three plunging hills; there seems to be much less stone, and you can get out of her so easily. In fact you *are* out of her, visually, most of the time; things fall away so violently that your glance goes straight out to the noble mass of the mountains, and rests there—on blue and violet slipping downward into valley green, or mounting to peaks of exquisite snow. . . . Memorable, in April or May, is the charm of that scene.

Yes, one can smell the snows from Perugia—or sometimes, when the sun is hot, a whiff of fragrance from her hillside flowers; but why not *be* in the country? Why sit and sniff and wish you were there? I would leave my stones, get up and go; lodge at a *podere,* and climb back (if I could not be without it) to my art, and my museums, and my Perugia.

Blashfield compares her to "the Griffin of her own escutcheon, crouching on her hilltop and extending long paws down the valley side"; a pictorial image, and quite true. Medievally, she extended those paws, with claws in them, much farther, clutching at her neighbors; even at little Assisi—so near, and, on her easier hillside, so defenceless. . . . The two, little and big, should have held each other's hands, but they did not; and it was to one of these quite fratricidal wars that young Francis of Assisi rode out, saying, as he looked back at his town gate,

"I shall come back a prince!"

All the young men of this region seemed warlike, even among themselves—in spite of Francis' later teaching, which they absorbed with the greatest piety. "Temperance," remarks Blashfield, "was never an Umbrian virtue. Massacre yesterday, and a procession of flagellants today . . . was Perugia's way of establishing a spiritual equilibrium"; for her citizens, "violent and devout," did not take kindly to ethical living. "Not even Siena," he says, "rent and tore herself as did Perugia. One reads of it all with bewilderment; Baglioni fighting Oddi till the latter were exterminated, then fighting among themselves, till in the late years of the *quattrocento,* the early years of the *cinque-cento,* they battled so constantly that one wonders how Perugino managed to reach his daily work upon the square, that centre of disturbance."

These Baglioni, "the Dragon's brood," were fierce and beautiful young men, it seems, ruthless and brave beyond belief; mostly dying young. Astorre Baglione, waking at night and hearing the enemy coming, and with no time to spread the alarm, seized his weapons and dashed out of the palace door in the darkness—fierce as a panther, beautiful as an angel, he was; met the first of these kinsmen creeping to the attack, and shouting, leaping and thrusting so that they thought he was an army, slew a score of them, drove off the rest, then fell himself . . . pierced with innumerable wounds!

At least a dear friend of ours, thrilled to the bone with this sort of thing, told us this tale; adding in a tone of immense drama and mystery—

"And, my dears, when I went down that hill there—you know, where the tram-tracks go—there, set in the stone of a palace wall, was a post-box with *'Oddi'* on it. JUST THAT ONE WORD—*Oddi!* . . . Think of it! After all these years!"

There must be one or two left, then.

We strolled on down to the Arco d'Augusto—bright purple in shadow, it was; then back, with some speed through the noonday heat, to a revivifying lunch at our table with the fresh and pretty flowers. An early *colazione;* for Nicolette was waiting for us. It was Sunday, and Assisi was calling us.

It was such a lovely day, too, we felt somehow just like St. Francis; the light on the hills was wonderful. Even the valley, fluffy with productiveness, yet braced with mountains, looked soft and cool, and Nicolette slipped pleasantly along its little roads. Mulberry trees and poppies, wheat and vineyards—all happy and flourishing and wonderfully tended; we even met a blue cart with four white oxen, out on some unusual mission. It looked as it were coming home from somewhere; beautiful, its pellucid creatures against that Umbrian view. We stopped for a picture, then drove quickly along; we wanted all the time we could have in Assisi—now approaching, on its mountainside.

Assisi, the beloved and long-dreamed of; to this day, merely a vision in a book . . . or books; Babs had a whole library on St. Francis. It was his winter; we had been to Housman's plays, given so well and charmingly at University College—the *Little Plays of St. Francis;* we had read most of the fresh things that Chesterton and others were writing about him; in fact we had soaked steadily in St. Francis for months . . . surprised at first by England's fervor about him, then not surprised at all. One simply needs to know about him; and with my child's love of things Franciscan, my own affection for the Saint began.

He had broken rather suddenly upon us, that winter; in America we do not seem to deal extensively with St. Francis. I remember hearing stories of his releasing cagefuls of birds, and feeling vaguely emulous of such fine deeds . . . feeling, vaguely, too, their romance and high import; wondering how much those birds cost—flights and flights of birds! and then dismissing the whole matter in a practical young mind, as beyond my reach. "Charming but impossible!" I should have said, had I been older.

To none of us, it seems, was he presented as he was to Chesterton, who speaks affectionately of a time

when long ago in those days of boyhood my fancy first took fire with the glory of Francis of Assisi. I too have lived in Arcady; but even in Arcady I met one walking in a brown habit who loved the woods better than Pan . . . and at no stage in my pilgrimage has he ever seemed to me a stranger. There is something of harmony between the hearth and the firelight and my own first pleasure in the words about Brother Fire . . . even the fantastic shadows thrown by fire makes a sort of shadow pantomime that belongs to the nursery; yet the shadows were even then the shadows of his favorite beasts and birds as he saw them, grotesque but haloed with the love of God. His Brother Wolf and Brother Sheep seemed then almost like the Br'er Fox and Br'er Rabbit of a more Christian Uncle Remus. I have come slowly to see many and more marvellous aspects of such a man, but I have never lost that one.

And tales of Francis might seem for children even an improvement on Br'er Rabbit, who is somewhat constricting to the imagination. No one that I ever heard of, went, or desired to go, any farther with Br'er Rabbit than Br'er Rabbit, in his very piquant actuality, goes; but these "sister birds" of Francis', his Brother Water and Sister Earth, seem to know, in their loving implications, no limits this side of infinity. Children being fresh from there, as Wordsworth suggests, have a scent for infinity; and if one learns to love the unworldly in this life, it is a long step toward realization of another.

But even England, indeed the whole modern world, has had a recent awakening to St. Francis. In a book of *Essays in Commemoration* published in London, there is one by the late Walter Seton, of the historic Seton family of Scotland,—"there was Mary Seton, and Mary Beaton, and Mary Carmichael and me"—also secretary of the British Society of Franciscan Studies, and dean at London University (where he was much beloved); and his essay is entitled "The Rediscovery of St. Francis of Assisi." In previous centuries there was no world-wide celebration, he says, because the world knew little of St. Francis. The Pope murmured a few things, a few of the devout echoed them, but that was all: "The whole world outside the Roman Catholic communion thought of him, if it thought at all, as a dead Roman Catholic" . . . whereas in 1926 a special series of Italian postage stamps was issued, because of the centenary—and if you are on a postage stamp, as Babs and I told each other, you are something. It takes a deal of popular sentiment and agitation to stir a government thus far; and the practical Mussolini himself, "ipse, ipsissimus!" the last man on earth one would fancy moved by a little person seven centuries dead—and while he lived, mad about unworldliness—issued a message "in which he compares Francis with Dante, with Columbus, with Leonardo da Vinci:

" 'Il più alto genio alla poesia, con Dante; il più audace navi-

gatore agli oceani, con Colombo; la mente più profonda alle arti e alla scienza, con Leonardo; ma l'Italia, con San Francesco, ha dato anche il più santo dei santi al Cristianesimo e all' umanità.' "

But the books about him were locked in monasteries and not available; "the priceless Fioretti," Mr. Seton says, "which have been a joy and an inspiration to countless readers of this generation, were certainly never quite forgotten, but in the first half of the nineteenth century they were known only to the learned." The first English translation of them was brought out in 1864; and twenty years later, in Paris, Renan wrote a study of him "which is a classic in Franciscan literature." Mrs. Oliphant also did a life of him; and Ruskin became deeply interested: "In *Deucalion* he wrote of himself as a brother of the third order, and he stayed for a long time at Assisi."

Then Professor Paul Sabatier was inspired by Renan to take up the Saint.

"The publication by Sabatier of the first edition of his *Vie de S. Francois d'Assise*—a book which was destined to go into forty-five editions and to be translated into many languages . . . was an epoch in Franciscan studies. Countless thousands of readers have derived from the writings of Sabatier . . . their first impulse toward interest in the saint, which has frequently developed into a complete surrender to his fascination and charm."

One is glad to know all this. It seems a subject one should always have known about—that it was a deprivation not to have known . . . and something, for the firesides of the future, should be done about it. Something as merry and actual and unexpected as Francis himself, a Francis who sang as he walked into the winter forest when things were at their worst for him, who not only leaped at what he did, but did what he leaped at; and whatever happened, smiled and sang and loved the world the more.

Oddly enough, Chesterton says, the world was ready for

him. It usually is not, when devoted people come along; but Chesterton gives some of the reasons, in a marvelous chapter on "The World St. Francis Found."

The end of the Dark Ages [he says] was not merely the end of a sleep. . . . It was the end of a penance; or, if it be preferred, a purgation . . . certain spiritual diseases had been finally expelled from the system. They had been expelled by an era of asceticism, which was the only thing that could have expelled them. Christianity had entered the world to cure the world.

The Greeks . . . started out with the idea that if man walked straight ahead on the high road of reason and nature, he could come to no harm. . . . The wisest men in the world set out to be natural; and the most unnatural thing in the world was the very first thing they did. The immediate effect of saluting the sun and the sunny sanity of nature was a perversion spreading like a pestilence. . . . In the Roman Empire also, long before the end, we find nature worship inevitably producing things that are against nature. . . .

What had happened to the human imagination, as a whole, was that the whole world was colored by dangerous and rapidly deteriorating passions; by natural passions becoming unnatural passions. Thus the effect of treating sex as only one innocent natural thing was that every other innocent natural thing became soaked and sodden with sex. For sex cannot be admitted to a mere equality among elementary emotions or experiences like eating and sleeping. . . . There is something dangerous and disproportionate in its place in human nature, for whatever reason; and it does really need a special purification and dedication. . . . The modern talk about sex being free like any other sense, about the body being beautiful like any tree or flower, is either a description of the Garden of Eden or a piece of thoroughly bad psychology, of which the world grew weary two thousand years ago. . . .

It was no metaphor to say that these people needed a new heaven and a new earth. . . . How could their case be met by looking at the sky, when erotic legends were scrawled in stars across it; how could they learn anything from the love of birds and flowers after the sort of love stories that were told of them? . . . We know what sort of sentimental associations are called up to us by the phrase "a garden . . ." melancholy and innocent ro-

A WINDOW IN PERUGIA'S CATHEDRAL

mances . . . some gracious maiden lady or kindly old parson pottering under a yew hedge perhaps in sight of a village spire. Then, let anyone who knows a little Latin poetry recall suddenly what would once have stood in place of the sun-dial or the fountain, obscene and monstrous in the sun; and of what sort was the god of their gardens.

Nothing could purge this obsession but a religion that was literally unearthly . . . and they wrote across that great space of history the text: "This sort goeth not out but by prayer and fasting!" . . . but out of Assisi—out of its deep gates under its high turrets was to come the message that was the gospel of the hour, "Your warfare is accomplished, your iniquity is pardoned."

Over those first beginnings of social reform, Chesterton adds, there was

still something of that ancient austerity that came from the long penitential period . . . something that is bracing even while it is bleak, like a wind blowing between the clefts of the mountains. That wind, austere and pure, of which the poet speaks. . . . It was the twilight of morning. . . . Gradually against this gray background beauty begins to appear . . . as something really fresh and delicate and above all surprising. Love returning is no longer what was once called platonic but what is still called chivalric love. The flowers and stars have recovered their first innocence. . . .

While it was yet twilight a figure appeared silently and suddenly on a little hill above the city, dark against the fading darkness. For it was the end of a long and stern night, a night of vigil, not unvisited by stars. He stood with his hands lifted, as in so many statues and pictures, and about him was a burst of birds singing; and behind him was the break of day.

That was Francis.

I suppose we crossed the Tiber, but I have not the slightest picture of it. Doubtless it was an unimpressive streamlet; perhaps it was even muddy. I do seem to remember something blue that went nicely with poppies; I know that Nicolette sped, and that Assisi was looking down at us.

It soon grew very large indeed; cream-colored and stony and important. We could see the great buttresses of the monastery straddling down the steep hillside for foothold; a wall jiggling up the hill, belfries against the mountain; then San Francesco again. It dominated everything.

San Francesco; his church. . . . As if trying to make it lovelier, a dark-blue cloud-shadow trailed swiftly across it, and over Monte Subasio behind it. This was another Umbrian sky today; we had had them for almost a week, and still were not used to them. Some of them had been Tuscan skies, to be sure, but this special blue—hot yet thoughtful, with vast white masses surging up and pretending to be thunderheads but not really being them, simply beautiful beyond belief, so enhancing were they to Umbria's charms and mountainous ways—seemed more a thing of the last day or two; since Umbria had been reached again. . . . Though little enough we had seen of it before—except the wild drive to Gubbio; we had flitted hastily through in a train, third class at that; choked with smoke and heat.

The sun was warm, now, on Nicolette's rim; it had been blazing, in Perugia; but a breeze was coming down from the mountain, and making the poppies dance. This green, fluffy valley was as cool and soft as it had looked.

Coming, through specially luscious vineyards, to Santa Maria degli Angeli on the plain below Assisi, in the bare uninteresting piazza of its tiny hamlet, we went in. That, said the guide-book, was the thing to do. We didn't care frightfully for Santa Maria, bare in spots, magnificent in spots, yet were very glad to have seen it. Outside it is huge and yellow, with a very tall tower, but inside is a sort of goldenness, from a huge and lofty dome, and a rather special feeling; for Francis is everywhere. His garden of "thornless roses" is here—the roses were budding, and one or two were out; the little chapel that he built, the cell where he died, and himself by della Robbia, touching and real. . . . Near the little rose-garden (*presso il roseto!*) is another statue of him with his robe, and sandals, and thin, gentle, yet keen face, bending to put one hand on a sheep's woolly neck, while the sheep, grazing on a hillside (if one may judge from her doubled knees) turns her nose up to him in surprised affection.

It is just the figure to have *"presso il roseto"*; a little figure that sent a great wave over the world. A wave of love and goodness.

For we had been reading the *Little Flowers of St. Francis,* which we had heard given as a lecture in London; and that sort of thing gets into one. *Fioretti* is such an exquisite word; we heard as we read the voice of its author speaking with charm and simple earnestness. The origin of the *Fioretti,* he says, is somewhat debated—whether or not it was written by one Fra Ugolino of Monte Santa Maria; another monk is mentioned in the manuscript, "an unnamed friar—*'ego qui scripsit.'* . . . In the first group of stories there is, no doubt, a purely fantastical element . . . but much is of genuine historical value . . . an oral tradition, coming straight from the memories, and perhaps the actual writing, of Francis's beloved secretary, his *'pecorella di Dio.'* Hence the singular beauty, the convincing Franciscan simplicity, of some of the stories in which Francis and Leo alone appear together upon the scene. . . . 'And so, in this humble contention, with many tears and much spiritual consolation, they kept vigil until day.' "

That sounds so nice; so homely and real. I like to believe all the miraculous things I can about St. Francis; and who would not believe what was told one by a *pecorella di Dio,* pronounced meltingly, Italian fashion, with many l's?

The preaching to the birds [the author says,] is nowhere told so fully or so beautifully as in the *Fioretti.* "Finally, having finished his sermon, St. Francis made the sign of the Cross over them, and gave them leave to depart; and then all those birds in a flock rose up into the air with marvellous songs . . . they divided into four parts; one part flew towards the east and another towards the west, the third towards the south, the fourth towards the north, and each flock sang marvellously as it went; signifying, in this, that . . . the preaching . . . renewed by St. Francis, should be carried by him and his friars throughout all the world; and these friars, in the fashion of birds, possessing nothing of their own in this world, committed their life to the providence of God."

There seemed a good deal of this still in Assisi; a sort of heavenliness. It was Sunday, and there were mild crowds in the street; we drove up the sharp little hill to the old Porta San Pietro, then along the cobbled stretch beneath the immense buttresses of the high, two-story church. A procession of boys in the dress of a monastic school was climbing the long flight of steps, Italian cars were driving up, and tourists, in moderation, were looking at the view, or coming with a strange quietness (for tourists) in and out of the old doors; but the certain something that belongs to Assisi was upon it all, something that Francis himself put there and which, like the enormous walls and thicknesses of his church, will remain.

Indescribable, but very real, it was in the guileless freshness of the air, the soft clearness of the Umbrian landscape; the very look and feel of the little climbing town and its pavements. For in this air were dreamed dreams; and those dreams still live. Things put upon the air have a way of living on—floating about; to be felt, now here, now there, as a breeze flits, or a loving thought comes by. A friend once said to me, "A poem is something you catch out of the air as it goes by" . . . and Francis' dreams were like poems.

Indeed, they were poems; in his young days he had wished to be a Troubadour. The songs of those *literati* of Provence and Languedoc had reached Italy and influenced Francis profoundly; he wrote, in French, his famous poem called the "Canticle of the Sun," and sang it, "wandering in the meadows in the summer season of his own career, when he was pouring upward into the sky all the passions of a poet." Mystical people are often annoying in real life, but Francis was not one of those; his sweetness and courtesy won him friends everywhere, and a remarkable following. In his early wanderings he had been given a rough brown tunic by a peasant, and had girt it with a rope he had picked up: "Ten years

ASSISI, AND THE SLOPES OF MONTE SUBIASO

From the Perugia Road

later," says Chesterton, "that makeshift costume was the uniform of five thousand men; and a hundred years later, in that, for a pontifical panoply, they laid great Dante in the grave."

Was all this in the minds of those who walked or climbed about the little town? We seemed to see a gentleness in their aspect not usual to those who explore ancient places; not only in theirs, but in that of the people of Assisi; and we were trying to be realistic and calm! For it is hard, in this magic atmosphere, not to fall into sentimentality over St. Francis; most of us have a vein of the mystic in us, and if one gave oneself up to it, there would be no stopping. . . .

Well, we didn't weep, as sentimentalists are accused of doing, and we didn't sigh; but we did feel Assisi very much. It is one of the places in the world where one goes not just to see, but to feel. We liked the noble Refectory of the monastery, with its look of high, vaulted distinction, and gorgeous old portraits above the long refectory tables—set now, even to manchets of bread, and water in the glasses, for the supper of the boys in the monastery school; we cared only moderately for the frescoes of the life of St. Francis, in the upper church; but all through our going about we were captured, laid hold of, by the little town itself. We had expected to be bowled over by the frescoes; but besides being damaged (all the rains in Umbria must have poured through that roof), they seemed too orange, and orange-purple, as if some one—not Giotto, certainly—had thought to cheer them up by a wash of yellow; a uniformity of orange glow unsuited to pictures showing such varied scenes.

And it is not a nice orange glow; a sort of miasma, like the enforced yellow of ochre that we met and heartily disliked in southern France, where even the hillsides and the dust (and Nicolette), were thus discolored. Sad, to want to like something and not be able to; both of us preferred the magnificent duskiness of the lower layer of San Francesco, its recessed chapels and huge low arches (almost crushingly low) under and about which, with renewed satisfaction and no disturbance at all, we now wandered. Deep beneath its rock foundation St. Francis is buried; everywhere one had a sense of the mountainous church above.

Candles flickered on the great altar, but a light was turned on for us. Exquisite faces came out; marvelous color; though it was almost lovelier when the light went off. One could still feel the faces, so strongly had they drawn themselves upon the mind—Cimabue's angels, the saints of Simone Martini, flat-patterned, alive with gold; richness of tint was still there, and the dusk brought everything together. Blashfield remarks that though the church, from end to end, is a delight to the eye, it is at first confusing; "everything is dominated by a sense of color, of warm dusky reds, of ultramarine greyed by the incense smoke. . . . The middle ages are calling to us with that color-voice which sounds from the walls of every decorative Gothic church . . . the deeply-chorded harmony of red, blue, and gold."

We strolled here or there, drawn by this bit of beauty, and by that; then out into the sane greens and blues of landscape, the hot and simple pavements of Assisi. Nicolette, both warm and ready, threaded us sweetly around its ancient corners; past the lovely Tempio di Minerva which, dating from the time of Augustus, doubtless once stood there alone, with due deference paid to its columned front and mellow steps, but is now crushed into the piazza's architecture. And it has been rechristened as a church; Santa Maria; by which *volte-face* a cherished name has been made ridiculous, and every one's architectural sense insulted. As well try, we said, to make a madonna out of helmeted Minerva herself; a temple this calm thing is, and will remain.

One cannot believe that Francis ever championed so foolish a change.

At the piazza's end is a fountain round whose upper basin the pigeons of Assisi drink, or preen themselves, where laden donkeys pass, and the cheerful picturesque peasants of Umbria, men and women, with their baskets, and faggots, and loaves of bread, chatter as they go. Peasant costume has survived, in Umbria; in Assisi's streets it belongs as nothing else could; its old colors, rose and brown, shrimp-color and blue, seem a part of everything. . . . Beyond the fountain we climbed, unknowingly, to the cathedral, struck by its aged façade and impressive sparseness of windows, its animals in stone; then on and up to many little churches, to trees peeping over a high wall, and, from this little *vicolo* or that, a far look at Assisi's view. . . . So many of these lanes, there were.

"Let's see where *this* goes!" Babs would say—and see we did, sometimes getting into odd spots or tight corners, and having to back out again.

Once, coming out from a lane of old houses, we saw a grassy indentation—you couldn't call it a road—diving into a sort of gully, then climbing along by a ruined wall.

"Let's go there!" said Babs, a gleam in her eyes.

For it seemed to go toward the high pasture land that mounts behind Assisi. Nicolette, much stared at by an old peasant woman, but undaunted by nothing her young driver asked of her, squeezed us (with subdued gasps from me) up the turfy slope by the wall—a goat-track, I was sure. Fragments of stone and marble were in our way, there was a downdrop on the other side, with barely room for our whels between it and the wall . . . but Nicolette made it; coming out at last by some ruins and, as we had hoped, upon a view.

Above us were the pinkish-brown slopes of Monte Subasio —decoratively dotted with rocks and hardy shrubs—in one of whose ravines is the forest hermitage of St. Francis; but the great sight was across the valley.

Simply more and more of Umbria; mountains of every color, silver streams, golden villages, the tender colors of the valley—wave after wave of it melting into dusty lavender, meeting at last the violet of the far hills; with St. Mary of the Angels "a tall and perfect lily in the plain." It is a valley, and a view, like no other in Italy; whose vines and olives are the softest waves, flowing, soundless, into an Umbrian clearness of color we had seen nowhere else; and over it all, the peace of Assisi seemed to brood.

We looked at each other; we got out and picked a small daisy or two—very white, these little daisies, untouched with any worldly crimson—then slid down again across the short grass, and bumped over the fragments, feeling somehow angelical ourselves.

You can't help it. It is Assisi. We slid along to Santa Chiara, lower down on the edge of the same view, its big flying buttresses boldly across the road. At home we had seen barns built across the road, but never buttresses; and Nicolette quite vanished in the enormousness of one of them. As by the entrance of Beauvais, or beside the iron palings of San Spirito, "I'm gone!" said she, disappearing in stone. And she was.

Pleased, we hastened in to Santa Chiara; looked lightly about, beamed at the rose-window, at a fresco which the sacristan, with a torch, was showing somebody else, and came lightly out. It was time for tea, and tea in Assisi there easily was; tea, in fact, shown by the agreeable outdoor wavings of yellow, blue, or pink table-cloths all up and down the sunny, cobbled hill, was being most bountifully offered. There were green or orange chairs to choose from, plants in tubs, and all sorts of simple pleasantness—very simple, as befitted the town, but active in spirit; and tea, in cheerful china with broad bands of rose-color (and roses painted on the rose-color), was soon being brought us. (We had picked out the place with the green chairs.) Monkish fare of butter and crusty bread went with it; no effeminate *biscotti* here, or cakes. Even tea, for a town so conscious of its Saint, was probably a concession; though one could not doubt that while rejecting it for himself, Francis would have loved other people to have it. That was one great thing about Francis. He respected other people's joys.

So we felt almost appropriate over the sturdiness of this meal, the stout padrone meanwhile eyeing us with a satisfaction which, we felt, was Assisian too; one is not often eyed that way by people beneath whose orange trees one is (so temporarily) sitting. *Hot* milk came with the tea—horrid but somehow heart-warming; quite as it should be on this hill above Assisi's wall, with its view stretching away.

That milk of Assisi never got cool. Over it came a wrinkled skin which fell back tactfully, *cortesemente* ("note the Franciscan word"!), as one poured; then resumed being a lid. Hot to the last drop, our lavender-tinted tea; and not otherwise would we have had it. . . . The padrone, though not reluctant about producing his bill, was entirely just; and he quite forgot to charge for atmosphere, which was our greatest indebtedness; for an air thick with memories—even for cloud-shadows in the valley.

A little wind got up, and dust started sighing among the leaves of the orange trees. We rose. Already the clouds were tinted; there would soon be sunset on those mountains. "While it was yet twilight"—the beautiful words came to me again—"a figure appeared silently on a little hill above the city, dark against the fading darkness. . . . He stood with his hands lifted . . . and behind him was the break of day."

We went away, wishing we might stay till dusk came down on Assisi. We had heard a soft bell ring from a tower; it was like no other bell we had heard, and we longed to hear more. We wanted to hear the convent bell ringing . . . from Monte Subasio.

Yes, we were being sentimental about it now; and a heavenly feeling it is. I had not then read Percy Lubbock's *Roman Pictures,* but nothing better expresses the beatific glow with which we drove along our little road than one of his paragraphs. It was at a dinner, in Rome, where the guests were exclaiming over the hill-towns: "The dear, sweet places, we name them in succession . . . assuring each other that Assisi—that Perugia—that Siena—needed no more words to express what we all agreed they were." A Miss Trumbull, it seems, had arrived that very day from Assisi, "where she had spent a fortnight alone with her feelings. These, she was clear, were unutterable; but so were mine, and when we threw them together the effect was instant. 'Assisi!' we both exclaimed in an outburst."

And Mr. Lubbock, I have always felt, is not being as wholly ironic about it as he would like to think he is.

A different little road we chose, for going back; a smooth sweet little road going along by a stream and big willows, and with nobody on it; bordered with vineyards, however, and looking back upon the late-afternoon loveliness of Assisi. It was sad to see it growing small behind us . . . fainter, almost fabulous; radiant still above its valleys.

I stood up in Nicolette and took a picture. Two peasant lads stared very hard, a mulberry tree emphatically shook its leaves, and on we went; hoping we had got something.

Nobody was on the road, we discovered, for the good reason that in the next village, a duck of a little round thing about an inch through, with its wall completely hiding it, was everybody. Rogation Sunday here was as merry as Easter day in France, flags and sports, bedecked peasants in gay mobs; worst of all, bicycles piled treacherously among them. We nearly ran Nicolette into a great heap of them; girls shrieked and youths leaped, but by nimble wheel-work Babs twisted us round it.

Some elaborate games were going on under the great gray walls, with colored ribbons and all sorts of prettiness; we wanted very much to stop and watch, but the crowd of joyful ones was overwhelming. It was their village, and their precious holiday; and though the handsome, laughing brown faces that turned up to us were alight with good-nature, even with a sort of uncouth welcome in their crude looks, we drove gently on. But they were beautiful people, gathered there; almost every face would have made a study; and the colors of the costumes . . . unspeakable.

Another adorable deviation we took, over the same good little white roads, to the east and north—how Francis must have loved this country of his: I remember great beauty, great trees and bubbling streams, old castles on peaks, and always mountains jumping up about us. As long as we dared, we kept on among them; turned reluctantly back. . . . Gorgeous, menacing clouds had suddenly arrived above us, rushing out from behind the mountains and flying away toward Perugia's hill—a marvelous sight, that city lifting itself above the shadows, with color increasing upon it, and a wild sky to set it off; as Nicolette climbed with us the long curves toward its walls, the vastness, richness, and wild beauty of the sunset took one's breath away.

A flaming rose blazed across the entire sky; the great clouds, with their purple underpinnings, were all lighted. As we looked, they went fiery crimson, streaked with bars of maroon and gold which stretched mightily from one horizon to another; a swarthy, long-lasting, Perugian sunset, splendid above her stony towers and walls, her darkening plain.

For a long time its distances, wave upon wave, were still shot with rifts of fire. Somewhere out in it, we said, though invisible to us, little Assisi must be twinkling away to itself; a pretty sight for St. Mary of the Angels, just below.

CHAPTER XIX

OVER THE APENNINES

THE sky was somber next morning, with a flush stealing along the mountains, and streams shining through the deep blue of dawn. The snow-peaks glowed a little, then paled; and I went back to my quilt. No use getting up yet; we had errands to do, and nothing abroad opens very early. Time to doze, to look out at the sky, write a note or two; even to worry a little about the weather!

"To Trasimeno, after a long bank job," says the diary.

Bank jobs in Italy *are* long; stately and decorative. This one took us up some old stairs into a hall of gilded carvings and frescoes, thence into a salon with all possible battle-scenes, very colorful and magnificent, around its walls; we were handed from one courteous Italian gentleman to another, and from room to room. Our whole progress indeed seemed to be through ball-rooms—I have a steady impression of pale-green velvet and crystal chandeliers; and to come at last, after infinite gravities, long searchings of documents and identifying of signatures, to a mere handing-over of money—crumply paper money at that—seemed an anti-climax.

As for a sad-looking elderly Englishwoman, who had been awaiting her turn, and who, after much whispered discussion with a friend, had decided to draw three hundred lire (about fifteen dollars) from her letter of credit, it scarcely seemed worth her while. . . . Nearly two hours we had spent in that stately though airless place, surviving quantities of both the French and Italian tongues; we walked out into the Corso, rich but exhausted.

"*What* a fuss!" said Babs, putting an arm through mine. (Such a relief to be affectionate, after all that.)

But the lire we had now would last us a long while, we told each other; and Nicolette, who had been waiting patiently in the street, skimmed gladly off with us.

"Clear gray morning," say my notes. "Found our way out backwards from the dear hill-town—curves and curves down, then along the most fertile of valleys. Like the one by Assisi. Perfect sequence of wheat, ditches, grape-vines in edge of ditch, green beans, poppies, and vetch; blue Apennines trimming the luscious prospect." And everywhere, as we went along, there were little wooden crosses set in the fields. We felt incredulous, a little awed, when we saw those crosses; but our imagination jumped at once to the solution—the peasants had put them there to bless the crops. . . . A poetic idea; and this valley surely leaped with vitality. My neighbors say that on a hot summer night "you can hear the corn growing"; in these luxuriant fields one could fairly see a vineyard unfolding.

A sweet spot; and everything about it went with our mood —the windless warmth of the peaceful morning, a touch of religion in the fields. . . . Did Francis tell the peasants to put crosses in their vineyards?

And we thought we were leaving the hill-towns, today, absolutely turning our backs on them—a tragic thing to do; but our road attacked some steep hair-pins and there was Magione above us, against the sky, beautifully hoary, with horse-chestnuts in bloom, a magnificent old castle, and magnificent views; we plunged down to Lake Trasimeno, long and light-green and water-colory, with a fishing-village on its edge—then sped north and saw Cortona high in air above us; very much a hill-town. We had forgotten Cortona.

"Lovely wall and double-barrelled church," say my notes. "It looked so perfect up there—why not keep it a picture?"

Growing bold, we swung into a cross-road (by Ponte Buriano) to avoid some of the valley road to Florence, which was suspiciously near the railway and looked, to us, manufactory-ish. It was; and it was the Val d'Arno, which sounds so lovely, and isn't. We were shocked.

Abandoning this highway at Figline we were able to take an unwordly little *bivio* which led us straight and handsomely across to Florence, via San Polo. Settignano, the birthplace of so many sculptors, was annoyingly over our heads, just when we had to get along to Florence before dark; but we were consoled when we drove into a dramatic and cliffy gorge with old castles, abrupt hills and a romantic village or two, and had thrills over real scenery once more. . . . We had not been parted long from scenery, but in Italy one expects it at one's elbow. So we gazed with fervor at the castles; the little river ran tumultuously through its gorge, but calmed itself after some downhill kilometers; landscape became orderly, a tram appeared—and we slid at last, feeling wise and accustomed, into beloved Florence by a southeastern way; wonderfully glad to be back, if only for a minute.

And the welcome we had; with the signora melting almost to tears of joy at our reappearance. Eager kindness and politeness we had had before, but come back a second time in Italy if you want to be overwhelmed with gratitude and joy from every one about the place. Such smiles, such rushings, such preparings of the very best! Our *cameriera* so glad to see us, our fat little waitress expanding in beams; there was "sheecken" that night, and I think there would have been if they had had to go out and buy it specially for us. . . .

We looked for a long time, that evening, at dusky San Miniato; breathing in what was Florence, and what tomorrow we must leave for the last time. The Arno's voice was quieter, its silver frill thinner over the shallow dam, but below the shadowy wall its gleam and classic presence had for us, as ever, something that no other stream can give. With its murmur of reassurance in our hearts, we slept.

Waking with the sun illuminating Miniato's heights, I had a sense of something about to happen. . . . The Apennines were to be climbed today! For the first time (in Nicolette) we were crossing Italy's range of mountains, though this ascent of them, and the looking back on Tuscany, had been our goal ever since we had once tunneled obscurely through them in a train.

This time we were to go flying over in all possible air and sunshine, up their purple sides and down, and had had great consultations as to which of the four or five routes to Ravenna would be the most rewarding. We wanted the most exciting and snarly one; the one thickest with brackets and red d's. They were all pretty well that way; also we knew that on mountain roads in Italy you don't get anywhere in a day, so we decided to make two of it, go a bit more north than was necessary, take a very grand road, and stop over at Bologna. For that was one of our triumphs, on this trip, to be geographically thrifty and include as much as possible on the way to something else. We *could* have gone across to Ravenna by way of Forli, or Faenza . . . in fact we need not have come to Florence at all, except that we wanted to start from her, as we had before, and cross the Apennines at this particular point—of beloved, if smothering memory.

Sheer sentiment; but we looked at each other with excited eyes. There was one very prickly road we should have loved to take, simply freckled with brackets—a climb after our own hearts; but it omitted Prato and Pistoia, two old cities we had rather on our consciences, and did look pretty bad for Nicolette.

"Can't do everything, you know," said Babs, very contentedly. "I think we're doing pretty well as it is!"

It was a morning that promised fairness, with clouds breaking away, and Florence, in gleams of May sunshine, was hard to leave. We crept along the Arno's entire edge so as to have as much of it as possible; then out into the mountains and the country. Near Prato we sighted a little construction of new boards and, never dreaming it was anything official, were sailing past it, when two smiling *dazio*-men ran out and threw up humoresque hands to stop us; apparently they were used to people who went sailing by. Nicolette nearly stood on her head; one look—*"Niente?"* (nothing)—and on we went.

"Took all that out of our tires—for *niente,*" said Babs; "next time I won't stop!"

And in Prato—a long, narrow, crowded old town, with fine Renaissance buildings and horrid traffic—they had, besides Lampo, only a Russian benzina; which we refused. "Fill Nicolette up with Soviet mud to cross Apennines?" say the notes, intemperately; "we couldn't imagine its being good. . . ." Out into lovely Tuscan country we went; alas, the road was "up." Stone-heaps and mule-carts for Nicolette; dust for us. Wishing to fly, we had to crawl; an awfully slow time. Some of the carts turned to the right, some to the left; the peasants are still mixed in their minds (and will be for a generation) because here in the region of Florence they and their forefathers used to turn to the left and now the whole country is to go to the right, and they can't get used to it.

Nicolette threaded her way among it all, bumping over rocks, settled-upon by her own dust; for the breeze was behind us and in spite of a desire to fly, we must crawl. . . . At last came smooth wide road: resume speed! Nicolette flitted by a donkey-cart and along between the lovely greennesses, when "Hu-ush!" she whispered, and slowed gracefully down.

"Petrol gone!" said Babs; swooped us into the gutter and leaped out over her door-edge. A long time since I had seen her do that.

Extracting a wrench, she unscrewed our tin-on-the-running-board from its iron straps, lifted it, and poured. (Attractive sound!) Lovely crops and mountains surveyed us; the donkey-cart passed us, greatly wondering, and in another minute we were passing *it.* There was still dust, but a cool fresh air; and how glad we were we had had that tin. This was the first European rescue it had accomplished for us, but more than once on English moors we had had occasion to be grateful to it. It seems entirely a British idea, every car has it there; even the most elegant Rolls goes by you with that unbecoming bump on its running-board. I suppose it is because of fogs; or fogs and moors mixed. A bad mixture.

But the Italian scene was fresh and clear, full of color; just as we were congratulating ourselves on the drive, more stone appeared in the road. We surmounted that; dust was resumed, the Apennines grew ever nearer—with the castle of Montemurlo on our right; a castle which saw the last, unsuccessful attempt of the Florentines to overthrow the Medici; and just as we began to wonder "Would there be any petrol in Pistoia?" behold a dusty stone house, and a scarlet-and-yellow pump decorating its wall.

Yes, decorating: did we ever not like the looks of pumps in an old country? This one positively glorified the gaunt old house it stood against.

But it looked closed; its red face was certainly shut tight. With a very hopeless feeling we sat there and tooted the horn, and from somewhere over our heads came a voice.

"Momento, signora!"

A face was shoved out of an upper window, boots clumped tumultuously downstairs; in an instant a tall and powerful Italian with flaming red hair was opening the pump and smiling at us. . . . We had liked red hair in France, we liked it now on the dusty road to Pistoia. Very honest and efficient; we told him to put in *cinque litri,* but he was convinced the tank would not hold it, nor the tin, and bent his bullet-head in anxious scrutiny. It did take it, and then he was delighted by our perspicacity; beamed upon us as he closed the front of his pump, and fastened it.

"Polvere!" he said, nodding wisely.

Dust indeed; the rich, three-inch sort. It pursued us along our charming way past shrines and classic remains, in deeply lovely country, with a stream running through flowery meadows; we agreed that for variety and antiquity we had been on no road quite like this one. . . . And it was not simply that it was a beautiful May day; it was that Angelo had wrought at Rome, and Lippi had been born near by, and every bit of the way one was conscious of them. Italy has her art by the roadside. What shrines these were; what snowy fragments against the dark of an old cedar!

And Pistoia was a surprise. All at once, out of the green

country, rose a thick, purple-gray wall beside us; leaned upon by greenery—and with a vegetable-garden in its moat! Beautiful vegetables; rows of light-green things just where you wanted light-green, rows and rows of maroon-stemmed, dark-viridian beets, so gravely handsome against that tremendous backing of stone—with trees looking lightly and democratically over the top of it, saying "howdy" to their useful relatives below. Why, I wondered, doesn't somebody do a water-color of vegetables in a moat? The wall rounded to a short fat tower; another similar tower stood slightly inside, round a sort of jog, and Pistoia's little roadway wound between them. . . . Very cautious. We had never seen towers arranged just that way, like shrubbery in an English garden, concealing its entrance; probably the shrubbery, in that privacy-loving land, took its pattern from medieval defenses—a survival, gentling down to mere horticultural definings. . . . We had never thought of that before; were entertained by the supposition.

"*What* jolly color!" said Babs, driving as slowly as possible and staring at the delicious walls; for old roofs now tumbled above them and a lofty campanile, graceful as a fox-glove, flowered against the Apennines . . . which were right on the town. Pistoia even toils up a bit of their amethystine slope, but soon gives up and runs down again.

We drove slowly on. A hum, a murmur, had come to us as we passed the towers, and well we knew what that meant . . . what black, loquacious masses; noonday is a bad time for narrow streets. Recalling Siena at that hour, we resolved to give Pistoia its dues (of inspection and appreciation) on another visit; and on, round the last narrow rounding of the fat wall, Nicolette conducted her exploring nose. Prato may have been a treasure-house, but we loved Pistoia—on the mere face of her, and her unspoiled antiquity; and as we rounded that wall, left a small piece of ourselves behind. You do, when you love anything and leave it. . . . The clang of armorers must have echoed in those streets with special vehemence, for the town, medievally, did ironwork; but though subjugated by Florence from its once proud state, it did NOT tear its wall down. . . . (Perhaps a nicer wall than Florence had.)

Up a white road under horse-chestnut trees, in little snow-storms of white bloom; then, with Pistoia charmingly below us, the climb began. We whirled at the first hair-pin. Some of them were steep, but not as much so as we expected, and we relaxed a little of the mountain-climbing tenseness we had acquired—since Radicofani.

"She's doing a grand job," I ventured.

"Isn't she—" said Babs, scarcely taking her gaze off the road. (This was the sort of driving that called for attention.) Nicolette sometimes whirled, sometimes struggled, past more d's and risky-looking places—I ready to step out if she seemed actually in trouble; both of us with one eye on the view, and one on her performance. For this *col* over the Apennines looked worse to us than those hills south of Siena; yet here she was, being gay over it.

"Never can tell!" said we; and the view was growing sublimer every second.

Even railway viaducts are romantic, in Italy. They now looped about us on the mountainside; beautiful, golden viaducts with mad little torrents dashing beneath them, each inside its guarding walls. No floods allowed on these nearly perpendicular slopes, fertile as they were, and abounding in joyous flora; one small torrent might devastate a whole mountainside, and the viaducts added immensely to the landscape. The golden diminuendo of those arches! the downward stretch of them to flowery bits far below; the grace of their retirement into mere mountainside; the black mystery of tunnel-holes. The fact of a hole in a hill that some creature goes into, is thrilling: and these were small ones. Flowers grew about them, in the distance they looked like woodchuck-holes; one wondered how a train got in. (Perhaps mountain trains were small, here; perhaps the engineer nibbled a mushroom.)

But no tunnels for us; no sudden retirement just when prospects were finest. Blue sky and fresh breezes, up and up and up; with Tuscany fast purpling below.

Cypresses and a classic fountain appeared, its roof and lovely columns against the dark foliage; glorious clear water flowed and splashed. A mountain washerwoman, her brown face framed in a blue kerchief, her brown arms busy in the basin, smiled gorgeously at us as we drew up, her white teeth flashing. Such a friendly face, she had.

I asked if the water were good to drink, and she laughed and nodded.

"Buona da bere—si si!" What a background, that scene, for the dark head.

I think she was the loveliest peasant we saw at all . . . and that water must have been from a mountain spring. It was icy cold; after the dust of the valley, just what we wanted. Nicolette had some, had a great deal in fact—and the green water-bottle all it would hold; that Cajarc bottle which had indeed come to Italy with us, though not to Rome. One hoped the bottle wasn't disappointed. We thought of Cajarc's poet, in the little café, and wished he could see his bottle in such far-away circumstances; maybe, someday, it would get all the way to Rome.

There are many fountains, there.

And although in the flaming sun all the time, as we moved or stood about in the white road, we climbed in again feeling mightily refreshed. Refreshed in spirit by the friendly woman and setting the lovely line of her face in our memories. She waved to us as we went; I had been able to say a word or two about the *bello tempo,* and since then the white teeth had flashed incessantly. . . . Sweet and gallant Italy, what beggarliness of phrase will not set you tingling with keenest pleasure? But Babs and I had done our best at smiling—our gratitude was genuine; and when my child smiles it goes to the marrow of your bones.

So the sky was bluer than ever, as we started, and Tuscany's great white clouds reared gloriously up. There seemed to be no side-road on this ascent; we looked for an opening to lunch in, but there wasn't any, so we drew up at a sightly turn and lunched in the very black shade of a box-hedge, with poplars fluttering above. The road was so *blinding* white.

"Italy is acting up to its reputation!" said Babs.

For we had put the top up in spite of scenery. The view of the valley was beyond belief; we sat there eating the signora's lunch—a little *fiaschetta* of her own white wine, she had given us—looking and looking. Almost icily cool, the little fitful breeze under Nicolette's top; and how jewelled the valley, with memory as with color.

"See that shadow?" said Babs, pointing; "that smooth bit, like a lavender balloon? That's the duomo."

"Why so it is. Good-by, Florence! . . . 'Can't see the Arno, can we."

"No. Too dim, I expect. . . ."

And we stared. Not a soul passed; the whole side of the Apennines was ours. A tiny Pistoia lay far below, purpling and jewelled like the rest of Tuscany . . . in which little pale bits were classic gems; a dot here, or a tiny, half-lost fretting which might be a columned front. Italy swept away, perfection under her warm sky . . . whose horizons purpled slightly to meet the distant scene; and to move from that hedge-shadow on up the white hill was a thing for fortitude.

"Ra-ra-ra!" said Nicolette, bearing us composedly away; did she know there was better in store? A swing—and we seemed to have surmounted the spine of the Apennines; there were snow-peaks on our left. Magnificent mountains, falling sharply, were draped like fabric in a showman's hands; lavender and gray, below the pearly peaks. And here was another set of valleys, infinitely far and straight below; heavens, what a country!

Along the spine we drove; it did not last long. There was bright sun-green velvet now, on the light slopes, dull purple in the shadowed folds. . . .

The new valleys looked so cosy down there, with roads and pink villages in the sun.

"Suddenly—up!" say my notes, for Nicolette did the last d with successful scorn. Water-cap very determined, today; very absorbed; boring busily around corners.

"What are Apennines?" said she. "Pr-*aff!*" and fell calmly into high.

For this was the top. Joyfully breathing the high air, we drove on along the spine—the real spine now, with terrific depths on either side, snow-peaks looking down, stupendous views tumbling confusedly away; and at the crest, a little hotel, or pension. There were seats under its trees . . . one would have loved to stay there; yet did it look the least bit brigandish? The host, in an apron, stared hard at us from the door. It was the loneliest of hostelries. . . . We ducked into a dark shadow of rock—round a rocky corner—and down.

Down and down! Apennines have brief summits. This was the descent into Emilia. A narrow cañon of a valley with a brook rushing, and beech-shrubs, brilliant golden-green, thick upon the hillsides. Was Italy reforesting, too? It was encouraging to see brush as high as that. Usually it is allowed to grow about five feet from its beginnings, and then pie-shaped pieces are cut out of it, leaving purple gashes in the green.

We dove down the narrow valley in great contentment. Cliff-houses, gray and angular, were built into the rocks above us, with patches of bright flowers tucked in among the rocks and old, paved cart-tracks winding up; by one house a child in a mauve frock, the sun on her bronze curls, stood on the cobbles in a dreaming pose, looking down over her shoulder at us. "Lovely picture. Gone in a flash," say my notes.

And Tuscany was really behind us now. We had never been in Emilia, except hasty pieces of it after dark in a train; greetings, Emilia. We like you very much so far.

So we plunged, in Emilia, always among pitching mountainsides and brooks and scarce hamlets; scenery very close and intimate.

Then it spread; we saw wideness; there was a river and a

hot afternoon sun—and Vergato, which I have forgotten. We went speeding on across the rich declensions of a landscape which, we concluded with little thrilled feelings, was already flattening for the sea. The towers of Bologna had been for some time before us; arriving, we found it long, yellow, and every inch arcaded.

Sunshine must be hot, in Bologna. We drove a long distance escorted by columns; sunny-yellow on the left, shadowy yellow on the right. . . . The town was decorated, banners were everywhere; the sidewalks under the arcades, the squares, the aged-looking streets, were alike crowded. This was only Tuesday; why should there be a fête in Bologna? It was ecclesiastical, evidently; there were priestly processions approaching; we appropriated our hotel (not far from the biggest piazza) and hastened forth to see these sights. I clung to Babs' arm as we edged along; we almost felt we might lose each other, such were the mobs; Italians were bursting feverishly past us. . . .

"It makes me think of what you said, ages ago, when we were on a riding trip and ran into a town having Old Home Week: 'Wherever we go, seems to me, we get into some sort of a 'citement!' "

Babs laughed. "But *this* is nice," said she. "Let's go into that old church opposite. Heavens, look at the candles!"

For through the color-draped door, we saw the altars one golden blaze. Mass was over and people were straggling out, but the big nave was still crowded; acolytes in crimson and white were busy about the chancel. This was the *duomo*—very Bolognese, we decided; huge, old, untended-looking, with vast plain spaces, its gloom beautiful with candle-glow. Its crimson drapings were beautiful too, with their alternate lightings and withdrawals into shadow; but the mood of the church was dramatic with worship. It was no time for spectators; even tip-toeings seemed a rude interruption to these glowing silences and far, soft murmurings.

So we came out again; under the immense crimson drapery. Round the next corner Bologna's leaning towers were in the air—old, plain, of rose-red brick; one tall, one shorter, both leaning extremely; and we had never heard of them. They were amazingly picturesque. Bands were now playing, and processions marching; the grave, close ancientness of the city was alight and astir. We walked around to a few piazzas, beheld the splashing fountain of Neptune, and vistas of campaniles down long narrow lanes; saw an ancient gate or two, and strove back to our albergo (Palazzo di San Marco!) which stood at the corner of the Via dei Mille.

The Street of the Thousand; Garibaldi and his dauntless thousand were remembered here, then. No modern war-name displaced theirs, or effaced the recollection of that vivid bravery.

But everything in Bologna had imposing names. There were not merely, as in every Italian town, piazzas Vittorio Emanuele, Umberto I, or Cavour, but squares unfamiliarly named: Otto Augusto, Aldrovandi, Minghetti, Carducci.

Only Carducci was a poet, and we should have known him. He lived till 1907 and seemed important in Bologna; and that diamond-shaped angle of the town where his *casa* stands might be its Poets' Corner, for across the Viale Carducci, dividing the corner into diamond halves, runs the Via Dante.

The whole city is a maze of recollection, its history can be learned from its nomenclature; yet it seemed different from any other town we had met. It seemed very bygone; and, except for that day's transient thrill of the processions, almost oppressively of the past. One is told it is a feast for archæologists; its solidity is surely of the unchangeable sort; if its towers leaned, one felt that they had always leaned. There were a few new names, but they too had become history, and Bologna, sitting heavily on its almost pre-Etruscan foundations, will thus continue to sit. Like a quarry pool, she has chiefly one dimension; she seems unfathomable, in depth . . . of time. The light of candles in her cathedral must have shone through the ages, her streets had positively a pre-Augustan air; and at dinner that night in our funny old *albergo,* it was almost a relief to watch an up-to-date young Italian officer being selfish about something as fresh and unlegendary as wild strawberries.

His wife, rather sad-looking and plainly dressed, was already waiting for him; she looked up, smiling a little as he came bustling in and with the air of a happy and triumphant child, laid a paper parcel on the table. It was only loosely done up, and the officer undid it, disclosing the strawberries. He gestured effusively over them, chattering to his wife; we thought, and said to each other,

"How nice! He has bought them somewhere for her, as a great surprise, and now they are going to have a wonderful time with them."

Not exactly. The officer sent the waiter for a soup-plate and busied himself arranging the berries as he wanted them, distributed with beautiful evenness over the bottom of the dish; put sugar on them, then with pursed lips and brow contracted poured red wine very carefully in, till the berries were barely floating; delightful-looking preparation. His brow cleared; he set the dish to one side—to soak, as it were—looked happily at his wife, and fell to eating his dinner. They chatted occasionally, she waiting for him, while he consumed quantities of rich Italian food; her responses were always milder than his remarks, but she had the air of one who had settled down to her life, whatever it was, and expected nothing more. . . . Just then the waiter cleared the last course away. The officer straightened himself, settled his collar more comfortably (Italian uniforms have fearfully high tight collars), paused an instant, then made a dive across at the strawberries; set them in front of himself, and rapturously began on them. All by himself. His wife sat quietly there, waiting for him; when we finished our coffee and rose to go, he was still eating and gloating.

Strawberries enough for three!

I began to believe what I had heard. My Italian teacher, a brilliant and attractive young woman, had raised hands of horror at the mere idea of going back to live in Italy. . . . I had asked her one day how she could bear to be away from her entrancing country.

"No, no, signora!" she said earnestly. "In Italy the woman is always in the kitchen! *Sempre, sempre, nel' cucina.* Meals and meals, for hours and hours—all day long. . . . Italy? *Mamma mia!"* (her exclamation for moments of dramatic horror). *"No, signora! Sempre, sempre nel' cucina!"* Now officers' wives, stationed about from place to place and living at hotels, cannot spend their days in kitchens; they make it up, apparently, by eating as little as possible and watching their husbands go gloriously through a menu. . . .

"Wanted to boot him—didn't you?" said Babs very gloomily, as we climbed the stairs.

But we walked to our window, looked down upon the roof that sheltered Nicolette and hoped she was being well-treated after her labors. . . . In the morning, though not a minute sooner, she was to be serviced, and have the dust washed off her; Bologna, less thrifty or less obliging than other places we had met, having declined to work on her that evening because of the *festa.*

"That means a late start in the morning," remarked Babs; "remember Montpellier—doing a tire for us on Easter evening?"

"I do! And that nice garageman at Albi, having her looked after the minute we took her in—"

Yes; there *were* things about France. . . . But then Siena had been wonderful; probably this was just Bologna's easygoing way . . . and we fell with avidity upon tomorrow's plans. Flat country, from here to Ravenna, lay before us, we knew; and the Apennines had been so marvelous, it seemed quite impossible to leave them, after that short glimpse. They ran quite close behind Bologna; we saw them from our window. . . . Coming with us, the lambs. Perhaps they knew how we adored them.

"See, A.B.," said Babs, "that road we were dying to take,

you know—over all those d's—well here it is, this end of it, coming down to Bologna from *that* place—"

"Firenzuola?"

"I guess so. Look at all those brackets! It's just all mountains. We could go up as far as there, and then take that other road back to Ravenna. A sort of triangle, you see. . . . There's a nice cross-road to Lugo, if we didn't want to go round by Faenza. Any road would probably do, down there. It's all level."

"How grand," I said, following her traveling pencil. "And is it far, Babbits? Awfully far? I don't feel, at the moment, as if I cared a rap if it is. . . . Only we ought to get to Ravenna tomorrow, I suppose."

"We ought," said she. "Let's see; it's fifty . . . and forty-seven . . . can't exactly tell about that cross-road . . . a hundred and sixty kilometers, about."

We looked at each other.

"Mountains do take a lot of time," I said; "but Nicolette's doing marvelously, don't you think?"

My child raised one eyebrow. "Rap on wood," said she, "yes, she is! And I'm beginning to think these d's aren't much. . . . That road does look spiffy, A.B. Shall we try it?"

"Let's," I said; "if it's a fine day. It'll be flat for so *long* now—"

"Though I love that sort; marshes, you know. . . ."

And we walked to the window again, smiling a little soberly. We knew more about mountain roads now, we knew our tendency to mad loops; but mountain-color still danced in our eyes. . . . And there was the grand line of them; silvered a little, yet dark beneath the stars.

CHAPTER XX

MARSH-FLOWERS AND RAVENNA

NEXT morning a discursive cab took us, by tortuous ways, to the Accademia della Belli Arti, daughter much thrilled by ancientness, both of us entertained by bad drawing. Some of the most appealing of the pictures had the weirdest drawing; and we loved the faint old coloring. . . . No new Italian color is faint, so one appreciates oldness.

Bologna, that "ancient capital of Romagna," is a little like Toulouse; much red brick (the ancient sort, different and attractive), interminably twisting streets, and an air of once-culture—the famous University was founded here in 1088; while the present state of the city, a little stagnant, a trace dilapidated, reminds one, too, of dear shabby charming Toulouse.

But there resemblance stops. Bologna gives one an odd feeling. Ruins are cheerful, the Colosseum makes one want to sing . . . but these buildings, not quite good, not quite contemporaneous, actively in use yet looking archæological and dim, depressed one a little. As with a plant after frost, its flowers still showing color yet ready to fall, one's gardening impulse is to pick them at once and be done with it: though we did not want to pluck Bologna from the map, still there was something about it which made us not sorry to go. . . . Miasmic? Possibly; although the region is not a swampy one.

Merely mental swamps, we concluded, induced by falling so soon from the mountains; for Babs, exultant though she was at the approach of Ravenna, felt it as much as I did.

But we had "enjoyed much" in Bologna, including our cab-driver, who not only told us his heart on all occasions, but as much of Bologna's as he could; a nice, opinionated old creature who returned us (lingeringly) to Nicolette. Alack! she was fatally bright with oil, or some sort of color-brightener with which the garage, unasked and officious, had rubbed her. . . . They were repentant, they rolled dark eyes and were desolated, they thought we should not want her so soon; but we had the luggage heartlessly piled in and, oil or no oil, turned down the Via del Indipendenza.

She looked lovely at the moment, like a wet water-color; but what would she look like in an hour's time?

We knew too well; for the sun was now brilliant, and the dust of Emilia glittering white. Perhaps it would get nice and marshy this afternoon; and we turned for a look at the towers. The best thing in Bologna, they are; really assisting each other's grace. They lean there in just the right relation, so slenderly, almost swaying; like two tall hollyhocks of a lovely, somehow fresh yet pale old red, so influenced by light that the towers are often of any tint rather than red—and always soft; a lavenderish rose, or goldish brown, holding the loveliness of a lighted side and darker one—of a tint flooding evenly to an edge and ceasing, in a long line of purplish shadow, on a spread of sky. . . . A tower is a strange thing to be made from stone or brick; illusory, somehow fabulous; and upon the warmth of Bologna's towers this morning was reflected a faint wash of blue.

Good-by, hollyhocks! wave safely, till we see you again. Fresh flowers, *you* should not droop. . . . And as we drove they grew small behind us; secure upon the heavy blue of that sky.

Suburbs today seemed even longer but at last we were out, swinging white curves, with green foot-hills coming nearer; Nicolette, though filmed with *polvere,* blithe and gay. She quite leaped along; and Babs let her leap. Higher before us neared the delicious mountains, but the sun was dangerously hot. Mountains or no, we halted and put up the top. . . . There was no choice about it; this was Italy, and a windless day. In some sort of shadow one must sit.

We continued to bound along. A very green bit of valley we were in, with a castle here and there aloft, and—ah, those purples and blues ahead of us; all at once our road swung to the left and went violently up. . . . Was it a d, so soon? Nicolette flew at it—an almost perpendicular pitch; I held my breath, actually feeling the heavy load she had, sagging heavier. . . . No! even in low she would not make it. Her gay tune failed, and she ceased. Babs jammed on the brakes.

"Dash her! and this is the first pitch too. She did dozens yesterday. . . . Can you find a stone, darling?"

For I was already out, and searching. I pushed, she stopped; several times I ran back for the stone and pushed again. Heavens, how the sun beat down! Babs looked out, made one leap for me and put me in the car.

"We'll try just once more," said my child very firmly, "but *you're going to sit in the car!* Mummy."

The steepness and the heat were too much. "I'm only a little Citröen," said Nicolette, relapsing in the white dust and intolerable glare; "a very little Citröen, and my load is getting heavier every day. . . . I'm awfully sorry—I really am, you know—but I'd ever so much rather slide down backwards. . . . Thank you. This is better. . . . Immensely better. *Now* I'll turn round for you!" and with a guilty look about her little bonnet she fled, bumping, toward Bologna.

Our feelings can be imagined; we quite gasped with rage. Never, except once in Dartmoor on a slippery, frosty January morning, had we given up a road we had started on. Nicolette had taken us in the wettest, the most impossible places; and our hearts yearned helplessly toward that loop by Firenzuola. We felt shamefaced, too; we felt like quitters . . . and yet we felt slightly relieved! It WAS so hot, the light whitish and bald; wouldn't it be pretty nice to be by the sea again? to smell marsh air, and get to that unknown ancientness we were both looking forward to? Perhaps, after all, Nicolette had delivered us from a foolishness.

"And we don't have to go way back to Bologna," said

Babs, swiftly passing an ox-cart. "I think we can cut across; I saw a road, last night. It'll be all new, then, you know."

And it was. We had never before seen Italy in a genuinely marshy mood, and it was a charming one; all little blue canals and luscious marsh-grass, little old bridges and tall blue and yellow flowers. There were no signs, but we found our way across; we took a wrong road from Lugo but it was perfectly lovely, and we thought it was the right one till we found ourselves coming to a little hill joining the dyked-up route that leads northward from Ravenna to Ferrara; were much surprised and quite entertained, simply turned to the right into a sky going golden over vast vineyards and marshes, and reached Ravenna by sunset-time.

Or rather by a dusky afterglow, very beautiful behind the black shapes of Ravenna. We were so breathless about getting there that I have no memory of our approach, except that it was short. Dusk was brown in the ancient streets, with their tiny cobbles, egg-shaped, set on end; Nicolette crept almost religiously along. More pale-gold sky and dark shapes, a few soft lights; but where was the hotel we had picked out—the Hotel Byron?

Where indeed was the Piazza Byron, on which the hotel sat?

Creeping cautiously, for we were entering a very Ravennese square with a low crenelated building against the sky and two Venetian columns in our way, we circumvented the columns, around which a smallish throng of black-coated citizens had congregated, and inquired for the Piazza Byron. A little *carabiniere* directed us, with important wavings, while the Ravennese ceased their chattering for an instant, to stare at us, and consented, very politely, to move aside.

Going through the narrow, scarcely lighted Piazza Alighieri into a dark via, we found the Piazza Byron, but no hotel. We stopped, in perplexity. The walls were high and blank, Ravennese dusk seemed suddenly very dusky, the antiquity about us inhospitable; we felt faint and weary . . .

somehow homeless. We had had no tea, as marshes and blue and yellow flowers had not offered any; and lunch, of which we had had an early bite in Bologna, seemed æons away.

Just then a light step sounded, and a woman came toward us; a charming Italian lady, slender and tall, graceful in her dark drapings and small, veil-drooped hat. Well-born! I thought, and leaned from Nicolette's edge, changing my usual abrupt query to a plaintive *"Per piacere, signora, dov'è l'albergo Byron?"*

To my surprise, she knew at once. She stopped, pleasantly, and smiled delightfully, her dark eyes taking in little Nicolette and our heaped belongings.

"L'albergo Beerong?" she said musically. *"Ma, signora—adesso non ch'è!"* (there isn't any now!) and she explained the mystery. The Hotel Byron was now the Hotel Byron-Central-Roma; quite at the other end of the Piazza Vittorio Emanuele, whence we had come; round the corner and to the right. *"Alle destra, signora!"*

She could not describe the way, but it was quite easy, she assured us, once we were in the piazza.

"Grazie tanto, signora!"

"Niente!" and *"Arivederci!"* she said very sweetly. Her friendly eyes, her cordial tones, seemed to invite more conversation; she even stood a moment, dark-robed and distinguished, watching us as we drove away.

"Now SHE was a corker," said Babs with warm emphasis; and we sat up extremely straight, feeling almost energetic once more. . . . We were at home, now, in the Piazza Alighieri; kind and familiar seemed a darkling Ravenna. A few more lights had come out; we accosted our *carabiniere* with gay certainty.

"Albergo Byron-Central-Roma? Si si si!" said he blithely, as one for whom a perplexing problem is solved; and waved us *destra,* as our charming friend had said, to a little old cobblestoned street with no side-walks. There, quite brightly lighted, it was—small, conservative, comfortable, with red velvet chairs set conspicuously about; and a staff speaking

French with a thick German accent. "Gummy waiters," say my notes. They could scarcely comprehend "our perfect Paris accent," said we grimly; and the headwaiter had a fearful time understanding when we wanted breakfast sent up.

"A wit hoores, au chambre?" he finally managed, the lobe of one fat ear colliding with his collar, his little gooseberry eyes staring dully at us; we climbed revoltedly upstairs. Our room however, fronting on a lively little lane, was long and clean and cheerful, and looked out at some great bulk against the starry sky—dark now, and velvet-blue.

"A church," I said, peering. . . . A church is a nice neighbor.

"Basilica!" said Babs, her voice deep with satisfaction. "They're almost all that here."

And we looked at each other with exultation. Ravenna, even in the dusk, fairly exhaled Byzantineness; Emperors, Ostrogoths, B. C., and all the rest of it, were ours for the taking, tomorrow. . . . And those mosaics!

"Nearly as good as Santa Sofia's—in Constantinople," Babs assured me, gloatingly. . . . Oh, there would be heaps to do tomorrow; we fell abruptly into bed.

And then Ravenna just began waking up. Its people, having dined late, now surged in the streets. Horns hooted, and church-bells rang—heavy, barbaric, Byzantine bells, booming here, clanging there. Our basilica joined in; its tones, suiting its size, were monstrous.

"Bowm-m-mm—BOWM-m-mm!" Ravenna shuddered with the din.

By a dim filtering of lights from the street, I could see the line of a quiet cheek in the other bed and knew that Babs was sleep, but for a long time lay broad awake, listening to Ravenna thronging by. . . . I thought it would never stop. This was not Saturday night, just harmless Wednesday; why were the bells ringing? And the feet sounded like Armistice Day in London—just boots tramping and tramping; never a hoof-beat or the rumble of a wheel. Up our lane raced the youth of Ravenna, in high spirits; sticks were being drawn along the slatted, metal shutters of shops, with the din that only sticks and slats can make. "Brrrrr-*aaaaa!*" Those shutters were a godsend.

Italian cities are splendid places for anything except sleep, we were discovering; the noises of each one are distinct. On the Lungarno it was a mixture of everything, with trams and cab-rattlings predominating . . . hasty, dashing noises; in Perugia there were stony echoes, lone clatterings; in Siena still stonier echoes, harsh and infrequent, with wild laughter from occasional mule-carts driven at high speed. . . . Rome's noises, as becomes a capital city, are sectional and various, the Pincian Hill region having one set (including ash-cans from pensions being rolled down the street in early morning) and the old part of town quite another; the ruins, stony and lovely under a night sky, doubtless others still—those of age and history, of a half-heard wonder at their own agedness . . . and one spring night a friend, in her high room near the Piazza di Spagna, heard in the city's silence a strange, small pattering going endlessly by—and there were sheep pouring along the pavement below, with their shepherds and quiet dogs. Thousands of little patterings, on their way to a more northern pasture after wintering on the *campagna*. Mesmerized by the stony silence, the strange, high walls about them, they were very quietly crossing the Eternal City at midnight.

Here, in Ravenna's frank tumult, I was thankful my child was asleep; and dozed off at last, only to be roused, very early, by an even more virulent onset of bells. They rang and rang. . . . Six o'clock, but bells must begin; "Up, up!" they clanged. "Ravenna had an awful time to get going," say my notes.

A bright little chambermaid brought our breakfast and the sad information that *oggi* was a holiday. Bother *oggi!* Most of the things we wanted to see would be shut, then. But there was always Nicolette; and Rimini, we soon ascertained, was to the south of us.

Rimini, of the beautiful and tragic story of Paolo and

Francesca; why not drive there? We fell on our maps to see. Nicolette was all greased and ready, the sun shone—"and in the book we read no more that day"; yes, we would see Rimini, for that haunting line of Dante's if for nothing more, as we had driven to Arezzo for Pompilia's, and Browning's, sake. Besides, there was this new and magic coast; for except in Venice—where it does not seem to matter—we had never really seen the Adriatic; and since turning north from Orvieto (and dismissing our sense of the necessity and importance of getting south), had felt its Eastern lure.

A deliberate lure; it lay there, we felt, half-asleep and lazy on its sands; and would so await us. We were in no panting hurry to arrive upon its edge, as we had been to reach our Mediterranean; was it because one hurries more to a loved association than to something enchanting and new?

Nicolette was already at the door, very restored-looking after a fresh wash. She had been fearful the night before—simply a ghost of a little obliterated Cit, with the dust of Emilia upon the oil of Bologna; so we had consigned her to the care of those who polish, and great had been their zeal. She shone, she was speckless, a proper bit of warm color in the little old winding street; seating ourselves with pleasure (no luggage, today!) and with somehow a very holiday feeling, we swung out into the strange quietness of Ravenna. There would be dust on the way, we told each other (with a certain flinching), but never mind; we were starting out immaculate, and that was what mattered.

Ravenna's people must all have gone somewhere; there was not a soul in the streets. We tried a church door or two, and found them locked; stared into the window of a print shop, also inaccessible, steered on down the Corso Garibaldi, lined with interest and paved with the industrious little cobbles, then out toward the Porta Garibaldi, old and brown.

Even in the light-minded morning, Ravenna gave us a hushed feeling. The sun was hot, and there were holes in the cobbles, but something in the austerity of those great plain walls, rough in finish, heroic in massiveness, gave one an odd thrill. Here anything might happen; heathenish things; here were the half-gods, the ancient idols, barely washed with Christianity. Something reckless and regardless was in the air of them, stone and inanimate though they were, blankly as they looked down upon us with their mysterious old faces. Mere spectacles, now . . . once they were not; and from their vast throats a sort of crypt-like growl arose. "No-ooo! Once, we were not."

But we bobbled lightheartedly along out the "Sobb. Garibaldi" and into marshy country, with a strong profile of pine woods between us and the sea. Dante's pine woods! Lovely atmosphere, across the fresh green of the marshes, a violet distance; also the campanile of solitary Sant' Apollinare, "tallest and most beautiful of all the towers of Ravenna." About three miles south of the city's wall, and obliging enough to be open: bits of its tessellated pavement (of the sixth century) are still there, while the basilica is impressive with columns—Greek columns, with Byzantine bases and capitals. Its dilapidated mosaics were the more fascinating for their dilapidation, and Babs' eyes, devouring them, I shall not forget. . . . At last, after all our journeying! For this smacked of her own world of archæological wonder; the studious world that had become her joy. . . .

It was hard to take such ardour away and set it out upon a mere, green-edged road with a wheel to look after, yet those eyes were still keen; a holiday morning is a holiday morning, and as we set off again, gaiety was making my child's ardour the more brilliant. . . . It was here, thick about us, that world of ancient magic—it would not run away; we smelt it in every marshy breath.

"We'll see how the Adriatic will be hitting it up for color!" said she; and laughed, from mere glee.

"But what's the matter with this road?" she presently demanded; "it isn't dusty. Oiled, by jinks! And what's that we're coming to; *grandstand?*"

It was; just being finished, and of new yellow boards; a

ST. FRANCIS'S HERMITAGE, ON THE MOUNTAIN

strange object with the walls of Ravenna scarcely out of sight. And here was the populace of Ravenna, already climbing into completed portions of the stands. . . . An air of tense excitement—low, powerful cars with drivers diabolical in huge black goggles: motor-races! We drove along, wishing to stare, but going as quietly as possible; even so, youths whirled to glare fiercely at us, the grandstand first muttered, then shouted, while *carabinieri* waved us hastily on our way; this was an important occasion, and persons coming from goodness-knows-where in little ridiculous five-horsepowers (even if clean and shiny), would better evaporate . . . because power (which Italians love) was in the air.

We fled on down the oiled stretch—Ravenna's best and flattest for a race—and paused at a cross-roads to look back. Stands were black now and the roar of racing motors beginning. What luck, that we had got through!

"It's the only road, too," said Babs, raising an amused eyebrow. "Hit it up, woman!" and she trod on the accelerator. We felt these roarings in our spines. Nicolette obediently leaped, crossing a bridge over a small canal, flashing on and away; the roars growing dimmer behind us.

"The woman's feeling fit today," remarked her driver; and once more peace surrounded us. It was not marshes now, rich agriculture had begun; but we were entertained by seeing, beside the square green fields, similar though blank-looking squares of water.

"First you raise a patch of wheat, and then you raise a patch of water!" said Babs; it was some time before it dawned on us that these were rice fields with the rice not yet up. Occasionally men with scythes were cutting hay—it was nice to see hay again; but for the most part the land was empty of workers. What peasants we saw were dressed in their delightful best and going along the road in little yellow donkey-carts, or behind good little bay horses. Near Cervia we met many little girls in white, very solemn-eyed, being driven by proud and excited parents to their first Communion. A pretty and touching sight; the peasant-father in his best black coat driving so intently, with glowing eyes; mother holding so cherishingly the little white-clad, dark-eyed daughters, with their gauzy veils and serious, impressed little faces. . . . Lovely faces, often, with a gravity that made us think of the pictured Ravennese saints. . . . After all, we said, what more natural than that these children should be descendants of men and women from whom the early craftsmen had modeled their saints' faces—that here or there, in this donkey-cart or that, was one whose likeness (of long ago) had been immortalized in nave or gallery?

We were going slowly now; this was too choice to hurry through—too special, and of this day we had so delightfully chanced upon. Whose day it was we did not know; but it was sweet. . . . It was almost nicer to see those little girls, than the mosaics they resembled.

And we were getting anxious to see the Adriatic; it seemed to stay indefinitely behind something. The sun grew hotter, but when it shone on the walls of little Cervia we were amazed as well as enchanted. A fortified fishing-village, with its old arched gate opening deliciously on a canal; never had we come upon a town gate doing that . . . and to a lovely smell of fish! Through the Porta we saw that here too a *festa* was vigorously going on, all down the vista of Cervia's close-built via—across the blue of the small canal, with brown crab-nets hanging in it; and when a narrow little old stone bridge (enough to melt the heart) led us across this most beautiful *rio,* whose clear water wound away to a glimpse of the sea, then took us beneath the arch and into the adorable little street with all its colors, salmon and pink and yellow, and the peasants, with their gigs and donkeys, *and* the little white girls—we forgot everything but a sense of reveling. Nicolette crept, she would have anyway, for it was thick steering . . . and we leaned out, avidly staring; clutching each other, giving little gasps of incredulity and admiration.

"Oh, to paint this!" I moaned—I, who hadn't really thought about painting for years.

"Yes, you *must* do it, A.B.," said Babs, looking at me with a smile, but very purposefully. "We'll come again sometime, with lots of time, and you can have your things—"

" 'Wish I had them now!" I sighed. "But we didn't know it was going to look like this, did we?"

A usual plaint of ours; but we had never seen anything like that entrance to Cervia. Never in all our wanderings. And the air smelled of crabs.

Disproportionately few ravings, it seemed to me, had been written about this coast. None, that I had read; and if things hadn't been shut tight in Ravenna that morning we should have missed all this. Verily—though we were disgusted enough about it at the time—some saint was kind. There was too much *festa* going on, unless we made ourselves horribly in the way, for us to stop for a picture, so we crawled on in the sunny narrowness and the crowd, nearly expiring with joy. And they were such nice people; gravely smiling, almost shy; the impressed and serious faces of the little girls seeming an index to the frame of mind of all the inhabitants along this shore. . . . We liked them; didn't mind how much we waded among them, they were so unnoticing and mild.

Few people from the outside world come here, it would seem; in twenty-five miles we met just three motors. A lovely region. Ravenna and her treasures may have been, for the moment, left behind, but as a friend later said, we were "seeing the art of Italy as she is. . . ." (That friend usually does "ring the bell" when she tells you anything.)

A cool wind now came to us; on it we sniffed the sea.

"Must be getting near!" said Babs . . . and after a stretch of marshes we turned sharp left, and into Cesenatico.

Another heavenly old village, built seaward along two sides of a canal; a pink and yellow village that was just an introduction to the sea. . . . A bit of blue horizon showed, with promise of more, the canal itself was a soft, pastelly blue-green; fishing-vessels lay in it, and the old weavering houses, following its slight curves, were set back across a little paved quai, the roadway of the village, upon which all Cesenatico's activities went on.

We drove out upon it; left Nicolette cooling her hot nose in the sea breezes and walked further out.

It was nice to walk, somehow a simplifying progress after getting through the crowds of Cervia; and this village didn't show a trace of any *festa.* Its fish-market, set back on a slight hill, was a white marble loggia of beautiful Greek pattern, as so many things are in Italy—she hasn't minded borrowing, Babs took occasion to tell me; it was open all round, and columned and fluted—an exquisite little temple of the sea. Toward it an old man and woman in peasant clothes (mostly blue and brown) were carrying a great brown-wicker tray heaped with little, wet, shiny, opal-tinted fishes; for a fishing-vessel, its patched sails still unfurled, was at the quai unloading.

Beyond the houses, a lovely gray bark with a high snub nose was unloading old iron into mule-carts . . . strange cargo for this unworldly-seeming shore, where everything spoke of times gone by. The mules stared at us with solemn ears, as if they thought so too; the pleasant, shy, fisher-people did not stare. We felt at home in their society, and independent of Nicolette; strolled very comfortably about. More of the red-and-yellow sails were coming in, drifting before the light breeze; the exquisite Adriatic was beyond. . . . At last we were near it; we walked as far as we could along the jetty.

Lovely, that pale, shimmering sea, delicate as the sky above it; more delicate in tint than our Mediterranean. Transparent over its pure white sands, it shimmers first topaz and silver, then opalescent; then by gentlest, most shining declensions, into emerald and palest blue.

That, at its deepest, seems to be all the Adriatic can do for color; perhaps it is never very deep. Its shore, at any rate, is so shallow that these entering canals have to be dug and guarded by jetties, so that the fishing-boats can sail in. . . . If only our picture of them could have been in color! Three of them now came past us, gliding silently along; then quietly

RIVER LEADING TO DANTE'S PINEWOOD, AND THE SEA

Near Ravenna

dropping anchor and nudging up to their places at the quai. The long blue lane of the village quite sparkled with color.

Only by the brush, we agreed, could Cesenatico be expressed; the endearing age of it, the high key of light, its look of solidness as well as of quite frivolous beauty; beyond all the gleaming and significant sea, father and mother of Cesenatico, its houses, and its people. . . . In a few mistaken spots the Adriatic is trying to be a seaside, with a sandy street laid out and grand names on pallid buildings, Ristorante Lido, Trattoria Milano; a large Hotel Britannia staring at the sea, very self-conscious and lonely and white, with box-hedges in small frightened patterns, and the sand creeping up on them. . . . Poor little box-hedges, endeavoring to be stylish; this long, pale coast is much happier doing pink-and-yellow villages—and does them much better.

We came back to Cesenatico and our road, barely missing an old woman who darted out from behind a high-walled corner.

"Good miss!" said Babs, coolly. But the old woman ducked and bowed and apologized, and wasn't annoyed at all. These Adriatic people. . . .

On, across level marshes; then with no warning at all (there were no warnings of any sort on this road) we came upon a curve and a low, grass-hidden bridge. A procession of mule-carts was half on, half off it; no drivers visible, and we going at a pace. . . .

"Wild vision, like Dante," my notes say, "with a sack over its head, rose and fished down wildly by his mule's tail for a rein; the rest of the carts swung with him, and we just squeezed by." Bright mules! A nice deep ditch was waiting for us, if those driverless carts had not turned out. . . .

More marsh-grass, then farming country; finally, over a low Roman bridge with a tremendous coping, we found the town. Pale, stony, and dusty, with a thick crowd in its streets and piazza. . . . We had somehow expected Rimini to be empty. We wormed our way in: cabs, a fountain, columned buildings, abominable paving. The greatest crowd was in a narrow street beside a building that looked like a *mercato;* being beautiful and stately, and its marble ornamented with fine detail, it was the fish market.

Was all this crowd just a noon mob, or still the *festa?* There were no little white girls here.

But Rimini looked favorable for lunching; we parked Nicolette by the fountain, with some worry about leaving her in surging mobs, and made our way to a *ristorante* in a lane near by. . . . Cool and lofty it was, with a clean, sea-smell about it, as of very fresh fish still wet with sea-water; and many large men were lunching. . . . Only men; we felt a trifle odd, but chose seats with as much composure as we could summon at one of the long tables, and the padrone himself, with something very nice and protecting in his expression, came for our order—a towering Italian in an apron; all the men of this region seemed to be both tall and broad. Gruff by nature he was, yet trying very hard to be polite; and we ordered omelet.

"Om'let?" growled the tremendous creature, seemingly displeased; and lurched toward the kitchen.

"OM'LET!" he roared, disappearing through its door; and as he moved about in his *cucina,* disgruntled bassoon-notes came from here and there in it: "om'let! . . . om'let!"

Not a popular order, evidently. We realized, too late, that in a fish-restaurant one should order fish; but when the despised dish came it was hot and golden and attractively garnished, and the bread of Rimini brown and crusty. Our neighbors at the long table were having crabs, or various sorts of breaded fish which all looked skilful and smelt very good indeed; other men customers, seating themselves heavily and confidently (though with slightly dismayed glances at us), ordered fish too. . . . Precedent, precedent!

And all of these good souls had a marvelous way of eating —the two-inch method, we called it; each large red-brown face bent down to within about that distance of its plate, when a mighty shoveling and savoring began. Well, these were hungry men; had probably been battling with seas and sails and nets. Sea-captains, they looked like; every one of them had an authoritative eye.

And everybody was so nice to us. Our two neighbors, who were having luscious-looking crabs, passed us everything they could think of; bread and relishes and salt, large ungainly bottles of whose contents we had no idea; they smiled at us guilelessly, like a pair of brothers, and spoke with bluff cheeriness of the weather.

"Bello tempo, non?" they said; and after an interval of politely concealed staring, lowered their great voices as they talked.

Indeed a gusty, outdoor amiability characterized the faces of these customers of the fish-restaurant; we liked their seagoing civilities. We were perfectly sure, by now, that they were schooner-captains or something interesting . . . and when we ordered *formaggio* to end with (an expensive choice) even the padrone grew pleasant, beamed upon us, and asked if everything was *buono*.

Nicolette was quite safe, as we might have known she would be, and we went off over Rimini's remarkable pavements to look at the Tempio Malatesta. This building, from being a plain thirteenth-century church, had been transformed into Renaissance splendor by Sigismondo Malatesta "and rechristened in his honour," he having been elected *podestà* by the people, after "centuries of strife between Pope and Emperor for mastery of the town"; Sigismondo was the grandfather of Francesca's glowering and unpleasant husband, Giovanni the Lame. At least for the moral of the tale let us hope he glowered. I am sure he did; it ran in the family. Dante mentions a glowering ancestor, and calls him "the old mastiff."

These Malatesti nevertheless were quite the great family of Rimini and kept on being powerful, and objectionable, until one Pandolfo sold the town to Venice, when, "after the battle of Ravenna . . . [1512] it fell into Papal hands and the Malatesta family passed into oblivion." One does not grieve too much—"bad head," their name means. One feels it a reprehensible thing too that a city could be sold, by one man—as Rimini was; but this seems to have been a medieval habit. Sedgwick mentions several such transactions. Avignon (in Provence) had been sold by a Pope, towns in Italy were usually disposed of by tyrants—one of the three evils, he says, under which Italy most suffered in the fourteenth century; the other two were *condottieri* and plagues. . . .

For I had been reading this "short" *History of Italy* of his, and found it both useful and entertaining; my child, in the recent light of British painstakingness, rather sniffed at it.

"Inaccurate and sloppy!" said she.

Now University books (from the Moccatta Library) are two feet by three; it used positively to frighten me, when she opened one on her study-table, to see it spread out and cover the whole table-top. Propping up one end of it with several ordinary-sized books, my daughter would sit down to it, or rather up to it, quite undeterred, and dive in. . . . Of course, the print in such a volume is large, and the full-page reproductions of ancient art it contains (or of inscriptions, or ground-plans) are frequent, and take much space; all the same a number of books like that piled about a room gives an appalling effect of learning; also one who has been for months digesting their well-vouched-for contents, naturally becomes critical of brilliant and witty generalizations.

"But anybody who can do anything short about Italy—deserves a crown," I said, reaching into Nicolette's pocket for our copy of the book. "Most books take you into such a network of dates and criss-cross rulers that you simply never get out again. And you don't remember one! *I* think he's done a marvelous job of sifting, if you ask me. Why, every town was a country then! had its separate wars and everything. It's a terrible mess to undo. . . . The only way was to do it in great swoops and swishes, it seems to me—the way he's done; with nice literary titles, you know; 'The Degradation of Italy'—'Last Flicker of the Empire'—that sort of thing. You almost remember the Empire *did* have a last flicker. . . . And a sentence like this," I said; "here it is: 'Genoa hated

Pisa; no Genoese sailor could endure the cut of a Pisan sail.' "

But Babs, though she smiled indulgently, still sniffed; she actually drew into the edge of the road, and scuffed pages in her turn.

"Look at that!" she said indignantly. "What does he mean by *that?* He just states it; gives you no sources, or documents, or anything. . . . What's that good for?"

"True darling," I said; "but I'm grateful to him, all the same. He's helped *my* inaccurate and sloppy ideas—very much!"

And we grinned at each other, and headed very cheerfully out of town, Rimini's streets being still crowded, thinking we might reach San Marino, that smallest of republics, somewhere up in the hills to westward. But it was the wrong road, and dusty, and very hot, so we desisted, and returned. Everything was at last empty and quiet; we explored with a great sense of freedom, jerking Nicolette round many small corners, and mightily admiring the Roman remains.

There are so many! all imposing, and all cream-colored. The great, single Arch of Augustus, for instance, that said "B. C. 271" on its top; for if Augustus had anything, it was a good one, and did not crumble. Roads in the Alps, walls and gates almost anywhere in southern France; and here he was, "embellishing" Rimini, as the guide-book called it; the nice sort of embellishment that lasts from B. C. till the twentieth century and looks better all the time.

It couldn't possibly have looked as nice in B. C. as it does now, we agreed; especially the Bridge of Augustus, whose tremendous coping, adorned with elderly Latin, had smitten us as we drove in, and was now smiting us again. Low, unbelievably massive, covered with dust of much its own color, it is worth reverence. . . .

Nicolette liked that bridge, we were sure, it felt so reliable beneath one; also she could see beautifully over its edge. One preferred, as one went (said she), to see things; and many of these old *ponti* had annoying edges. . . . The one at Avignon, we remembered; though that was recent and trivial compared to this of Augustus's, and quite to be excused for its youth.

While I dismounted to take a snap-shot of some of the venerableness about us, Babs did a little dusting; whereat a polite and foreign-looking gentleman, tall and fastidiously dressed, who had been walking along in the dusty road, raised his hat and began speaking to her in smooth and beautiful Italian. She looked up at me with humorous eyes, but great calm.

"I am being addressed in a foreign language," said she. "Quantities of it. Will you tell him what he wants to know, A.B.?"

He wanted to know if we had come from Monaco; was positive he had seen us there. . . . Sorry, I told him, but we had not been in Monaco; he might have seen us on the Grande Corniche. . . . True. *Benissimo!* A thousand pardons, ladies! Bowing charmingly, he withdrew. We grinned at each other.

"See what you might have met, if we'd only gone to Monaco."

"Uh-huh," grunted Babs, peering wickedly over the coping of the bridge. "Wot a loss!"

And I wonder sometimes, as I think of our two selves there in the dusty road—so surrounded by Augustus, so unpromising in our tweeds—just what was the motive of the polite gentleman in speaking to us. Was he, with his beautiful voice and his elegance, the last of the Malatesti? It is fun to imagine that he was; to remember that we quite refused to have been seen in Monaco.

We climbed swiftly back into Nicolette; glad, as usual, to be in her. The "canalized" river Marecchi that runs beneath the bridge was not much to see; rivers, we decided, have an ill time in Italy. Here, at least, they wander sluggishly through plains or marshy, lagoony districts near the sea, where the lagoons and marshes stop them up, and they have to be dug out and canalized by man. . . . We disliked canalizing. It isn't pretty; and it mixes you all up on your map.

River so-and-so, it says, to be met at such a point, and you meet a thing like this, meandering along as if it didn't know its own mind.

"River?" you say: "this is a canal!" and proceed to search for the river, which does not reveal itself.

We went on our way. We had seen no traces of Paolo or Francesca in Rimini, but that, in an Italian town famous for literary romance, we had grown to expect. Rimini and Ravenna were both silent about Francesca, so far, though she was born in the latter town, of the house of da Polenta that sheltered and consoled Dante in his bitter exile; and Dante, who lived and walked in these towns, wrote tenderly of her.

Seeing a sweet little side-road, we turned toward Rimini's beach. Colored sails were on the water beyond it; we explored these lanes near the sea. "Hot here," say my notes; "but with a clean white sandy look, and little roads, and little dunes . . . and the silvery-grayish things with pink or purple blossoms, that grow on dunes; very pleasant, to us dune-lovers." None of the little sandy roads went far in any direction, but turned insignificant small corners; we followed, pleased, in this land where one must dwell so much on great things, to be doing something insignificant." "Cosy *little* homes for the peasants," my notes say; "charming!" For Italy is many and wonderful things, but not often cosy, and here, with the lapping of the Adriatic so near, was a sweet spot for homes.

And it was not all retired and simple; we met two stylish young peasant-girls returning from the beach in yellow blouses, white skirts, and patent-leather shoes. Young Italy is certainly modern; but patent leather, in sand?

"I expect they think it's just grand!" said Babs indulgently, as we turned toward the highway, now very visible across flat fields—no getting lost in this section, with a large opalescence on one side of you, and your road on the other; and we had wandered, in the dreamy sunshine, to our hearts' content. But the two girls did not look dreamy; they eyed us with very sparkling eyes. After we passed them I looked back, and their heads were close together; one moment they would shade their eyes and stare after us, then the heads would go together again. . . . These *donne Inglesi,* going about all by themselves; on a feast-day, too! And one of them —the young signorina—doing the driving. . . . Dreadful! yet how one would like to do it—eh, Pepita? *non?* And their young laughter rose.

Not a wealthy region, but rich, one fancied, in content. Peasants were now happily loafing, everywhere. A few of them had cut loads of branches and were carrying them home —faggots for the evening fire; but nobody was really at work. Even the donkeys were still in gigs on the road, going visiting. The plump little horses, driven by proudly-smiling owners, again passed us; some of them had a colt trotting beside them. One bay colt with a large white star, a charging, up-headed little fellow, was taking enormous steps and keeping up with no trouble whatever; when he met us he did a fine gambol in the air . . . out of pure joy, apparently.

We looked back, laughing, after that colt; for if ever we saw one, there was gimpy young stallion in the making.

A white mare with a fat black colt was staked out near the sea, on nice pasture . . . the baby stared hard at us. Next came a mule with a baby—a velvet-coated thing with the sweetest white nose-end; mule-colts are adorable, with their baby look, and the wisdom of great ears above. This one pondered us a minute, then skipped in the air and ran twice round his mother! A *macchina* was a fine joke.

Nicolette fled along over the bumps, leaving a trail of *polvere* behind her. There was no wind, and it floated off sidewise across the green fields, being as deliberate and objectionable as possible . . . and the fields looked so fresh. Clover, scarlet poppies, and sky-blue corn-flowers rioted in them; stimulating fields! We tried not to object to this intimacy of scarlet and clover-color, but felt as if our hair were all being rumpled the wrong way; then a soothing bit of dark green came along. One man and a scythe were tackling a very thick patch of alfalfa-looking stuff, a mule and a wagon waiting for a load; two stocky peasants were carrying in a tray of it and staggering with the weight.

"Green feed for the cow—and it's heavy!" said Babs, her accustomed eye taking in these combinations; for memory assailed us. These fields, foreign as they were, spoke to us like old friends; every one we passed received tribute from us. Pollen flying on the wind, clover wagging at the sky, a small ditch shining—even every wriggling weed that pushed, for foothold, out upon the dusty margin of the road, we were sensible of; breathed the salt cool air and sat up, exulting. What a day! how grand it would be to do mosaics, after this.

"We're almost at that bridge—you know, where they were having the races," remarked Babs, with a look at the map. " 'Like to go round, A.B., and avoid them? I believe I saw another way, west of Ravenna. . . . 'Thought there wasn't any other road, but—yes, here it is, by a river with a curve. . . . . Or do you suppose they call this *canal* a river—the one the bridge goes over?" The old perplexity.

There was no way of telling but to go, and Nicolette hastened across the marshes. . . . Ah, there were the pines, coming between us and the sea. Nice pines! and just then we heard a faint roar; the races must still be going on! Yes, the bridge, just ahead, had a crowd filling it, and far up the oiled road was a flash of scarlet. . . . In an instant it grew large—a racing car, coming straight at the crowd. Was it going to take that corner, round the building? Whoo-OOF! It did a racing skid, and took that perilous bend at full speed, skidding half round, nearly overturning into the canal—but flying on. A man and a girl were in it; in a moment they were a scarlet speck.

The crowd took a breath. . . . Roa-*oar!* A purple streak was coming; it likewise flew at the corner, careened, and smoked on . . . a light blue, which, coming like a small typhoon, hit the low bank of the canal and nearly tipped over (gasps from the crowd) but tore on; an emerald green, flashing round the danger-point with a horrid squawk of tires, then vanishing, like the others, in a wild mop of its own dust.

The crowd moved a little; nodded heads, murmured wisdom to neighbors. Were there more racers to come? The sun was hot, even this late in the afternoon, and tea-hour at hand; could we not get by somehow? If we could turn westward as the racers had, and swing north to Ravenna. . . .

But we couldn't risk being overtaken by one of them; one felt one's hair rising at the idea. There was something terrifying, Massala-like, in the ferocity of these young drivers, black hair flying, goggles glaring, teeth set for victory or death . . . at least that is how they looked; and I appealed to a sweet Italian in a brown suit, with a blue band on his arm and a note-book in his hand, who seemed to be directing things at this point.

"Per piacere, signore—altra via per Ravenna, non?"

And at this everybody crowded round, leaned affectionately on Nicolette, and poked at my map; their entire interest was now diverted to us, and Italian interest is a whole-hearted thing.

"Si si si!" cried a half-dozen voices, as kind brown fingers tried to trace out the way; the medley of advice was bewildering. In the midst of it I asked the young Italian how much longer the races were to last; but before he could answer, a large man in a wide black hat, convinced that I didn't know numbers in Italian, pulled out his watch and leaned in to us. *"La mia ora!"* he said proudly; "my watch!" then illustrated, with a broad thumb-nail and smiling, insistent glances, on the face of the watch . . . something about three, and eight, and five! I smiled at him, but shook my head; again he earnestly pointed out numbers—which meant nothing to either of us. Good soul; he was replaced by the Italian in brown, with the well-bred face and smile and soft delightful voice, who made us understand that it would not be safe yet to take either road—perhaps an hour and a half before we could start. Meanwhile, he pointed at the marshes, where a little road led to the wood of pines beyond.

"Bello posto," he suggested, with smiling gestures; *"dove Dante scripsit!"* We could go there, he said, *"per passare il tempo!"* To pass the time; a beautiful place, where Dante wrote. Charming of him, to think of it; we looked at each other with hope. Why not? It was a sweet little road, with the stream beside it. Thanking everybody, we made our way through this courteous crowd; they stepped quickly aside to let us pass, smiling, and bidding us farewell. Nice, NICE people by the Adriatic, we said; and Nicolette twisted softly along the little sandy ruts that led to the wood.

Dante's pine wood; Garibaldi's too; Mazzini's, perhaps; all three had taken shelter there. . . . By the little river and its crab-nets; then into lovely pines and woods, the late sun glorifying them. May was in bloom, honeysuckle on the trees, orchids beneath them; unknown shrubs were flowering. We crossed a shaky wooden bridge. The shallow, clear-brown river was going very straight for the sea, a path on either bank; beside it we bumped along over tree-roots (how good it was to feel a tree-root again!) and at last saw a peasant's cottage.

Would there be tea here? We alighted with a sense of pleasant leisure, but immediately fell on Nicolette and began dusting her—think of dusting anything in Dante's pine woods; while the young peasant and his wife, doing little jobs about their fenced-in yard, looked covertly at us, serious and shy. . . . They were caretakers of the *pineta,* no doubt; cleaners-up of the cherished forest, and tea was probably the last thing in their horizons; we went to walk in the wood.

A lofty, breathing wood, pleasantly open; no wonder Dante could write here. Clumps of shrubbery interrupted it; rare flowers, large of their kind, delicate and greenhouse-like, as wood-flowers are, grew here and there. Very large mosquitoes ventured out from the shrubbery and paid us tentative attention: like the peasants, they seemed serious and shy; their ways were meditative. . . . An Adriatic pine wood might have that effect; we stared up at the tops of the trees, which swayed thoughtfully, as if aware of the magic of their past.

. . . Dante, at any moment, in his dark hood, might come strolling back from the sea, a *canzonetta* in his hand, dozens in his head; loving these woods, yet sighing for Florence and the dear forbidden life there. . . . We picked a flower or two; met more mosquitoes, who grew in sociability as we went farther among the pines; the wood was beautiful, but somehow very solemn; after a time we turned back. There was only a slight breeze along the river, but too much for Adriatic mosquitoes; with one accord they retired to their solitude, their clumps of shrubbery and wild flowers.

So we sat pleasantly on the bank and read, leaning against a huge pine; then bent forward to watch a most humorous procession of crabs on the bottom of the river. They were large crabs, very busy with this and that, dashing here and there, charging delightfully sidewise at each other and waving their claws, but apparently heading for the sea. It must have been the right time of the tide; visions of wide beaches to play on and plenty of sand-fleas for supper, stirred their crabbish minds. The stream moved placidly onward—and so, except for their dashings at each other, did the crabs; soon they were beyond our sight, however, their wide brown shells mingling with the faint ripples of the river. . . . Cows were browsing on the other bank, and fisher-people occasionally passed; the sun shone, a sail was on the sea; this was indeed a *bello posto*.

Three tall fisher-lads went by on the path below us, their blue trousers well rolled up, their legs and arms very brown; they had to stop and look at us, but instead of openly staring, as the other coast of Italy would have done, they pretended to pick bulrushes while casting shy glances up at us through their eyelashes. . . . Then *"Avanti, avanti! La-la-la!"* chanted the eldest in a high, pleasant voice; and they all started briskly on.

"Nice of 'em!" observed my daughter, pulling a grass-stem and looking affably after them. For it all went with the Adriatic—with the courteous gentleness of Dante's wood; we could not imagine any one's being rude or shrill here . . . our own voices lowered as we talked. It was the sort of place one sees no real reason for leaving; but our hour and a half was more than gone.

" 'Don't hear anything now—do you?" said Babs, rising, and staring down into the water.

"Not a thing."

"It *is* lovely; but I suppose—oh, there's a sail!" for across the stretch of turquoise at the river's mouth went a bit of bright color; then another and another. . . . Flowers—of the sea. And the sun full on them.

Nicolette bumped us very leisurely away over the roots, but we stopped on the bridge to look down the stream as it went, between dark stone-pines, to the sea. . . . Good-by, *pineta!*

No crowd was on the roadway; even our sweet Italian had gone. We turned confidently toward Ravenna.

"It's all over, now," said Babs.

At the grandstand, to our surprise, a few people still lingered; as we approached, from somewhere behind it came a tremendous roaring. It increased, seemed over our heads . . . everywhere . . . a cloud of roaring! Yet we saw nothing; the track ahead was absolutely clear—when before we had chance to think, or even gasp, three red demons leaped from behind the stands and bore down on us full speed, roaring terrifically. One of them, striving to pass the other, let off a great burst of black smoke and leaped in the air; side by side they were, rushing at us, filling the little road. . . . Babs jerked Nicolette almost into the boarding of the stand—there was a babel of screams and horns; the racing-driver, suddenly seeing us, dove back again behind the other, and like a dozen nightmares and a thunder-storm mixed the three roared by, covering us with smoke and dust.

It all happened in such a flash, we had scarcely time for fright, or even thought, but I found I had cowered instinctively down beside Babs. The demons were roaring away, tiny in the distance; but my child, sitting up very straight, with flashing eyes, was looking warlike, and some bewildered officials who had started out toward us in an indeterminate sort of way, merely stared hard at us, their dark eyes large with alarm, and went back again. . . .

"What the *deuce,"* began Babs furiously; "letting us through like that—?" and whirled on.

I of course felt as if we had disturbed the balance of Europe—or done something criminal like that; and yet it WAS all their fault. Easy-going Adriatic, indeed! and it took me all the way across to Ravenna's walls to get the quivers out of my elbows and some breath back again.

"Well!" said daughter at last, turning to me with a smile, and one eyebrow lifted; "thought we were gone for a second —didn't you?"

" 'Did, rather!" I said, smiling back.

"Decent of him, to get behind the other one like that . . . it spoiled all his chances for the race, of course."

"Yes. . . . I didn't think he would, did you?"

"No, I didn't," said she frankly. "That's why—"

"Exactly," I said, and we grinned at each other; but Babs, as was her way when things happened, laid a hand on my knee and kept it there a while.

Yet we liked these people, we reassured ourselves presently; if they had been half as kind to Dante as they were being to us, then even exile must have had its mitigations; poor Dante, whose every likeness reminded us of what a friend said of a Portuguese housemaid—that she had a "long, melancholy nose with a tear-drop on the end of it. . . ."

And when we drove in through the old gate, all Ravenna was on its door-steps. It was near twilight, and we went slowly; people were sitting in their porches, or in chairs on the cobblestones before their doors; old couples, parents, young people, digesting the holiday and discussing the grand events. They looked at us benevolently. Pleasant, on this home-coming after a long day, to be thus looked at; especially in the mood we were just then in, with our realization of how a touch of fate could shatter all one's world. . . . But the piazza was strangely empty, the little *carabiniere* smiled as we passed him; even the Hotel-Beeron-Chentral-Roma (to give it its true, Ravennese pronunciation), ordinarily unemotional, seemed in its thick way, glad to see us.

Waking early next morning I saw the old church pale gold, with light shadows; another—earlier—was the softest rose, against a still blue sky.

Pigeons love these unfinished walls of the churches, the jutting timbers, and dark holes in the old stonework; there was a nest in every timber-hole. The birds walked up and down, bowing and pirouetting. A baby, high on one of the timbers, was shaking its wings imploringly; a horrid parent pecked it, then returned to strut. Their coo-cooing was soft and constant on the air.

Our little chambermaid was much thrilled with our map, when we spread it out on tables after breakfast.

"Firenze?" she cried rapturously; *"ah, si si si!"*

I explained about the French names, which of course she did not recognize, and delighted laughter greeted this information; we then told her about our drive to Rimini, the day before.

"Rimini?" she exclaimed. *"Cinquante chilometri? Ma—c'è un poco!"*

We agreed with her that fifty kilometers was not much, though much may be contained in them; and to extend matters a little, showed her our projected route north. I did not think it necessary to tell her we were probably *not* going to Venice, and when she saw it, her face lighted wonderfully.

"Venezia!" she breathed; then very wistfully, *"Venezia—la piace, signora?"* I assured her it did; and she sighed for joy.

"Una sola Venezia," she murmured. *"Bella Venezia!"*

For she had been born there . . . and had once lived in Arezzo; all the romantic places. Her eyes sparkled joyously as she pointed them out to us. Enthusiasm is a delightful thing, and even a little *cameriera's* helped send us on our way rejoicing; we had grown very fond of this one, she threw herself into our concerns with such delighted ardor.

But the soda-water donkey, another enthusiastic soul, was

outside as usual that morning, and awful sounds arose from him. Every day he had the same lovely, frost-colored load of green and white; while his driver went inside he lifted his nose and howled—always in the same spot, under our window. He would sniff the pavement a moment, then throw up his head and vehemently "fry an egg"—as we used to call that equine process of curling back the upper lip and making sizzling sounds. . . . "Gi-a!" called his driver; and he went obediently on. He was a large, black donkey, very intelligent; crossed the busy lane when he saw fit, dodged carts and people, then stopped, of his own volition, at another door. He knew! knew his route like a milkman's horse on Beacon Hill—and made even more noise about it. He had a fine red brow-band on his bridle, and he owned Ravenna. We thought him one of the sights of the town—which we were now off to explore.

"Half a day—will that do it?" I said, climbing into Nicolette.

" 'Must," said my daughter calmly. "*We've* got to be humping along north, you know, A.B."

"Yes—" I said; "and Ravenna is, really, rather one sort of thing I expect. Basilicas, you know . . ." and just then we stopped before the august front of one. Dust-colored, ancient; Sant' Apollinare Nuovo, very hot in the sun.

Ancientness, indeed, smote us at our first footfall on its half-sunken pavement. Greek columns stood in mellow perspective, and above the nave, high along the walls, ran a row of mosaics; one felt that one had never seen mosaics before. Life-sized, ascetic figures in greens and blues or dove-color, with touches of orange-brown; grave of face, appealing and real; incredibly achieved with little pieces of colored marble. For all their size they were done with extraordinary style; the scant flow of their garments ravished the eye. . . . And this kept on, all around the long nave.

We were silenced; stole around in a sort of breathlessness, as if an uttered word would bring these heart-searching beauties down about our heads. A cloister was a relief—an incredibly solid and ancient cloister with low heavy stonework, heavy bits of sculpture lying rather shabbily about, and behind the columns a neglected but somehow sweet garden, with a corner of sunlight on sparse greenery. We escaped into the street; but in spite of the bright assistance of Ra, had a complicated time trying to get a picture of the very tall, colonnaded, slightly leaning and entirely glorious campanile.

San Vitale, our next church, that "most precious jewel of Byzantine art in the west," was even more silencing. Babs walked about—my scoffing child—simply breathing it in; dreams and the realization of dreams, in her eyes . . . for again, everything was "different." (Ravenna was *not* "rather one sort of thing" as I had expected.) We had always liked anything octagonal, there is a completeness, an enclosingness about the shape, that suggests treasures within; and here they were. Babs had a perfect time going round identifying them. Triumphal arch, fragment of Roman frieze, four columns from a ciborium; one "Of green breccia—very rare; from *Egypt,* A.B.!" and so on. . . . All so strange, so absorbing; as things were too in the marvelous little fifth-century mausoleum in San Vitale's rear, across a nice bit of bright grass with stepping-stones in it.

The little building has already sunk (crookedly) several feet in the ground, which gives it an engagingly coy look; one hopes it won't sink much more.

The greens and blues of its mosaics are fresh as yesterday —green and blue, brown and cream-color, in robes of saints, or in landscape, seeming to be favorite tints of their creators. Just right, we told each other, for deer drinking at a Holy Fount . . . charming deer, that would have done for an illustration in *Bambi* . . . They and a woodland background in the slight roughness of mosaic, seemed very specially right; and in another lunette were some most lifelike sheep, pasturing on grass and flowers. I never enjoyed a mausoleum before.

But we loved these outdoor colors; went around, the notes say, "in a sort of bath of being suited with what we saw."

There seemed a most unusual lack of scarlet and crimson in the ecclesiastical decoration of Ravenna, and we were glad; these old interiors are soothing, almost, as a soft landscape on a November day.

And the rude outsides of the churches looked so abysmally old; as if they, as well as the green *breccia,* belonged in Egypt.

Ecclesiastic chill was welcome after the hot streets. We careered from one old *chiesa* to another, seizing hungrily upon chance guides—Ravenna is not over-full of these; seeing everything, we thought, including the "scarcely adequate" tomb of Dante (really a feeble product) in the Piazza Byron. But it is "a sacred shrine of Italian patriotism. . . . Since September 1908, a lamb of remembrance has burnt here continuously, the gift of the Società Dantesca . . ." and when Michelangelo offered, in older days, to build a fitting tomb he was not allowed to; so that it was only in one or two of his sonnets he was able to express—"to some extent in verse," Professor Gardner says, "what he was not suffered to do in marble:

> From Heaven his spirit came, and, robed in clay,
> The realms of justice and of mercy trod:
>
> * *
>
> I speak of Dante, whose high work remains
> Unknown, unhonoured by that thankless brood
> Who only to just men deny their wage.
> Were I but he! Born for like lingering pains,
> Against his exile coupled with his good
> I'd gladly change the world's best heritage.

Hard to realize that Dante's work was ever unknown or unhonored; but Angelo's noble spirit would be one to acknowledge, and appreciate, unhappy greatness. . . . One wonders that the "thankless brood" did not consign *him* to the pine woods.

And I became perfectly mixed about Dante's actual tomb. He was put in one; then they wanted him somewhere else, and put him there; and was he ever put back again? I asked that twice, but the guide instantly told such a long story about it, and in such rapid, Ravennese Italian, that we came away wondering where, after all, great Dante now is. . . .

Theodoric's mausoleum stood at a little distance outside Ravenna's wall, past the Rocca di Brancaleone—a somehow heroic name that goes with the "rugged bastions" of that fortress; we debated for a minute as to going, then were most glad we had. The round building was impressive, in its pretty setting, with a suggestion of formal garden about—most of the ancient things in Ravenna have that; it is "of unhewn stone without mortar," topped by a most huge and remarkable monolithic roof, and was "begun by the great Ostrogoth himself." Theodoric had the bright thought, too, of using a porphry bath for his sarcophagus—at least one hoped it was Theodoric, not some scornful descendant. . . . But porphry is beautiful; and why not a bath?

Far less depressing than most sarcophagi. I felt that the great Ostrogoth had a sense of humor, as well as a love of Persian antiquity and soothing richness of color . . . and never before had I stopped to credit a Goth with these amenities.

In short, it was a morning of enlightenment; and on our way back we gave a lift to a distressed and conversational Englishwoman who "found walking about in these streets *so* tiring, my dear!" She wished to share the nearest cab with us, but leaped with surprise and pleasure on learning that we had a car outside. I suppose we did not look as if we had. We smiled together, *en confidence,* at the sudden change in the lady's manner, which had become reverential; when she saw Nicolette, she relaxed a little.

"Oh! You are driving yourselves, aren't you!" she exclaimed, with recovered sprightliness. But she climbed with real gratitude into the comfortable rear seat of our cloverleaf—now fortunately free of luggage—and rode off with us in much ease of mind. . . .

"She expected a Rolls, at *least,*" said Babs when we had deposited our loquacious passenger in the square—she had talked, with great devotion, in our convenient ears all the way back; and we went off, giggling at the ways of humans.

CHAPTER XXI

THE GREAT DIKE, AND PADUA

HASTILY collecting a lunch which the Hotel Byron-Central-Roma had put up for us, we set Nicolette's nose northward toward Ferrara; now, for a day or two, we were to go skimming up the Adriatic shore. At least we thought we were going to Ferrara, but as we drove the country intrigued us, and we felt more and more reluctant to reach that inland spot, only seventy *chilometri* away; for what, on a morning in mid-May, were towns—to this sunlight shining radiant and transparent through grape-leaves, or on the brilliant roadside flowers, and picking out a glint of blue across the marshes?

On our right were miles of vineyards with the vines trained on poles, or running exuberantly and beautifully from one mulberry tree to another; sometimes depending from a wide circle of wooden arms attached to the mulberries . . . an original pattern and most picturesque, as one looked down their far-stretching vistas toward flatness and the sea.

The peasants were hard at it today; spraying was furiously going on. As we came to a lane by a cottage, a spray-tub was being drawn into its shady yard by the pale-blue figures of three men: turquoise hats and shirts, faces as solid with it as if it had been painted on. They grinned cheerfully at us, out of those unrecognizable faces; we did not see how they could bear it . . . or breathe. But the little grape-blossoms were just out. This was the moment for all these miles of them to be cared for at once, and the peasants, with all their genius for leisure, had almost an air of haste.

Hilarity went with it, however, and one trio, after working through a long morning, were just coming in for their noon meal. They had drawn, as was their fashion, the stained and picturesque spray-barrel into the wide yard of the vine-covered cottage, where two hearty-looking peasant-women were at the door to greet them, their broad faces creased with mirth; the youngest of the men rolled up his blue shirt-sleeves and, to our amazement, began washing vigorously in a trough near the front fence.

The trough was brimming with beautiful clear water . . . and to wash off all that poison, in there? Would the oxen drink from it afterwards, the family's pots and kettles be filled —or was it simply a place for outdoor washing?

It needed plenty of splashing to get off all that blue; the young peasant was gradually turning a ruddy brown, emerging to laugh at us even more freely as his features released themselves—for we simply had to slow down and watch this fascinating process. It was so nice to see a handsome brown Italian face dawn out of that mask of expressionless blue; gave one positively a washed and relieved feeling about one's own mouth and nose, to see that young peasant's once more appearing! The two older men approached the trough, grinning with anticipation; little children ran about like lively flowers, hens picked morsels here and there, the two women, picturesque in their yellow kerchiefs, waved to us from the doorway; even the donkey came strolling round a corner of a wall to see what it was all about.

With a last glance back at the good-fellowship of that yard, we got up speed once more. It was growing late, considering our early and hasty breakfast—with all the treasures of Ravenna awaiting us; but before choosing a lunch-place, we first wanted to get past the more ardent regions of the spray. The very air seemed full of it. Grapes were even growing beside us, on a steep bank, with a peasant standing below shooting at them; the spray fell only whimsically on the vines—sometimes it blew away, sometimes the stream did not reach.

"*I* call that sloppy!" said Babs, with vigor.

"Don't you suppose he's going to climb that bank?" I said —though the man had a lazy, sleepy look.

"Hope so," said she; "he's doing a precious poor job where he is!" And we laughed. . . .

Criticizing again! Well, if farming is in one's bones, it is; and there was plenty of it along this road to draw out opinions. Whole books had been written about the agriculture here, mostly by English travelers of an older day, "the type of the honest squire venturing abroad," and Emilia had long been famous for rich lands.

But the level of the fields was sinking. Banks beside us went down instead of up, vineyards were amiably giving place to the wide green of the marshes, to lines of tall poplar trees, and dykes, and wild flowers. We must be nearing the cross-country road we had come on from Lugo.

"Here it is!" said Babs, steering down a little hill to the grassy bank of the canal, and coming to rest under leaf-shadows. "How's this?"

"Divine," I said—for a bird was singing loudly in the poplars; and after a morning of chilly church smells, this interlude of sunshine was the more precious. . . . Lovers of sunny grasses we are and always shall be; of ribbons of blue water, and tall, strange, paintable flowers waving in an Adriatic breeze. Marsh flowers are always lovely, with a quality of rareness in their wavings; we sat on the bank and ate, and looked—and decided very suddenly that we would go to Comacchio.

There it sat, on the map, with the letters of its name in the sea; almost the last outpost of everything, away out across a lagoon . . . and how we loved lagoons.

It must be a fishing-village, on that lagoon; perhaps we could stay there! We hastened our lunch. A slight mistiness had come over the sun, to be sure; leaf-shadows about us had grown first faint, then invisible; but a gray afternoon over marshes would be lovely. We quite preferred it gray! Color in the marsh-grass would come out, and the sky come down cuddly and brooding; if the lagoon had gone gray it would have silver on its surface, and any low line of dune beyond it (the Adriatic usually had dunes) would be blue-gray and charming.

So through little Alphonsine we sped; through Argenta and Portomaggiore—hamlets, magnificently surrounded by marshes; then on across more marshes to San Vito, where we struck into a fine big road seaward for Comacchio. At least it was comparatively big; but during all this drive everything was so flat and open that one had wide feelings anyway. . . .

Far away the marshes were purple; sometimes a lonely little narrow-gauge came near us as if for the pleasure of our society, then wandered off in its concealing grasses again, beside half-seen lagoons.

It was a gray gravel road we were on, punctuated with sharp little stones; and a great wind had come up, as winds do over marshes. . . . Nicolette didn't like winds. Wider spread the soft marsh world before us; farther and farther away seemed Comacchio. We passed Ostellato, a huddle of little windswept houses: somewhere between there and San Giovanni, another ancient huddle, the ground lifted a few feet, ceased being marsh—and we could not imagine what was the tiny crop we saw growing in the vast fields. . . .

Radishes! Miles and miles of those little hors d'œuvres, an inch or two high; it gradually appealed to us as immensely humorous. We first smiled, then chuckled, then, as they kept on and on, and the wind blew ever harder, fell into helpless laughter at the silliness of them. . . . They didn't *last* long enough to be grown in fields! They'd be two feet high, pretty soon, and in blossom; and to think of anybody's growing them by the mile—out by that limitless, sea-going marsh, oh ha ha ha!

It is easy to laugh, with the wind blowing so it almost rocks you.

In a field by a peasant's cottage, however, some big oxen were standing on the radishes—which was a sobering sight; right in the middle of a flourishing growth of them.

COMING IN FROM THE ADRIATIC

Cesenatico, enroute to Rimini

Had the peasants gone mad? There the great creatures stood, chewing cuds and stamping at flies, squashing any quantity of crop . . . we were convinced their masters had had sunstrokes or been carried off by a plague.

But the day was grayer and grayer (no excuse for sunstrokes!) the air was splendid, on this slight elevation, and we soon came to a more rational sight: rows and rows of peasants down on their knees picking radishes, as radishes should be picked. Young and old, the pickers were in bright-colored shirts, or dresses and kerchiefs, laughing and chattering at their work; they sat up and waved to us—a most sketchable sight, with the low, gray-pleated sky so near them, and the great marsh beyond. Yet no Italian Millet had painted it; no painter at all, that we knew of, had come here, as Sorolla among his people on Valencia's coast, and done immortal landscape-with-figures. Babs and I agreed that this whole section was strangely unfrequented by artists.

We now entered the vast tracklessness of Comacchio's marsh. Wind was still blowing, the cool, ferocious wind that loves to blow across such stretches; Nicolette shook as it struck her. Gray, ruffled lagoons came in sight—and far, far off on a rim of nothingness, was a line of blue-gray nubs, almost lost in the purple of that distance. A gray-blue spire stuck up—that must be Comacchio, no other town was as far out . . . enticing it looked, but very lonely; and where would one stay, in Comacchio?

"I forgot to look," I murmured.

Nowhere, apparently. Not an inn, not a lodging-house was to be had there; indeed, almost nothing was said about Comacchio. "From Ostellato there is a branch-line to Porto Garibaldi, a harbour on the Adriatic, *via Comacchio* (8700 inhab.) in the midst of the Valli, or Lagoons of Comacchio, noted for their eels."

"Eels!" I said; "probably right here, in this creek. . . . But what do you think, lamb?"

Babs slowed down while we thought. The little spire, the

gray-blue nubbles, sat there looking impossibly far away; the sky was darkening, the wind was cold; lagoons looked somehow uninhabitable. Nicolette halted, in a very strong smell of tide, beside tufts of violently-blown marsh-grass. Not a sail was on the water; little hasty waves lapped and lapped on bumps of dead grass or sea-weed; little wreaths of foam bobbed up and down upon them or attached themselves to the marshy shore, even dangling from blades of its coarse grass, where they had been lifted and blown.

That wind grew colder every minute. . . . Would the village be like the one where we bought the peasant bread? One surely could not have slept there. . . . There might not be a spare bed in all Comacchio; more likely, not a spare half or quarter or eighth of a bed. And village food?

Had this been France we might have gone on, in a sort of faith; but the wind whistled suddenly in my other ear as we swung round. . . . A pity! Those nubs still allured us, and the feeling of the edge of everything; but we were on our way to Padua and the Lakes, it was better to stop experimenting, and go. . . . Much better! we said, staring back at the vanishing romantic nubs.

"Glad we've had this bit of it, anyway," said Babs, pulling her hat down. "Now we'll hump along, darling, and get to Ferrara."

North of us, I discovered, lay Codigoro, that "largest land-reclaiming installation in the world"; and eastward of it, standing on what was once an island, is Pomposa, the famous Benedictine abbey. Was Pomposa's island one of the things reclaimed from the sea, we wondered? The abbey now stands on the edge of an inland lagoon; and farther north of Codigoro is what our map called the *"Ancienne lagune d'Ambrogio,"* a large piece of very dry land where once was shining water. Italy, one gathers, is finding ways of extending her territory other than by war; a very industrious one is filling lagoons. . . .

And it shouldn't have seemed long, but it did, exceedingly, before we sighted the great red walls of Ferrara. Only forty-nine kilometers, but flatness is flatness; sometimes, with twilight coming on and a strong wind blowing, you have had enough of it. We had a detestable time getting into the town, with mobs of black-coated men filling the wide street in front of the cathedral—they were much annoyed, and glared at us when we tried to pass. *Women* driving, and at that hour!—and there wasn't a *carabiniere* to be seen, nothing but hotly-arguing frock-coats, and our ill-timed selves advancing . . . and a well-fed Italian is somehow too fat to push; and when at last we did arrive at the quiet courtyard of the old Albergo Stella d'Oro, we had a detestable night there.

We were tired that night; our room was large, the beds were good, but there didn't seem to be any air in Ferrara, and through the lace curtains of our windows strolled very large mosquitoes. Babs can sleep through any mosquito, but I lay awake . . . deeply wishing to turn Nottingham lace into screens.

Next morning we found out why the creatures had hummed so. Across the piazza from us, invisible in the dusk of last evening, was the huge Castello Estense, "an imposing pile surrounded by its ample moat and bridges"; the moat was ample indeed, the bridges delightful, but the water in the moat looked as old as the *castello* itself; green and stagnant. We had to go round the unwholesome thing on our way to see the "empty *palazzi*" that are supposed to give Ferrara an "air of solemnity"; it made us feel like holding our breaths.

Is stagnation solemnity, then? Ferrara could not please us. Its air seemed that of vacant gloom rather than of solemnity. Our guide-book insisted that there were streets where "the handsome fronts of *palazzi* alternate with verdant gardens," but we saw no gardens; and one of Ferrara's dukes had imprisoned Tasso as a madman, which didn't make us think better of the place. Poets, in any epoch, should be allowed to be a little mad. . . .

Strange what a sleepless night will do. I have felt really

apologetic about the town since, for on some other day we might have found it charming. The cathedral did impress us—huge, bizarre, and heathenish-looking, and very hard to take a picture of—ladies of Ferrara would get in the way. The cathedral is too long (for photographic purposes), but with a truly magnificent perspective along one decorated side, and lovely beasts in front of it; imaginative Persian beasts who are anything and nothing, and are wonderful. They had been hidden by crowds the night before, but now showed us their true delightfulness.

That was all, however; and my penciled notes of the day, scrawled while Nicolette was in motion, begin, "Escape from Ferrara." The town was founded merely because the Veneti and other coast tribes were driven to escape from barbarian invasions by settling in the marshes—poor things, in all the mosquitoes; we much preferred, as a residence, the Valli di Comacchio. I'd sleep on a tuft of grass ANYTIME, rather than listen for things coming in through Nottingham lace . . . and out there toward Comacchio where winds blew and eels flourished, the marshes were salt and invigorating.

The way out of Ferrara was not easy to find. It was a cool gray morning, there had been rain in the night, and Nicolette, who had slept (doubtless very badly) in an open courtyard, was damp and balky. We all felt damp. Everything in her, she told us, was sticking to everything else; and Babs persuaded, and coaxed, and used a few of the milder University oaths (I quite enjoy placid swearing), finally dismounting on the cobbles and putting oil in the transmitter, which seemed to be what was needed. Nicolette went round the next corner with some zeal.

Ferrara had infinite corners, but at last we met a nice bright boy who told us the turnings. Such a rosy-cheeked, brown-haired, cheerful and polite boy, who quite made us like Ferrara; we went on our way with pleasant feelings. . . . Out toward Portelagoscuro we trundled—the Gate of the Dark Lake, which sounded quite Dantesque, but was merely "one of the ports on the lower reaches of the Po"; we glimpsed its smoke a little way upstream, saw no lake, bright or dark, but came to the gate of a toll-bridge. The toll-bridge man, who was rosy-cheeked and brown-haired like our boy, was also most cheerful and merry and polite (toll-men usually are); observing our G.B., he made smiling signs and held out three shining *lire* in the palm of his hand to show us what the toll was.

And then the magnificent river. We were not prepared for that. One had always read of the Po, and thought of the Po, known that the Po had a lot of mouths, drained a tremendous extent of territory, and finally ended in the embrace of the Adriatic; but we had not realized how it would look.

While we were still gaping, Nicolette slid us off the bridge and on to a magnificent dyke. It had steep grassy banks and was at least forty or fifty feet above the river; a grand wide road sailed along its top, which curved as the river curved. We had done some triumphant motoring on the high deserts of France, on mountain descents, or swinging along the Corniches; but this was almost the most so. There below one was the mighty river, deep, rapid, almost envenomed in its vast rushing to the sea, its mood powerful, unchanging, inimical to man; like a solid creature, forever streaming past, yet never passing; and here we were, safe and high, coursing along the top of things. . . .

There had been rains, I suppose the Po was in flood; whatever the cause, it was sufficiently impressive. We gazed down upon the monster below us, and kept pace with its racings; we seemed to drive faster and faster.

"Go it, Nicolette!" I cried, patting her; and Babs smiled at me.

"Like it, A.B.?"

I did, but we could not race all the way. It was too charming. And interesting. Charming wild flowers grew upon the dyke; and the river, for all its bodeful pace, was a noble, full-hearted river, with no reefs of protruding gravel to mar its look of mass, of swift and vast intention.

One could have watched it . . . by the week.

Occasionally, on the dyke's inner and protected side, houses were set far down below; not even their smoking chimneys reaching our level. They had gardens and vines, with animals and children running about; "actually vegetables!" say my notes; and beyond this pleasant domesticity was the rich grass of the plain, with little roads winding and a dot of a village here and there, or a curve of blue from a canal.

This view of the country was lovely, but the river was the thing. Fishing was riskily going on in frail, black, Eastern-looking shallops ("Venetian influence?" my notes ask); they had slim blue sails and, assisted by oars and the shouting and gesturing of brown-legged fishermen, were laboring mightily with the current. They were charming, light-hearted shallops, friskily pointed both fore and aft, their small blue sails lightly tethered to a slim mast and swelling far in advance of the bow, below which creamed and foamed the hungry wavelets. There seemed very little of these boats in the water; they skimmed about the surface of the river like blue-winged dragon-flies. They should do no such utilitarian thing as cruise about for food; how many fish could such shallops hold?

But the shouting fishermen did not enlighten us; gaiety was in their shouts—joy in riskiness, and in conquest of the rushing river-thing they battled with. A thrilling sight, those ceaseless skirmishes; a battling of azure-winged butterflies . . . brave ones.

The dyke magnificently curved, the river ran, wild flowers continued to bloom; and girls were getting water from the Po. Three of them came up the steep bank, following a little well-worn path, with wooden yokes on their shoulders and full buckets dangling.

"Poor girls!" said Babs; and then—horrified— "Do you *suppose* they boil macaroni in Po?"

But they must. It was so obviously their only supply; the yokes and buckets, the well-worn path, told their story. Farther on, some girls were bringing washing up the bank in wheelbarrows; heavy wet washing, scarcely wrung out from the Po—and wrung by hand. Some dressed-up men (dressed up for peasants, that is) stood idly by, looking on; was this another holiday? Fishermen were fishing, but probably they always did that; fishermen, in any clime, have no holidays. The girls struggled up the bank, laughing, but resting now and then—one could see what hard work it was; and the men watched, complacently. . . . This is the land, to be sure, where a housemaid seizes your trunk and carries it up three flights while the cabman looks on; but these particular men were so idle, so complacent. . . .

More groups of them we passed—yes, surely, this was a holiday; and every group faced the river as the men chatted. That was the thing one watched, when one lived beside it; one stood on the dyke and speculated. . . . There was a fearful current by this bank at every curve. "Pulleys, etc., on the fishing-nets," my notes say; for all rigging on the poles had to be very strong, and strongly secured, before any net could be dipped into this vast rushing.

The blue sails flitted about; a slender pink campanile, tall and lovely upon the green country, raised itself from a village church. We stopped at the next village for benzina—a very smiling, holiday performance, with pump-handles being worked with extra fervor by a young Italian in a brilliant necktie; and here a pink-and-white campanile was so near the river that it looked like a lighthouse. If little churches on the Montagne Noire were used as forts, why not a belfry for a lighthouse? It would make a good one, at this bold curve in the river—which now swung across fields and left us.

"Blue flowers we didn't know," say my notes; "daisies and huge buttercups, where we got water in winding canal." For I have a picture of Babs, wading through deep grass, reaching down through still deeper grasses and flowers to bring up a saucepanful, and coming carefully back, carrying it, with pollen and buttercup-petals on her skirt. Nicolette seemed to use a great deal of water nowadays; could that radiator of hers be leaking? We looked, but she was dripping with canal-water, and foiled us; so we climbed in, hoping for the best.

Men were mowing beside the road, on this gray day with rain threatening; laying the grass down in rich, heavy swathes—four stocky, broad-shouldered villagers, having such a sociable time. Never mind rain—which was now gently falling; this deep grass would take more than a day's drying. Mow, men—mow! They did; and for all their merry talk, the swathes fell fast. . . .

And here was the Canale Bianco on whose banks stands Adria, "the ancient town that gave its name to the Adriatic"; it seemed very odd, and all wrong, to have a sea named from a town . . . the Adriatic is a small sea, but somehow enormous in its suggestions.

"Nice old Rovigo," say my notes. "Porta very old. Brownish brick and stone. Rovigo brownish. People so docile—leap from puddles. . . ." There must have been a hard rain in Rovigo. Puddles gleamed and shone before us, they shone, mud-colored, beside Rovigo's nice narrow square—with a very old clock-tower, a Renaissance palace, and the fattest, most jubilant statue of Victor Emanuel we had seen anywhere. There are so many of these—most of them equestrian, all enchantingly fat, yet so different in their degrees of aplomb, pomposity, and conscious virtue, so reflecting Italy's absolute suffocation of pride in that energetic ruler—that they are worth making a collection of.

But we had to find a way out of that square; our road seemed to curl round and end in the façade of a delightful, warm-colored building.

"Can we go *there?*" said Babs, peering into the most imperceptible of lanes.

Yes indeed! A helpful cab preceded us and we went patiently behind it. The lane spread itself into a street, and a wide road started north; our road, we inferred; it had no sign. (One's powers of inference grow, over here.) "Gardens," say my notes; "nice villa with roses; then straight road, with poplars. Like France! Didn't expect to find it in Italy. We arrive at the conclusion that everything is everywhere.

"Boulevard, dyked up; high above crops. Great leafy poplars. Yellow iris, by ditch. Very rich fields, bosky with willows and grape-vines. . . . Pale-pink house set down among its vineyards; it had columbines, and a great climbing rose. Beans, growing in corn. Nice to see real corn."

For this was not wheat, or any European substitute, but plants of actual two-bladed corn in rows softened by bean-foliage. Gardens here, of course, must think of the furious summer sun; and beans do thrive so delightfully.

Crossing the Adige, we found ourselves in Stanghella; a circular town. Its streets went in circles, it had a circular piazza with fresh grass and a splashing fountain and we did gravitory system round it—much wondering if our direct progress were ended and we should now wander and divagate as Italian roads usually did; but the circles, accompanied by nice clear signs, were just to conduct us out of town—into the marvelous straightness again. Oh, we liked curves best; but this straightness, escorted by trained trees and with all sorts of crops making a design below, was interesting for a change . . . and so easy to get along on. Once more the high-dyked road, the richness and wetness; but the leafy poplars had changed to skeletons. They had been espaliered like pear trees on a wall, their great branches going north and south only; desolating to have them cut, but they made nice patterns.

"Sharp, barbered line against the sky—architectural effect, like columns; 11 kilometers of it. . . . Rare villages, with separate campaniles by the churches. Separate ones all the go. Venetian influence?"

For Venice was closing in upon us, and Venice was one to make herself felt. Her lion's paw was upon everything. Ever since crossing the Po we had been in her province; no wonder things had begun to remind us—by this slight gracefulness, that bit of ornament—of the magic creature of the seas. . . .

We were not going there—oh no; we remembered it as if it were yesterday. There was so much ELSE we wanted to do up north here. . . .

Yes, we knew Venice; we must waste no time on her this vac. Righto! And under a gray tumultuous sky, quite alone on this fascinating and strange road, we flew absorbedly. Easy going; the mud of Venetia is shallow mud, Nicolette told us. Swwrr-ssss! went our tires, sloshing along; casting gray mud upon trunks, or showering it shockingly near a roadside shrine.

By and by we saw the poplared straightness ending, and after that we curved and were natural and Italian; landscape was on a level with us, and we turned across bare, marshy openness into a confusion of weather—and scenery.

For some time a tumultuous sky had been blowing up, and now an amazing hill was dawning under the clouds. Hill? we thought it was all flat, up here. A castellated wall led stormily up its side, and in and out of the clouds—half-seen, cloud-wreathed—was a castle.

Castle! We drove amazedly into its little village; Monselice. "Dear little old town; nice donkeys, clean market, church with round loggia and square clock-tower, Via Venti Settembre, and all. . . . More humps outside—with walls and castles; Nicolette flying into fierce head wind and flying puddles." For the sky would be puffy and slate-dark, then brilliant with bits of illuminated cloud, or slanting and yellowed with a wild space of rain; changing, purpling, bowling about, but always driven and hurtled, as we were, by the furious wind.

"Is this a revelation—or a cyclone? . . . Such a mad day!" said Babs, gripping the wheel.

Humps and sky and furiousness kept on; Nicolette bounced and scudded, and we, as always in a storm, were vastly exhilarated. It really did not rain much on us, and areas of wild rain somewhere else are delightful to see. We eyed these celestial discriminations (going on so gorgeously for our benefit) with gratification.

"The Euganean hills, these are," I said, feeling lukewarm on information and very gladly closing the guide-book.

It had been most difficult to read it with Nicolette plunging and bucking about, and when we drove into Battaglia, beside a deep little walled canal with the road sunk unimportantly beside it, my notes simply say: "Battaglia—must have a history."

For Battaglia means battle—a drum-beat of a word, in any tongue; and the canal was the Canale Battaglia too, but what battles it meant except that the Venetians were always attacking some one hereabouts, no book disclosed.

And the canal had a little arched bridge like those over side-canals in Venice—the sort that Henry Irving used in the first act of his *Merchant of Venice,* with soft lights and lovely gloom, and gallants in rose or plum-colored satin coming and going—a marvelous night-scene.

It was daylight in Battaglia now, but the little bridge got us by the throat. Horse and mule-loads were in the way as we approached it, and we could not stop—they were having a hard enough time in Battaglia's deep mud; yet the blue-green of the canal, the pinkish color of that bridge—its balustrade of pale stone, its shallow steps, made us feel Venice in every pulse of us . . . Babs turned to me.

" 'Expect we *must* go there, after all," she murmured. I nodded, we clasped hands, and it was done.

Joy seized us. Venice! how could we ever have thought of leaving it out? And we saw a niche to park in.

"We'll do Padua," I said, "and go on to Vicenza for the night, as we meant to; and then get to Venice round that northern loop. . . . Oh goodness, Babs, I suppose we'll have to leave Nicolette in Mestre!"

" 'Suppose we shall," said she, glancing with some apprehension at the map. . . .

Our precious Nicolette; and would there be an honest garage in Mestre? Our impression of the Venetian populace was a somewhat light-minded one; and leaving her—for days?

"Oh well!" I said, "we'll see what it's like when we get there."

"Yes—" responded Babs; "and you know those garage girls in London said it was all right. . . ."

The "garage girls" were four plucky young Londoners who had driven ambulances during the war and had since conducted a successful garage in Kensington; they had helped us buy Nicolette the autumn before, and given us quantities of wise advice about the trip, so when we now recalled that they also had jumped off at Mestre and deposited Chubby there (an ancient pet of theirs), we felt better. Chubby had been all right, though there was some sad tale of the petrol's having been poured out of her overnight . . . but that wasn't anything vital, we assured each other; and nobody could help being nice to Nicolette. . . .

Our bridge had a statue, we now saw, and turned to stare at it; the dear simpering statue of a Pope or Bishop or somebody. A white marble person, charming, slender and informal, in the most amusingly natural pose; coming smiling down the steps holding a green umbrella over himself—a bronze umbrella—picking up his robes with one slender lifelike hand, and tipping his head to one side with the most engaging simper. . . . He was entirely real; I have seen people at parties coming down steps just that way, a little fussy and self-conscious, but very pleased with themselves and the world. There was not much rugged character in the face, which was that of a somewhat sinuous personality—compliant, graceful, full of a kindly wit, agreeable always; he looked as if he had just been received in audience by a great person, not quite as if he were the great person himself. He was doubtless the genius of Battaglia, however; very great in his own domain.

We started rapturously on; did not even detour to Arqua del Monte where Petrarch lived for three years, and died, and where Byron and Mozart, so Baddy tells you, have their names in the visitors' book. "His house is in the upper part of the town, with painted wooden ceilings, and faded frescoes in allusion to his poems. . . ." How nice to have faded frescoes in allusion to one's poems . . . but I did not discover all this till next day. Nicolette had begun bouncing again.

We seemed fated never to see a house of Petrarch's. Only a few weeks ago we had spent a mad afternoon in the neighborhood of Avignon, on a fête day, trying to find his château, and it had "disappeared"; so now we sailed serenely and ecstatically through this small and simple Battaglia, crowded merely by a few orderly mule-teams, quite unconscious that the great lyricist had lived near by . . . and this really was a house, with ceilings and reminiscences and all, not just a mythical something on a crumbling crag that after all wasn't there.

It was delightful all the way to Padua. We followed the blue-green canal—a navigable one, with canal-boats in it, and lively bits of the Euganean Hills jumping up about us . . . the marble for St. Mark's piazza came from these same hills. The old villas were delightful too; one small one had great climbing roses over it, and a formal garden of rose trees and gravel walks, with three stained and mouldering statues, very noseless. Very nice! There was lichen on their curls—of an antique gold; those soft gold heads made them go with the garden. Across the canal was the yellow château of the Obizzi family, very mellow on its fresh green background; set well back against trees and the humpy hills, residential and yet warlike, with fortified edges and great stone gates beautifully thick with statues; hints of such gardens and treasures within! It had a shut-up look, however. . . .

A straight road, and more great villas—were they Paduan summer residences? beside the pretty little Bacchiglione; then the towers of Padua, gray-blue.

"Since the founding of its university in 1222 . . . an important center of culture, patriotism, and liberty of thought . . . it has earned the surname of *la dotta* (the learned)." We expectantly entered Padua's old wall by, a Barriera, drove along the Corso and came to the Prato della Valle—once "the pasture-field of the valley (or dale)"; "an oval plantation, originally a grassy dale."

None of these phrases, though culled from various books, convey the ancient charm of the Prato; the murmur of its waters, or its lofty trees that meet overhead. Such trees are a treat, in Italy. "Melodious marble bridges," say my notes; "nice clean water all around; marble railings, ancient marble of Roman-draped worthies, in two circling rows above the bright little canal. Tasso, Petrarch, Galileo; insignificant Romans, appealing but quite bad. The whole piazza abounded in charm."

By one of its edges, a great church backs away into its own greatness—San Giustina, many-domed, brick-façaded, bare of front; with steps across its entire width. We drove respectfully before it; then turned into traffic.

For a short Paduan tram-car was preceding us—short but mighty; it stopped, and we with it, all along the narrow delightful main street of the town, which curved and had arcades and was altogether proper for Padua, but a bit thick, on a Saturday, for navigating.

The clouds had been newly gathering and now rain fell, shining on the stone pavements. We stopped by a convenient widening and flung up the top, then prowled on. Umbrellas went up, the crowds thinned to hurrying figures; Padua was pretty in a rain, though slipperier; and one could not stick one's head out quite so freely to stare, prognosticate, and inspect, because the moment one did, Nicolette dripped down one's neck. But fascinating glimpses were everywhere. Padua is a sweet old town, with the narrow arms of the Bacchiglione winding through it, and little bridges dating back to Roman days; there was the University courtyard, with columns, sculptured arms and entrances; then the *mercato;* finally a round old wall, partly ruinous, but pretty with roses, and enclosing a sort of park or public garden—once the amphitheater.

By this time we were up by the Via Garibaldi, looking

for a restaurant, and beyond the garden was a horrid grand one with a light-green sign saying "ORCHESTRE." Fancy an orchestra—in Padua; and from the large windows, the idle faces of lunchers stared and laughed.

Padua shouldn't stare. . . . Misliking the faces, we turned abruptly round. But the rain was slackening, and across a paved space we saw a decent-looking *trattoria*—a striped awning, a woman with a white napkin in the open door, a glimpse of oranges on a white-clothed table.

"Won't that do?" said Babs; and steered for the red-and-white awning, whose edges exceedingly dripped.

We made a bolt inside. Sawdust on the floor, a welcome from a polite padrone in an apron; we liked our *trattoria.* The keen wind and storm had made us hungry; we had marvelous oily ravioli, of which a lusty, blond peasant-farmer—or drover (to judge by his powerful build, jolly red face, and weather-beaten but adequate clothes) was also partaking; then while listening to his jolly talk with the padrone (he had, it seems, been bringing in a load of calves to the market), we had *frutti* and all sorts of things, ending with great cups of *caffè latte,* all garnished with courtesy and kind attentions . . . in fact I have a pleasant, blond memory of the whole place; blue aprons, white linen, crusty golden bread, oranges in piles. A peasant youth looked at us once or twice, but with vast respect; the gay drover, luminous with wine as was his world just then, toned down his tremendous voice and conveyed to us some few comments on the weather.

"Tempo orribile!" he pronounced, smiling tremendously at us; stamping his great boots under the table, shoving, with a giant's gesture, his hat further back upon his head. Whatever he did was tremendous; he would have been almost alarming, had it not been for his good nature.

"Molto fango!" he shouted; but I was quite up on mud (of which we had been through a good deal that day) and could answer with some surety; at which our good neighbor burst absolutely into fugues.

We quite understood him! Perhaps farming Italian was our sort; at any rate the dear soul seemed to think it was and had a beautiful time, and so did we; so apparently did the padrone and his wife, and a rustic *convivale* or two, who joined in. It was a social occasion. With a great sense of achievement, and great appreciation of every one's kindliness, we rose to go. . . . Vastly un-Paduan, that *trattoria;* little of "*la dotta*" could be recognized in those plain-spoken guests from the farms outside; but we had liked their society.

The rain had ceased, and brightness lay upon the pools in the paving; in the smooth brown paths of the arena garden, a lean, bronzed old Italian was sweeping up white acacia-blossoms torn off by the storm. With the roses, and the old wall, it was a pretty sight. . . . Brooms, with us, are not much used out-of-doors; but they sweep, all over Italy. All over Europe, in fact. English gardeners are forever sweeping their paths; and this old Paduan, pausing in the collecting of long creamy frills of blossoms, smiled sociably at us. . . . Gardeners and roadmen are a cheery lot—especially roadmen; their labors are not too difficult; we had seen them lifting three small stones on a shovel and calling it a load, then looking expectantly up at us as we drove by.

"They seem to think every motorist ought to stop and say 'Cheerio'!" said my daughter.

But we had little time for locust-blossoms, and put Nicolette into the mazes of Padua. . . . Into its bits of scholarliness—such as were visible to the cruising eye; or crooking in and out of less crowded regions, where we followed Mantegna, and his mentor, Donatello. For that alert and vivid person, coming to Padua in the fifteenth century, was able to give it a new horizon of "liberty in artistic thought," Muirhead says, so that its school of art resisted, for a time at least, the powerful influence of Venice. . . . That was nice; so many things in this region had tried to resist Venice, and failed—bridges, and villa windows, and coats-of-arms; not to mention ourselves. . . .

The Byzantine look of Sant' Antonio, in its roomy square,

allured us, as did the whole, imposing piazza, where Donatello's huge equestrian figure of Gattamelata—an armored person on an armored charger—glorifies everything about it. It is nobly placed; there is room for mane-flyings, and document-extendings, and the curling of noble forelegs; and, like the horses of St. Mark's—or Verrochio's glorious figure near San Giorgio Maggiore—this conspicuous bronze, the first of its size cast in Italy after the Renaissance, was sent to Rome for safety during the World War. . . . We wondered where they put it.

After gazing at the bunched Byzantineness of Sant' Antonio's six domes (San Giustina had had eight), we went to look for Donatello within the great church, too—especially the "little wild player of cymbals." One rarely mistakes—or omits—a Donatello, and the little wild figure is full of charm.

"Worth tramping after!" said we, retiring swiftly down the long aisle. We loved a wild angel.

Nicolette, in a little ray of brightness, was waiting for us in the vast piazza; away we went, bumping gently over the mild Paduan cobbles, and around, once more, our cherished Romans, in their robes of stained marble, looking so benignly at us across the little bridges and the stream of clear brown water. We *may* see you again, Prato! said we, circling it fondly; if we come back this way . . . but it was four o'clock, and we scudded off across flat country and swollen rivers, with green hills interestingly on our left, and popped into Vincenza just as rain came down in torrents.

CHAPTER XXII

VICENZA IS NEAR VENICE

NOBODY goes to Vicenza. Everybody looks blank when you mention it.

"Vicenza? No, we didn't go there—?" with the little upward inflection which means "Now don't begin to be enthusiastic about something I don't know anything about!"

For we loved Vicenza from its first cobblestone, on; and at our first glimpse of that astounding spot, the Piazza dei Signori, we fairly gasped.

"Babs! It's like Venice."

"So it is! . . . The Doges' Palace!"

Really stirred, we forgot that we were making our way sharply down an unknown hill; all our architectural feelings were roused, and we craned our necks, narrowly missing a hand-pushed milk-cart full of bright copper cans with brass edges, also going downhill . . . but then the rain drove us remorselessly on.

The Albergo Cavaletto was a cheery place, even if in a stony hollow behind the piazza's architecture; it had plants and a welcoming air, and a dear old porter in a worn brown coat trimmed with gold; we were impressed, too, with our ecclesiastical furniture of inlaid wood, Gothic bed-heads, bureau-top and bedside tables, all carved, and all matching.

"No tin beds here!" said Babs, with a grin; for the north of Italy is fond of progress and dreadful new ideas, and our previous night had been oppressed not only by moats and mosquitoes but by metal furniture painted to resemble wood—and one doubly hates to lie awake in a bed that goes "bong!" when you move. Our quilts, too, were of gentle yellow satin instead of blaring red; and the north of Italy redounds with red.

Altogether we felt blessed and charmed; and outside our windows lay the Piazza dei Signori. Its rear portion, to be sure, rather the rear of its architecture; but who wants to be completely blazed-at in one's bedroom? Dusk was coming on and we stared, in the intervals of hair-brushing, at the piazza's classic pavement, from which rose dusky columns with golden edges; for here and there about the square were soft old lights. Just right for columns; right for Vicenza, too, and her evening quietude. . . . A worthwhile place for Sunday, and one that gave us no need or excuse for motoring away from it. . . . If it had been Ferrara, we shouldn't have stayed; and what a bore that would have been. For we felt like a bit of a breathing-spell before plunging into Venice; we knew, by the unexpected fervor of our feelings in Battaglia, that we should probably be done in and finished, this time, by Venice, and Vicenza was a good place in which to prepare oneself—to knock, as it were, the edge off a little—because of Palladio.

"Palladio by the mile," says Babs' Diary. Quite true. This last great architect of the later Renaissance is Vicenza's boast; he was born here, planned all her palaces and some of the loveliest churches in Venice, then returned to do Vicenza's basilica, a glimpse of whose windows had so taken our breaths the night before . . . the chief characteristic of his school, Baddy says, being "a studious adherence to impressive simplicity of form. . . ."

"Just so, Baddy," I said; and gazed out of the window.

This was next morning after breakfast. "Sunday after Ascension," says the diary; "rained—poured in buckets all day."

Babs was in a comfortable green-velvet chair by the other window; we watched, fascinated, the soaking silver veiling the columns and pounding upon the pavements, whence it bounded in a wild gray dance of "the little men," as we called its populous jumpings from anything stony. People had gathered to see the Italian flag go out—which, in spite of the rain, it did; drooping its great folds against the rainy columns, its colors magnificently becoming to the square; purple and gold streamers were hung from the balustrade—poor streamers!—and the decorations for the day were complete.

It was the wettest rain. In the midst of it a little boy in his Sunday best—blue suit, new straw hat with a blue-and-yellow band—dashed out from the arcade and the care of a sister to capture a wad of white paper; he picked it up and dashed back, laughing, to put it under a spout, or down-pipe, of the basilica. ("Spout very busy," say my notes.)

Soon it was white no longer, soon it was pulp, soon it was nothing; the spout had won, and the little boy, instructed by sister, and waving his straw hat to dry it, gave a leap of joy and was borne away.

The shower died down; there was peace for a time in the puddles of Vicenza. They even shone a little, in the yellowish way puddles have, with a sort of fleeting brightness; we went expectantly out. . . . The beauty of the colonnaded basilica held us for a time, but most of all I remember our surprise on turning into a narrow and darkish *contra* (as streets are called here) to see exquisite though dusky palaces lining it. . . . Utter quiet—the quiet of ages, in that street; a slight greening of moss on its pavement, even on the walls of the *palazzi;* and in their upper storey, placed rarely and with distinction, those same Venetian windows of romance.

Palladio by the mile, indeed. Vicenza's simpleness was a rest. We loved the lanes and the little old palaces; wandered on to the *museo,* where, in its three-cornered garden, with antique fragments scattered about, and the faded color of the museo's walls as background—a sort of *bois de rose*—the young wife of the custodian, herself rich in dusky beauty, a carnation tucked in the soft charcoal of her hair, insisted on picking us a whole sheaf of long-stemmed red roses, very fresh of foliage, from her rosebush by the old portal.

Everywhere we went, Vicenza was kind like that. Even the crowds assembled at every point to watch the scary rushing of the floods, were as unnoticing and friendly as if we had been old residents. It seemed a prosperous, contented, self-sufficing sort of place, untroubled by tourists, and with plenty of normal things for its people to do—not merely a huddle of abnormal picturesqueness, like many towns in southern Italy, useful for the traveler but hard on the inhabitants. . . . More and more we enjoyed Vicenza's twisting cosiness and pretty trees; its dipping streets ending in gardens or quaint bridges, its mountains jumping up, in such a lively way, all about it; and we enjoyed its mentality too . . . its psychic ego. . . . Even Palladio's architecture is affable. I always did like a two-storied town with its beauty down where you can see it, and mull over it; for then any belfry, or other aged thing that sticks up, has such effect.

Everything in these streets has its full value, therefore, and presents it to you with both hands . . . and if Vicenza can serve it up on roses, or across a vivid garden with a twist of river to run wetly through it, so much the better.

She finds it easy to do that, thanks to the Retrone and Bacchiglione within her—dear, verdant-edged and convoluting streams, both owning plenty of militant water; and in this May freshet, the rise of it in an hour or two was unbelievable.

Sand-bags, piled at corners, were being inundated, lawns and gardens disappearing under the disconcerting yellow floods; one or two bridges were already under water.

Should we be held, in Vicenza?

The crowd was being kept back from the one bridge, the Ponte degli Angeli, over which lay our road to Venice; for every moment new motorfuls of excited Italians raced up, and deposited spectators. Girls, gay in Sunday pink or scarlet, rushed about holding each other's arms and shrieking; everybody confided, or shouted, the worst to everybody else; it was delightful; the authorities might worry, but Vicenza's citizens, pointing out horrors and clutching each other, were having a glorious time.

The lakes in the piazza were undiminished, as we returned; sawdust was thick on the marble of the hall floor, and Babs, twirling gaily at the stairs, slipped on that treacherous footing and fell flat. In the sawdust! The old porter dusted her, stockings and all, with such concern. . . .

"Sticky, getting started to Treviso," says the diary.

The floods had fortunately subsided but their muddy traces were left, and Nicolette's tail slipped and slewed as, hurrying across the Ponte dei Angeli, we twisted through the Porta San Lucia and out into the dyked road beyond. . . . And then it all grew so lovely that I took notes as we drove.

Glimpse of mountains! Wonderful blue and white day. Sun just right, with the top down. River gone down, but all fields flooded. Poor beans and leeks, looking up at us through a foot or two of clear water! Pretty torrents by our dyked road; children and ducks having wonderful time in the floods. Ducks swimming in and out of rows of bright-green vines, in vineyards. Women busy on edge of things—washing in flood. One of them (in faded blue, and lilac apron; fruit trees over her, sunshine flickering through) was dipping clothes in a stream by her door—a stream never meant to be there, but deep enough now for energetic dipping. . . . She looked up at us, smiling.

Lovely trees here. More green in sky, as we go north! Branches and twigs allowed. Locusts not shedding here, as in Padua; blossoms beautiful among gray-green foliage.

Fragrant. . . . Every sort of team in road.

For this was the land of tiny donkeys and their two-wheeled carts. One white one, all curly, came placidly dotting his little steps along, a dear old peasant and his equally sweet and smiling old wife sitting side by side in the cart. All three looked complacently at us. . . . It was a region of serenity. Just this one road, which everybody followed; so no one could get lost, and everybody met everybody. We felt exceedingly serene, ourselves.

"We've got our two jobs pretty well in hand now," said Babs, smiling at me as we passed a shrine; "I drive in Italy with calm, you find our way with great calm!"

More donkeys we met, paddling valiantly along in the

drying mud; was there to be an event of some sort in Vicenza? Perhaps they were all going in to see the sand-bags. But there were floods everywhere; maybe they were just doing marketing, in those tiny carts.

"Crossed the Brenta. At Fontaniva, beautiful old brick campanile beside a white church. Charming, in sunlight." Beyond this was flat green country, then— "Wonderful wall and gate of Cittadella."

We slowed down. Oh, for water-colors; for anything that would show that medieval island of a town, its round wall rising from meadows, under a brilliant sky; the rose-red battlements, the wide, gently-circling moat with shining water in it, and rose-red reflections; poplars on its banks; then the miniature view through its huge old Gate . . . for inside there was a market going on. . . . Ah, this was where the donkey-carts were coming from.

And it was all a perfect surprise. None of our friends had mentioned Cittadella. Baddy mentions the fact that in the cathedral is a "Last Supper" by Jacopo Bassano—by which one infers that there is a cathedral; Muirhead says, "a picturesque walled town"; but that falls a million miles short of Cittadella. We joggled amazedly through the great gate, and at once into the market—which filled the town from edge to edge. Wooden things came first, tubs and chairs and baskets—a whole acreage of tubs; then the street swelled out into a square. We edged gently through dry-goods—bright-colored stuffs, under awnings—then through booths of straw hats; hats of every color, laid on canvases in the roadway or under a small arcade. We wondered who would buy so many.

The crowds were not bad at all, or over-merry; this was a sedate northern market. There were knots of peasants here and there—"bright-looking people, brown-haired and gray-eyed, as often as dark," the notes say.

Nicolette made her way very comfortably along. We went slowly, wishing to take in this sight—the home industries of Venetia, evidently; those hats and baskets were made by peasant-women sitting in their doorways, as we had seen them—keeping an eye meanwhile on the pot of *fagiuoli* stewing on the charcoal fire. . . . And the tubs and chairs were handmade, too, nicely solid and simple. We could have used some of those chairs on the farm; went by with regret.

Cittadella, like Vicenza, had the air of never having seen a tourist—of never having conceived the species; of being a normal, self-sufficing place with industries of its own, and gave us a happy feeling, just driving through it. It was one's ideal of a little medieval town—"moat and all," the notes say. "Loveliest color; a perfect water-color everywhere. Its gardens and fields were just outside—and the freshest green; locusts, full brooks, mountains just under the edge of pearly clouds . . . lovely peaky ones, velvet-blue—or moss-rose green in streaks of sun."

We came out upon all this through the second *porta,* where a ravishingly beautiful girl in peasant dress was offering green-and-silver leeks from a basket on her arm—a fitting farewell for Cittadella; beyond her, in a corner of the gate, two fat little yellow calves were tethered comfortably in the shade. Animals, as well as peasants, were well conditioned here; we met a fat and shiny donkey, just outside, who reared with the greatest spirit. Babs laughed, seeing him in her mirror.

A road led northward from ours; the road to Bassano. Napoleon, interfering with other people's destinies as usual, defeated the Austrians there in September, 1796, "having marched hither from Trent in two days." Marched? He rode, and his army tramped. "The covered wooden bridge over the Brenta"—we had crossed that stream a few miles back—"occupies the place of one which the French blew up on that occasion"; and this fine bridge, of a single arch, was designed by Canova, and built with money which he left for that purpose. A public-spirited artist, Canova; even his name has a noble ring to it.

This region, like Provence, beseiged one with detours. Straight north from Vicenza was a road to Torrebelvicino

(Tower of the Beautiful Neighborhood!), off in the edge of the Dolomites; and now, only fourteen kilometers away, was this birthplace of Jacopo (Bassano), containing most of his works, and those of his father, Francesco, and of his son, Leandro—nice family party; "a charmingly situated town . . . surrounded by old ivy-clad walls. The houses of the market-place show some interesting remains of the early façade painting which was so common in the towns of the Venetian Terra Ferma."

A new term to us. We were glad to know Venice had some; and the façade painting sounded seductive. . . . Well, we should see some of that in Treviso. *Avanti!*

Lovely farm-houses now reposed by our dyked and shady road—or below it, nestled among vineyards; mellow houses, each with a grape-vine trained carefully over it, every shoot where it should be, also with beautiful old stone flights of outside stairs and charming arched openings, like loggias. These houses were mostly rose and lavender, with blue patterns from the spray; fascinating implements sat about under the arches. . . . Oh dear, this road; painters should have been painting it by the mile . . . and its flowers and gardens, sunshine and shadow; the brookfuls of white, yellow-billed ducks, the little donkeys poking their noses out from behind a grape-vine or a soft pink wall.

Castelfranco was a rose-red island too, with its ornately battlemented wall rising from bright-green meadows—and a most moving moat. . . . Not quite so perfect as Cittadella, since it had been unwise enough, on its further side, to grow a little outside its wall; were we getting fussy about our medievalism? Quite a town, it considered itself, within the wall: *Albergo Roma!* said a sign; *bagni, garage, ternie!* —whatever that last may be. At any rate one could stay in Castelfranco; and again, we had never heard of it.

At the end of this fine street came the eastern gate; the show gate, one judged, splendid, clock-towered, and machicolated, with the winged lion of Venice conspicuous upon it in white stone. Perhaps Venice built it; it was at her end.

And then in a wink we were in the open country.

The lovely winding road again, locusts so charming, mountains keeping track of us, then shying off. . . . Toward noon the roads became clear; every donkey was having a siesta, and we could have hastened; but Nicolette was "skipping."

"Carburetor I expect," said Babs easily; "we'll have her all done, you know—in Mestre."

Feeling somehow quite secure with this idea of spare time ahead of us, we drove placidly along. We hadn't had a day like this for a long time, it seemed—with just such mountains and vineyards; since Massa, perhaps. The poplars were still allowed to be spreading trees, and beneath their shade were the most remarkable shrines: no small, weather-beaten fresco or little plaster figure framed in a wooden box, but much-dressed Virgins, one after another, set back within deep frames and almost life sized, usually in brilliant red and blue robes. Little cupids with silvery wings were dangling beside one of them; this Virgin was attired in purple and rose-color, trimmed with tinsel, and had curtains guardingly around her . . . 'mustn't fade the Madonna!

Often, in this part of our drive, a campanile would be seen rearing against sky and mountains. "Every little town had a grand one. Big bells." Venice had one, these soaring outlines seemed to say; what was a village without a campanile? Venice, Venice—and your outstretched arm. . . .

But farm-houses faded; fields began to wave up and down and have woods. Estates set in. Luxurious ducal estates of the sixteenth century, these were, with rich-looking farms.

One after another these estates came into view, looking not only columned and magnificent, but spruce as to lands and buildings. Dairying, of a ducal sort, must be profitable here; and fine herds were in the fields. Concealed cows are common enough throughout Italy, cows living inside dark little stables, yet producing calves that grow up to be the enormous white oxen—strange, we said, that they ever could grow, raised in the dark like that; but where Italy does any visible dairying, she does it superbly and on an enormous scale. Nicolette forgot her desire to skip and went evenly along; the roads, of smooth gray gravel, were good here; we leaned back, appreciating our upholstery. (On some roads you forget you have any, and sit up as straight as possible, bouncing.)

"Treviso—nice old gate as usual," say the notes. We drove through empty streets, then a crowded one, from which we turned into the great Piazza del Duomo, with its enormous cream-colored church. We had decided to have a last roadside lunch, before going where no roadsides were, and crept on down the sunny sloping yellow piazza, looking for shops. Were they all closed for siesta?

No. We perceived a sardine tin protruding under the edge of an awning, the red-brown kind that hangs straight down and is very preventive on looking in, as well as against sun—Italy is strong on awnings—and found a nice shop, clean and prettily arranged. The padrone had a great stock of delicacies, tinned and otherwise; he put up my parcels with expedition, and told me where *pane* was—just up a cobblestoned lane, the Via Ricati, round the corner; a lovely clean bakery it was, smelling of crusts. Such warm smiles, from the good old proprietress, went with my crusty loaf; I was shown benedictorily to the door and went out, wishing Babs had been with me. (The Via Ricati had the sweetest roofs against the sky, balconies, and a bit of façade-painting.)

But Nicolette had followed me, and was waiting outside; we both stared at the little street. Poor Treviso! It is a town of painted gables and bomb holes. The Austrians had dropped fifteen hundred bombs on it, and the façades of the precious houses were a good deal damaged . . . "especially during the last year of the struggle, when Treviso stood midway between Venice and the Piave front."

That fateful river, we found, was only a few miles away, running down from the Carnichian Alps and the wild slopes of Monte Paralba—white with snow they would still be; crooking on through magnificent Alpine scenery, past Monte Schiara and a succession of *cols,* down into the plain, then taking itself and all its woes into the Adriatic, just above Venice. Those who have read *Farewell to Arms* will never forget the Piave.

Treviso sees two little rivers twist about and then meet, within her—the Sile and the Botteniga; also a winding canal or two diversify her quaint streets, so that one is always crossing water-ways.

"Nosed our narrow way out," say the notes. For we headed Nicolette across a series of small bridges into a most narrow stony turn, or stony squirm, in the last one—in which we prayed to meet nothing and nobody, and did not, except a luckily slim young priest who shriveled himself and his cassock into a sort of crease in the wall, and was slender enough to escape. Then we were out at last upon the veritable way to Mestre. We are always going to edges, panting as we go; and Mestre was an edge that—oh well! We had to lunch first. We would keep an eye out for a place. . . .

"Road to Venice!" say the notes. It was lovely, stealing upon her by road. A straight, widish, quite unsentimental road at first, not very well cared for, and escorted by shrubbery-strangled estates whose rather mouldy houses peered at us out of nests of shrouding foliage. . . . It was not far to Mestre; we began to wonder—should we find any lunch-nook at all? Ha! was that a side-road beyond? It was; or a side-lane, tree-shadowed, and across a small brown brook.

"Sweet place after all," murmured Babs; and swung in.

The lane was damp, so we ate in Nicolette, trying hard to be calm, and much pleased by the behavior of passers-by. Bicyclists were especially polite; they maneuvered past, apparently not noticing us; a little boy walked very closely by, simply dying with curiosity—indeed, I could see the hard-held flick of his nearest eye—but never once looking over Nicolette's rim, which he might so easily have done.

Putting away some uneaten lunch, we backed out into the road again. . . . "More villas; a shower from a round cloud just overhead, then Mestre and mud," say the notes.

Tooling along the slimy road into Mestre's grimy outskirts—heavens, was this what the town was like?—we saw three long-legged and shabby-looking youths leap out from beside a bridge and come racing toward us; to our amazement and disgust, they all three leaped on the running-board and leaned impudently in, sticking their ragged elbows into us, breathing in our very faces, shouting in barbaric young voices . . . *What* was this? The eldest of them, clinging to Nicolette's door, a wild-eyed ruffian of a lad with a hoarse voice, was on my side.

"*Vade via!*" I cried indignantly, shrinking back from his odoriferous shirt-sleeve; but though I commanded and Babs frowned, he clung the tighter and bawled the louder.

"*Gar—aage, signora! S'nora, molto buono! Ec-co, signora! G'rage moderno!*" and so on.

I understood. These howling young wolves had been set upon us to advertise a garage; just as I was thinking we should never be rid of them—and longing to do something really ferocious, like pushing them backwards into a ditch, —two more raced out to us, the three jumped off and began a passionate quarrel with them, Babs stepped adroitly on the accelerator—and we darted along, free at last.

Whoof! That had been an unsavory welcome to Mestre, and a dismaying demonstration of its methods; but as we swung the wide corner by the station, behold a row of most dignified petrol-pumps, and tall board-fences very soothingly surrounding the big clean yards of garages.

"Looks as if any of these would do!" said Babs with relief; and whirled into a yard.

Everything was most official. A lock-box for Nicolette, to which only ourselves (said they) had the key, and into which we drove her . . . scarcely realizing, until the actual moment, that this meant separation; we locked her beloved pockets, folded the rug, seized the smaller suit-case (especially and craftily packed for this occasion) and tore ourselves away. . . .

Strange, to be walking across the same damp cinders we had just driven in on; strange to be buying a railway ticket—*"Due per Venezia* . . . third class will do, won't it?" muttered Babs, hurriedly stuffing things in her pockets; stranger still to see a funny short train waiting, some distance down the tracks, and to have the guard racing up the platform, smiling affectionately but calling to us as he raced, *"Partire—signora! partire subito!"* and hurrying wildly to catch the little puffing thing . . . (It ran often; but why waste an hour, a moment—in Venice?) Babs caught up the suit-case and fled before me; I galloped after her.

Stones flew behind my child's athletic leaps—there was blue cracked stone between the tracks—but we never stopped for a wooden crossing; up steep little steps—bang! went the suit-case on the platform, and just as the train started, into funny little wooden seats we subsided, breathless. . . . Great fun to hurry; we had hurried so little on this trip.

"Jolly little train," said Babs, beaming at me as it lurched importantly along. "Suppose we *might* have gone first, Mummy. . . . D'you mind these wooden seats?"

"Love 'em!" I said. "Anything for variety, you know. . . . Wasn't it luck we caught it? I can still see your skirts flying down that track, my dear. And stones! You did make time."

"So did you! Yes, I was bound we'd make it. Decent of that guard to run and tell us, wasn't it. . . . Look, A.B.!"

For marshes were going by. Water was coming . . . low lagoons, then a clear shallow rippling. We were surrounded by water. Far across it lay a low, blue-gray nubbly line.

" 'Venice rising from the sea,' " I said. "But not very far! Doesn't look much from here, does it—" and Babs smiled; a blissful smile.

"Not yet," said she.

We gazed fixedly across the rippling water.

"Isn't that domes sticking up?"

" 'Expect it is . . ." and I felt myself sighing a long sigh of content. Venice! She hides herself nicely from you, but it was she; just those nubs; the bits of half-seen domes. It was raining a little, but never mind; before we had really relaxed from our train-catching, we slid under a platform roof and halted.

Half in a daze, we dismounted.

A tenor warble from the cab of the engine, a handsome young face smiling down at us—a face that went with the voice—was our welcome to Venice. Holding very tight to our bag we marched through the station's dusky rooms; such freedom, with that one bit of luggage. A big, arched opening—a somehow watery light—there was the canal before us, and a wall of porters waiting. Ignoring them, we picked out in the most superior manner our own gondola from a number of them bobbing at the steps—how wonderful they looked!—stepped proudly in upon its red carpet, sat grandly down . . . and floated off.

Ah! Black seats and little brass horses, black prow so far ahead of us—how right this was; how delicious, this watery way of being rowed from the station . . . no, not rowed, but swept melodiously along, with yowls when we wanted to pass anybody. Such a simple way of getting to one's hotel . . . whereat in a moment we were looking at each other at first blankly, then with great amusement; both of us had forgotten the name. At the steps, I had simply said *"Avanti —Schiavone!"* to the gondolier, so as to get off as quickly as possible; I knew I had forgotten the name but thought Babs knew it, of course—she always did; and now—ha ha!

For a pair of traveling English friends had casually told us of the place two years ago; and we had not written it down.

Well, we'd know it when we saw it. We were sure we should know it; and the gondolier, obviously thinking us a little mad, did as I directed: kept on rowing toward the Schiavone. We met frequent launches dashing along, their flags and varnish cursing with everything, their wakes slapping at aged palaces; madly rocking the waiting gondolas at their doors, profanely splashing at the old, shallow, marble steps on which, with unfailing charm, the water of the Adriatic gently rose and sank. . . . But the rain had stopped.

"See—a bit of blue!" said Babs pointing. Venice "seemed better than we remembered," my notes say. "So much color. Gardens! Palaces more delicious."

And the quietness of this splashing along. . . . We swished past the ever-glorious whiteness of the fish-market; confronted the Rialto and were staring at it, rejoiced to see it again—far more rejoiced than we had expected to be—when, with one push of the great oar, we were switched into a dark side canal.

"Perchè?" I asked—we didn't feel like side canals; and the gondolier, reducing his showy pace to one more applicable to narrowness and corners, explained that it was shorter.

We moved soothingly along. No wakes here, no modernness. Silence and age, water-worn steps; a tiny piazza with a bridge. . . . *"O -hè!"* Right-turn, on and on; a shadowy bit with green mouldering old walls and (*"O -hè!"*) ineffable dusky doorways. More corners, on and on; another vigorous swing (the gondolier was hastening now) and there were Gothicness, white marble, and a bit of bright blue beyond. Good man, to bring us out this way . . . The Ponte dei Sospiri was over our heads, beside us a dreadfulness of dungeon windows, heavily barred; San Giorgio across the water, magnificent steps, magnificent everything, a sea of rocking gondolas—and here we were, out by the Palace and the Schiavone.

Really, how splendid it all was . . . and now seriously, *what* was the name of that hotel? We felt suddenly rather lost, sloshing along out in the broadening lagoon, among the active little steamboats, with a scandalized gondolier rowing more and more slowly, and wishing to land us somewhere. The hotel we wanted was beyond the one we were in before . . . it was not the Danieli, as our gondolier, with hope in his eye, had suggested; but we'd know it when we saw it. Ah—Yes! *Là, là!* I waved joyfully at the boatman. There it was, its sweet Gothic windows and nice narrow little front looking so choice; the Beau Rivage, of course.

In an instant the old landing-man was hooking us to the

steps, and a surprised porter was rushing out. Had we engaged rooms? No? Whereat he helped us out, in great amazement. We paid everybody too much, and inside glass doors a dark-eyed padrone, quite unsurprised, was welcoming us as cordially as if we were old friends. Yes, by good chance he had one room left—just one, looking out on the lagoon; and we caught each other's eye. That was what happened to the Dovers. They came here, unannounced, and got a perfectly lovely room. Dear me, how remarkable!

Ecstatically we climbed, behind the elaborate porter, a flight of crimson-carpeted stairs, and were ushered in. The door closed; we rushed into each other's arms.

"Darling—what luck."

"Just *look* out of this window!"

We ran to it. There it was, everything we had come for; with Victor Emanuel and his horse so gorgeously being a foreground to it, yet just not in the way. What luck—oh lamb, what luck.

"Gondola to hotel," relates the diary. "Tea, St. Marks, dinner, gondola, divine evening—" a list almost sufficient in itself. Blissful but swift tea in the piazza, a straightaway for the doors of San Marco—my child leading with her long stride; a stunned halt within the doors, gradual recovery of breath, a quiet going here and there among the dusky gilded glories. A crimson light or two came out in the flickering silver row above the grille, candles bloomed from some of the chapels; I thought the face beside me lovely in their glow.

Wherever light was, the walls gleamed; then vanished into dusk. . . . The little *duomo* is magical at such an hour. We stayed till all grew evening-like—till lights were really lights, not mere color-enhancement; then strolled out, pausing at the door as always, to look affectionately back. Outside, a new and empurpled air was in charge of the piazza; a different Venice, this, from the daytime one we had lately left. . . . The whole great space was drenched with lavender, fringed with dottings of pale gold; beyond, through the *piazzetta's* opening, a dark-blue lagoon was exquisitely splashing, with the light-touched, wing-summited column of St. Mark's clear-drawn upon it; to the left an exquisiteness of palace-columns, tinted with afterglow, and opposite, the noble shadowed perspective of the Libreria.

Thus unspeakably escorted, we paced toward that opening where one feels the breath of the sea. Gondolas were thickly flapping, the waters darkening—but with a gleam; was it a brightness of architecture still glinting there, the water, all to itself, celebrating the last daylight . . . or just Venice being indescribable? We agreed that it was probably just that; sauntered along an empty Schiavone, with the lights of San Giorgio looking sociably across; past the King on his rearing horse, darkly splendid against an evening sky; and so to dinner.

The night turned strangely cool, but, panoplied with winter coats we walked out past the brilliance of the *piazzetta,* one spot where Venice has said to herself, "Well, I'll be light here anyway!"—then along the garden (we like that quieter bit) and found "a small gondola with no nose," my notes say, for an evening rock on the canal; the inevitable, looked-forward-to rock. . . . We liked our little boat, and the honest-looking Italian who rowed it—very brown he was, and with a cheerful snub-nose; asking him not to go too near the *musica,* we were given a push by one of those grumpy old men always found on Venetian steps—one feels, at times, that Venice is made of old men—and floated off. . . . Is there any motion so lovely?

Far away the song-gondolas were already making a warm orange spot on the dark waters, also very hot sounds; it seemed, when scraps of their tenor orgies were wafted to us on the wind, that the temperature of that bit of the lagoon where they nightly sit—or is it the Giudecca, out there?—must be permanently raised. We were wary of them.

Warily we were sculled up and down, the water slapping and lapping; past a romantic Salute with domes very dark, gold on its doorways; up a moonlit canal, deserted and lone —palaces all dark, a moon dodging the clouds, swift beams and shadows beautifully chasing each other across the blue-black and silver that is Venice at night . . . then swinging about to see Venice golden-edged, her waters sparkling with gold. Chilly, infinitely contented, we leaned closer to each other, in a little league against the breezes; asked the gondolier to stop a while, and just looked. . . . Who does not, on a night-lagoon? Those shapes on shore; hints of them on the water—columns, mazy with gold, laid down in twinkles and glitters. . . .

The whole lagoon glittered. Gleams sparkled toward us at a great and promising pace; broke, sparkled again, and ran the more swiftly at us, to be lost in our craft's shadow. Poor gleams, they meant to land in our laps; and across them (if we drifted at all near), across domes, and water-music, and all—a part, by now, of Venice's evening architecture, of her very air, came the rasping nasal melodies from those song-boats.

When that happened, I said a word over my shoulder; the gondolier obediently dug in his oar, marveling at our taste meanwhile—he would have liked, of course, to be near the excitements of that heaving, orange spot—and shot us, with one stroke, toward duskiness and peace.

That was grand. We were especially glad when it was toward San Giorgio—San Giorgio's columns were so wonderful, rising there in aloof Palladian majesty yet collecting, whether they wanted to or not, a slight warmth and obviousness from the mere, unaristocratic, jostlings of the tides below— "Almost a vulgar glitter, my dear!" I fancied one great white stately beauty saying to another as she held, so high and still in air, her faultless, white, Corinthian curls . . . (Is Palladio Corinthian? I have a very Corinthian feeling about that front, but am dim about details. So is Muirhead.)

We were very quiet, watching; so was our nice gondolier, rowing us with perfect gentleness, whatever his opinions; his rugged face and bronzed throat touched by the lights as nicely as any column. At last we asked to be taken back. Wafted shoreward with swift and apparently rejoicing strokes we were hooked up to the same dusky steps; rewarded our deserving friend, also friend's friend who did the hooking, and staggered away, soothed to beautiful sleepiness by the Adriatic air; by the rocking, the dusk, the gold, the lappings —everything seen, unseen, or half-seen that one had been absorbing with greedy pores. A very ordinary evening, for Venice; but is one in Venice every moment?

And until you have stepped into a gondola and are once more gliding on those age-escorted waters, you do not remember how it will seize you. Venice, her lights and waters . . . different from all other lights and waters; in their own way they approach you . . . in a night-dream all their own, they fade away. And if it had not been for that bridge at Battaglia, we should have missed all this. Neither of us could imagine staying long here, or doing work; but for exquisite drifting about, for looking and re-living, it is *the* place.

We woke to a bright day, and a stuffy feeling in the head. Intending to walk this affliction off, we didn't help it by first standing about in the raw wind of morning, watching two thousand tourists (or so it seemed to us) land from a boat that had come in in the night. "Ship from Egypt," say the notes. "Disembarkation of tourists in fleets of gondolas with ship's flags. Tremendous time to disembark them."

When we went out, the first ones were climbing onto our *riva* and looking about them with pleased eyes. We walked on, at last, and spent the rest of the morning in the *accademia* —coming out rather dazed, after all the Bellini and their ilk, and taking the little hustling steamer—and on our way back we passed the first instalment of that fleet of tourists rocking in the canal just outside the Salute, six to a gondola, waiting their turn to land. . . . All along the lagoon we met relays of them, just starting out; it was lunch-time, then. At the quai-edge, the very last ones were coming ashore; and a small crowd of patient ones, trying to make feeble jokes while their faces turned lavender-blue and their raiment fluttered in the cold wind from the Adriatic, were still standing about waiting to be taken off in the sight-seeing gondolas. . . .

For they were brought ashore in one fleet, and laboriously transferred to another. And they were to have two days in Venice.

"Poor things," said Babs, as we turned away: "I wouldn't do that, if I were paid to. . . ."

And from our room, with wonder and compassion, we regarded anew the big gray ship. Very nice she looked out there, with her flags flying; a great addition to the shipping of the lagoon; but—our scooting little Nicolette! the blessedness of going where we wanted to when we wanted to! We sighed; and went down to an excellent lunch.

On our visit here two years before, we had explored a great deal on foot. Baddy expanded on the extent and interest of the walking to be done, in this city of waterways, so map in hand, we plunged into her labyrinths. Not without their thrill, these *calli,* some five feet wide or less, with the peril of windows above from which a pailful of slops might be cast upon your head; in the darkest ones we admittedly hurried, catching a breath both of air and relief on coming out into a shut-in *piazzetta,* or upon a little canal. Sometimes a sudden turn would bring us to a church-front or an old palace, gazing rather blankly on its little waterway . . . and we could hardly bear the bridges, the vistas from them were so unforgettable. One of our pictures, almost the only one that captured some of Venice's romantic feeling, was taken from a bridge.

The peak and summit of these walks was usually S.S. Giovanni e Paolo and the ample pavement of its square, where lovely old women sat with baskets of oranges under their great umbrellas. We were quite divided between the church and the look up its little canal to the shining aquamarine of the bay—where the red sails of fishing-boats came by, or fleets of them went drifting out, past the mirage-like islands, toward the Alps. . . . Never was such shining water as on that flat, flat shallow bay. On a bright day it shone like glass; on a gray one it still remembered that brilliance, and brought down silver and lemon-yellow, or pearly white, from the sky. . . . There was also the arched bridge below which the gondoliers were always congregated, gabbling together, or prinking up their craft; across it we discovered a most useful little street. It was ten feet wide at least; it had fruit and book-shops, and vegetables, and a stall for flowers. Melted by the freshness and fragrance of the narcissi—so white and pure in these lanes—and overjoyed by the few lire asked for them, we carried off a bunch; we knew we should love them in our room, but long before reaching that haven they proved their value. Going through one of the worst of the *calli,* I buried my nose in them, then hastily offered them to Babs; and this became part of our regular program.

"Pass the flowers!"

But today it was to be canals; the *piccoli canali,* Venice's Left Bank, always beckoning us, unexplored. We found a noseless gondola again; took no flowers with us, having faith in the airiness of *canali* as compared to *calli,* and our boatman, though not the one of the night before, was similarly snub-nosed and burnt just as beautiful a golden brown. We made our bargain with him, then—*"Sinistra!"* I told him, *"piccoli canali!"* and he nodded and grinned, setting off with the purposeful, magnificent stroke which all gondoliers practice along the lagoon.

There was a brisk breeze and colors were at their liveliest; waves were hopping up and down in a most stimulating fashion, as was the fleet of gondolas moored before the *piazzetta.* Not altogether a banal composition; I sprang up, set a foot on the gunwale and, just as a wave gave us a large lurch, took a picture.

"Look *out!*" said Babs, "don't fall in, A.B.!"

I laughed and took another, then fell—but back upon the seat.

Great fun, having the lagoon so frisky; we sat up, enjoying the slaps and splashings. Such a tonic, dark blue day; it made one felt like seizing the oar and doing the rowing. . . .

And colors seemed brighter, every stroke the gondolier

AN ANIMATED HOUR, AT THE MOLO

Venice

took. The canal sea-blue and emerald, dashed with brightness from the palaces, and vivid, even in shadow, with flashes of silver; azure and emerald complementing the warm tints of the gaudy mooring-poles, then disappearing, with a certain darkening of shadow and quieting of waves, between the walls of side canals.

Their high walls now closed about us, walls at first rosy or orange, then quieter, less beautiful in tint; on and on, under bridges and round corners we went, losing direction entirely —almost losing a feeling of Venice. "Slums and industries mostly," say my notes. The wide doors of workshops were open, on a level with our heads, along these canals; woodworking seemed a favorite industry, and shavings floated lazily about. . . .

Venetian slums are less obvious than those of ordinary cities, being less articulate; there is a hush, a blankness, about them. No children play in the watery streets, few inhabitants lean from the rare windows; but the occasional doorways did look slummy. They had no Gothic ornament, no ameliorating gardens showed above the old walls; Palladio had been busy elsewhere. For this is not a region of run-down splendor, Venice's magnificence is magnificent still; we began to discover why so little is said about this Left Bank. There is little to say! Its ways are somnolent; one floats along in a sort of inferior dream.

Yet it was interesting to know it was blank, if it was. "Enjoyed slipping out of it into select region, up near station," the notes say. Bits of beauty seemed newly remarkable; our gondolier, now aiming homeward and feeling discursive, told us nearly all the things we knew before. He showed us Byron's villa and Desdemona's (presumable) palace—which Baedeker does not mention; a slim, graceful one with embroidered windows. Those windows, we thought, had a yearning look; was Desdemona sorry to leave it—if it *was* her palace? Byron, however, should have had a more floral front on his *palazzo,* the poet not being one to hide his romance, or his magnificence . . . probably it was all in the rear. This is a rather plain bit of the canal, too, leading straight, and a trifle bleakly, from the Rialto. Yes, Byron belonged in a pink-and-white curly one, we agreed; Venice has plenty such, and it is a pity they and he did not coincide. But plain old *palazzi* have their purposes; that famous fighter, Doge Enrico Dandolo, Admiral of the Venetian fleet (and the first person to use carrier-pigeons), had lived in a very simple little one, farther on.

It was pleasant, by the way, to realize that Doges were ever admirals, or generals; during a childhood's visit, I had pictured them merely as proud creatures in velvet robes who did little but sit on gold-fringed cushions and send people across the Bridge of Sighs; and behold them, warriors subduing the East! Cuirasses instead of cushions; galleys and the difficult seas. Yet my childish horror and hatred of the dungeons in their infernal palace are vivid still; it is not hard, even now, to loathe a Doge.

Returning, we had a fine battle with the gondolier about the fare—which he wished to increase by half. The old person with the boat-hook was appealed to and backed up his comrade, barking out short, crusty asseverations in wrathful Italian. . . . Of course! all that distance, rowing and rowing. *Sempre, sempre, tutto il mattine!* Of *course* it should be more—than the price agreed upon.

"*Non basta!* No no!" and they shook their heads sourly.

The opinion of the molo seemed to be against us, in the offing I could see other gondoliers pricking an ear and preparing to come over; soon the dark, gesturing crowds would be about us—it was simply too much fuss; we put the lire in his conscienceless brown hand and stalked off.

"Beast, wasn't he?" muttered Babs, looking very disgustedly at the winged column.

For there had been an ugliness about this encounter; none of the smiling wiles, the hands laid on the heart, the sweetly persuasive guile of southern Italy. Gondoliers were a bad lot, we agreed; desperadoes with sashes on; good-looking brigands! For we had been determined not to pay those unjust lire, yet we had paid them; a submission which did not taste well in the mouth. . . . Pah! we'd have some tea.

We stalked past the Piazzetta, still casting glances of dudgeon at its innocent architecture, and reached the beginnings of our *riva.* Why not sit here? we asked each other.

"Detestable tea on the riva!" say the notes. But any tea was inspiriting with the lagoon to look at, and afternoon Venice going by. We had sat down to dark clouds over the Salute, and rose in a gentle drizzle, making for San Marco. Beautiful, everything about the piazza; we got damp, staring at it, then took sanctuary in the cathedral. It was wonderful, in that gloom. We had a heavenly time with details; Babs knew what everything was.

"Stone in marble, you know—very difficult!" she said, leaning affectionately over a bit of marble inlay. . . .

I didn't know, but was charmed to find out; and was led to a little Gothic banister near by. It was also of marble, and like a cloister in design. There are few places where one really cares for marble—a substance that seems to need just the right treatment . . . too brown and mottled, one finds it, in restaurants in London, too cold a blue-white in our libraries, excepting the one in Boston; in Venice it seems to have found its real home, and the detail is always exquisitely worked. Color and all, this little banister was most satisfying—a porphyry-like purple, with pale dove-colored, or lilac, inlay; it and adjacent charms delayed us till shadows were falling thick in the corners of the *duomo,* and our damp ankles grew chilly. Shivering, we hurried out; and our landlord, whom we met in the hall, was all sympathy and concern; indeed gloriously, expressively *simpatico.*

"Si si!" indignantly; this weather was *"brutto"!* It was *"come Novembre, non Maggio!"* (like November, not May!) he cried, spreading out both arms in a generous expostulation with fate. After dinner he would send us up something, yes; *limoni,* hot water, a decanter. *"Sola cosa è!"* The only thing, signora! But after dinner. . . .

We climbed upstairs, gondoliers forgotten; delighted with this graphic kindness. Dinner itself was a restoration, choice and *soigné* among the flowers and mirrors of the cosy *sala;* and later, upon us and our books entered the headwaiter, pompous but unbending to smiles, setting before us a tray with covered silver jugs and everything needful, including enormous native *limoni,* and disposing it with care.

"Let's put in lots of lemon," I said rather nervously, a ghost of my Puritanical upbringing standing behind me and trying to shake its head; I gave it a dismissing frown however—imagine having a cold in Venice—and we mixed and stirred.

"Not so bad," said my child composedly—this particular brew was new to us. "Here's how, A.B.!"

"Yes," I said, striving hard for commonplace intonation. "To the rain! If it'll stop tomorrow. A little is very nice, but—"

"Just so," said she. "A bit moppy, getting about. . . . But the pavement will be lovely, darling; all reflections!"

And we went to the window.

We loved that window. It was luxury just to lean there with a friendly shoulder beside one's own, and have Venice and her tides beyond; night-hints of her, always the best. The column, faintly lighted; somewhere a slim sail, which we sensed rather than saw, slipping along in the roughening and mysterious waters that so soon darkened into the wastes of the Adriatic. . . . Tides are blessed things; and architecture on the edge of them is as much improved as when backed by trees or mountains. . . . We had said this above Buonconvento, and now reiterated it with fervor; even Rome, we agreed, would be the better for waves, instead of pavements, clasping her ancient steps. . . . Venice, of course, was not put in waters because it was going to be lovely to have her there; those who founded her were simply driven out here, as other tribes had been driven inland, by the assaults of the barbarians.

It seemed, after all, a sort of justice: the Veneti had inhabited the mainland, the Romans took it from them; then the Romans, fleeing in turn from their imperiled towns, Aquileia, Padua, Adria, perched first on islands in the shallow lagoons—the *laguna morte*—till finding even these unsafe, they took a last, desperate leap across the *laguna viva* and settled on the present islets (117 of them).

Through force of flight, therefore, this beauty was accomplished; a difficult beauty, with water prying at the cracks in its walls.

The palaces, to us, still looked impossible; especially in a *rio piccolo* with no quai to protect them, where you steal intimately along and can reach out and touch the handsome green sea-slime on their sides; amphibian, they look, with their great flat cakes of stone going happily up into air and sunshine—yet reaching, with no apparent change in mood or well-being, down under the corroding dull green water. They rise with almost a monotony of preservation above one's prowling gondola; and on coming out into the comparative liveliness of the Canale Grande it is with a shock, though a certain sense of justification, that one sees something at last tumbling into the water . . . though it be only a corner of that garden-wall caved in by Austrian bombs. And as far as we went, such bits here and there seemed the only infraction time—and brine—had made upon these ancient structures.

At least we thought so that evening. On the morrow we were to hear a different tale, but just now—what were falling palaces to stuffy heads and a weight on the chest? We fled to our waiting quilts. . . . Crimson ones, here; warm and cheerful, to match the carpets; we liked them. Gleams from the quai-light by Victor Emanuel still shone in at our window, and flickered on the wall; said a cosy voice from the other bed—and from the blue, as usual:

"Maisie says, you know, you must take enough so you see two bedposts instead of one. . . . I almost think I do!"

CHAPTER XXIII

ART AND OTHERWISE

THE big liner, with not a tourist in sight, looked very far out, and chill, and lonesome, next morning, in a gray and empty lagoon; for it was raining. Victor Emanuel reared grandly, all alone on the shining pavement, with just a woman in black carrying a bundle and a man under an umbrella hastening along; the reflections were so splendid that, grayness and all, we took a picture and hoped for the best.

"Recovered from steps we had taken for cold," says the diary; steps might be one name for it, I suppose. We still felt strange in the head and were almost glad of a cosy, letter-writing hour or so, but the sky was brightening after all; we set out for a walk by the longest possible way to find Titian's "Assumption," which was not in the *accademia* but had been transferred to San Tomà.

"Rain in Venice," the notes say; as if that were something special.

It is, by morning light. The piazza was gleaming with wet brightness—it and San Marco; San Marco beautiful in the softening rain. We had never seen it so beautiful. The graying of the rain muffled its sometimes too apparent facts; dulled the pinks, softened the gold of the mosaics, combed lunettes and pinnacles into one loveliness. The dark arches of the square were also brought into oneness by the falling veil; we stood under the Florentine umbrella, enchanted by the look of it. . . . *Not* a post-card this morning—poor Venice, as on distinct days it occasionally is . . . though waves, boats, shouts, and chatter do their best to redeem it.

Chatter was not needed now; poetry was in this quietness. The vast space was empty.

A RAINY MORNING FROM OUR WINDOW IN VENICE

In our nostrils the scent, the feel of the rain—on our cheeks the fresh breath of it: clean, wet stone—never had Venice smelled so nice, looked so unforgettable. Sparrows were bathing in the very flat wide, pools, trying so hard to grovel in them, shaking their wings with such pleasure; a few pigeons were about, damp as to feathers, but pecking the pavement undismayed—turning their bright feet this way and that with the humorous, flat-footed quickness pigeons have. . . . Genealogical pigeons these are, lineal descendants of Admiral Dandolo's that were sent back to Venice with news of his victory over the Turks. Out of the clouds of battle we could see them flying—high above the burning galleys; once in clearer air, they circled, got their skyey bearings (miraculous creatures), then with one impulse darted westward. Fast, fast! the seas beneath them, their keen eyes unwavering; at last across pale twilight waters a thread of something upon the sky; a tower—their campanile, behind the safe lagoon. . . . One would have liked to see the welcome they had as they swirled down, those first news-carriers of the air, back-watering gracefully, lighting in the piazza; just the same pretty colors and innocent pink feet (in the thirteenth century) as were here before us, and bearing the weight of messages in Latin.

And then (still under the green umbrella) we discovered that St. Marks had not always been the *duomo,* but the chapel of the Doges, ever since anything churchly was demanded of this spot, and it ceased being a sandy bank, with marsh-grass. . . . Those potentates, of course, made it flower sumptuously, with a beauty borrowed from the East; and for centuries a great bare thing out on the Isola di San Pietro, turning its back on Venice and looking abstractedly at Alps and fishing boats, had been her cathedral. Strange!

But we found our new and longer way to reach the Rialto (the sun had come out, and everything looked joyful); swung dozens of corners, at last coming upon a wide inland thoroughfare which wound most conversibly along . . . and we had never seen it before.

A motley crowd was here. Nuns, jackies, quiet English,

roystering Tedeschi; a harried Venetian dodging along with a tray of *fiaschi* on his head, hatless mothers carrying babies; shoppers, citizens, and youths, youths, youths. Venice seemed to be full of the young of the male species, some borrowed, some indigenous, but all callow, and, like the youths of Siena, hastening gibingly along. . . . Baskets were being let down from fourth-storey windows, and newspapers going up in them—in Siena it was always bread that was ascending; other large baskets were sitting on window-sills—full of stock, or purple cinerarias. . . . "Baroque going quite mad, in any little back square," say the notes; indeed, the church-fronts were a mass of curly stone, solid with decoration—foliage and busts: stately, Jovian persons with curled heads and wreaths. Hair-curling must have been a great art, in old days; trees were pollarded, men were waved. *Antichitè,* beads, and plants were being sold in booths; by a little canal and its bridge, some kerchiefed, sensible-looking, motherly women were in charge of book-stalls, while high overhead flowers and vines in pretty leaf drizzled sweetly above the green water. . . . A nice corner for books; nice to see books, in Venice.

All along our thoroughfare, too, the nurse-maids were coming out, bearing their charges; the superlative nurse-maids of Venice, with their great head-dresses and trailing ribbons, frilled aprons, fine shoes, and pink or scarlet dresses—though some were of brilliant plaid. . . . When groups of these are strutting in the piazza it is a sight, for often a nurse-maid will have children to match; if she is in watermelon-pink or scarlet, they are too; glowing flowers on the *pavimento*—usually surrounded by pigeons.

And Venice has a leaning tower, tucked away here by the church in the Campo San Maurizio: a charming pink belfry, slanting very much; behind it, in the engaging tiny "Campiello Dietro la Chiesa" (Little Field behind the Church), we peered into the water of a small canal where its leaning foundations were being assisted by great stone props.

"Dozens of these leaning *torri* in Italy," say the notes; full of wisdom today. "This is an old country. Things sink."

In San Maurizio's pleasant, irregular Campo, now warm with sunshine, was a six-sided well-head; a youngish Venetian was having a nice nap against it—the only person we had seen that morning who wasn't bustling about something. One of the cisterna's sides had an inscription, and a little old worn relief; as we stopped to look at it, the air in the Campo was resonant with the song of a boy leaning over a high balcony, its rail brilliant with his mother's washing; he leaned on a dry towel and sang lustily. Just beneath him was a window of plants, mostly cinerarias, crimson and purple—favorites in Italy; brightly surrounded, the boy smiled down at us, and sang as he smiled, a canary on the balcony, also rampant with cheerfulness, apparently trying to rival him.

The Venetian having a nap on the cisterna's sunny side roused a little, and smiled sweetly at us; bending to investigate the green bronze spout of the well-top, which was dripping, and evidently in use, I asked him if the water were still good.

"Si si. Buona, madama!" he said pleasantly.

"È—molto antica?" I ventured; meaning, was it the same old water they used to use.

"Si, madama—antica!" and he smiled and half rose, lifting his old torn cap, as we left, and murmuring a soft-toned *"Arivederci."* Once more, sweet Venetians.

Delicious, this sunlight on the stone of the old Campo, the sweet fresh air with which Venice had so far greeted us; this walk was a great success. To cap it, we came out upon the canal almost where we thought we were going to, climbing the worn, beautiful steps of the Rialto and passing its insignificant tawdry traffic with quite the careless unnoticing air (or so we flattered ourselves) of old residents. . . . We had been over this thing before, and only wished we had not . . . that we had left it in Shakespeare's pages forever. Rialto; what glamour in that name (*Rivoalto* originally—high bank—but softened by a lazy Venetian dialect to this) and, except for glimpses of the canal, which the stalls of cheap wares mostly hide, what stodginess in reality.

Yet these were old stones we were treading on; old, and often tragic. We walked thoughtfully away. . . . Inland, we found a cleaner region than on many of our walks; more open spaces, and frequent churches. Pavements were drying in the sunshine; we strode along, crossed little canals, twisted here or there and lost our way; for the more lost you are in Venice, the more twistings and turnings you seem to have to take. What a long walk it was. The "Assumption" we knew had moved; we began to think the Rialto had too—backwards.

And had we really lost San Tomà? Some of the *calli* had names and some had not; but my child's trail-finding sense came to the rescue.

"I think it's this way, A.B.!" she would say musingly, at some particularly unnamed and stony corner—so like many other little corners—looking about her, then up at belfries and cornices, as if they had been mountain-profiles or the tops of woods; "this looks like that little canal we passed yesterday; I *think* I recognize that doorway!" For thus in our mountains, when slightly lost, did we look and deduce, and then decide; so now, though much more lost, we set off in some faith.

"You're right!" I said; "that last church was San' Aponal, and this one—by jinks, it must be San Polo."

"Then this is the Campo San Whatever!" swiftly responded Babs—who, too fastidious to pronounce Italian wrong, never attempted a syllable of these unfamiliar names; we went very gaily over the Rio San Polo, swung to the right, then to the left— "*Is* that the back of the Palazzo Pisani? It ought to be!" —then across another tiny *canaletto* and into an open space, showing, at its end, ecclesiastical stone: a doorway with columns.

We hastened to it. A leather flap-door opened for us, with the charming ease flap-doors have; an aged wooden one declined. *Chiudo,* said a sign.

San Tomà, one inferred, was closed. Since when? The pinkish stone, the pavement of the little square, said nothing. . . .

Inside was doubtless what we wished to see, tantalizingly illumining some dusky wall. No, there was light here—a bit of space before San Tomà's side windows. The picture might be quite visible. . . .

We sat down on a little *cisterna,* in the sun.

"I think the canal's just out *there,*" said my daughter, pointing.

We squeezed between two old palaces, and there it was. Blue, now; and sun on the palaces. Charming, in its recovered brightness, but we strolled away. . . . It was nice, here; we'd explore a bit more, now that we had found where the boat-landing was.

So behind the Frari we came, quite by chance, upon San Rocco and the Scuola—having wandered round the Frari's picturesque apse mostly because we love apses. . . . All sorts, old ones in Italian hill-country, or the little wooden attempts at them in our South, on gray, darkey churches far back in the pine woods—a tiny, nondescript, cabiny thing perhaps, with its chimney propped up on sticks; one would scarcely think it a church were it not for the touching and ever-sacred bit of bulge on one end. Must be ecclesiastical! For even out there in the woods, reached by a poetic little rooty road all pine-needles, with violets growing under the trees and moss and bull briars hanging down from them, that particular architectural urge is still evident in the human mind.

The Frari's apse, of course, is a dream. And in the Scuola, some wood-carvings of the life of St. Roche are worth study.

"Sweet figure of St. Roche," the notes say. "Cat sitting on an open *cisterna,* with realistic rope hanging over the side; cats sat on wells, in Venice, even in the seventeenth century. . . . One relief shows the visit of an angel: the Saint, with an ankle secured to an iron ring in a step, sits enraptured while a beautiful floating creature in a tunic tucked up by a draped sash, approaches with a tray (refreshments?) jauntily in one hand. . . . In the previous scene, St. Roche comes to his imprisonment—meek, his hands roped behind him, the rope held by a jeering centurion; he bends his head to enter a fortress tower, its small door open, every stone in its wall outlined, and the top of a palm tree wildly waving."

A bodeful wind should be blowing, when saints go to jail; for he was a good saint. "Gives all to the poor"; "saves everybody"—during the plague—while a peasant girl, her water-jar fallen from her hand, is perishing by a tub of water, and discarded buckets are lying about, their rope handles trailing among wild flowers. In one of the last scenes a hasty and acrobatic angel, nearly turning a somersault, reaches poor San Rocco in his extremity . . . finally, *"Sepultus est Honorifice";* a stone is held ready, labeled "Rocco," to mark his grave, while indignant emperors and ecclesiastics, a little late, hasten from the rear.

These carvings are of beautiful old color, and dotted with pleasant wormholes; protruding bits are brightly polished by centuries of dusting, or adoration, and around San Rocco's hall, at intervals, stand great canopied gold-fringed lanterns or *baldichini,* for his procession in August.

"Si si! nelle strade!"—in the streets! said the old custodian eagerly, when I asked if the procession really went far; the *baldichini,* it appears, are borne (with great honor and difficulty) over bridges and through *calli,* all the way to San Marco and back. We liked the figure of Tintoretto, too, carved in golden-grown wood; a caricature of him as an intense, large-headed little creature shriveled down in his painter's robe, one veined and nervous hand grasping the palette, and a pail of brushes at his feet . . . by the size of the dark frescoes almost swamping the church across the way, one might infer Tintoretto needed brushes by the pailful.

Out in the warm sunshine again, we strolled to the Frari's landing and stepped on a boat. We had walked enough. It was early still, but we would lunch and come back again; that lane by the church looked too charming not to see more of.

It was. But we took a detour, first, past some shadowed, romantic, old terra-cotta walls and a heavy stone loggia in the rear of our *scuola*—which, we discovered, is in the Parrochia Santa Maria Gloriosa dei Frari . . . melodious mouthful. One would like to live in a parish called that. It was sweet back out here; surprising with waterways. We sat lazily on a step and regarded them.

"Pleasant canals, green water, rosy color, iris on a balcony," say the notes. "Boat, loaded with vegetables and one enormous wine-flask (wicker-covered), nearly as wide as the boat, slipping down a little *rio* under the iris; a young gondolier sitting on its stone steps, very contentedly polishing his brass horses. Ivy and plants are in windows, the bells of San Rocco ring; faded amber curtains wave, a noon gun (in the safe distance) goes off; canaries sing . . . on the way here, we had heard a nightingale in the piazzetta garden. Children in pinafores played in the court, where grass was growing between the stones; beyond it was a specially sweet arrangement of jade-green canals avoiding or twisting into each other, one at the left disappearing in washing and a pink bridge—under which a blue work-boat came, pushed by two stalwart Italians.

Some one above was practicing exercises on a piano, everywhere was the goo, goo! of pigeons (only a wood-pigeon says "coo"); and on the quai-wall a gray cat was eating something out of a paper. The paper blew over, hiding its contents and the cat, with the well-known feline distaste for actually pushing anything, had a time getting it reopened. She put back her whiskers and delicately tried; shook her head, used one paw and then another; finally, with the help of a breeze from the opposite direction, succeeded in uncovering the morsel.

Some Venetian boys passed, without annoying her—indeed they looked kindly at her; a woman in bright blue had a smile for her as she filled a flask from the spouting lion-head by the court's rosy wall. A subject for a sketch, that was. . . . Water pours and runs away from similar lion-heads all over Venice—good water, silvery, with blue in the shadows. A school-boy came by and drank of it with gusto.

Revived by the leisure of the little court, we set off along the Calle Tintoretto. Fig trees were in leaf over its bulging wall; then the lane swelled out, vase-fashion, to hold a *cisterna* with a sort of stone dimple in its rim, for cats and pigeons to drink from. . . . A kind-hearted dimple. The *cisterna* had a pump attached, with a design of fish for a cover; the spout was another curly fish, and on the four sides (old and worn, but in the same delightful greenish bronze of the fishes) was a relief of the Venetian lion. Just half of him, sweet thing; with his paw on his book.

"Such pains, for a pump in a back lane!" my notes say; and the stone top of the well-head, as always, was of beautiful design. (I saw some in an antique-shop, later, and the shopkeeper said he couldn't get enough of them—to send to America. I suppose they'll all be gone, someday.)

A canary overhead, sang especially loud here, looking down on some fluffy greenery that hung over the pinkish-gray wall —it seemed like bamboo foliage; all in all, a pleasant basking corner, with the belfries of San Rocco and the Frari high in sunshine beyond, and the marble figure of the Saint, snowy against the blue, perched airily on the tip-top of his church. . . . Strange things they seemed to do, to San Rocco.

Round the corner, we greatly admired a cat with a white bosom sitting in the doorway of a nice neat *pizzicheria,* against a sack of dried peas; two Italians, workmen carrying a board, laughed in sympathy as they went by and saw us aiming the camera at her. *"Inglesi!"* said they. (English fondness for cats is common knowledge, in Venice; we, therefore, must be *Inglesi.*) A few more corners, and we came to a series of small gardens behind a neat row of houses. Vines and lilac, birds singing; a clean and pleasant quarter. Wisteria, a shiny shrub, and more lilac; four cats ran out of one of the gardens to stare hopefully up, when some one raised a window—to take in a plant! "Do these people throw out food for cats?" my notes ask; it certainly looked as if they did. For the cats were all fat, glossy, and clean, and the woman who opened the window spoke pleasantly to them, I noticed. Venice must like her cats. They sit on every *cisterna,* in the little courts; except for pigeons and canaries, they are her only animals.

Groups of boys were now coming from school—the polite well-dressed sons of Venice's respectable, but little-seen, middle class—and in the Campiello della Scuola near by, was a relief and its inscription set in the school wall; a row of little kneeling figures of boys, with the master kneeling at their head, and St. John (I suppose) looking down at them. Very sweet. . . . The tiny Campiello San Giovanni, beyond, had "lovely marble doorway and windows; a belfry high against blue sky in the rear." Of gray, veined marble, this archway was, with narrow insets of bluish stone; exquisite tracery adorned it; little reliefs of San Giovanni's eagle, and small Corinthian pilasters. A beautiful little Gothic court; we adored pilasters. "Lovely!" repeat the notes. "Just one more of the unnoted corners of Venice; and beyond it a square of garden hung over a wall, with a tree in lemon-colored leaf lifting its round head. Really a big tree!"

I don't know that a square of garden can exactly hang over a wall, but the notes start off again, undeterred.

"In a little *rio* were lovely bridges under which came gondolas with canopies. Rio di San Giacimo dall' Orto, it is called; lovely name, lovely *rio;* and more gardens hung over its walls."

Humbler streets now began. In a dusky downhill dip—exciting to see a downhill, however slight, in Venice—were little vegetable-shops with very purple artichokes; a small dark hole of a wine-shop had the cryptic sign VINI—DOLCE NERO, PER ESPOI. Sweet *black* wine? said we. Remarkable; like the *vin gris* in the south of France . . . only gray wine sounds more haggard and disenchanting even than black.

Beyond the wine-shop our little *calle* became slimy and slummy indeed; we turned back. But how homelike and agreeable was this part of Venice! By a particularly peaceful bridge, to be sure, we had been depressed by the sight of a tablet to one Enrico or Vincenzo, a Fascist, who had been killed there . . . which in that basking emptiness seemed impossible and all wrong. But the air was bright and fresh; one could almost fancy, if there were a nice pension, staying here a while and growing very fond of it and its people.

One would never imagine it from a gondola, we told each other—or else the gondolier didn't take us this way; but we were sure he did. We simply scraped this section. . . . Nothing like walking, after all. "At Venice," said the Türistiche pamphlet reasonably, "even the coldest observer is subdued by the graceful harmony of the surroundings. Therefore he should stroll listlessly along the byways of Venice."

We had, only not very listlessly; we were not sorry to reach the Frari's boat-landing. Sun on the palaces again, puff-puff, a swirling of waters, and we were scuttling down the canal. We went forward in the little craft, glad of a rest, and sat sidewise, our elbows on her rail; water busily splashing, and palaces scooting by—pink and cream-color in the sun, shadowy on our right.

That left hand (or northern side) of the canal, it seemed to us, was the more frivolous of the two, thicker with color and decorated *palazzi;* perhaps the more frivolous and fashionable of the old Venetians preferred to live in the sun. And its marble steps, at once dimmed and freshened by the transparent tides, are such a beautiful mellow color; like submerged alabaster. Our boat scuttled hectically yet softly along, puffing out much more smoke from its low stack than seemed needful; scooting excitedly, as any Venetian boat should, past the bright, traitorous terra-cotta of the Cà del Duca (a one-storied house begun for the Duke of Milan, but left unfinished after his downfall); curving very suddenly in to the *accademia* landing, puffing an instant, and with no hint of what was in store for us, making the usual precipitate departure while passengers were still staggering forward to acquire seats.

"Let's sit on the other side—before those seats are taken," murmured Babs.

For we always liked, from here down, to be on the St. Marks's side, and had risen to accomplish this, when . . .

was it *possible?* Could this be our Viola, whom we knew was in Italy somewhere? Our most special person, our incentive to all things artistic? A little unworldly charming figure in lavender, with a wide-brimmed black hat and long drizzle of carelessly-tied black lace—limp, friendly, old lace, pleasant on the soft lavender, was coming toward us; edging its way along, a cloak on its arm, bag and umbrella and blue guide in hand, a smut on its cheek, the precious darling; was actually beside us, looking up in momentary stupefaction. . . . Then the keen eyes lighted as only Viola's can—they are cornflower blue too; and she was seizing a hand of each of us.

"You—you here? I've been hoping— I've been wondering . . ."

Ah, that deep, satisfying voice; not too deep, not pompous—I have known voices I wanted to hit in the eye; just blessedly full of *timbre* . . . full of variety, too! nods and becks and wreathed smiles (as it were), with a good snappy Southern *a* thrown in for a tonic; an utterly honest voice, humorous or dramatic as the moment demanded. . . . And she'd "been wondering" about us.

"So have we!" I cried; "it's too marvelous, here on this boat; of all the chances. Darling, let's sit down!" for we were clutching each other, and being lurched about.

" 'Must put my cloak on—" for indeed the wind was chill; we helped her on with it, then in the happy triangle we three always make, we furiously talked and planned. . . . We'd have tea together; and she must try dinner with us at our hotel. Where was she staying? Down this way?

"No, I'm at a pension," she murmured, "farther up the canal. . . . 'Been here a week—and feel as if I'd done nothing yet. There is so much . . ." and she looked absently, almost bleakly, about . . . "But I've been hoping to hear from you!" she said, turning vividly to us again; "There's a letter for you floating about Europe somewhere—"

"Is there? And here she is with her Muirhead, just setting out; and we're interrupting—"

"But to meet friends!" said Viola, looking affectionately and somehow humidly at both of us; "friends, in Venice! That, my dears, will make a day to be marked with jewels."

Landing at the *piazzetta,* we walked off, Babs and I in a sort of concentrated bliss. We were leaving tomorrow, dash it, but—

"What *luck,* that we came to Venice!" said Babs, her eyes eloquent.

"We so nearly didn't, you know!" and we told her about Battaglia.

Viola beamed upon us. "I'm blessing that canal . . . that bridge!" said she. (Ah, that gallant Southern way of hers, of saying nice things! We sighed, from mere pleasure.)

As we were passing the stout columns of the palace, our companion paused, her attention caught by the carvings on one of them; old stone, wrought skilfully into foliage and little figures; implements, symbols, ideas of this or that, different on every column; on every one, a happy medley.

"What fun the *small craftsman* must have had, in those old days!" said she, with a positive blaze of her blue eyes at us; looking fondly up, going on to the next, and the next, delighting in every petal, every stocking carved on a little leg, every little grotesquerie. We gazed fondly too; this sort of lingering was what we most loved; but coming near the side portal Babs led the way wordlessly, as if by a sort of instinct, into her beloved St. Mark's. . . . Mosaics, mosaics; the East! I can see her now, striding up those steps in front of us. Viola and I followed; but in the first rich duskiness our friend paused, looking (for her) quite hesitantly about.

"Not this—I think. . . . Not today," she murmured. "One must take a long time for it. I—it—" and she glanced humbly, almost helplessly, up at us.

We understood. Nodded at her, smiling. Dusky, solitary—St. Mark's is for long musing; for time-forgetting gazings. We had had ours (or a little of it; one never has enough) in that solitude *à deux* which, to me, was solitude made doubly rich. Doubly? A thousand-fold! I thought—while the object of these reflections stood, grinning wisely, at my elbow . . . infinitely, immutably rich and cherishable.

We tip-toed out. Gleams of light were still among the clouds, but a softening color on the palaces; it was time for tea. We chose seats in front of San Marco, with lunettes and pinnacles looking down at us; in spite of their loveliness, and a hint of apricot beginning to come in the sky, there was scarcely anybody in the piazza.

"Silly people. Afraid of more rain, I suppose," said Babs, with scorn.

Pigeons stepped about us, bobbing their necks; away toward the lagoon was the usual beauty—and behind us, and around, and everywhere. Our friend ate nothing, as usual, but in intervals of eloquence stared devoutly here and there.

"Just old stone is so charming!" murmured she.

And we rose and strolled away, listening to Viola's latest Italian tale of the "little dim Englishwoman" and the "terrible tea," where they entertained her "with fearful labor. . . ." Babs and I, at this, exchanged a smile. Our friend is so eloquent, so emotionally dominant, she may well live in an overwhelmed world; it already made us feel crude, even guilty, to be bumping about Italian roads and adoring landscape instead of spending all our time—like our beloved friend—idolizing art. (Her phrase.)

"I am starved for Art!" said she; and looked hungrily about her.

So had we been; but there is something in us that must now and again see green things and sky, or we perish. We had tried to explain this a year ago, but felt we did not quite "put it over."

And little Nicolette, waiting so patiently for us behind the *laguna morte*—was she a crudeness too? Just think of the things we had probably motored past and not seen, said our eyes guiltily to each other; the probable galleries we had skipped, the insides of villages we just worked our way through, thankful to be out at any cost. . . .

Alack! and yet we somehow felt incomparably cheerful.

For years we had been dying to see the hill-villages, and now Nicolette, bless her forever, was giving us the chance. Art? Of course. But–slide about in the sunshine too? Rather. And as we wandered toward the rear of San Marco, the tale of the terrible tea went on.

"That little old Englishwoman–she was so dim, so ill-dressed, if you met her in the piazza you'd give her a penny! yet she had a flat in that palace, with twenty rooms–as big as this!" and Viola motioned at the little Piazzetta-with-the-beasts, where we were now standing. "And she lives there all by herself; one little old Englishwoman, and twenty rooms in Venice. . . . I never *had* such a tea!"

Strolling past the campanile we stopped to stare up at the little *loggetta* and its ornate attic–which Babs does not like. It *is* rather crowded with figures, but as Viola murmured, "By a master hand!"

"You see, darling, you *should* adore it–an attic by Sansovino!" I said, smiling, and putting an arm through my child's.

"I insist it's a mess!" said she cheerfully, but looking up at it with that simple benevolence of hers; and Viola and I shouted. One has to do something–fall on somebody's neck with fearful hoots–when Babs looks like that; and when we calmed down a little,

"Go off a bit–you two," I said, undoing the camera; "I'll take your picture, against that doorway."

They turned to me defensively.

"Terrible object . . . I," murmured Viola; Babs raised a despairing eyebrow. But they obediently retreated; and on that lovely background–unposed, hatted, clothes baggy with the damp–I took them, umbrellas and all. Frightful of them both, it came out, with scarcely a vestige of our friend's charm, or the amused tenderness lurking in my child's face; yet something about it makes it a precious record.

Just behind them were the two affectionate porphyry gentlemen, set into a corner of the *duomo,* that had charmed us the day before—one always sees something new here; two little ancient figures clad all for battle in reddish-purple armor—and yet they have their arms round each other's necks. We really felt bright to have picked them out, for Viola hadn't noticed them before and rushed to exult over them; and Babs knew at once they were Persian.

And then we had a sunset walk along the Schiavone—and further, along the Riva Cà di Dio and the Riva S. Biagio; in fact as far as the *rivas* go, in a seaward direction, where Venice grows indigenous, and a bit business-like. Amber, copper, and green—of sea and sky, there were; a lovely lowering of tone everywhere; and a fleet of sand-boats, with their sails furled, was tied up alongside the Cà di Dio. A bit of real life, in Venice. A young woman and two children were stepping about the boats; a man with bread under his arm was climbing up a small ladder from a row-boat, and a little yellow dog running to meet him, barking joyfully.

Dusk was now falling, the afterglow deepening; it was frightfully beautiful out here. . . . Sand is one of the things that must be brought to Venice, it seems—though her islands (and her glass) are made of it; how pleasing that it is still brought in this ancient way, in slow, blunt-nosed, low-gunwaled, flat-decked boats, very homely and wooden, with simple sea-faring life going on on board them. The young woman called the children and they disappeared together, chattering; the man smiled as he took his loaves across the darkening deck and down some cabin steps, the little dog hectically following him; the last we saw of that dog, as he tipped himself down the companionway, was a tail wagging so fast that, though in perfect order, it was a mere blur.

We walked on, all three of us arm in arm, in deep content; and meeting nobody at this hour. Domes of the Salute looked alarmingly far away, but—

"I can walk, you know!" said Viola suddenly and courageously. "That's one thing I *can* do!"

The afterglow was dull red across the lagoon; every sort of

reflection was on the water, and along the *riva* a light or two had come out; by the time we reached the Beau Rivage they were all out, twinkling goldenly.

Viola loved our room; sank down, entranced, before our window. At dinner, in the *sala* (where she accomplished a bit of Adriatic fish, and a few wild strawberries done with sugar and red wine), she "was listened to by the entire dining-room," my notes say. "Such conviction, such understanding, such breadth. No one has such understanding. Admires the English—'no people so great, with such a genius for governing,' she said; 'and yet [with amazed eyes] the English people in this pension here—the ordinary courtesy of a morning nod at the breakfast-table—they look through you as if you weren't there!' "

We exchanged indignant glances. Yet her generous heart held no grudge—unlike another friend of ours who can't bear the English, or their institutions, just because of what Viola presently called "their snobby mediocrities who travel." As Babs remarked,

"Yes—if you meet one that smiles at you, and wants to talk, it's sure to be the cultivated sort . . . or a duchess!"

And then, just to even things up, we fell to telling the usual stories of our compatriots; especially of the young women who said, of Venice, "Oh yes, we were going to stop there, but they were having such bad floods in the streets! We just looked at it from the station and came away." Viola, however, vouched for the truth of this tale; and we for the story of the two middle-aged and querulous women-travelers whom a friend had heard talking as they had tea in the piazza—discussing evidently, a member of their party.

"It's funny; Matilda don't seem to care a bit for Venice."

"Well . . . you know at home; she never *did* like Atlantic City!"

We all laughed; and the evening fled as with wings.

"So late—for me!" murmured Viola. "It is hard to tear myself away from two such friends; but I must!"

HALF OUR GONDOLIER

A Side-Canal, Venice

Alas! and it seemed only a minute since we had found her; impossible, to let her go like this. . . . And had she a little air of dread, going out alone? We dashed for our coats. We would see her home. . . . Travel is an egotistic thing—one never does anything for anybody; it would be a nice feeling, to escort somebody somewhere!

The *piazzetta* was well lighted, and nearly empty, though voices still came from around the corner; but it did seem a trifle spooky, at that hour. . . . It was warmer tonight—very pleasant; delicious, the air. We found a small gondola waiting at the steps, and beyond the first bright usualness, the lights and distant music of the Canal, our gondolier swung us into a very dark small one that Babs and I were not familiar with.

We glided between the great moist walls, a light shining dimly at a far turn.

"The past rises up so, about one!" murmured Viola.

A point of green moved silently out of the dark—another gondola, darkly gliding. A quiver of gold, a lance of green on the water beside us—a shadow stole by; was gone. . . . Mystery of the past; of ancient glidings that had come and gone about these corners; of the immemorial sloppings on these old steps and mysterious doorways. Darkness was thick about one's hands, about the gondola's rim, but opposite me was the dim oval of a young face, with hair slightly ruffled off the forehead in the little breeze; eyes dreaming, a little upward, hands around her knees, Babs was leaning back, silent, happy. I felt I knew what she was thinking. Nothing around us but shadowiness, and gleams of green and gold; lovely night-world, with no red in it, and no noise!

Venice, for quiet . . . at night in a side canal.

Not a dry quiet; a moist, slopping quiet, with fresh soft air and just enough reflected light to show how beautiful the darks are. A square of soft gold, high up; clean-cut shapes of water-gold, beside us—scimitars and witching curves of pale gold; then emerald breaks in once more, on the shining black. . . . *Such* a shiningness! You rest on luster; are borne on gleams.

"M'yo!" from the lithe form behind you; at least it sounds like m'yo. I've tried to make sense of it and turn it into *"rio,"* or *"gia,"* which they are supposed to say; but it won't turn. If ever a cat said *meow* (which they do), then a gondolier says m'yo. It sounds nice and yowly, too, like a cat . . . but even "m'yo" was soft. No need to be loud, in these lanes where everything carries so,—where every little wave is an event.

Viola was very quiet now, and just as the dark silence had begun to seem a little long, out we came into the bright big Canal again, finding it empty, and rather a let-down. Water was visibly slopping here—pleasant, but a fact; and we had come into it out of a dream. . . . A few entrances down, and we landed at the pension steps, dismissing the gondolier—once more a nice snub-nosed creature, so pleased and honest over his money. Was he a brother of No. 4, our favorite? Viola thought it likely.

" 'Expect they do it by families," said Babs, watching him row away.

Anything so skilful must run in the blood; that beautiful back-swerve. He leaned forward, pushing gracefully, yet with great strength, his back hollowed, his shoulders straight—then came the magic twist of the whole lithe form, the long leap-forward of the gondola . . . and they slid into glittering dusk.

"Marvelous!" said Viola, smiling at us, her face softly lighted from the gleam of the water. . . ."Yes, this is our little garden! It's really pretty, if you could see it—but how are you getting home?" she asked, suddenly concerned; for we were on the wrong side of the canal.

"Walk!" said we as one man.

"We'd love to!" I added.

" 'Know the way 'pufficky'!" grinned Babs.

"Wonderful," murmured gallant Viola; "you two. . . . You're not afraid—at this hour. You'll stride along, I suppose, and think it nothing!"

Leave-taking was difficult; we clung to one another's hands.

"Bless you—my dears!"

"Good-by! good luck, darling!"

A fortunate bit of pavement led from the little garden to a wider strip in front of some *trattorias*—the Riva del Vin; toward this we briskly departed. What fun! a walk in Venice at this hour. I wondered a little what the *trattorias* might say, as we went by so close to their awnings—which projected above the tables where dark-faced Venetians were sitting, almost over the water, their wine dark in glasses before them. Would they call out to us? I thought of Monfrin, and the Gallic tumult there. . . .

No! These Italians looked at us quietly, and said nothing. "Respectful *trattorias,*" say my notes. "Back alleys of Venice bright and alive at night."

For we crossed the dusky Rialto a shade hurriedly; then, expecting similar darkness, found ourselves in animation: the youth of Venice, talking and laughing as they walked briskly, yet with a somehow classic grace—ah, that grace of Italy!—along the little arcades; whose shops were all open, bright with lights and color.

How delightful. Venice seemed more alive now than we had ever seen it . . . and with its own people. They were such nice people. One reads, in guide-books, about a large portion of her inhabitants being "paupers"; these attractive young people surely were not, and their looks at us, as we went enjoyingly along, were both polite and kind. . . . We twisted and turned; all too soon came out through the arch under the clock-tower into a brilliantly lighted piazza, seeing St. Mark's in a new glow. A few lingerers were still in the cafés; the great clock said eleven-forty.

Gold was in the air, on the gray arcades, on what our friend called the "rhyming repetitions" of St. Mark's; that lovely, airy flinging of one lunette over another. For Viola had once told us of her visit to a town in Surrey called Limpsfield, and the "horrible mile of villas" made lovely by fog; rhyming repetitions, indeed.

The piazza did not need fog. We stared at it romantically.

Good-by Venice, being so golden— San Marco, best of pigeon-perches. . . . For the pigeons had all gone to bed, huddled among the minarets.

Good-by, lovely dark hopping of water; our little bridge, the empty café chairs; Victor Emanuel, alive and dark as ever, but flashing bits of light from his helmet, an elbow, a hoof of his horse; and somewhere down the darkness of the Cà di Dio, a yellow lantern gleamed.

" 'Night, sand-boats!" said a voice beside me.

CHAPTER XXIV

MANTUA IN A FLOOD

NEXT morning, however, we looked forth on Victor Emanuel as on one already left behind; even the colors of a Venetian May were on their way to becoming part of the past.

"Now *this* is the way to travel!" said Babs, shutting our one bag with satisfaction.

We felt like picking it up and running abandonedly downstairs and across the quai with it, without waiting for porters; but that would never do. We descended in the usual order. The water was lapping at the steps, the gondola moving restlessly; I had my coat on my arm, the camera and a Sheila Kaye-Smith novel laid absent-mindedly on top of it; I bent to step in, with the porter in possession of my other elbow, and—plop! went the camera into the lagoon. Only that Kaye-Smith cover, with a fine sense of self-preservation, clung to my sleeve. . . .

Alas! our precious camera; and there was a half-taken film in it.

The porter burst into lamentations; was wringing his hands helplessly, when a youth, and a little boy with him, came up to us. He was about nineteen, a tall lad with a meager face and great golden eyes, cleanly clad in a skimpy but fresh shirt and much-shrunken trousers of coarse linen which clung tight to his thin legs, but had very new creases; evidently Mama had just ironed him and turned him out on the quai, beautiful to behold. . . . At least he would have been handsome, in the thin, undeveloped way of the Venetian under-classes, had it not been for his utter callowness, and his look of the confirmed loafer, half-bold, half-shrinking: the sort of youth whom the medieval Italian would have kicked and sent about his business, and who would have gone slinking and whining off.

But here were women, and ingratiation was joined with a becoming degree of boldness. I wondered what he wanted.

"Signora, signora—!" and he gestured toward the canal.

He wanted to dive into that water for the camera! Babs and I were delighted at the idea of retrieving it, but our concierge eyed the youth, as one poacher might eye another; disapprovingly, up and down. Interfering with his prerogatives? Yet no concierge could precipitate his beautiful uniform into the lagoon; *bene!* this fellow in a shirt should do it then . . . and great bargainings followed. I offered fifteen lire.

"No no, signora!" very earnestly.

Twenty, then?

He wavered; glanced at his little brother—who was dancing with impatience and begging, in loud whispers, to be allowed to do the diving himself—then asked if he could go home and change his clothes. No? The signora had not time? *Allora* . . . long explanations; and we finally settled on twenty-five. That water did look horrid, heaving up and down; and nobody knew how deep . . . at least we didn't. With an eye gleaming with satisfaction he retired across the pavement to roll up the valuable trousers. They would not roll very far, but with brown shins somewhat bared he advanced to the edge, hesitated a second, seized his nose in one hand, and dove.

We watched, in fascinated horror, for him to come up; which he almost instantly did. (I felt quite defrauded. It wasn't deep at all!) Up came an arm, streaming, and holding the camera, all blue mud; the porter seized it, gave it one disgusted wipe, and before we even dreamed what he was going to do, opened it and gave it a thorough swash back and forth in the sea-water.

We shrieked at him—poor camera, as if it hadn't had bath enough already; paid the now blue and dripping youth,

"I'LL TAKE YOUR PICTURES—AGAINST THAT DOORWAY"

San Marco, Venice

whose teeth had begun to chatter; and all the pleasant way to the station, shook and wiped it.

"Dashed ass!" muttered Babs, still in a state of fury with that porter; "if he hadn't done that it might have been all right, but now everything will rust of course. . . ."

I offered to hold it in the air as we drove. "But it's horrid to have no camera," I remarked, as the little train jostled us along. "Probably, now that we can't use it, we shall be seeing things we want to take, every minute."

"Probably!" said Babs. "Well, here's Mestre, darling. . . . Wonder how Nicolette is!" and we debarked, both of us smiling involuntarily at the thought of seeing her again.

We need not have worried; there was no trace of the methods of the wolves in her appearance or behavior. All fit, and nicely washed, she backed ably from her lock-box; the little suit-case quickly joined its fellow, the padrone tucked us in, the bill was a fair one, and in surprisingly few minutes we were wheeling away for Mantua.

Delightful to be driving again! we beamed at the Canale de Brenta. A new idea, getting to Garda this way—and a little jog southward—but we had never been to Mantua; Mantua was a University town, and meant Virgil and Mantegna, and Babs wanted to see it.

A sweet morning, calm and palely blue; I held the camera in my lap. Fine villas bordered the pretty canal; fields beside us were very moist, there were pools in the road, but Nicolette splashed serenely along. Great trees there were, cows pasturing on nice fresh grass, many-colored boats moored in the canal, ducks swimming in its clear rushy water—all the atmosphere of fishing and liveliness, leaf-shadows and aquatic charm that accompanies a canal in peaceful country. This canal was once a part of the serious waterway between Venice, Chioggia, and Padua, and somewhere below, where it joined the river, Mastino Scaliger, a tyrant of Verona, had once infuriated Venice by building a salt-factory "where every Venetian vessel as it passed along the Brenta was called on to pay a tax. . . ."

Great oaks, from little acorns, etc.; this small affair of the salt-tax turned out to be a grievous affront, occurring on territory which Venice regarded as her own, and led to the forming of an anti-Veronese league between herself and Florence, which resulted in the ultimate downfall of Mastino. Verona had owned ten cities, and the Scaliger's blunder lost him six of these, together with the tremendous income they brought in; as Villani, a Florentine historian, wrote, "the rents which accrued . . . from those ten towns and from their castles, were more than 700,000 florins of gold, which no Christian king possesses, unless it be the King of France . . . never were there tyrants in Italy possessed of such power."

Mastino, after these humiliations, "became suspicious and irascible," says Wiel; in a fit of fury he murdered Bishop Bartolomeo de la Scala, a member of his own family, with his own hand, and there was a legend in Verona that after this, "Mastino never showed his face again even to his faithful and beloved wife Taddea de Carrara." The statue on his tomb, at any rate, has the visor of the helmet drawn down. And all this came from a mistaken bit of enterprise on the Brenta.

Crossing that uneventful-looking stream, down which so much bitterness had drifted, we were soon, with a sense of pleased familiarity, driving through Padua again. The "faithful Taddea," it seems, had come from Padua's reigning house, the Carrara family; we hoped she had had some happy hours in Verona—so soon to be the scene, for her, of loss and tragedy. . . . We had to linger a little by the entrancing Prato; found a new gate, crossed the little Bacchiglione by a different bridge and continued, all in small roads and among the pretty green Euganean hills, to Este, or Montagnana—some lovely old walled town, where I remember being crushed with regret because we had no camera.

For this was Virgil's country. We seemed to drive a great deal through a rich, uneventful region, wonderfully taken care of and planted with vines and mulberries; I have no memory of anything in particular until the dyke-country began, when everything becomes extremely clear. The roads toward Mantua are all lifted on tremendous dykes, and we were bumping across a brown and heathy stretch, on one of them, thinking of nothing except that this wasn't very interesting, when all at once the moor-like landscape dipped, and we saw a sight . . . Mantua! We drew up, thrilled.

Mantua was sitting in a huge sheet of water, shining and satin-blue, above which its brown walls and towers stood picturesquely out. The rains, we said, that had swollen the Po to dangerous magnificence, were here having their widest effect. For Mantua sits on a promontory dividing three lakes, or rather three broadenings of the river Mincio—so is advantageously placed for being cut off; and the Mincio, it struck us, was doing well at the moment. Babs lifted an eyebrow at it. Would Nicolette have to go into that? The immensely long bridge ahead of us soon disappeared under water; not a cart, or a car, was on the road to inquire of. We scanned the waste of waters a moment, thinking how unattainable (and how desirable) the town looked; then dove into the map. Yes, there was a little road that branched from ours, and led toward Parma; we ducked into it and set off over excruciating bumps, hoping to find a bridge, or a *bivio;* bouncing along with the tops of bushes, and floods, on each side of us. After a while trees arrived, and into this jungle vanished a lane of deep red mud. A twisting cart-track was in it.

"It's only for carts," we said, looking wistfully down it; and drove on. A priest was on the road but we did not stop to interrogate him—he looked as if he wouldn't like being asked. Besides, the town was right out there. . . . But it grew discouragingly out of sight behind us; I began to wish I had asked that dour-looking padre. The water was so persistent; we should be in Parma presently, if we didn't stop. Could the road have been that cart-track under the trees? And Nicolette, as if cheered by this small hope, hastened back with us.

Heartening to see Mantua growing bigger and bigger across the water; on reaching the muddy track we found an actual, live cart turning into it, and the carter said rather gruffly that *si, si,* this would take us to Mantua. A horrible mud-wallow! Nicolette slewed, roared, heaved herself out—and there we were on a high-dyked bit of red gravel road, still going downhill, with the flood escorting us. The tops of maple trees were showing beside us; round mounds of green above the satin-smooth water, with ducks bumping into their foliage! And where our road dipped to cross another, a tongue of water was already creeping over the gravel. . . .

The flood was rising, then!

But an upgrade followed, and on its bank Italians in every style of dress were seated, dangling lines in this new and clear lake. Round a point of trees we came in sight of the ramparts again; and more fishermen. Half Mantua was out, making a holiday of it; gabbling and gesticulating at the flood, or angling lightheartedly from its edge. They looked merrily up at us as if about to speak, but did not; went on with their angling, or their conversation, and were most polite. Many of them indeed were well-to-do Mantuans in broadcloth and Fedoras; officials of the town doubtless, out to see about things and gabbling as hard as anybody.

We looked back at the thread of mainland, and wondered about getting to it again. We had thought of staying overnight here instead of at Verona, where we had been before, but if that flood rose many inches we should be immured.

Immured, at Mantua? We were not thrilled enough about it for that. Garda was calling us; Bogliaco and the snows and the red fishing sails. . . . And Mantua, said Baddy, had mosquitoes.

We would see. These ramparts surely were imposing; we entered their great brown gate. Tram-tracks, and a thick bit of traffic—Mantua is the center of Italy's silk trade, though she doesn't look it; perhaps this was silk we were in the middle of. In New York, we knew, there is a most annoying section given over to silk—not attractively displayed in windows, but in paper-clad bales and names over doors; possibly Mantua's silk is also thus concealed. At any rate, Nicolette took us round a narrow corner (we were sure she had an ecclesiastical sense, by now), and there was the great portal of Sant' Andrea, with a gaudy officer coming out of it in scarlet and medals. Beyond, we sighted something huge and brownish; went gingerly through more narrowness and out, to our pleasure, into an enormous space—now the Piazza Sordello. It had been only recently renamed.

"Who will may hear Sordello's story told," says Browning; but why should Mantua re-name itself about a troubadour who lived in 1250? Why not do it a little sooner? For he was mentioned by Dante, and Dante is dear to the heart of Italy —dearer, as I had discovered, than Robert Browning, whose poem had been written so much later. What reminded Mantua of Sordello? We scented something interesting here.

Around us were more great things with battlements, and more officers hastening up their steps; indeed our whole impression of the town, except for the red and white of Sant' Andrea, was of hugeness, brownness, and battlements.

And we had not expected officers in Mantua. They brightened it up, but they interfered; mentally, that is. For we had expected Virgil and quietness, Mantegna and grave beauty, whereas here, as I have said, were battlements and officers. The entire present tone of the place seemed to be gay and hurrying officers, the churches a thing of the past—as much a background in reality as they were in color and agedness; standing there unchanged, unprotesting in their medievalness, yet somehow blunted in their intentions, unsure in their appeal; not quite reaching you. Was mass ever held in this impassive bulk, unkempt and shabby? Was that one a palace, or a barracks?

Mantua, with perhaps a breath of weediness in the remote edges of her cobblestones, has a way of looking at you a little helplessly. She craves something—or you crave it for her: point, a scheme of things, more fuss about her entrances, a little topographical enthusiasm, even tourists and noise; for all the local enthusiasm, just now, seemed to be outside catching fish. We gazed, we drew up, we said, Really, this is fine;

but the Mantegnas had somehow grown dim, inside those great façades; and as for Virgil, he didn't exist. . . . We wanted tea, but did not stop for it; whirled past Sant' Andrea again, had a lively, friendly, and most satisfying conversation with a tall jolly red-faced colonel with a gold sword dangling.

He was dashing down the church steps but stopped and assured us, with great kindness and cordiality, that we had better go on at once—presto; adesso! as the town would certainly be shut in by morning.

He looked amused and amiable, sketched the beginning of compliments, twirled his mustache, and glanced admiringly at Babs—evidently desiring to see more of these bold traveling signore; wished us a gallant farewell, saluted, turned smartly on his heel, joined a fellow-officer who was hastening by and went decoratively and jinglingly off.

"Well!" said we in one breath; then laughed and drove on. "Wasn't he nice," I said.

"But *where* do they get that uniform these days?" asked Babs; for there had been nothing of the "black shirt" about our friend; he was resplendent in crimson and blue and gold. "Perhaps it was a special day," she suggested; "perhaps they were going to have a review."

"Perhaps he was going fishing!"

We lingered a little outside Mantua's walls, but saw not one mosquito. Bother the floods. But for them we should have stayed here and seen Virgil's birthplace, a few miles away; perhaps even Gonzago, ancestral home of the Gonzagas family who ruled Mantua for 380 years and made their city *Mantova la Gloriosa.* But blood thinned out at last, history took an ill turn, and the duchy "came to a miserable end in 1708, when Mantua passed to the Austrians."

Most duchies came to a miserable end about then. The time of Italy's sturdy glory, of rich burghers and flourishing art, was nearly over, and foreign domination setting in. For decades Napoleon and the Austrians played a sort of ball with poor Mantua, extending her fortifications and using her as a southern corner of their battle-ground; she was not really liberated until Italy's great day of liberation in 1866.

Across the sheet of water Mantua retreated behind us, brown and walled, full of unseen treasures. These northern cities, we were finding, have a richness and fascination all their own; and for all our dash southward across the floods, here we were omitting Parma entirely, and those "finest Correggios" it holds.

Va bene! It had all been interesting, the floods not the least so; here were the ranks of fishermen again and, where our road dipped to cross the other, not a trickle of water as before, but a lake across which ducks were now swimming. . . . Quite a fleet of white ducks, very pretty on the pale satin-blue and much pleased with this extension of their privileges; navigating about, making a dash for a particularly splendid worm or gobbling a minnow. . . . Some hundred yards away the red road came out again, and disappeared in the jungly trees; but a shining and fearsome surface lay between us and them.

"It can't be very deep," said Babs, peering, however, rather earnestly round her wheel. "I'll put her in low, I think."

Roaring, and effectually scattering the ducks—who rose on their tails and fled, in a pictorial muddle of wings and water—Nicolette entered the lake. We had taken her through a flood in Cornwall once before, and went gurgling and splashing along; sinking alarmingly, and much faster than I had expected. . . . The tops of the trees had disappeared, there was nothing about us now but shining water; nothing, except my child's sense of direction, to prevent our running off into it and joining the roots of trees far below. Nicolette's gurgling was growing thick, and she was beginning to falter; just as I was convinced that the half-choked motor would stop and the water rush in about our feet, a blessed up-slant began; Nicolette recovered, gained speed, and roared up and out, flinging water wildly about us.

"Well done, lamb!" I said.

"Just as well we didn't stay in Mantua!" murmured Babs,

doing what she could to help heave Nicolette through the mud-hole. "Lucky there's that bit of branch road, isn't it?"

For Verona was now our destination, and the real road to her, also the bridge that led to it, were submerged. Poor Mantua! We could see round her last corner now, and it was all lake. . . . Well, here was our *bivio;* brown and muddy, like the one by the Lago Inferiore, but soon reaching a village and the fine smoothness of the Verona highway.

Now we could buzz along. Smooth, rapid motion was a joy; the country was darkening, purples settled on the mountains, a light or two came out; we knew we were in the midst of historic, battled-over hills, and wished we could see them better. . . . Those hills which, "thrown up by the ancient glacier of the Adige, have been the theatre of many battles"; but we simply fled along. Nicolette, indeed, as if forgetting that she was mortal, forgetting and forgiving her earlier troubles in Italy—her faintings on the Sienese road, the sad gear-twisting in the mountains, today's muddy bath, the storms and dampenings of our Paduan days—flew as one rejoicing; in fact she had been flying for so long now that we quite forgot we had ever been perplexed about her; ever downcast or full of foreboding at some bit of inexplicable behavior.

"*Ra*-ra!" said she complacently, whirling a steady little bonnet round the corner of a great wall; and here was Villafranca di Verona already.

Historic ground still, for Villafranca has the ancient castle of the Scaligers and their great wall known as the "Serraglio," begun by Mastino but finished by his son; a "stupendous work," says Wiel, "consisting of towers at stated intervals, with ditches and moats behind which to shelter the peasants with their flocks and herds. . . ." It also "brought Villafranca almost into touch with Valeggio . . . and acted as a mighty rampart between the territory belonging to Verona and that owned by the lords of Mantua."

This castle of Valeggio, too, looks out not only upon a lovely distant view, but on the high Torre di San Martino which commemorates the victory of Victor Emanuel, "that honorable, bold, shrewd, resolute king," in 1859—and south of it is a tower marking the field of Solferino where, on the same day, his ally Napoleon III put the rest of the Austrian army to flight.

A view, in short, that means something. Topped by the later victories of Garibaldi, these battles in the hills now purpling about us had given Italy her freedom . . . and there was heroism in the air.

Dossobuono; Santa Lucia; a turn north, with long dottings of lights; tram-tracks, a bit of fine intermediary darkness, and a mass of something rose before us, dark against the goldenness of the town; something half-rosy, half-dusky; Verona's wall, and the Porta Nuova. Did the Austrians fortify this, too? A stern-faced dazio, stern as if thinking of Austrians only, and (strangely enough) not realizing the extent of our pro-Italian feelings, approached from his guard-house; quite refusing to smile, as if no little muddy G.B. were going to get the better of him, but allowing us grudgingly, and after much interrogation, to enter. . . . Unlike Italy, this was; yet the northern part of the peninsula has had cause to be stern with invaders.

Verona and her hubbub! We should have known it anywhere. Almost immediately you are in the hospitable heart of the town (or one of them), the Piazza Vittorio Emanuele; and an entertaining heart it is, full of voices, band-music, and an air of uncommon rejoicing—which happens every evening.

We were late in entering, so the rejoicings were in full swing; inattentive crowds beset us, gay youths sang at us—or stood straight and saluted with mock valor and were generally helpful. But we knew the way if Nicolette didn't, and ambled easily along, pleased, after our darksome arrival, by this brilliant sociability. Past arcades, and the gorgeous, half-seen wall of the old arena; then a turn into the most extraordinary darkness— "Lucky we know this place!" muttered Babs; feeling our way along, and halting with a sense of suspended triumph before a dim doorway; the dimmest that ever thought it had a light and was ready for guests.

And we ate in a dim dining-room with a dark and spooky wall-paper; the one bright thing about that meal being the retreat of a tall and grizzled spinster in black who rose, clutching her bottle of Evian water (she had just corked it with care), and sending at the headwaiter as she walked off a glance of purest malevolence. . . .

Here you are, Verona; nice gay Verona . . . and the great Diocletian wall, whose rough projectings, remote though they are in the ages—and rounding tremendously away into Verona's darkness—were touched with a present prettiness of the square's orange glow; Italy, thank heaven, not being given to sky-signs that nullify and disperse the charm and mystery of night.

But both of us were tired; Verona's evening air grew chilly, cafés and *sirops* (except in Venice) do not allure us, and we had had one of those wandering, fresh-air days that all too early put a timber on one's eyelids. . . . After all we were in Verona chiefly to sleep; the lakes, tomorrow, were the thing. After trying our best to stay up a while and be amused, back into the welcome darkness we went; and slept late next morning, and didn't write a note.

THE COMFORTABLE PERGOLA OF THE LOCANDA

San Vigilio, Lago di Garda

CHAPTER XXV

VERONA LEADS TO GARDA

A FINE early start, and a lovely morning. Alps and rose-color were confronting us; here we were, all packed and ready, but—

"Want to just go and look at the Adige?" said Babs.

"Yes!" I said, with all the alacrity of one who had previously determined not to look at anything. "It's *that* way, I think!" and we began to go past the Arena; both of us staring very hard.

"Oh dear," I said . . . "*Would* you just like to go inside?"

A whirl of the wheel was the reply; once within the great walls, we began climbing fervently. "That view from the top!" for the much-towered city is lovely from there.

Today it seemed more than ever so. The Arena is still used, "for lyrical purposes," the guide-book sweetly said; so we gazed with calm—it had once seen sights like the burning of 150 heretics by Mastino. We had looked at this view by a primrose sunset before, but morning blue was enthralling; there were the green meadows, the Alps and the Adige and a bridge or two—of the five Verona has; for this lively river makes an S through the town, as it is so sweet of rivers in old cities to do. . . .

We had always loved the Adige. Verona of course must have it within quais, but still there are its golden pebbles and stones (of a pleasing size); its bright color—blue, on this day, with pink and purple in the wavelets—and always its ardent friendly galloping, busy, so busy on its curly way half across Italy, where it becomes large and calm in the marsh-land above Adria, refusing to relapse downwards into the omnivorous Po, as most northern streams do, but persevering onward to the Adriatic, which it meets with great suddenness.

And we found we knew Verona's streets so well that in a moment we were out by the *duomo* again—"That stunning portal, you know!"—loving its twelfth-centuryness, and the beasts outside the door. . . . And the sculpture on the tombs; especially our little man on horseback, with the broad grin, and the eagle on his back (it's his helmet, hanging down).

Art owes very much to the passion of our race for tombs; the Scaligers have a group of gorgeous ones by the church of Santa Maria Antica, and that little man is Cangrande I; the "Story of Verona" thus interprets the grin: "The rider turns his face toward you and smiles, an indication it may be that Death, of whom he had no fear while yet in this life, has equally no dread for him now that he is to meet him face to face."

The young ruler, greatest of the Scaligers, seems to have been an attractive soul; brave in battle, considerate to his foes, a patron of art and learning. He quarreled with Dante, to be sure, toward the last of that great man's stay; but the unhappy poet, spending his first year of exile there, was probably in a frame of mind with which it was easy to fall out, and Cangrande was tremendously busy; digging "the great moat out of its rocks," as Ruskin says, building Verona's walls and towers, and acquiring cities; Padua, Vicenza, Bassano.

Cangrande "died at thirty-seven—of eating apples when he was too hot," Ruskin adds; and his death was a catastrophe for Verona. Youthful as he was, and blithe of spirit, he had labored for the good of his people, and his successors were "men of a different and entirely inferior order."

Juliet's tomb, of red marble, being entirely legendary, we did not again bestir ourselves in its direction. It is in a pretty enough setting, under cloister-arches, with shrubs blooming and vines drizzling, but we preferred to linger at this northern bend of the Adige. The nicest bridge of all is here, partly because it is Roman, and many-arched, partly because things on the banks are deliciously old and pink-and-yellow—Verona's oldest corner, this is, and too delightful for words;

though the Adige chatters and tries to give you even those, and the Alps look immortally down and tell you you don't need any.

But downstream is the lovely apse of St. Anastasia, and its tower; opposite, the verdant and blossoming hill goes steeply up with its fortifications, merging into a glory of Alpine summits against the blue; there are old, old churches, and gardens with cypresses . . . and the ruin of the great Teatro Antico, within whose enormous construction the river itself used to be turned on, "to aid in whatever scenery required water effects"—which sounds like magic but was merely Roman brains. . . . Not even anything as recent as Scaliger brains; and architects nowadays, given rivers and hills, seem still less to realize their possibilities.

For Verona deserves chapters; books—I had just started reading one about her; and Ruskin, with an excitement that one quite understands, calls it "a city which in sooth is possessed of conditions so estimable as to cause it to rank among the best in Italy."

"*That* place has atmosphere," said two very calm Cambridge friends, who had spent some days here and wished to spend more.

And I must not forget the balconies; lovely old ones of carved marble. They hang over one's head in the least likely of places; as the great English appreciator again says, in one of his precise yet oddly malleable sentences, "The chief city of Italy, as regards the strict effect of the balcony, is Verona; and if we were to lose ourselves among the sweet shadows of its lonely streets, where the falling branches of the flowers stream like the fountains through the pierced traceries of the marble," etc.—I have not room for all of it, nor do I know just where Ruskin was when he saw his flowers streaming; but it sounds as if one were en route to the Piazza delle Erbe, whence run "sweet shadows" and "lonely streets." . . .

For all its dazzling architecture, this space is Verona's market, "almost the most picturesque piazza in Italy." A fabulous skyline and painted façades, it has; a tower, a Venetian column and delicate old palaces; above all, the charm of its long wriggling shape, careless and river-like, with the white market umbrellas clustering thickly about the aged fountain; while beneath the transparent shadow of the umbrellas—beneath towers and romanticism—sit the peasants with their flowers and vegetables and bright wares.

A busy place, but we inserted ourselves through a minor piece of it; on our way out I glanced up at the house-tops of a little lane and saw mustard, in two pots, growing against the stuccoed chimney of a tiny roof-garden; branching upward, doing splendidly. They would have something blossoming, these Veronese housewives, if they had to go out in the fields and dig up a mustard-plant . . . sweet, on an Italian sky.

Beyond the vegetable end of the piazza, the lively, gabbly end, was the most dignified of squares; literally a square, unusual in Italy, with chaste entering arches, grave fronts, pure stoniness, and Dante, in robes, mournfully in the middle; high and unsocial on a pedestal. A really hushing piazza —the Piazza Dante. Verona for variety! we said; and on nearing the grim old Castel Vecchio chanced to look down a crack, and there were forked red-and-white battlements that we had never seen. Wildly forked, they were; we drove cautiously down the crack, finding that they belonged to a simply tremendous old Scaliger bridge, and how we had failed to notice it we could not imagine. Cangrande II, a bad Scaliger and an oppressor of the people, had built it, having first in fear of his enemies erected the Castel Vecchio on the bank, and moved into it for the rest of his life; he then felt that with a bridge leading directly across the river at this point, he could summon aid from Germany whenever needed. (He seems to have had a crony there; doubtless a pleasant creature like himself.)

A long way for aid to come—from Germany; but the old structure is most conspicuous. No mercenary would mistake it, even from a distance, with its hectically forked stone, and two equally forked and feverish turrets midway across; he would have no excuse for not hastening straight to the castle —which was why Cangrande wanted it red and white, I expect. But it retires enchantingly, with its warm color and exclamatory shape, across the bright running of the river, to the green and melting meadows of the other shore.

Anything so spiked should end in something melting, we said; and the Scaligers, terrible as some of them were, had surely done things for their town. Even Cansignorio, last and worst of them, who killed one brother and was responsible for the death of another, the much-beloved young Paolo Alboino, did a conspicuous service to the people by bringing in pure drinkable water "by means of leaden pipes laid down to the Piazza della Erbe, where the beautiful fountain . . . stands as a record to this day of the good deed wrought for the city by Cansignorio della Scala."

We came to the hill of Verona's garden, the Giardino Giusti, and climbed its infinite flights of steps to the view; the "blue Lombardic plain, wide as the sea, and . . . a little cluster of domes and towers, with a gleam of white water around them" which is Mantua. You can see the hills about Padua, Ruskin says; the "gleam of the horizon" in which Venice rests, and the snowy Alps of Frinli, "touched into a crown of strange rubies as the sun descends. . . ." We liked strange rubies; sunset ones, that is.

Off again by the river, after a long stare at lovely San Zeno, with its lions and its glorious rose-window; then out the Via San Zeno, and the Porta San Zeno, for out that gate ran the road to Castelnuovo—and Garda.

Beloved Garda! In our minds we could already see that shining water, and went bouncing along a dusty road, hotfoot for our first love in the way of Italian lakes—its lemon trees, and blue, and shining white upon the sky. We were only going to glance at it this time, stay there the night, then on for Como; but going to it by road, we should see it so much sooner. See it longer. . . .

The road to our satisfaction was almost straight. Country, as if preparing to be shut in by tremendous bumps in the shape of Alps, was quite intelligently flat; and somewhere out here lay the great plain where a Dominican monk got together an audience for what Sedgwick calls "an emotional peacemaking. . . . The monk preached from the text 'My peace I give unto you,' " and 400,000 people said Amen, wept, and embraced each other.

Waves of a passionate desire for peace, Sedgwick remarks, ran through Italy in the thirteenth century—as waves of reform will run; " 'Oh, when will the day come that Pavia shall say to Milan, Thy people are my people, and Crema to Cremona, Thy city is my city?' " In Florence, Pope Gregory X "pleaded with the Florentine Guelphs to take back the banished Ghibellines . . . and one hundred and fifty leaders of each party met and embraced on the sandy flats of the Arno."

"It is hardly necessary to say," he adds, "that these peacemakings were soon followed by martial emotions . . . and sword and halberd were picked up with appetites whetted by abstinence"; and Babs and I agreed, as hotly as was compatible with the present gaiety of our feelings, that it was simply sickening (and fatiguing and ridiculous) how history repeats itself.

But Nicolette, in her most amiable mood, was hastening. We could almost smell the lake. The end of a deep-blue bay crept toward us, narrowing into the glorious deep swift greenness of Garda's outlet—which turned out to be the beginning of our Mincio. Smooth-sliding indeed; Virgil must have stood here on its brink, when he named it; and into it Peschiara's fortress was magnificently jutting—the same fortress in which Cansignorio imprisoned his beautiful young brother Paolo.

"Well, Mincio," I said, as we crossed it; " 'can't say that we've exactly seen you before, because you had smothered yourself in lakes—but you were there somewhere, buried in all that water about Mantua. . . . Good-by, Mincio! Don't be too deep. Mantua wants its bridges, sometime!"

But what a place for a sketch this was; green and silver,

rushing round the old ivied stone and towered bastions; pinkish-brown, this fortress, as most of them are hereabouts, unless some one got fantastic, like Cansignorio, and wanted red brick. "Peschiara, a darling place," my notes say. "Albergo 'Bel Arrivo'! Casermo, with huge chestnut trees in bloom; one rose-red. Five rosy arches over stream. Lovely!"

Sirmione's peninsula now stood out into the lake, with a belfry at its end. The belfry was charming from where we were; we thought the peninsula was just scenery, and went on,—and there is a particularly fine castle at Sirmione, on the edge of the lake. Also Catullus wrote his poems out there. . . . And there *is* a road; I wasn't looking its way when we passed.

Garda grows broad here, with low wooded shores, but one begins to see how superbly it winds away among grand and snowy mountains. . . . All that northern country is inspiriting; and we had been surprised to learn (in Venice) that Titian was born among the Dolomites, at Pieve di Cadore. Someway one does not associate Titian with mountains—though it needed almost a mountaineering strength to paint as he did. He was "much interested in pure landscape" too, another thing we did not associate him with. . . . But probably mountains did that to him; they do something unforgettable to one, of beauty or of valor, and a picture of his now hanging in Buckingham Palace—odd, I told Babs, we hadn't seen it—shows "an extent of wooded hills after a storm."

Perhaps, we said, the great Venetian would have liked to keep on doing hills after a storm; and they kept him in a city, doing portraits. Oh, grand faces, grand faces . . . but what is a face to a Dolomite? Giorgione, we knew, had an interest in landscape, and possibly communicated it to Titian—who was known to be a follower of this young, romantic and gifted painter; but one liked to feel that in one canvas at least, a memory of the hills among which he was reared, and the storms and sunsets behind their peaks, had returned to invade his work as they once possessed his heart.

Desenzano's hillside gives you a great sweep of these peaks, and of Garda, narrowing fjord-fashion to the north—as water among mountains always seems to narrow; the heavenly recessional of an Alpine lake, blue and violet and silver . . . only you must leave it and plunge down a mile or so to get to the little town and the water.

We plunged; to the very edge of it, where the white steamers set off from a homely, rather shaky wharf; there was a nice cobble-stoned quai, and a fruit-stand, and tables with travelers having golden, froth-edged beer in the open; most of them with their backs to the lake. There it was in its beauty; there were they, humped over their glasses. "What is man, that thou art mindful of him—?"

But they *were* men, and there were only a few of them; they looked like bagmen at that.

Nicolette thought the lake was worth looking at; there had been a blue sail in a little harbor, and a tiny blue speedboat called "Ahi! Ahi!"

A wise little inn had arbors, climbed over with yellow jasmine. Alps were in the sky, and villages made pink or golden spots along the shore; the colored sails of fishing-boats hung here or there. Reflections were marvelous—and very long, for all this wide part of Garda shone; the scarcely moving sails rose from their own pictures. No danger, said we, from Garda's systematic winds today—though the lake can be as rough as the sea, Baddy says. We sat under our arbor in great peace; decided that we remembered Desenzano's church too well to walk uphill and visit it again—we had once seen it with its stone columns blazingly wound with crimson—and set off for Salo.

Through Desenzano's cosy, arcaded streets—a pleasant old place it is—and into the country. Hay was being cut, the first we had seen; we looked out under the shady branches of chestnut trees at fields of cocks, pretty in the sun; the peasants here were all in blue or rose-red. "Blue like the sail!" say my notes. Beautiful in the meadows; also the rose-red.

The lake sheered off, and we attacked a hilly peninsula; were amazed at the precipitous climbing and descending (Garda's waves were all on shore, today)—with an immense view every time we arrived at the top; at last the road curved steadily down to the lake.

Lovely that descent, with pink Salo opposite in its wooded shore, and the deep, green-blue bay between; the Alps that guard and glorify this bit of Italy very snow-peaked, to the north. The road runs by the water—it would be heart-breaking if it did not; along Salo's edge we drove, past boats, colored table-cloths, orange trees in tubs, and pink buildings, till the quai ended and we had to turn inland up into Salo's hot little piazza, then along behind "a succession of villages . . . embowered in cedar and olive groves. The steamer skirts the shore."

Yes, but the road doesn't. "Embowered" is right. Glossy, pampered-looking foliage hung over us, foliage in marvelous condition; but we drove along with a steady sense of bafflement on the right . . . of promontories, which we were not on, standing out into the lake. There were bits and spots where it came in sight, of course, then all was foliage again. (Garda's well-known luxuriance, this was.) "Even the sensitive lemon comes to maturity here," as Baddy explains, "but the trees require to be carefully covered in winter. . . . The fruit is more bitter and aromatic than that of Sicily, suffers less from carriage, and keeps longer."

The sensitive lemon was now on every side of us. Salo and Gardone have hillsides of them, and their fragrance; farther along, "most of the lemon gardens belong to members of the Italian noblesse."

Nice to be a noblesse and have lemons. We even remembered a village called Limone (because its *limoni* were the first grown in Europe) in a bay a little way on; under mountain cliffs it had its terraces and white posts, smothered with glossy foliage and hung with phenomenal lemons—about four times as large as most. From its enchanting shore came row-boats waving branches of lemon trees at you, the fruit in clusters of four or five on a small branch, as conspicuous as lanterns against the cobalt water. . . .

Maderno, Toscolano, Messago, with scarcely a view out . . . and mountains in wild Alpine color towering ever higher above our heads; at last a blossoming meadow, and Bogliaco's dear stone jetty out in the water. We crept expectantly down its tiny lanes to the quai, the hotel, and its little rose-garden with a parapet fascinatingly over the water; but on a balcony women were beating carpet. Long crimson strips of it were on the grass of Bogliaco's little green, beside fishing-nets and boats turned bottom side up; alack, were they closing?

They were. They had closed yesterday. Smiles and regrets; the women were sorry; but even the little water-front looked deserted. No fishing-boats, with high red sails drooping, lay at the stone jetty or were making their way across the lake; our mountains were all there—the snow peaks opposite, the far purple ones; the great shoulders of blue-velvet surrounding the bay, and the near, green one we had climbed; but Bogliaco itself seemed strangely dead.

Had it ever been so magical? Did it all depend on the presence of our English friends—and carpets in their proper places? It had been a pretty story, our finding Bogliaco; we would leave it unspoiled. Besides, there was no place to stay! We felt a little dashed.

We stepped into the rose-garden; that too seemed empty . . . but—the view from that stone parapet! Far down on Garda's other side we could even see San Vigilio's point of cypresses; it was too far (all around the bottom of the lake) to drive there now, from Bogliaco, but if one could just hop across! Around that point, beneath the Duke's garden, one could feel how the lovely shrine of the chapel hung over the water . . . and then the terrace, where, under great horse-chestnuts and their domes of white bloom, you eat, in all simplicity, good bread and butter, good Italian food . . . with great purple fishes wagging their fins and being incomparably lazy below; then comes the gray-walled *locanda,* beside which the big fishing boats slip softly into a tiny, stone-bounded harbor. (It holds two of them, close together.) They have a trick of coming in at twilight, or early dawn—when a fisherman's voice may rouse you, or the sound of oars in rowlocks; if you have the courage to get up and look from a window, you see the nice thing just below you, furling its great sail—ones with yellow sails always seemed to come in at San Vigilio—with fish piled in baskets and its bowsprit almost, though not quite, in at the door of the little wine shop, but poked very nicely under the grape-vine that flourishes so there against the locanda's gray wall, above its old, rounding, stone steps that go down into Garda's water. . . .

A dear spot, San Vigilio; but the afternoon was getting along. . . . We returned to Nicolette, suddenly feeling less dashed.

"This road goes a little further, you know—shall we go on?" said my daughter, starting the motor with great briskness. "Perhaps it goes nearer the lake, now."

It did; first getting us to gray old Gargnano—a fishing-town, rather thick driving—then into a much smaller road, but still beside the water's edge. (We were determined to see as much of Garda as we could.) A charming road, informal and up and down, with lovely Italian ruralities going on—donkeys, fishing-people, flowers, little pink houses; lemon trees bright with lemons, the blue water always beyond; it revived us instantly. Up! up, it must presently go, with the lake below it, and a white billowing of mountains. Visions assailed us of reaching villages no car had ever reached, views no motorist had set eyes on; and Nicolette was gaily climbing a dark-earthy, scrambling ascent toward a corner enclosed in crumbling walls when—alas! we saw that half of it had been washed away.

Ah, chestnut trees, high villages and romance! We must leave you, just as your lure was greatest. . . . But mule-tracks were mule-tracks.

Ec-co! And we *had* seen a sweet little inn at Salo.

Back there again, a smiling waiter with a napkin on his arm was waiting for us to have tea among his orange-tubs. Waiters by a lake always do that—and by the Thames . . . (oh, our garden in Kew!)—it seems to be a waterside custom; and it is pleasant, after a long drive, to see some one so ready for you, proprietary smile and all. This *cameriere* was particularly sweet; sat us where we could see the very most of the lake and the mountains, and hovered faithfully over us. We liked being hovered over, liked the simplicity and neatness of the little inn, and decided to stay there—though anything on Garda would do; it is a spot that removes criticism as if it were some malign thing in one's organism.

Our room looked out over gay awnings and little orange trees to the lake and its enchantments. Light had lowered, sunset was coming on; we ran upstairs and changed hastily into tennis-shoes.

We were going out in a boat! The padrone himself untied one for us, a nice dry boat that rowed easily; in a few long strokes Babs had us well out in the bay, with Salo just part of the view behind us. Even out here where the lake-water was so alarmingly deep, we could see how absolutely clear it was; something to look down into . . . but not for long. Up, was too wonderful; and we were far enough out now to see around Gardone's promontory.

Surrounded by rosiness and mountains, we floated on. It was a pink sunset; with snow-peaks against a belt of turquoise-blue. Far out, the lake was pink and satin-smooth; shores were reflected in it—cypresses on a point, a village, an old tower; near us lay rosy reflections of snow peaks and clouds. . . . Rose-color grew flaming; sometimes Babs moved an oar to keep the boat from swinging, for the sky was most marvelous across the lake in the east, where the highest mountains were, and the most snow.

Evenings on Garda we had known before; but there is no imagining a sunset. You may conceive a sky, such as you have already seen, but what it will do, how glorify, on what its enhancings will most fall—what its particular fantasy and superimposing of colors will be, its keenness and softness, its gleamings here and lightings there, its withdrawal into dusk —no one, however rich in sunset-memory, can foresee. We simply floated there in our nice dry boat; floated on sky color. Sometimes Babs turned her eyes from the mountains, in a quiet look. Ourselves floating there—beauty everywhere; that is how I shall always see Garda.

Dusk was coming, doing marvelous things to colors and reflections. Velvet brown with streaks of copper-red and gold; blackish-green, with streaks of rose; orange-brown villages, blinking with topaz; and the reflection of one cypress was a mile long.

Poems had been written under that cypress. A fitting spot . . . I remembered how at San Vigilio the little pale man with the dark glasses—a writer, and friend of the Docteur Mario who was staying there (and who had won the Prix d'Oro, Italy's Victoria Cross, three times: *"C'est un héro! Dans son pays, il est renommé!"* said the little friend, very earnestly)—had talked to me, on two minutes' acquaintance, and with such simplicity and fervor, about the beauty of this country . . . and was kind enough to do it in French. One sentence of his fluent and fervid speech, as we stood looking out at Garda, is still in my mind.

"Dans ces paysages, belles et tranquilles, on cherche les âmes les plus grands—les poêtes!"

"Yes, little man!" I thought, touched by his pale face and his fervor; and longed to tell him about Babs.

Not being an Italian, however, I did not; to my everlasting regret.

Yes, poets belonged on this lake, and exquisite verses; yet, "Boat and sunset," Babs wrote that night in her diary. Somehow it seemed enough.

It had grown dark now, except for touches of light on the snowy creatures up in the sky. A star had come out. With some quakings, out there in the very deep water, we changed places; Babs leaned back and looked, and I rowed home on a kind gleam of light that came all the way out from Salo to show us the path in.

And then we slept most wonderfully in our clean room, with fresh Alpine air blowing in; breakfasted outdoors in blue and green and gold—as one so often does on the Lakes—then got ourselves away, in sunshine and over dusty roads, for Brescia. Were surprised by Brescia's lovely loggias, wandered a little, admired more loggias, and had Nicolette greased while we lunched—a combination that always pleases us; then leaving the good town and her heroisms (she had once held out for ten days against "the Austrian general Haynau, nicknamed 'the hyena of Brescia!' "), started off northwest again.

We had entered by the Via Venezia and went out, with equal logic, by the Via Milano; but not to Milan. We already knew that cathedral, having seen it by sunshine, moonlight, and a most moving rain.

"Out there," said Babs, gesturing eloquently, "is Baynesie's plain. We want to avoid that."

"Do we?" I said.

"Yes. It's absolutely flat, all the way to Milan. Baynesie was always talking about it." (Baynesie was an instructor in history.) "Marvelously rich, you know; but you don't want to drive over it."

"No," I said; "don't let's!" and we struck into the road for Iseo.

A short, pictorial drive, with a violent thunder-storm in the middle, nowhere to take shelter, and the best lightning and sheets of rain we had met; then the sky parted, blue showed, the sun came warmly out, and the world was all one drenched, glittering beauty—that soon dried (as we did) and brought us to a tempestuous hill-climbing Iseo, gleaming with color.

A jumble of wild little hills were escorting us—dark, or waterily lighted; also a flock of lop-eared sheep. They looked funny with drooping ears. There were little pink churches on dark hills, against other hills almost sunlit . . . a vivid pale green; and in that dish of light sat a pink village. There came a flash of vivid blue, through trees—just iris, by a brook (one blossom and a bud; a most Japanese arrangement). Honeysuckle was in the hedges; white daisies and a dark-blue, spiry flower scattered themselves in rye-green under the shade of mulberries, with sun filtering through. "Lovely!" say the notes.

I remember looking back at it and wishing the dark-blue spiry flower—and the daisies—would grow in our rye at home; we don't encourage daisies in rye. Too bad. They seemed to be doing it no harm; and probably the peasants make something thrifty out of the intruders, or they wouldn't be so cheerful about letting them grow there. Daisy soup! Blue-flower salad. . . .

We met another big flock; and shepherds with short yellow crooks. Their dog, shaggy and iron-gray, took his charges to one side of the road and stood between us and them, not moving; not making a sound; just lifting his lip a little. . . . "*You* look out for my sheep!"

He could scarcely have done a more eloquent thing. We went by, liking him so much . . . and the way the shepherds left it all to him.

Iseo is the lake with the deepest, most concentrated blues and greens, we decided; the best island with a half-hidden villa (we could just see the balustrade of its garden); the most jagged, mixed, and tumultuous mountains leaping up around her; we thought it merely our usual luck when we found, a mile or two up the shore, a little Italian *albergo* (very Italian) all alone by some meadows with its feet in the lake, and its own garden with red roses blooming in arbors. It had a sort of pavilion adjoining, in which dinner for 250 people was being rather alarmingly laid; also our room was a little —unused, one might say; its yellow satin a trifle sad, the prodigal lace of its curtains—why are Italian hostesses so fond of Nottingham lace?—the least bit dingy; but we leaned out its window at the mellifluous view and said,

"What do we care? We shall be out all the time anyway!" and felt we wouldn't move for a kingdom. This was a grand place for over Sunday. . . .

A young Italian seemed to be the proprietor and we had much amicable conversation with him—stood about, quite comfortably gabbling. The padrone was nice—tall, thin and humorous; he had a younger brother, an old father who stood in the doorway and looked amiably on, and a dear old peasant-mother, kerchiefed and immensely aproned, scuttling about the kitchen—its open, vine-wreathed door fronted on the yard; a glorious, old-time, Italian kitchen that occupied the main wing of the house. It had copper pots along its walls and pleasant large windows looking both on the lake and on the garden. Bright charcoal fires were burning and huge pots stewing; garlic hung about, pans of vegetables and orderly piles of fruit were on the two great tables that went the length of the room; some peasant assistants, their old heads in bright kerchiefs, were sitting by the tables peeling and preparing . . . and a lively chatter going on.

It wouldn't be bad, we said, spending "hours and hours" in that kitchen. The other rooms were quite subordinate to it; small, a trifle musty, little thought of.

And then occurred an incident very characteristic of this naïve delightful land. Not having found upstairs anything resembling a bath-room, I approached the old peasant-mother. "*Si si!*" said she heartily. To my dismay however she spoke in no uncertain tones to her old husband, he standing about unoccupied; he brightened, and shouted something to his sons; they approached (*bon Dieu!*) and he waved me to their care. There was no retreat now; smiling and bowing—*ec-co,* a service he could render the signora?—one son planted himself in the driveway, gladly gesturing, the other took his stand by a vine-clad building opposite (idiot! why hadn't I seen it myself?), also making signs of welcome; and through this avenue of masculine cordiality, papa still beaming from his doorway, I took rapid steps.

FROM OUR BALCONY IN VARENNA

Lake Como

Utter peasant simplicity this was, terrible, but without guile, for when I came out, prepared to perish, both chaperones had gone their simple way.

Nicolette still stood in the yard: "It's early yet; want to go for a drive round the lake?" said Babs.

I did. Neat, delightful villages, with gardens by the water, were hiding in tiny coves; there was a belfry on every point; and a moss-rosebud of an island, not the one with the balustrade, but a bigger one—was the island of one's dreams. It had a mountain in the middle and a medieval castle, with a profile of perfect evergreens declining, and a windmill on a rock; its fishing-village was below on a bit of beach. . . . Moss-rose mountains rose from the lake with old houses clinging to them and a wreath of snow-white cloud across their middles; on one very dark mountain a white church showed above the cloud-wreath. . . . A devout region, here; on our road the large shrines faced both ways, so that fishermen from the lake could see Madonna, and be blessed.

Wild flowers . . . the air was sweet with them; aromatic with wild thyme; and a rose-pink flower with long stems and fine silvery foliage hung out from the cliffs in great clumps. It was a feature of this drive. Nowhere else but on Iseo did it seem to beautify the cliffs, and Iseo is beset with cliffs; the road had to cut its way into some of them. Oh, a jewel of a little long lake—not so little either; we thought of course we were going all the way round, but on crossing its narrow tip came to an *impasse.* The map had said there wasn't any more road—that it went off inland to Bergamo; but as at Garda, we felt there ought to be a road. Perdition, there must be a road! We crawled up a cobbled hill beside little fish-smelling buildings, then slid down slimier cobbles; *did* the road go round that red fish-house?

The cobbles did, on a slant; deep water was just below it, and Nicolette's forefeet on its slope—when we stopped so suddenly that I found myself in the wind-shield. The cobbles, round that corner, shrank to half their width! This was another mule-track—or a foot-path, alas; and the mountains ahead were so steep and blue-green and heavenly, the islanded lake so enticing.

The cottages here were stony and aged, with boats slopping in the water below, and blossomy fields beyond—Iseo's fields of buttercups and forget-me-nots, dark columbine and white orchids, lovely but tantalizing—and the road could just as well have gone across them. . . . Yet everything smiles, about Iseo, no matter where you are—colors and flowers and little white villages, cosy and informal, fishy and farmy . . . for except in spots at the far end, Iseo is mostly Italian and of the people; refreshing for that.

Colors, dropping toward sunset, were even lovelier. We had tea in a fortunate garden; and everything looked different, going this way. The bit of road under the precipices seemed wetter and more winding, the water a more fairy green; the rose-colored flowers stood out differently against it, or drooped in new perspective from the cliff; the villages, with their big old catalpa trees in lavender bloom, did almost a better job of hinging mountain and lake, while the mountains themselves, showing the same rock-strata in waving, purple bands along their surfaces, seemed saucier of outline, more scarred or velvety of sides.

And the Saturday party was arriving, as we turned in at the *albergo's* gate.

Youths and girls were clustering under the rose-arbors; simple light dresses or blouses with dark skirts, the girls wore, but their vitality and sparkling eyes made gaiety enough. The young men were graceful; I remember how one of them reached above his head, picked a red rose, and with charming play of eye and hand, offered it to his lady. A perfect little act.

During dinner some thumping music arrived, and they danced; we betook ourselves to a little red-and-blue boat. The padrone gave us a push-off, and a laughing caution about something—I did not quite catch it; Babs settled back into the oars, the water widened between us and shore. . . . Ah, this was the way to escape; the hilarity came more faintly out to us.

"Splendid, darlings—" I thought. "Have a wonderful time, dance and scream, but let us be out here!"

Starlight was on the lake, the dark mountains; it led us far out. We rowed quite round the island, sculling along under the shadow of its overhanging trees with the water lapping on its old wall—we could just see the beautiful balustrade, as we floated below and beside it. The scent of roses came over it; from somewhere, a nightingale sang.

We went twice around that island . . . its cypresses sharp against the starry, velvet blue, roses in the darkness; there may have been a thousand roses as big as cauliflowers—the dark hid them, all but that fragrance. Very shadowy, this far side. No light came from the hidden villa, though we sometimes caught a gleam of its closed front; very black trees hung far out over us, making exotic noises; black lappings, shiny as jet and touched only rarely with silver, crept mysteriously about us. . . .

Was this an "Island that Liked to be Visited"? we asked each other; and thought of Mary Rose. An odd effluence seemed to come from it, exquisite, incomprehensible, but somehow hair-stirring: sounds, now and then, that might have been the sob of one tree upon another, or of a soul close-pressed. We were not at all sure the island liked us; not sorry, as our boat rounded the last bit of balustrade, to let it drift out a little; out of the blackest heart of the shadow, away from the tones of the water as it met the old wall. . . . Lovely, they were; tuneful, varying—and astonishingly human.

It was magical, out in the friendly star-gleams again, with a wide sparkling going off to an abrupt wall of mountains.

Iseo is nobly walled. High against the manifold and glittering stars they flung themselves, less dark than the cypresses, more akin to stars. Their tops almost vanished in silver; darkly silvered the whole range of them, as if the starlight were falling on moss . . . which it undoubtedly was. The island was an island now—it had been a continent when we were beside it; Mary Rose's island, we were sure. It sat there, a cypressed shape in the star-gleams, drawing its fragrances about it. Even the nightingale's song had grown dim; but the water-voices had followed us, and were all under our boat. All there were, on that silent lake; and they, so light and lulling.

We drifted a long time. So many twinkles led to those mountains! Lights had gone down, on the shore; managing, in that noble starshine, to get a gleam on the face of Minnie, we were amazed to find it nearly midnight and rowed back, dew and peacefulness to the roots of our hair, watching the glorious retreat of the mountains. Babs "lined" a cypress and stretched out—gladly, for it was growing chill; a swift wake we made, without a swerve, but even so were met by worried hosts on the dock. From the *casa* to the water's edge they had been going—back and forth, they told us . . . did they know that was Mary Rose's island? They could not imagine any one's wishing to row for hours on "a dark lake," and with smiles and great relief bowed us to our beds. But I shall never know what it was the padrone tried to tell us that night, as he pushed us off from the little wharf.

CHAPTER XXVI

AS A PRELUDE TO COMO

May 23rd. Whitsunday. . . . Pilzonè, Bergamo, Varenna. Very thick driving; bicycle-races," says the diary; for we had decided to go on to Como.

It was one of those long-distance races that Italy adores, with thin lads in gaudy jerseys, and with numbers tied on their backs, making what time they can over Italy's sharp hills and through dust and roughness. Every little town was jammed, but it was at Ponte San Pietro we had our first real taste of what a bicycle-race means; roped-off crowds, flags, booths, and shouting; all the paraphernalia of holiday, including hoots of disgust at the sight of little Nicolette creeping into their midst. The road took a sharp uphill turn, carrying crowds, ropes, and booths with it; and the instant Nicolette came in sight, fresh snarls of what sounded like hate, rage, and disappointment broke from the throats of hundreds of spectators who had heard the previous shouting and thought that a large squad of racers was about to burst upon them. Arms waved, chins were furiously stuck out at us, epithets flew; feeling hot and superfluous we went grinding up the hill, and were attaining a slight zone of peace, when a roaring behind us announced the coming of the riders at last. Roars, whistles, hoots!

"And here's the Committee," said Babs. "Behold the armbands!" For three important citizens were capering before us.

"Sinistra! sinistra!" they shouted. Left, left!

Very well, we'd *sinistra;* keep your hair on, darlings. We looked back, expecting thunderbolts and lightning-flashes at least . . . and behind us in a sort of harmless jingling and crinkling, with a low murmur of talk and in entire amity, with nobody apparently trying to get ahead of anybody else, came a bunch of seven or eight riders, all hung with different colors and spare tires; all unanimously humped over their handle-bars, unanimously pedaling and perspiring, but smiling at each other and chewing peacefully.

"That's funny," I muttered, staring after their departing backs; "but then they couldn't rush all the way to Lecco, I suppose—or wherever this thing ends."

"Hope it's Lecco!" murmured Babs; for more shouts were greeting us. "Here comes another squad."

Another cross-road impended; but this time friendliness predominated. Two squads of racers had just gone by, and here was a little red car close after them, obviously unable to catch up. *Benissimo! Viva l'Italia!* And they waved hats and handkerchiefs, smiling gorgeously up at us; we smiled back. . . .

After that the crowds, watching passionately, were pleasant or not as the mood took them, but more disorderly; they burst from their bounds, and driving grew perilous. . . .

We descended into a valley, with a pretty green stream widening over the flat bits; was this Como's outlet?

"Those mountains there—the ones that are so much bluer —they *must* be on the other side of the lake."

"Yes, and all that opening-out. . . . I'm *sure* it's the beginning of Como!"

In spite of these excitements, and the lovely way great thundery-looking clouds were rearing up, matters in the road still took our attention till we sighted the tall chimneys of Lecco and entered that industrious town. It wasn't as unpleasant as we had expected, but had a lake-front with a park and flowers and many boats, and manufacturing poked away somewhere; here we really left the last of the racers and the crowds behind, and peace fell. We could scarcely believe it.

We climbed steeply up through Lecco and a few more of her little afterthoughts, warehouses and such, then turned away from them down a long, gradual hill with a flowered and bushed mountain on our right, going straight up, and at the bottom of the hill, over a little low wall and a flower or two, Como at last beside us.

She was clear, she was deep, she was the color of mountains; and she stretched vastly northward. Snow peaks looked at us over the heads of others—a noble company. The confusion of them was lovely; dark-blues and purples, climbing to forget-me-not, and to snow.

We had come to Como by train before and had a stormy day-and-a-half in which, with awful thrills at the wharves, yells and splashings and losings of ropes, we went round her by boat and decided she was the most marvelous thing we knew . . . especially in a storm. But now we felt it was going to be different; weather and all. "Now," said Nicolette, bobbing contentedly along, "owing to me, you'll stay a while, perhaps!" Owing to various things, O Nicolette. . . .

Como, in places opulently lovely, is yet wide-flung and diverse enough, with her three arms, to give one long stretches of simplicity, and simple villages. Opulence touches the Bellagio side, but soon thins out—to nature's opulence of orchid studded pastures and forest-scented cliffs; the true concentration of it is opposite, where the Villa Carlotta sits in her fat gardens staring at the white lake-boats that skim so busily by, and transfixing the souls of tourists ("Oo! Look at the azaleas!") so that they walk obediently down the gangplank, in at her elaborate gates.

We had done that ourselves—though hastily; but there would be more time for things now, we told each other. We could go exhaustively around that garden—six times round each azalea, if we wished. . . . And as we spoke, the purples came down over the mountains; the lake, though twinkling with silver near us, had their vast purple shapes upon its forest tints and twilight blue. Nicolette was very quiet, a bird sang, and we stole blissfully along, in wild flowers and under great mountainsides; into dripping tunnels with little brooks splashing down their rocky sides.

"Bump *wump!*" said Nicolette, as she came out of one; and kept on bumping, over a bed of rough stones, until it occurred to us we might have a puncture.

We had. We found a dry spot beside the wet cliffs and got the spare on; not with any great speed, we were out of practice now. But colors look wonderful after a tunnel. Blues never were so blue; you stare at a single poppy by the roadside as if you had never seen one. . . .

Como was overwhelming, but we bore up well; even listened for the noise of the Fiume Latte when we came near its village. There it was, milk-white and roaring; nothing had been done to the village to hurt its age and charm, and the breath of the torrent greeted us as before—the Fiume Latte shoots out an icy finger and grips you as you go by; then the road lifted us into a scented blackness of cypresses above a grand little villa or two, whose lights twinkled through shrubbery below us. . . . Ah, but in Varenna we were going to be grand too. No little pier-side *albergo* for us this time, but the town's upper levels; a salmon-pink hostelry, and gardens over the lake—we had seen all this from the boat and vowed to stay there one day.

This was the day; and strange enough it seemed. . . . We were growing so very magnificent! This summer had been the best year for the farm, a good year for books (three out and one in the works), and our letter of credit holding out amazingly; why should we not go to a hotel with a hyphenated name? and if we had been a pair of parrots sitting there in Nicolette we should no doubt have made proud, objectionable noises and stuck out every feather we owned.

Well, we'd done it, with infinite faggings; the darling ponies had trotted their small legs over hill and dale—they ought to be here too, we said.

The bare church, the straggling triangle of piazza; women standing in doorways, little girls carrying loaves of bread . . . and down every steep little lane a magic glimpse of lake and mountains; yes, this was our Varenna. Whirl in to the left, and here is your grandeur, looking (on its street side) ordinary enough; I went in. Nothing extraordinary here either. The little padrone listened courteously to my Italian but replied, as they all burn to do, in voluble English; no doubt was left one that he had in readiness for us a plenitude of magnificent, indeed of indescribable rooms.

"Momento, signor!" said I; and dashed for the door.

Go through those gardens without Babs? That wasn't the way we did things.

Blissful, we descended steps in the wake of the padrone. He led us, it seemed to our expectant hearts, through the clean prose of mattinged halls into a sudden, aged poetry of gardens. Silently we went down its terraces, under the roofed banksias and along by the balustrade of its wall—below which lapped the water of the lake and where, on a tiny beach, fishing-boats were drawn up. On some old steps a woman artist in a red smock was cleaning a palette; across the lake the mountains loomed above their bright villages.

We hurried to catch up with the landlord.

The wall, which crooked outward round a great horse-chestnut, led to a shady walk roofed with a luxuriance of everything that waves or scrambles nimbly toward the light (blooming beautifully in the shade meanwhile); there was a bit of mossy fountain at its end, then mossy steps up to a sudden brightness, where the salmon-colored front of the Dépendence looked down upon a pergola of wisteria. All the lake was beyond; in face of that, salmon-color and wisteria seemed somehow to melt, to retire, to be unable to wound. . . . Varenna, especially if seen from the lake, is mostly bright tints of an orangy-pink order, or pale yellow, or (rarely) a lovely old faded color like clove-pinks, but all so trailed over by rose-vines, shielded by mountains and repeated in the water, that one doesn't mind its rifts of brilliance. We gave one gasp at the bright front—for it was bright after that dim path; and climbed to our room.

A large room looking out on everything, with big tables to write on, and soft color, and a great soft rug—everything somehow rich and spacious and soft, as Como demands. The chestnut tree composed, the old roofs were divine, a hooded fishing-boat was going slowly by. Age and deliberation were everywhere. Across the water, the deliberation of mountains. . . . Also pleasing to us at the moment was the hint of frivolity at their feet—little dabs of pink and white, the white steamers plying about; on shore an ordered frivolity, classic and reposeful, housed year after year in the same tinted stucco, shaded by the same rose-arbors. . . .

"Va Bene!" I said, with the feeling one has that one should never praise a room too highly, yet with a sense of horrid stinginess in not praising it more; and Nicolette was soon in care of a young mechanic. Dark-eyed and bursting with enthusiasm was he; he thought our little *macchina* was *"graciosa, bellissima!"* and fluttered about her like a desirous bee confronted with the first larkspur of the season. *"Lavare?"* He would begin this very instant. *"Olio, non?"* The signorina thought not?

That was a blow, but he bore up under it; pounced on the carburetor and fluttered still more.

It was some time since anybody had been so enthusiastic about Nicolette; we smiled all the way back to our room. Difficult to dress, with lights coming out across the lake and a nightingale singing in the chestnut tree, but we descended at last.

Dinner, as far as human atmosphere went, was amusingly frosty because the guests were mostly English, of correct middle class, with one or two mistaken Ja-Ja's in a corner, subdued and almost furtive; the flowers were lovely, the food cordial, and if "coffee in the lounge" was frostier still, with little glances, correct silences and little, well-bred clinkings, it was no more so than we had expected, at this sort of place.

A sense that starlight was waiting for us, cut short my reflections; we went out to be in it. . . . Incidentally, to drift along toward our wisteria. How bright the stars were! Those lights opposite must be Menaggio; the little ones above were farms on the mountains, perhaps. A few, very soft-orange ones blossomed on the dark point that hid Bellagio—villa-lights, probably; and there was the boat gliding along, a little, fat brooch of lights above its reflection.

How sweet that wisteria was, over our heads, its mass of bloom thick and pale in starlight. A thousand other scents were in that air, weighted with richness; but we staggered up the flights of shallow old stone stairs. . . . Even stairs were soothing, on Como; and outside the nightingale sang.

CHAPTER XXVII

TEA AND PEACEFULNESS

HE sang, at intervals, during the night; sometimes another answered him.

I don't know what woke me, I think it must have been a sense of beauty outside, marvelous beauty, going on through the night; and the morning was no change. Beauty came out a little from her mysteriousness, put on a brighter dress; but the depth of her was still there.

Night had a great round moon that came up behind the mountains, down the lake from our garden; but days on Como are very beautiful. We had breakfast at a little red-and-yellow table under the banksia roses; other guests were at other little tables, and the scene was gay.

"Read in A. M.," says the three-line diary.

To feel leisurely enough to do that on Monday morning! but that is what lakes are for. Clean air, and color to lean one's soul upon; great clouds over great mountains. . . . And we didn't feel like very much else that morning; needed all they had to give us, and more. We had found a black-bordered letter waiting for us, telling of the death of a gay-hearted and gallant friend who had been devotedly kind to Babs during that winter when I had to stay and take care of the farm, and she in town was equally lonely. We sat under the chestnut tree and tried to read, but my child's grief as well as my own was in my heart; the water lapped sadly on the old steps below.

Yet Como was there; we must go out into her uncomprehending brightness. Bellagio? Yes, we felt like Bellagio, as much as anything, and took the boat across for tea. A very

THE TINY CHURCH WITH THE FRESCO, BESIDE LAKE COMO

spruce boat, with all its brass glittering; we sat by its rail, soothed by seeing Varenna dwindle picturesquely behind us; seeing new shores unfold, and mountains change and grow steeper. The boat stopped at Menaggio; we stared at every detail. Pollarded trees along the quai, and awninged boats drawn up beyond reach of the wildly splashing water; calves being persuaded over the gang-plank, peasants coming aboard with flowers and fruit, and making their dignified way forward to second-class seats in the bow; peddlers wheeling on loaded bicycles, soldiers in green and yellow, Alpine tourists in strange array, parties of women in the full flower of summer dress; a gay and varied traffic.

Cadenabbia's tea-places looked charming, all roses and vines and with the beautiful mountains opposite; but we sat still and let ourselves be taken across to Bellagio—with *its* beautiful mountains opposite, and its gay lake front.

Quite a crowd was waiting, and porters were vociferating. It was pleasant to walk through them, hatless and empty-handed, simply on one's way to tea; past the purple-faced old cab-drivers in the same way . . . they know enough in Bellagio not to bother leisurely-looking people with no bags. Expensive luggage and travelers to correspond were being helped into the Serbelloni bus; we made our way across to a loggia where we always have a first tea in Bellagio. Enormous cakes are passed around and cut to your order; tea indeed is on a rather overwhelming scale, but the waiters are genial, the prospect interesting; we somehow liked the clatter of the Hotel du Lac, and its medley of people having tea.

For Como's confusions are all pretty, and really orderly; Bellagio was merely being very busy today. Every nationality was under that loggia, the usual amazing resident conglomeration, family parties, couples, solitary spinsters reflectively sipping; stray wanderers, like ourselves, driving up in splashed motors—and every table seeming, in its own way, to enjoy itself.

A party of Englishmen in mountain climbing clothes, evidently just back from an expedition, came silently in, however, and sank into seats near us. The headwaiter bustled up, full of suggestions about dry Martinis, etc., but one of the Englishmen said wearily,

"No. Hot milk."

But tea-hour is a luxury, almost anywhere on this lake; quite one of its specialties. If you want triviality, there it is; if you want sublimity, look beyond. Beauty you cannot escape—Como seems to blossom in a pleased consciousness of this; and here Bellagio's color and gaiety were against it all. Tomato-colored boat-awnings under flat-topped, very green trees—a street full of people, arcades full of shops, and always the boats coming and going, churning the water to a rush of silver, then skimming quietly off again.

We strolled about, in a reaction of after-tea gaiety, wantonly poking scarves and purses, exasperating the women in charge of the souvenir-trays; found a photograph shop to which we entrusted the camera and our films, and skimmed off ourselves.

Varenna is sweet, to draw near; sweet its roses looked, its bunch of dark cypresses; the pink belfry.

"A.B. walked to Fiume Latte," says the diary. I suppose I did; but like most things I did without Babs (and they were few) I don't remember it, while that evening, which we spent together, is like yesterday. . . . Mountains were dark, the moon large and golden; its path across the little bay golden too. Moons usually change to silver, but this one didn't; and everything seemed to have a special softness. Was it mist from the water, we wondered, or something else that just belonged to Como? That night was as clear as a dark jewel, yet its lights were soft orange; the moon kept her glamour of being just risen. . . . And the ripples in her path, breaking silver on our steps; the chestnut-leaves, black and five-fingered against them! We strolled up and down the walks, aware of each other's mingled feeling, breathing in the balm of water-lapping peace—a peace as tangible as the scent of roses in the air about us. Sometimes a boat went by, with a boy's voice singing; more often the lake was quiet, leading away to its moonlit distances.

More leisure, and rose-foliage, next morning—with all Como's impersonal happenings going restfully on beyond; in the afternoon there was the Villa Carlotta, with a person explaining every bush.

"Arocarria! Monkey puzzler!" said he brightly, turning to see our astonishment. But there were hundreds of things we didn't know, information was a good distraction, and for once I listened intently to one of these expounders.

"Bumbooze!" he joyfully told us. *"Arba japonica! Calceolari!"* But the hillsides of color were the thing: those azaleas, a little crumpled by the last rain, yet in sheltered spots still perfect. . . .

One wall of a great winding room, this hillside is and Como is its floor . . . that floor now active silver along the edge, with rufflings of sapphire; amethyst farther out.

"Rowed to Lenno, expensive tea," says the diary.

Exactly. Tea on Lenno's lawn (with choice arbors) cost as much as a dinner; perhaps because one rows from there to the wooded peninsula of the Punta Balbionella, and turns in at its old water-gate, and that is the most perfect thing in Italy. Dripping silence surrounds one—a smell of moss and oleanders; above is a balustrade with a mossy statue of a little saint on each post, flowers and jasmine drooping; an old stairway climbing to a circling low-walled terrace shadowed by great trees, scarlet flowers brilliant in their shadow, and the marvel of the Como arm winding away beyond.

Another water-gate, closed and rose-wreathed, keeps its own silence below. One can but be silent, with the beauty about one.

For Balbionella occurs at the lake's most magic curve. Here water is deepest, and mountains steepest; here the oldest villages perch—pink spots, high up—or are crammed in gray rock-cracks by the water. I talked a moment with the gardener, who had been showing us a vine that has a lovely blue blossom yet is a relative of the potato, and he pointed out a village opposite which the peasants call Lezzina della Mal' Fortuna, because the mountain overhangs it so that no sun shines there for three months.

"Non splendet, per tre mezzi!" the gardener repeated in awe-struck tones.

The mountain was very purple, we could see that, and very sheer; and in a strip under it, cramped and lean looking, was little Lezzina. A beam of sun was on the lake but Lezzina lay in shadow; she even has taken the pains to have a Grotto, "darkened artificially, to imitate the one at Capri." If I were Lezzina I wouldn't darken anything at all, in my neighborhood. . . .

We could scarcely bear to leave that water-gate, its silence and its age; its beauty that birds sang at, that one could linger by in a boat. Its charms hung over us as we glided out; good-by oleanders; good-by, little mossy saints.

And to think we nearly hadn't come; for as we sat in our arbor at Lenno, beauty there seemed enough, and it was mostly the prospect of rowing again in one of Como's delightful cushioned and awninged boats that had lured us over here.

Swish-swish! back to Tremezzo, admiring the wisteria; past the azaleas again, with late afternoon on the mountains; then the wharf at Bellagio and myself doing the "camera-dash," as the diary called it; flying to the film-shop, gaspingly flinging down money and racing back again before the boat left . . . my child's face, a bit anxious, lighting as I came in sight, hurtling through the cabs. I never ran faster. Just why we had to stay on that same boat I don't know; we just wanted to. It seemed a neat way of ending our afternoon. . . . And they were waiting for me, the ducks! the captain had his eye on me, and one hand on the bell-cord; the grinning sailors, their arms braced on the gang-plank ropes, grinned still more as I panted across it—and then how they pulled it in!

Possessing herself of my packages, Babs conducted me forward to our pet seats where, with our chins on the rail, absolutely at home now, we once more appropriated Como: the tiny white church on the way to Menaggio, for example, that is so high on the mountainside, right over one's head; that cliffy bit is one of our favorites, it *is* so cliffy and pink-purple, its little farms so unbelievably high. Nice Menaggio again—nice to look at from the boat, that is; and then a swift-away across the Lecco arm, heading for two snow-peaks.

Sunset was across the water from us, but then Italian sunsets seem to be everywhere. Color was often just as wonderful in the south-east—and that, from Varenna, would have been over the land, only a lucky little bay made in there, so not even the south-east reflections escaped us. Bellagio, of course, has indescribable sunsets; I daresay even Cadenabbia and Menaggio, with their backs to the west, have all of it they want; but there was something about Varenna, the way our garden hung over the water, and what we saw from it, that we found nowhere else. The padrone (whom we had come to like very much by now) said that those two other places, Tremezzo and its neighbor, were spoiled by the road; he made us a long speech on the subject while escorting us up from the garage.

"Those veellages, it is beau-tiful place, but they have road between them and the lake. It is ruin them! So many pipple; and cars all the time. A peety. They had great fight over that road; English pipple not want it. . . . Here, the road go behind—in veellage. It is *onlee* place, signora! Varenna is not spoil; it is sah-vage!"

We agreed with him, if not with a traitorous dictionary that had given him "wild" and "savage" in the same breath; and tramped back through Varenna's savageness, admiring the flowers in an old wall. It was a high wall of rough gray-brown stone, holding up the mountainside at a curve of Varenna's hill. Arbors of red roses were visible from below, but what most pleased us were the clumps of crimson-tipped daisies like the little English ones, only an Italian version with stems six or seven inches long, so that they hung gracefully—yet being daisies, were not too limp to stand up from the top of the clump, thus making an attractive rock-plant. . . .

Their colors were a hint sunburnt and different too—they may have been from South Africa, for all I know—but the crimson tips were English, as was the thick fringe of little petals and the clear gold center . . . only more important, and in a wall; one charm about the arrangement being the contrast between the small neatness of the daisies, and the toweringness of the mountain that went up behind them—of which they constituted, as it were, the flowering start.

Flowers in Como's villages often do that; even the villages themselves are a sort of blossoming introduction to great, green sides with tips of snow peeping over them. . . . Worth while being a flower—or a village—in that connection.

And in our garden the chestnut tree was murmuring a little, so that its candelabra moved; blooms whose petals were like smooth heavy cream, with, at the heart of each, an oddly bright blotch of rose, edged with buttercup-yellow.

This tree, Como-like in its splendid luxuriance, was a joy to us always. Beneath it the lake was ruffling now in a twilight breeze, and a purple and gold sunset dimming over Monte Crocione; though to the southward, over our dear mountain known to the map as M. Fop, the colors were strangely brightening . . . very different colors; silver and peach, primrose and turquoise. Horrific purples were chasing them; was there to be a storm? We almost hoped there would be.

But the hurtlings went on, finding destinations of their own; flitting here or there into mere beauty, and a background for snows. There was no storm.

Next day, indeed, dawned fine and hot; was by turns dusty, interesting, beautiful, tiresome, and enraging—all because I had a sentimental idea. In my childhood we once drove by extra-poste, with four horses, to Colico and Chiavenna, north of the lake, and thence, the next day, over the Maloja Pass into Switzerland. My sister and I during this drive were perched high in a sort of hooded rumble at the rear of our huge conveyance, whence we could see delightfully over our parents' heads, and the horses', out to lake and mountains illimitable; and the memory of that day had since been clad, to me, in a sort of glory. After the hot road, we drove romantically into the courtyard of an inn at Chiavenna, which I remembered as huge and cool, all stony arcades and trampling steeds, and with a noisy stream rushing somewhere . . . and when I told Babs of this, it seemed to both of us that the one thing to do was to repeat that trip as far as Chiavenna—and on up into the Pass, as far as we could? said we, with shining eyes.

The padrone had a lunch put up for us, and off we went. Wet cliffs reared romantically up, with a lolling cream-white flower growing on them, exactly like fat clusters of acacia blossoms that some one had stuck in the rock; the cliffs were reddish-purple, and slim white cataracts came down them; when they retreated, meadows began, and little blossoms of villages. The soil here must have been curious, we agreed; the roadside poppies, usually so immense, were small and pale . . . but the villages throve—like rock-flowers; sticking themselves in anywhere. The more they were pushed into the lake the prettier they were, with little gardens out on stone quais, and stone arms to hold their fishing-boats.

The boats sat there, very sweet, with their sails up—colored sails; and flowers and vines from the gardens drizzled almost into the water.

Some villages had plenty of room; one with a nice open water-front—trees to shade it, and boats drawn up on a real sand beach—had a lace-market going on. Half miles of lace, wide enough for tennis-nets, stretched in every direction, with trestles holding smaller pieces; the piazza looked like a cobweb. Boat-noses were drawn up near it, and donkey-carts made their way carelessly past, but Nicolette went very gingerly by the fragile stuff. Fancy driving into lace! And it was odd, seeing it outdoors, subject to sun and breezes. Lace is such indoor stuff.

But the nice, kerchiefed women in charge of it glanced at us in the most friendly way. They didn't think we were going to snatch threads out of their precious product; probably they hoped we should buy some of it . . . the last thing in life it occurs to us to want. Especially by the half-mile.

Somewhere along here there was a marvelous village on a point; it had cliff-walls, black cypresses, pink houses, a battlemented castle; all the charms. I have no idea what its name was; Borgo, or Ogliasca; the way it piled itself above the lake was the thing. Colico, however, was scattering and gaunt, untidy and queer; we bought petrol and bumped on. The road was a rough and careless one, deep in dust; it soon dampened, pleasantly, bringing us to a most exquisite swamp. The lake narrows almost to nothing, here; there are rushy stretches, buttercup fields, and wide, dark pools bordered with yellow iris. Water-lilies were floating in the pools; against the fields brilliant with buttercups were masses of pink ragged robin . . . bright pink! As a child, I had adored ragged robin, which grows (temperately) in English meadows; but here were wild effervescent masses of it, pinker than anything in the world—pinker than the insides of watermelons! The buttercups effervesced, too, as did the groves of little locust trees in the meadows; Italy's morning having raised all this brightness to a pitch which, against the purple of the mountains opposite, took one's breath.

And then we came to Chiavenna; a nasty town, dusty and nothing in particular. There were no cool courtyards or stone arcades, no green streams rushing; and in the very whitest and dustiest spot we had a puncture. It was our second one that morning, so we took our invalids into a garage to be mended; seeing us stationary, who should come strolling along but an official of some sort, an unpleasant creature in a blue shirt and suspenders, and demanded to see our papers; and we found we had left them at the hotel.

Well, that became an international situation, of course. . . . It was no business of his, we told each other indignantly, when we were just getting mended for a minute, and Chiavenna wasn't a frontier or anything—or was it one, come to think? . . . At any rate, "Great fuss about driving passport," says the diary. More officials were called; they sat us down in the stiff little parlor of a house and gave us a nasty time. Even the mayor was called in to help bully; and nobody, of all the accusing ones that sat on the parlor's hard chairs and glared at us, spoke French. I talked to them as best I could, explaining that we were just out for a drive, that we always locked up the portfolio when we came to a place to stay, because we were afraid of losing it, etc., etc.; but for a ridiculous hour or more those officials were as grim and portentous as if it were wartime and we female spies.

Growing a little angry at last, for I could feel how Babs was worrying, I took bold tactics; turned on them and demanded that they call up the padrone. Yes, be so good as to telephone him! He knows all about us; *he* can produce our papers; and how pleased he will be to have his guests, just out for a drive like this, held up and worried.

At this their faces changed; they reflected. One or two of them went out. Evidently the padrone was somebody to conjure with. . . . Yes, they said reluctantly, that could be done; but we must wait for the call to be put through. So they all left us—glory be—and we sat and conversed in low tones, wondering if we should get out of this without paying a fortune, as our dear friend in the shirt hinted we might have to.

We paid nothing at all. After a long wait, he came grudgingly back and said it was all right and we might go.

Might go? 'Thought he could keep us here, did he? We went out, the hackles on our Yankee necks fairly bristling. . . . Of course we knew we ought not to have risked leaving the silly thing behind us; though not till we had swished the last of Chiavenna's dust from our tires did we exchange little grins of conscious guilt.

But—did they ever do this in France? We had gone on any number of portfolioless drives; *had* anybody asked to see our papers? Not a soul. Confound Chiavenna, said we heartily; drat the place; for now that we were free again and scuttling along toward the mountains, it was pleasant to rave a little, on our own behalf. . . . A nice time to be looking for a place to lunch, we grumbled; middle of the afternoon . . . and gone, gone, were all my childish predilections for Chiavenna. Fancy, I said, being sentimental over *that* place!

"Lunch in pass," says the diary; "back in a lot of dust."

Undoubtedly; but I don't remember anything more at all that was nice that day, except getting home to Varenna, and that was heavenly. The padrone was as beautifully wrathful as we knew he would be; his eyes flashed, his gestures flew. He would see about it; he would indeed.

"Those offeecials in lil' town, signora—they like make trobble," he said scornfully.

And we went to our room, complacent. The moon had waited for us, the garden said it was glad to see us, the mountains told us (as they always do) that they would take care of us; and this time, we almost felt we had needed it.

* *

That was May 26th; but May 27th more than made up for it.

We had, for one thing, a frivolous morning in Bellagio, climbing its steep lanes and shopping; going into wood-carving shops, which we love, and buying a wedding-present to send home. I still have a miniature easel with "Ritornero" on it, that my father got me when I was a child, from these very shops.

The lanes are enchanting to prowl in, with the gorgeous floor of the lake always below you. Flowers, balconies, bright colors; open doors, with nice industries going on where you can walk in and buy things. And Bellagio's people do not seem spoiled. They offer you things as you go by, but gently and agreeably. One likes being offered things, in those lanes; and what a comfort, when shopping is done, to be swished smoothly back across water and lunch in a garden.

For we had decided to drive round the lake that afternoon. Really round; about eighty-five miles, in all; and it was a day of sun and towering clouds and all that Como does to herself to be enchanting. . . . From Colico on, it was to be all new;

and I wrote notes as we drove. Fearful scrawlings; but Babs, who sympathizes with work as few people do, always looked approving when I did that.

The lace-market was gone today; but we went through the iris-swamp, and it took our breaths as before—also the buttercup meadows against the mountains' deep purple-blues—we were driving *at* the mountains now; and haying was going on, as peasants do haying; a different way in every field.

"Colt, haying with mother, in pretty meadow on left. Two peasant-women leading Swiss oxen, on load of nice green hay —" a beautiful bit.

And the peasants were all beautiful, in this region. Either of the young women leading those oxen could have been a madonna—not a Raphael, something more interesting; and another madonna—or saint—middle-aged, kerchiefed and benignant, yet vivid still with the grace of youth, was walking in front of a high-heaped wagon holding up the tip of its pole. A peasant was driving these oxen, but it was the woman who was helping them—sweetly, heroically, taking half the weight off their necks, and any one who has even felt of the tip of a loaded pole will know what that means. Yet she was advancing quite easily; bracing her beautiful lithe figure back a little, but throwing up her head to smile idyllically at us. . . . Ah, the beauty of the world around Como.

Sorico is at almost the head of the lake on this side. "Picturesque Sorico," say the notes; "stuccoed houses stained faded blue; big trees, old street, then pastures to lake—donkeys, cows, black pigs, peacefully grazing; fields were flooded, so the fishermen could bring their boats in under the mulberry trees."

For this stretch from Sorico down is quite the place to see peasant activities. "Impossible to describe all the things these lakeside people do, or the picturesque way they do them; the animals they goodhumoredly deal with, under the heat of an Italian sun; the back-loads they cheerfully carry." The fishing-boats, when not sailing, used their bits of sails as awnings; one fisherman even had a tiny triangle of canvas rigged over his head as he stood up to row. . . . They all stand and row, here; looking very intently forward, but pushing easily at the oars; a pose most becoming to the scenery.

"More romantic from this side," say my notes.

It really was. Of course there were more fields for haying, up this way, and fishing was a serious thing; for though some fishing goes on, off Bellagio, it never seems real or necessitous, mixed with steamers and dressy tourists—tourists should be enough for a region to live on.

Up here the polite boats skimmed by and did not stop; we waved to one of them. *"Pax vobiscum,"* said we. "Don't stop, darling!"

At Dongo a dozen women dressed in sackcloth were unloading iron from a stout, unpainted old schooner, the *Antoinetta, Dongo.* They walked strappingly across a plank which sloped upward from the *Antoinetta's* stern to the quai; a difficult slant, if one had no load on one's head—and a sight to see the line of them doing it, for they stepped lightly enough along; heavy, man-like creatures, a bit Rabelaisian in mien, staring at us and laughing hardily. . . . They had those piles of rusty iron weighing them down—Babs said it made her think of a Pharaoh's slaves building the Pyramids; and that laughter of theirs, abandoned yet somehow fatalistic, was doubtless their defence against an ill fate.

Nicolette swarmed up a steep hill; and from here until the descent to Menaggio, it was almost all a high road along a wooded cliff. Brooks were dashing out of that precipitous forest—they splashed almost upon us; one could have touched the masses of ferns, the gray rocks and golden indigo. Thrillingly far below was the lake, and across it, keeping us fine company on our lofty little road, glittered the line of snow peaks. . . . What a drive! But we wondered if they stayed snowy in July.

The road whirled out toward a promontory. "Rezzonico, perfect old place," say the notes. "Ivied fortress, steep purple-roofed houses, groups of cypresses—all falling down to the lake. (Place we lost the rope!)

"Hot peasants haying; beautiful old woman in a blue kerchief, Rembrandt color; just shining in full sun!"

For she was doing a little field all by herself, alongside her cottage; beside its blossoming hedges, and with the cobalt lake beyond. She heaved up a basket of hay in her strong old arms and smiled at us so; a picture that Rembrandt might have gone far to seek. . . . Up a little gorge with a brook stood a frescoed shrine; and from further up that ravine came the pleasant sound of a cascade. Roadside banks were deep in grasses and blossom—maroon columbines, almost black, and blue-violet geraniums, lightened with foamings of Queen Anne's lace—an exquisite arrangement; white, slender-stemmed lilies, strange pink things, and tall, transfigured Italian forget-me-nots. Not only the lilies but their neighbors swayed in the afternoon breeze, and throughout the grasses ran steadier undercurrents of smaller flowers—rosy cyclamen, orchids, blue harebells; infinite others.

The bump of Bellagio was now plainly visible across the water; Varenna, too, with its one belfry. Most of Como's villages, we were discovering, have just one belfry. . . . We entered a short tunnel, its rocky arch enchanting with flowers, and framing a view. "Superior tunnels on this side!" smiled Babs; and below us was the most perfect little wooded cove with deep green water, rock edges and ferns, and woods coming down to a bit of white sand beach; a place to cruise into. . . .

But we drove rather quickly through the ancient windings of Menaggio.

"Same smell as two years ago," say my notes. "Permanent!"

It was indeed a strong and incomprehensible reek, which lasted through several twists of the old street, then ceased, at sight of a piazza and the lake, as if reluctant to enter Menaggio's nice water-front. The same little toy train was waiting on its track, with frisky white curtains looped back, and one car marked "Riservanta!" (Cook's); the tourists, all alpenstocks and Tyrolean feathers, were hastily eating at little outdoor tables . . . glancing up at us, then bending and gobbling again. . . . We had taken that Swiss train once, and knew how they felt.

Bellagio was now shining very intimately at us, from across the water; "awning-colored boat (plus awning) in a very blue spot of the lake," the notes say. . . . Bluer than Capri, the water here seemed; and lake awnings are tomato-orange.

On the other side of us were walls and shrubberies: "Everybody's villa, keeping out the sun!" I complained; and Babs laughed. But sunshine was so nice, today.

This, of course, is the most gardened stretch on Como. Wonderful roses hung over those elaborate walls, gray lichened cupids sported on their posts, curlicues and trimmings tormented their tops, but they and their shrubbery nearly hid the rococoness of the villas, and that was a boon. Lovely balustrated old steps, somewhat cupided, went down into the water beside us, but Como took care of them . . . drowned them in silver and topaz, sank with them through a palette of greens and blues down, down to unfathomable depths—and fishes, and sunken palaces.

A lake should do that. Here and there man has done awful things on Como's edge, but she melts them—and him; pulverizes and mountainsides them, twines vines over them, and, whoof! it's just Como, and you love it.

We really liked the atrocious curlicues, even while abusing them; and no one could help liking little crowded Cadenabbia. The arbors and tea-places belong to the hotels, but you're not conscious of them; everything in Cadenabbia is so polite and prettily colored, the voices of bartering ones so sweetly modulated, the roses so profuse, that you sit under your arbor and forget everything—but beautifulness.

"Tea at Cadenabbia, lovely!" says the diary.

A canopy of rose-foliage spread itself over the tea-garden, every leaf shining and bright. "Everything fresh as fresh," say the notes. "Such pure sugar, the lumps had glacial blue between! We watched the fishes, their backs purple under the blue-green; they swam slowly about, in the friendly way lake-fishes have. Small trout don't like chocolate frosting; a big one gobbled it."

A sound recalled us; the orchestra had filed stealthily in behind a rose screen and were gently tuning their violins; looking nervous, for they had to sing too. But it was "all soft and nice; hushed voices and extreme sentiment, suited for 40 feet away in a Como tea-garden," the notes say. "Rector's party, from hotel, having strawberries. *They* know where it's good, and cheap!"

We stayed on, luxuriating in the heavenly view, in Cadenabbia's air . . . so soft and warm yet cool and watery; but Nicolette, looking very open-hearted with her top down, was waiting for us beside Rodrigo's hedge. Sweet and neat, Tremezzo's water-front, merely more of Cadenabbia, only it was Tremezzo and not *quite* so nice; we passed the Carlotta entrance—then on into the magnificence of just Como, and mountains, and old villages.

A solid, mountain-shadow was now over us, but sun lay on the mountains opposite; and the villages were perfect. Brienno (I think it was Brienno) had a tiny uphill piazza and a statue of a bearded soldier throwing a rock; a middle-aged man in a cap and a torn winter uniform gazing fiercely down, the jagged rock held high over his head, ready to hurl.

" 'Expect it's what they did here," said my daughter, gravely.

The Alpine troops. Somehow that figure gave one a picture of everything: the wintry heights, the desperate, primitive battling—with rocks or anything that came to hand; the privations, the prolonged, unbelievable heroisms. . . .

But the lake unfolded and brought us to waterfalls. The villages just here were built steeply into the lake, or on shelves above our heads; "Ossucio a picture," say the notes, "with its tall pale belfry against the mountains; and one old iron-gray village was simply made of stairways. Under arches, through holes in heavy masonry, they went; and if donkeys in this town were hitched to anything, it was to rude sleds. One was resting on a cobbled stairway, with his load of firewood."

The peasants, coming down from some mountain field,

were carrying baskets of cut grass on their backs, and by a little bridge we overtook a slender and sweet-faced old woman thus laden, who stopped to let us go by, leaning her burden against a walled bank. The grace of her! She had a kerchief over her silver hair, and from her shoulders hung the tall basket of weeds, freshly cut, with a sickle on top; such a sweet little old smile was on her face, as with the beauty, the pathetic patience of age, she waited for us to pass. . . .

Argegno had wreaths of little fishes hung rather sadly on wires above a wall that held in a bursting torrent; with twigs through their little gills, they twisted slightly in the breeze. . . . But Argegno had a sweet frontage on the lake with roses and little *ristorante* tables, and beyond this was a winding cliff road like the one above Menaggio; forest, flowers, bushes and rocks reared enchantingly above our heads, as usual. . . . The woods ended, and we tried to get a picture of a tiny church wedged between us and the lake, its frescoed apse all gold and blues and browns, its Spanish belfry cutting water and mountains; we got it by climbing impetuously upon a wall—and nearly falling off into a dizzy drop on the other side. The little thing was lodged just where one of Como's loveliest bits stretched away, beyond a castle, to a new magnificence of mountains.

The lake had now swung so that sun was upon us; but the road, which had been good, became terrible, and a road-sign high up at a turn said very musically, "Adagio! Svolta pericolosa!"

We drove *adagio,* as indeed we'd been doing for some time, and zigzagged through Como, missing the cool green and blue and violet of the water frightfully, as we set off behind a flange of mountains. We *could* have followed the lake back to Bellagio,—a high and romantic way, with break-neck views down to the water—but alack, there was no road from there to Lecco. Behind the great barrier of the mountain—a fine purple one with vineyards at its foot—were dust and potholes and a leaning tower: "the little old leaning tower of Albese —and nobody looking at it!" say the notes. Rosy against a mist of olive groves, it leaned engagingly, and we felt somebody should be looking at it; but vineyards kept on, and we at last reached a consoling view: the walled and winding lake, rich and shadowy; a rock-peak beyond Lecco, rosy in light.

"The light on that rock makes up for all the bumps we've been over," Babs said. . . .

And then there was sunset, for her; all the way up the lake.

But as we came out of a dark tunnel Nicolette stopped abruptly. Nothing would budge her. We stared at each other in horror.

"This is the same place where we had the puncture," remarked my child; "remember this cliff?"

I did; and glanced dismally up at it. Were our inexplicable troubles to begin again—and with Alps before us? But from Babs, bent over the dash-board, came a sudden shout of laughter. "I turned the power off, when I switched off the lights!" And the relief was so great that we roared in unison, while Nicolette crossly proceeded.

"Funny, isn't it?" she creaked, coming groaning out of a pothole. "Pffwish!!" and she sent mud flying at the cliff.

For we had never done that to her before; and when we reached Varenna at eight o'clock after all that extraordinary road, and with no puncture, the padrone warmly congratulated us.

But no matter what difficulties hedged Como in, one would find a way round her somehow; and as late that evening we went out on our balcony, the night-sounds, the balm of it, entered my child's heart. She sighed, and took my hand. Later I saw her busy with something under the lamp; but not till months afterwards did she give me what she had written that night.

It happened to be the poem that later on, when her book of verse was published, *Morning Moods,* our wise and genial friend, Clarence Day, liked so very much.

"Those last three lines, Anne," he wrote me. "I think they're marvelous."

Of course I thought so, too.

Como pondering under her moon,
And I weighted with my pain;
The mountains sweep to glorious heights
And the waves lap in broken golden shreds;
How can the world be all shattered chords,
With nature
Climbing to these hills of harmony?

CHAPTER XXVIII

MAGGIORE AND THE SIMPLON PASS

LEFT 11:30. Lecco, Como, Varese, auto-*strada*. Blast! Sesto, Baveno, Hotel Suisse." Thus the diary, fairly rhythmic in its disgusted brevity.

For we were going on to Maggiore for the week-end; leaving our garden. . . . We halted in Como for tire-mending—one of the poor things had finally succumbed to a fresh batch of stones—also for agreeable coffee in the piazza, with a blue table-cloth, and boats coming and going, and much conversation about how there's always somewhere to go and sit, outdoors—somehow to spend time, in a foreign city, if it's nothing but a sidewalk café or a quai. (U.S. please copy.) Then we rambled a little, and took a picture of the cathedral doorway just as an Italian strode by on a pair of very long legs, taking enormous steps.

"Funny that Como should have a cathedral!" said my daughter, winding up the film.

Indeed it seemed all wrong to be turning one's mind to doorways here, yet the rather square little cathedral has a beautiful one—Lombard-Gothic, "altered to Renaissance." . . . And we thought we had left Art permanently behind.

But then we gratified the nice policeman by taking his road to Varese—he had been quite worried about us because we stopped and turned off another way; everybody went to Varese! A tense, winding, and confused old town, we found, where one goes straight south in order to turn northwest and up the shore of Lake Maggiore. . . . The new auto-*strada* (Italy's pride) led south from here, but we did not want to go by the auto-*strada;* we inquired for the old road,—and came unexpectedly out on two large toll-gates.

"*That* thing?" said Babs, wheeling Nicolette around. "I think not!"

We inquired again, but nobody seemed to understand. What was the matter with Varese? People usually stood on their heads to understand you, in this country. . . . We fought our way through slummy intricacies, bumped curb-stones, and got very hot, conducting our researches, but find a little dusty road we *would;* a road that led comfortably away through flowers and donkeys and villages, the sort of road we had always taken. . . . One very promising young Italian who seemed to understand what we wanted, headed us straight back to the toll-gates; we returned, wrathful but persevering, took a bright-looking boy on the running-board—and arrived at the auto-*strada.* (The boy had made speed back into town.)

By this time the officials were looking curiously at us. What was the matter with the signore? Did they not like the beautiful new road?

"Time's getting on," said my child, glancing at Minnie with a sort of sigh. "What do you say, A.B.?"

So we wheeled up; were given a green ticket and several honey-sweet smiles from the now busily kow-towing officials —they'd drawn a fish after all, from what looked like reluctant waters. . . .

Bah! this auto-*strada.* We went swiftly along, despising it. Occasionally we caught glimpses of the other road that we had so wanted to be on, curving through villages and sweet land-scape as we knew it would; sometimes we even saw a faint cloud of its dust where an ox-cart went along . . . and that was especially maddening; for the *strada* was cutting straight through thin-looking fields or high sand-banks. But the banks began to be planted with rye, the fields became prosperous and swam beside veils of rye; mulberry trunks shone through rye, poppies flashed in it, undertoned it—a new kind, short-stemmed and salmon-tinted. Huge, scarlet poppies grew among white daisies, "a peasant with an eye," as the notes say, having cut around a particularly glowing patch of them and left them to be a joy; while clumps of phenomenal bachelor's buttons shouted "Here's blue for you!"

But here was our turn-off—it had only seemed a few minutes, in the rye; Nicolette, though hissingly warm, was complacent, and beyond Sesto we had a mild thrill on coming in sight of the end of the lake; a mild bit, much inhabited. Mountains were yet to come. Foot-hills arose, with M. Mottarone behind them; across the broadening lake were sweet blue peaks; but Stresa from the road is not Stresa glimpsed from the train—mimosas and peach trees in bloom, the castled islands in deep water, snowy things beyond; we had once gone by on an express, and nearly thrown our bags out of the window, we wanted to stop so. . . . But there were too many hotels. The darling islands were there, but you saw them better from further on; we continued along a delicious bit of shore road under immense trees and with the lovely view beyond, feeling happier the more we left Stresa behind. (Travel often is like that.)

What would Baveno be like? It was not far; a nice old town, we saw, with its market-place right on the lake. The little pier had shady trees overhanging it—a new thing, for boat-landings; a homey spot, Baveno, staring at the Îles Borromées. . . . And an Hôtel Suisse, we saw, stared at them harder than anything else did, across its graveled garden, sociable with little tables and enormous flowers.

We drew up by its iron fence, enchanted.

"Sisignora!" A nimble young padrone was upon us in a second; past the pansies, across gravel, under rose-arbors I was hastened, up the funny, twisting, carpeted stairs—jolly stairs—into a room with intelligent large windows. They gave on the garden, on the lake, on the Îles Borromées. . . . Sufficient! I ran down again. Simplicity was in the air of this place, comfort and simple charm; Babs, I could see to my pleasure, was already relaxing; leaning dreamily back in Nicolette, lost in islands. (The snow peaks came *just* to the left of a castle. . . .)

Luggage? Oh, possibly! we let everybody else do the work. It seemed country-honest here. Como, as far as concierges went, had been all suavity and gold braid; Baveno was broad shoulders, informality, a limp, and kind smiles. . . . Babs liked our room as much as I did, but in a twinkling we were down again and by the preposterous flowers, having tea and breathing sighs of joy. We hadn't expected to like it as much as this; we hadn't expected Baveno at all. "Did you ever *see* such pansies?" For they were rearing against the fence, masses of purple and yellow. "And every leaf in that rose-arbor, so neat?" "And I can hear the water splashing—"

"Shall we take a boat and go out?"

We did; in watery quietness. Water was deep, under us; soon it was unfathomable; we headed for the Isola dei Piscatorio, where the fishing-village is. Old houses, with lanes climbing between; nets drying; fishermen and their boats in a little bay; on the point, a pension with a sweet garden. Yellow umbrellas on the lawn! And such a view; snow peaks, and the Isola Bella just beyond.

"Would you have liked to stay here?" I said, a little inclined to be jealous of the beautiful site of that pension: Babs shook her head decisively.

"Couldn't have had Nicolette with us," said she.

"That's true . . . but I adore an island."

"So do I," and Babs looked fondly at it as she sculled along—you didn't really seem to have to row, here. . . . Trees in another instant hung over us, scents as from a greenhouse poured down, water was lapping everywhere on stone, and—"*Look* at this!" said she in amazement.

Isola Bella—from the very water's edge, a fantasy of baroque. Mossy balustrades and urns and vases, exotic flowers and vines; terrace upon stone terrace (ten of them) "wonderful in a riot of fancy," climbing to an unfinished palace drowned in ivy, more flowers, and statues. From a little way off, age and romance are all one sees, but with our boat softly bunting the lowest terrace. . . . The faces of the statues were too horrid, for one thing; I remember Pannish creatures, grinning distortedly. Fancy, expecting to live with all that; yet as we left it, it again became as beautiful as "the noble Italian family of Borromeo" had doubtless intended it to be.

"Probably they thought it was—" suggested Babs, in charitable tones.

"Maybe," I said very seriously, racked by the romance of it as its colors ran together, and it rose flower-like from its own darkening reflection.

A woman boarder on the Isola dei Piscatorio was sitting in the garden, staring at us very hard; we stared too, as we rowed by, feeling, in our small craft, and out on that twilight silvering, somehow released from all obligations, all sense of manners. . . . We stared at the village, at the fishermen fussing with their boats; listened to their bits of gabbling talk. Poor fishermen. They sounded happy; but the noble Italian family of Borromeo still own the fishing-rights on all the lake. Quite a few rights.

I suppose there is a tax on every fish.

Sunset colors were coming, and Maggiore is meltingly lovely at that hour. The air was warm, our shore very dark green, with purples shrouding it, and in it, with a light coming here or there, sat the easy cheerful little town, so old and yet so gay. Sounds from it were strangely clear.

The padrone was in the garden, groping in his pond, which was thick with the agitated purple backs of carp; extracting two, he came over to a table by the wall where a young and stylish Italian motorist and two companions were seated, and exhibited the treasures.

"Bene!" cried they with great laughter. *Pesce* for their dinner—*si si!* fresh and fresh! Broil them, *amico!* they cried; and the padrone, laughing and nodding, hurried off.

Should we eat outside too? The dining-room, all lampshades and flowers, looked uncommonly pretty and cheerful; in spite of lights in the garden, outdoors had suddenly grown very dark, as Italian evenings do, and the pansies had lost their color. We went in; and spent next day driving to Locarno.

In London we had seen posters of Locarno, all mountains, apple-blossoms, and bright blue lake, so above Baveno we were astonished to come upon immense quarries and sheds full of marble-workers. The noise was deafening. Blocks lay about in the road, teams were struggling, blasts were going off: an exciting passage. Willows, lovely huge ones, and a stretch of the lake, looked doubly peaceful after this; then came a stretch of sophistication, but at Brissago, a clean-looking village with white houses, we were pleased to find ourselves in Switzerland. The slopes were still soft with olives, pomegranates, and myrtle; on this warm day, we found the air so mellow as to be positively relaxing.

"Whoo!" said Babs energetically opening the wind-shield; "*I* think Maggiore's hot!"

We did not find our postery bit of apple-blossoms, but Locarno was old and interesting, its views memorable; we started back by a wild little Swiss road through mountains and gorges, and just as it was at its wildest, and we exulting in it—"Road broken!" says the diary. . . . We had to return. Couldn't dodge the sophistication of that upper shore after all. But we had a sightly and pleasant tea in Locarno; and going home, there was the lovely shadowed color of everything. Our porter gave us a great and excited welcome in the garden, for he had just discovered we were from Vermont—and he had worked in a quarry at Barre! For a few years, poor fellow; then a block of marble fell on him.

"No good now," he said ruefully, yet with his nice cheerful smile. "Come back here—carry trunk!"

And next day, which was a Sunday, we had to spend largely in agitated preparations for getting into Switzerland. "Great mental disturbance about passes," says the diary. For they were mostly closed, still. . . . Should we have to ship Nicolette tamely through a tunnel? We had so looked forward to the thrill of driving our little five-horse-power over the Simplon, but the padrone discouraged us; there were still avalanches and "landslips," he said—and here it was nearly June.

"DID THEY PUT HER HERE, SO THAT THE MEADOW COULD OFFER HER FLOWERS?"

Mountain Road, near Macugagna

Annoying! We couldn't believe it; and drove to Stresa to find out.

"Very hot and very much world," my child's diary observes.

All the cars in Italy, overloaded with exuberant Italians, seemed to come whooping and hurrahing through Baveno that morning, but as we started, a bit of peacefulness occurred —and something else, resembling magic. An old horse from the country came into the market-place with a big woolly sheep trotting beside his legs—we could hardly believe it was a sheep, but it was; and when their peasant-master hitched the horse to a post the sheep, like an attentive dog, lay down on the hot pavement beside his friend, panting quietly. The peasant strolled away, but the sheep stayed; then and there we went back and asked the padrone about this amazing thing . . . for what a brave sheep, coming through traffic; trotting calmly and one-idea'dly beside the tall legs and resounding hoofs of its friend! But the padrone, accompanying us to the gate, said that in the mountains hereabouts a sheep was always kept with the horses so that they wouldn't go blind; that it got very fond of its companion and often refused to be separated from him, going with him on the road, in the fields, and everywhere.

Mystery, said we. Why should a sheep prevent blindness in a horse? The padrone shrugged his shoulders and said he didn't know why; the peasants did it in these mountains, and always had, and there must be something in it. . . .

The hotels in Stresa, this torrid morning, looked even less to our taste; and we had an exasperating interview with an agent in a "bureau," a pale and sulky young man who gave us as much misinformation as a young man well could, in a few minutes, but he told us that the pass over the Simplon was closed.

That settled it. It would take time to get to the other passes. Zermatt was our objective, and the Simplon led us there. Nicolette must go through on a flat-car, alas.

Oof! such heat, and whizzing cars. It was good to be back

in Baveno again. The sheep was gone—back to some cool mountainside, we hoped; we sniffed our garden flowers, lunched beside them, and when shadows lengthened, went out in our boat.

Out—far out, this time, with islands left behind and a glory of mountains lifting; for to westward of Maggiore are grouped "the thrones of the mighty," and as you get out in the lake you see them, towering wonderfully. So pure, on a sunset sky. The five-peaked summit of Monte Rose is there, and "the snows of the Mischabelhorner and the Weissmies"; we had never heard of the Weissmies, they sounded gnome-like and fascinating—especially as we couldn't find them on the map; and somewhere over there, behind Monte Rosa, were Zermatt and the Matterhorn. Soon, oh very soon, we should be starting for them. . . .

Meanwhile, coolness was coming down; twilight and afterglow were on the lovely world. We said good-by to the islands, sent love and farewell to all sorts of things—for this, though it seemed quite impossible, was our last whole day in Italy. . . . Arrangements were all made; we were to drive to Domo d'Ossola next morning. Palpitations assailed us as we thought of a new currency; of another border to surmount, the dear Italian tongue to leave behind; and heaven knew what sort of language we should run into crossing the line, for we had heard that speech in southern Switzerland is extremely mixed.

A gray, dour morning, threatening storm; the valley was magnificent. Great peaks towered up—and so did the clouds; above Premosello, or was it Vergogne? was a sweet little half-ruined castle on a small, isolated peak. It looked lonely.

"Take care of yourself, ruin; nobody else will," I thought. . . . This was a grand bit of valley now, comparatively a crack among mountains—though immense poplars and willows were still with us; the river beside them was blue-green and clear. "Glacial!" said we inspiritedly. . . .

"The crack to Macugagna!" say my notes.

It led to such dark-blue of ravines, and cliffs, that we took it for a little way—the back-road to Monte Rosa, only that superb creature would probably be hidden in clouds. . . . But there was a shrine in a meadow with a pretty, frescoed madonna with golden hair; did they put her here so that the meadow could offer her flowers? Alpine things—dark-blue and pink; golden balls, like globe-flowers; rare, clustered, white lilies, that hung their heads like woodlilies. I think the crack to Macugagna surpassed all the places we had been in, for flowers.

Clouds were now hurtling even more magnificently; down they came, whirling grandly into the ravine, smothering everything, finishing our hopes of Monte Rosa; we turned and went flying down. . . . In the bigger valley, the mountains showed only ghost-peaks now—they had faded, since we left them. But the domesticities of the wayside were all there; ducks marching across the road to a brook-pool opposite their cottage, taking thankful sips, wagging their tails as congratulatorily as if they had never seen a brook before (that is an engaging habit of ducks); a cow, led along a lane by a boy, with a pet sheep closely following it—more sheep-magic? And then grayness closed down on us; the torrent roared, rain came in a gray wall. . . . Never mind, we had seen the magnificences, and were nearly there. Arcaded streets met us—muddy, twisting streets with peasant-women selling bunches of Alpine cyclamen; poor wild things, squeezed so tight—then the station, in a splendid expanse of mud.

We wheeled up to it, feeling fluttery. Nicolette was to be torn from us, here; and a sharp-eyed interpreter approached . . . suave, however; would Mademoiselle be so good as to drive the lil' car to the end of the station—*par là, mesdames*—and up on the platform?

Mademoiselle would. She even drove Nicolette off the platform and on to a vile and perilous flat-car, its floor thick with nails—you'd think, we said, they might pull a few out; after which we started off with the interpreter on a series of constitutionals down endless platforms. It was lucky there was plenty of time for everything: for the signatures and stampings and payments (127 Swiss francs, by jinks! as the diary remarked) and last but not least, the great bundles of receipts that go with shipping anything through an Alpine tunnel. We were pale and weary before it was over . . . and *all* the time, the interpreter talked.

The season, he said, was very late this year; the ladies were very wise to send their car over by train. . . . But—the Simplon wasn't open? I said, puzzled by this remark. . . . Oh yes, madame! It opened yesterday, he said.

"Opened? but the man at —'s told us it wasn't. . . ."

And then the little interpreter turned dark-red. He thrust his thin face into mine.

"—'s is *ee*diots!" he hissed.

I fervently agreed with him. We had wanted to turn dark-red at that young man several times yesterday; felt really obliged to our hot-tempered friend, especially as he proceeded to dilate on the dangers of the pass at this season . . . the rocks that fall from the cliffs, the likelihood of blinding snowstorms, and so on; which made us feel better about it. But we were not yet free of worry as to how the flat-car was going to treat Nicolette; we hastened back to watch her being spiked down to that moving floor. . . . Poor dear, that sooty tunnel; all by herself in the cold and dark! And she might have been climbing into glories by now.

A guard shouted at us. " 'By, Nicolette! Take care of yourself!" and we bolted for our seats. (Actually, it was good to sit down after all that racing.)

"Rather a bore not to drive her over," murmured Babs, placidly lighting a cigarette; I smiled at her—for going over the Simplon had been one of her dearest plans.

We were winding along the side of the valley, against a wall of cliff; but it was Italy still. Beloved, ill-treated Italy; we had had scarcely time in all this deciding and arranging, and being so hot yesterday, to say a proper good-by to her, and felt again as Miss Raby did, in Forster's delightful story: "They had come to the land of *Ach* and *Ja*. Miss Raby sighed; for she

"NICOLETTE LOOKED PATHETICALLY SMALL, IN ALL THIS VASTNESS"

Just over the Jaun Pass

loved the Latins, as every one must who is not pressed for time. . . . 'They still talk Italian for seven miles!' she said, comforting herself like a child."

For we felt romantic and sorrowful, as we stared from our window. What purple cliffs! and how the rain-gray valley was falling away below us, its river, still faintly blue, winding scenically along. But the cliff closed in, and wild flowers looked in at us from chinks in the rocks; a dark hole was ahead. Guards hurried through, shutting windows. . . . Lights were on and thick darkness was about us.

Woo! We could feel the train twisting, like a worm in its hole. The air was sulphurous; lights were unwholesomely dim. . . . The conductor came through, a nice, jovial, fresh-faced one with underlings attending him, jotting down things in little books; he regarded us very kindly as he took our tickets and this, for a moment, was comfortable; but it seemed a long time before passengers about us stirred, a faint blueness arrived on the Simplon's sooty walls, and we pulled slowly out into railway yards.

Seizing our things, we fairly tumbled down the steps.

Clearest blue sky; dazzling snow peaks upon it; the storm was left far below, and sunshine flooding this very Swiss valley.

How beautiful. We nearly fell over backward, staring at those peaks. How clear and sharp the air was; we shivered, and put on more coats. It was cold in Brieg! Such a change from languid Maggiore; we briskly followed a porter up a hilly street which, after widening into a *place,* came to its end apparently in the most lofty mountains. Swiss neatness was everywhere; the street's edges were adorned with neat round flower-beds of geraniums and balsam—bracing flowers, there is nothing languid about a geranium; and Brieg's houses and hotels were all freshly, sometimes astonishingly, painted—brown and sky-blue, salmon and nile green.

And from our corner room, a suddenly Swiss room with a shiny white stove, what mountains. The Rhone Valley, we were in . . . though it felt too high for any valley; and Brieg is perched a bit above it. Sunset light was on the peaks now; the blue behind them was dazzling. Ten and twelve thousand feet, those peaks of the Lötchenpass; and that evening we read how the road over the Simplon, built by Napoleon, was "a lasting memento of his genius and energy. He desired to have a great military road into Italy, and his constant inquiry was: '*Quand le canon pourra-t'il donc passer au Simplon?*' " When the artillery can it get over the Simplon? Yes, the *canon*, sweet dear; his one idea was to lug them over terrific mountains, killing men and horses en route, then do in as many people as possible on the other side. . . .

His road was finished in six years; scenery from it must be surpassing. It goes by Refuges, Alpine roses, and glaciers; "a gorge of the brawling Diviera, one of the wildest and grandest in the Alps"; and if we had come up over it, instead of under, we might have been reposing comfortably in an avalanche this very minute. . . . We gazed out at the starlit peaks, consoling ourselves—the peaks did a good deal toward that; and how we slept that night in Brieg's bracing air. (It was a nice hotel, by the way.) That air took the regrets out of one; and everything was so vivid here, so uplifting; we absolutely ran down Brieg's hill, to greet Nicolette.

A black, despicable object stood on the freight-platform. . . . Was that she, blackened from bonnet to tail? A windshield so smoked we couldn't see through it . . . and in all this mountain purity?

They *might* have thrown a tarpaulin over her. Pouf! We made faces over her; took out all the cloths she owned, and scrubbed and dusted. There wasn't a soul around to help; nobody even to take all our fabulous papers. Very well! We took her back to the hotel, ran upstairs and washed profoundly, collected bags (especially the rucksack we had packed to take with us to Zermatt) and started up the Rhone Valley . . . hardly looking at it, we were so thrilled with getting somewhere else. Stalden, our map said, was as far as you could drive; a carriage road used to climb all the way, but now you go up to this first village and jump on a cogwheel train. . . .

We were not at all sure we should take that train; the map merely said the trail beyond Stalden was "impracticable."

"What does *that* mean?" I said, as we twisted along by the nice torrent, with great heartening mountain crags above us. "Probably we can drive all the way up."

" 'Bet we can!" said Babs.

"Route interdite aux automobiles," the map also said—chiefly because of red brackets, it seemed to us; hadn't we done thousands of those? We passed, just here, a little old peasant-woman, staff in hand, trudging sturdily up with a load of zinc on her back; a bag of something on top of the zinc, and loaves of bread on top of that—load enough for a donkey . . . but she seemed quite unaffected. We sailed hopefully into hot little Stalden, around small Swissy corners, and down to the brown chalet that is Stalden's inn, pleasant with vines and a broad piazza. *Oui, madame!* and a large garage key was forthcoming. *Non, madame!* The path beyond was not for motors.

"By bicycle they go sometimes," volunteered the stout, red-bearded host; unbelieving still, we climbed out to investigate for ourselves.

Well, no. Frankly, no! Over rock ledges and round little gardens went the dwindling path, then beside a cliff; a sweet trail—but if Nicolette had gone along it, exactly half of her would have been upon the air.

So that was what "impracticable" meant. We stepped reluctantly down across the ledges— "She wouldn't have minded *those!*" murmured Babs—took the large key and shut her safely in. Daughter shouldered the rucksack—she looked so natural with it on; tall and competent, striding along. Ah, this felt good, said we, climbing hardily in the hot sun; bumping the rucksack doughtily down on the porch floor and demanding lunch. We felt like mountain-climbers already; had a great deal of lemonade with our lunch. Lemonade somehow "went" with the sudden simplicity of our feelings; with basking in sun, smelling gardens and hay, listening to bees, hearing the clatter of mule-hoofs on the road . . . then strolling down to the *bahnhof,* where a mule-train was loading up. "Nice brown mules," say the notes; "the lead-mule had a bell on." Off they filed, a bearded mountaineer striding after them very calmly smoking his pipe; over the track, down across the torrent the mules went—knowing all about it—then up the winding sunny trail toward a village called Saas.

"Must be hot over there," I said; for this Swiss sun penetrated.

On the station platform, climbers were sitting at little tables, their ski and huge packs beside them. Swiss platforms are always pleasant, full of friendliness and sun, alpenstocks, golf-stockings, and beer, and this one had a view, but when we went in to get tickets, we were astounded at the tremendous price. *"Pourquoi?"* I said; and the old, German-looking ticket-man, glancing sourly at me, replied in a rumbling great bass voice somewhere down in his beard—everybody had beards here—that it was because the railway had such a short season.

"Cela ne pas—en hiver marche!" said he disgustedly; in such perfect German-French that I made a note of it then and there. Smiling, we went out onto the platform again; to the pleasantness and the sun, the golf-stockings and beer.

"One could have lunched here, apparently," I said, gazing about.

There were trees of ripe cherries close by the track, and across it now tramped our old peasant-woman with the load of zinc on her back; she went pelting along downhill for the valley of the Saas. Seven kilometers yet to go, up that mountain path; and she had walked from Brieg with that load. . . . Our cog-wheel train was late.

"Ah, here she comes!" Babs said; for a puffing approached; round a curve, the head of our conveyance. Cog-wheels came grinding along; jolted to a stop. Third class, everybody! No such thing as first, in Switzerland, and inside one finds bright varnish and bright, new, light-colored wood, slippery but comfortable: a long car all big windows, mostly open. Everybody piled in—and opened the rest of them; rucksacks were flung into racks, ski stood in corners, heads were out of windows.

Sunny meadows, dark little Alpine huts; flowers beside the track, the foaming torrent below; crags looming, cascades filming down from the cliffs—and a big snowy head, high on our left. Was it the Ulrichhorn? Some sort of Horn they all were, here; Tasschorn,Egginerhorn, Rimpfishhorn! We passed San Niklaus, and began to climb through a larch forest still in feathery spring green, and with a close-woven carpet of larch-needles . . . pleasant, short, little needles.

"I love this larch forest . . ." I murmured, leaning out.

"Yes—" said my child, with the unflinching realism of the young; "there's a woman sitting in it, biting her nails."

"Any other occupation?"

"No. Got a kerchief on her head!"

Cog-wheels were working hard; we moved slowly. Larches, rocks, the bounding torrent—one could be intimate with them, realize each wild detail. At a swing across a bridge, however, the gorge-like valley turned, and a great shout went up from the climbers. To the platform they rushed, waving hats, hurrahing, pounding each other on the back; the Matterhorn was in sight! We hung far out of the window; yes, there he was, clear on blue sky, rocky, snow-streaked; above the rockiness, a finger of pure snow, pointing . . . beckoning.

Did they mean to tackle *him,* these boys?

The valley opened a little and he was still more in sight; sometimes behind a big cliff, under which we had to wind, sometimes peeping over a lesser summit, but always there; always in one's mind. Ah! a broader widening; larch slopes, chalets, hotel-roofs, wide meadows; this must be Zermatt.

Leisurely we ground toward it; a cog-wheel never hurries. The impatient climbers hanging from its steps, hurled themselves out as it slowed; we hastily followed. A nice chalet-ish station, then Zermatt's little street. A big hotel, set back in its grounds—closed; another, ditto; little shops for wood-carvings, curios, post-cards, groceries, climbers' boots—altogether a cosy, gossipy little Alpine street, with guides leaning against its wall. Our first guides.

We devoured them with our eyes—spare, shrewd-looking men with snow-burned faces, hobnailed boots, a coiled rope, woolen shirts; a humorous, clean look. . . . And the people of Zermatt, turning to stare interestedly at us and our rucksack, were trundling wheelbarrows, carrying armfuls of wood or cans of milk; stopping to talk comfortably together. A restful little street—more a promenade than anything else; ah, the peace of getting away from a world of motors.

Let's find some place more outside the village, said we; not a hotel, but a little place; and just then a tall young woman, brown-haired and hatless, came up to us. She had been standing in the street, looking station-ward.

"Would you like a nice pension?" she asked, in French. "We have a very nice one, just a little farther on. . . . Good meals!" she added, smiling.

I liked her friendly face and way; Babs and I exchanged looks of consultation. "Let's" they said.

The young woman, who must have been a psychologist, reached promptly for our rucksack.

"No—I can take it," protested Babs, backing away; but on that strong Swiss shoulder it went, preceding us into a lane that twisted round some wide-roofed and balconied old chalets dark with age (or wintering); geraniums were on their railings, their roofs weighted with rocks, woodpiles stacked under the balconies, and each with its little plot of garden. . . . Beets, we noticed, were barely coming up.

"It *is* late here, isn't it," murmured Babs. "Nice, to see things just beginning!"

It was. Somehow a bracing change from the vegetable luxuriance we had been in so long. Marvelous, this clear mountain air; a brook was dashing beside us. Meadows and snow mountains were beyond this small torrent as it cascaded down, and above it stood a pale-brown balconied chalet on a little high terrace of its own, with cheerful flowers, an orange umbrella, tables set out; the Pension Triftbach. Our rucksack, and we after it, climbed the stone steps—then an intriguing flight of carved, wooden ones to an upper balcony, and a sweet little room all Alpine neatness.

Snowy white muslin, shiny light-green walls; big beams, very close over our heads, painted shining white—they shone, like melting ice-cream—and patchwork quilts on the narrow beds.

Ah, this was what we had wanted to find; and the little torrent roared avidly below. Across Zermatt's valley our windows looked—low-set little Alpine windows with heavy framework—across the old chalets, across a flowery bit of hilly meadow, with a goat in it, away to the purple, snow-streaked precipices of Alps.

It was just tea-time, so tea we had, under the orange umbrella—a generous Swiss tea; and set off up the valley trail. Gentle, flowery meadows with the river dashing below; nearer came the Matterhorn's silver peak, gloriously clear on the blue. Very real now were his rocks, and snow-filled cracks; "cracks!" I thought; they were gorges, near to. A big glacier was at one side of him; more glaciers dribbled over heights on the other side.

Our path went up past little Alpine barns, heavy-timbered and windowless; eloquent of the bitter cold, the eight-foot snows, they combat. Was anything in them? Two calf-tails showed through an open door; tan-colored babies, very hollow-sided, were turning moist little grayish noses at us—noses that moved entreatingly, expecting their supper. We rubbed their little foreheads—but that, they told us, should lead to something more. . . . Grass and flowers were just outside the door; where was Mother, we wondered? For we saw no cows pasturing; then remembered that this conglomeration of blossoms around the little barns was Zermatt's hay-crop, and not to be eaten till winter.

Larches were very near us now, beautiful great feathery light-green ones; also a waterfall and a dividing of gorges, with glimpses of snowy things beyond. A charming trail. Under the larches, by great boulders of the tumbling stream it went; two peasants presently overtook us, climbing rapidly onward with the enviable strides of the mountaineer, and with bulging packs on their backs. . . . This path was a real one, then, going on to a village—a cluster of huts somewhere far above (we had seen a dotting on the map); sunset was coming, and we hadn't time for anything very long, so though the larches towered ever higher, and the torrent made splendid thunderings, we tramped back to the waterfall and the other trail. (It looked as if it might have briefer ideas.)

Steep, this was! Very white and plungeous the fall—either the noise or the light of it, we said, would tell us the way back; on up through dusky, pungent forest went our rooty trail. We stopped to sniff the perfumed larch-needles, and peer at yet another torrent in an abyss below—every trail has its torrent here; and saw above us, at the top of a bank, a grassy opening by a little gray Alpine barn.

That sort of opening is irresistible, leading uphill out of a wood. You can't quite see where it goes to; there is clear sky above it, and usually raspberries or a view behind the gray barn—both of them equally neglected, therefore uncommonly fine. We sprinted expectantly up the slope and rounded the barn, but stopped; feeling devout. . . . It was a meadow of Alpine crocuses that stretched off to a wall of dark spruces, the Matterhorn, a silver rapier on clear blue sky, towering above; beautiful, terrible. Just the Matterhorn; even its glaciers were shut off by the great fir trees.

The best sight of him that could be had, rearing so perfectly above that meadow. A calf loo'ed in the barn; farming in sublimity, this was.

And the flowers; that crocus meadow! Its whiteness stretched away toward the fir trees—only it was not white. The slim, rather tall little flowers, much slimmer than domestic crocuses—truly wild, and rejoicing in it, and with the unnameable *cachet* that wild things have—were delicately veined with pale violet; the whole field had the slightest, coolest tinge of lavender. The most spiritual-looking little slim flowers I ever saw; each one looked like a little message. They were

THE MATTERHORN, BECKONING ALOOFLY

lightly closed for evening; tiptoeing, ready for flight; if they had risen and winged off like skylarks, on some high quest, neither of us would have been really astonished. . . .

A rosiness was coming on the silver Matterhorn, shadows across the meadow . . . more violet on the crocuses. A rapier of flame now, our mountain, above the dark trees; solemn in its greatness. No cloud was near it; solitary it glowed, the one bright thing in a twilight world . . . yet softened by approaching night.

Flowers at our feet were feeling the unearthly glow; what with staring about us, and fearing to tread on something lovely, we hardly dared move. By and by my child wandered off a little, and stood in the flowers. "Lorna in the crocuses!" my notes say—it is not everybody one would want in a field like that; her young figure in its gray-brown tweeds and a bit of soft old-blue tie—this was a day when she felt like old blue . . . . above it her face, like an Italian boy's. . . .

When she came back, and turned to look at the mountain, I could see her better; knowing, perhaps, after many candle-lighted moments in old churches, what to expect. Any face would have kindled, in that glow; and when it is your child's . . . gazing up, very gentle with its love of beauty— I picked a crocus and had another look. A Matterhorn seemed to suit it.

We smiled at each other. If it hadn't been for that fiery thing up aloft, this Alpine meadow and its fir trees would have made us think of the Shrewsbury hills and their wild loneness. Tops of blue spruces, romantic against a clouded sky—there always seemed to be clouds—and when you smell blue spruces you know you are high up; somewhere in their shelter a white-throat singing . . . another thing that made you know you were in the wilds. We used to camp there, in forgotten swampy meadows and pink hardhack; a cold, high smell in the air, a lost brook wandering somewhere, and the smoke from our fire drifting off. . . . Gli beside us, our horses roaming about, and that white-throat singing. He sang sometimes in the middle of the night, a full grand song—that is, if sounds and fragrances were too lovely to let one get to sleep, or our tin cups of coffee had been too large—which they frequently were—for me; they were huge cups.

But purples were coming now; they stole from under the trees.

"We'd better be getting down that path," said Babs; and the meadow was so lovely yet, with the crocuses still holding a little light—fir trees refusing to harbor any and therefore very black; the mountain brilliant. . . .

Seriously dark along the rooty trail, which dove at once into shadow; if we could have moved the Matterhorn along, and so had it shine down that glen! but mountains have a lofty way of doing things for themselves alone. Guided not a little by the roar of the fall, and with one or two large stumbles over unseen rocks, we came out from under the trees in valley light once more. Glad to see it, we were. A lovely light, mostly afterglow—from the row of rejoicing glaciers, who were having their chance out here, and being as rosy as anybody. The Matterhorn still burned, dimly. . . . What a valley! And the sound of the stream was so loud.

The little calves were being fed, from a brimming pail—no mother visible yet; and comfortable, warm-milk scents were on the air. In another little barn two red-and-white babies, plump-sided and happy, yet (evidently) with a sense of having been defrauded of the fearful joy of sucking something while their meal went on, were busily and pervertedly sucking each other's tails. . . . Wicked babies, we informed them; who would come to no good end!

And as the chalets of the village drew near, there were cosy sounds of evening; clink of dishes and milk-pails, the sound of wood-chopping, thump of wood falling into boxes; a laugh, as one home-coming peasant greeted another. Men sat on their porches, smoking reflectively, talking little; women were leaning over the gates and chattering, but with an eye on the mountains . . . not uneasily, but with a somewhat harassed look of habit, it seemed to us. Some of those men on the porches were guides—many of them indeed, and the thoughts of the women dwelt aloft. With reason; what tomorrow would bring, or the summer, only these heights knew. People's lives in Zermatt are lived in that shadow; and when next day we walked into the little cemetery, there was the long, much-decorated row of climbers' graves, facing the silent precipices. Famous names were on those graves, young Lord this, the Honourable that; and then good Swiss names. . . . At our pension a tall young woman, a daughter of the family, walked quietly about, helping with the work, often carrying a flaxen-haired child on her shoulder; a baby of a year or more.

"What can she do?" said her sister, sadly. "Last year her husband was killed. Last June. He was a guide, yes. . . . Young, and most pleasant always—so good a young man; they were the happiest people, those two, together. . . . He was just up here—" she waved a hand toward the glacier behind the Gornergrat, "and he slipped. . . . They never found him. It was very hard for her."

And the tall, fair-haired figure in the black dress was sitting among the flowers of the hillside meadow, early next morning; playing with her child, picking flowers for it, lifting it for a sudden kiss.

But this evening, the young climbers who had been on the train with us possessed the place. A party of rather pale-faced students, chattering German, they had come thronging up the pension steps at dinner-time with their ski and packs; the sisters' old father, blue-eyed and hale, had been a famous guide in his day, and this, it appeared, was a rendezvous for climbers. Laughing and voluble they were, about their intended exploits; one especially lavender-faced lad tossing around some flat loaves of a durable brown bread which, he said, was the thing for their trip . . . and three Austrians at a table near by sat and listened quietly—two men and a girl, lean and hardy-looking, quite blackened by sun on snow; worn down to mere muscle and sinew. (Not beautiful at all; quite ghastly.) The girl was wearing a knitted, sleeveless, lemon-colored frock, against which her thin arms looked like black sticks, and she and her companions listened, scornfully, to this flood of talk. . . . They had done it all, early in the season, their glances at each other said; what would these pasty-faced ones, white with town living, do on the heights? (They were planning a four days' ski-trip, it seemed, to a hut on Monte Rosa, carrying on their backs everything they would need.)

The Austrians went up to bed, we really thought, rather than listen to this foolishness any longer.

Next day we took the train up to the Gornergrat—its first trip this year—and there they were, with their enormous packs, boarding it uproariously. . . . Slow progress, that climbing from the valley; through larches and purple cliffs with great icicles dripping; then out on the vast snowy wilds.

It wasn't a good day, not a blue-and-white one, that is; stormy-looking and with visibility poor, but all the grander for that. . . . We were above the gorge of the Matterhorn; its glaciers looked across at us, its black rocks and snowy crevices. An unreal, Titanic world; a world of icy impossibility; we watched its great panorama unfolding. Beyond the endless snow-fields through which we crawled, their drifts high above us, it seemed all glaciers.

But there was one actual touch; we came in sight of a wooden hotel below us, deep in snow; just above the precipice. . . . Foolish, it looked. Trivial! The climbers craned their necks at it. . . . Summer must bring about a great change here, if that place was ever to be inhabited.

Near the last station, with workers still digging at a huge drift, we all piled out to walk some hundred yards up the track in wet squshy snow, ankle deep; Babs and I were in low shoes. One guide was already by the station-shed, waxing several pairs of ski which he had up-ended against a wall; the climbers stopped with him and did likewise, and we tramped on. The Gornergrat's low, prison-like hotel of gray stone, entirely snow-girt, was some distance ahead; from there would be still more view.

There was; even with snow-storms in the offing. I shall not forget the feeling we had there, looking miles down (it seemed) to a sea of blue-green ice; looking off over whirling wastes to more seas of broken ice and cruel white peaks—brushed by storm, or showing bare teeth upon the clouds. . . . I suppose Monte Rosa was one of them. A ray of sun burst through, and vanished—marvelous, as it raced over that scene; then we had to start down. The lavender-faced boy, ski on, his tremendous pack shouldered, was striding somberly away at right angles to us, up across the waste of snow; a companion followed likewise silently, all gaiety gone, and as we reached the little station, two more set morosely off. The guide, talking very casually with one of his kind, was apparently waiting for the last to go before starting after them. I hoped he knew what he was in for.

And those awful packs! Would these boys—only now looking as if they at all realized what was before them—be able to endure it? For four days; and suppose a blizzard caught them?

Perhaps it is not anything to go across those glacial wastes to Monte Rosa; on that dour afternoon, with snow hovering, it looked like a fearful exploit, one that only old climbers should attempt . . . people like those Austrians. In fact, now that we had been up to the Grat and seen what one sees from there, Mount Everest could look no more terrifying.

But our shoes were snow-soaked and icy cold; we were not a bit sorry when the train started down. We felt reflective, and a trifle fatalistic; very glad we had come up (at the pension they had rather discouraged it), even gladder, when a snow-squall came whirling down; the Matterhorn was even more beautiful, with this veiling. We crawled along, impossibly intimate with the dimmed purple of its gorges; down and down, seeing larches through snow-storm, the emerald of the valley through it. . . . Big flakes they were, visibly spotting the far cliffs. Babs caught one on her cuff; it was immense, but dissolved quickly.

Purely a mountain storm; Zermatt's roofs were not even whitened. We emerged into a village as dry as when we had left it. . . . Tea in a warm dining-room was comfortable; Babs elected a book and a rest, and I strolled out again.

"A.B. took a gorgeous walk up the valley," says the diary; interested and sympathetic, as ever.

Drops of rain were falling, but I somehow had to go up that valley; I did love those little barns so, and the flowers. A clear stream came bursting down to join the tumultuous Visp below; the path wound upward, the larches came down, the Matterhorn called you on. This afternoon the Matterhorn was a sweet ghost, but beckoned even more; the torrent was very loud. On the heights, clouds were shifting and whirling; snow-squalls flitting about; what *would* become of those boys, striding across the dreary wastes?

All about me were farm-scents and security. In one barn a fair little calf had been fed, and looked round at me happily; I hoped my red babies were not chewing each other's tails again. The meadows seemed even more frantic with Alpine flowers, scentless, mostly, but making up on color; I gathered some to take back to Babs. A johnny-jump-up stared at me through the fence with such sad hopes; bitten on one upper petal, he was, but the only one I could reach.

"Come along," I told him; "somebody's been eating you, but never mind!" For the johnnies here are very appealing; what they lack in size and velvet they gain in anxiety, and an anxious johnny goes to one's heart.

My child was sauntering to meet me. "Thought you were lost!" said she, banteringly. "It's been raining; did you know that?"

And past milk-pails, and little porches, and flowery banks, we made our way back. Along the level bit—with forget-me-nots by the fence; past the little path we always wanted to take across somebody's uphill field, but felt it was private property . . . you had to climb a fence; around the garden where the beets were so small . . . and home.

Really home, the chalet now seemed . . . how bright-faced it was, up there; and a sister was out on the terrace looking for us—another homelike touch. Supper was ready, she said, smiling.

Supper? It was a banquet. Everything so rich and home-made and good—and more than any soul could eat.

Basking afterwards by the hot stove, we fought through a chapter or two of books, and climbed early to bed under our ice-cream rafters . . . well that we did, for we woke to a blinding snow-storm. Zermatt's landscape was under inches of it already. Boo! what could one do in low shoes, in Zermatt, in a snow-storm? With sudden resolution we leaped into our clothes, rammed things into the rucksack, swallowed breakfast, settled with the astonished but ever good-natured sisters, and in thirty-five minutes from the time we first peered from our Alpine window, caught the early train down.

The sisters didn't think we could make it, so we lifted heel and ran; dashed, laughing but determined, through the four-inch snow, past peasants with pails of milk, defeating barrowfuls of morning wood; got there just in time and climbed aboard ticketless and panting, elated with our feat; happy to feel ourselves jerking and grinding along toward Nicolette.

CHAPTER XXIX

THE MATTERHORN BIDS US FAREWELL

THE shrouded valley was beautiful.

After a little, the flakes ceased falling. At Brietermatt—or was it Herbriggen?—the larch-needles were brown again.

"Let's walk the rest of it!" said Babs, who had been leaning out of the window. "Grand idea!" said I; and we jerked down the rucksack and jumped off. Jolly, to be able to do this, even at the sacrifice of some of our expensive ticket; the guard stared in stupefaction, but he would anyway.

We felt, as we watched the cog-wheel joggle off without us, a little adventurous, having no idea how many miles it was to Stalden; our map was in the car. A path led down through the delicate greens of the larchwood; how much lovelier to walk . . . how much more of it one got. Especially overhead. Beside us the torrent rushed among its boulders, there were moments when the sun came out and fell dapplingly on our brown path, on the rocks and mosses about us, the little wood-flowers—but above was the real world of glory: summits, cliffs and filmy waterfalls. Sometimes we went through a bit of flowery meadow, and then the snowy heads were all the more thrilling; the Breithorn was up there, the little Matterhorn, and the Rifflehorn; and glacier streams came bursting down to mingle with the already furious Visp.

Such white water and big boiling pools—there are no better companions for a mountain tramp; to their rough tumbling, with the fresh flower-faces to escort us—and that upper world of an Alpine valley, the distance seemed nothing. We kept our faces mostly upward, while our intelligent boots took care of things below. If you are in the habit of looking out for a horse's footing, you can memorize a stretch of path at a glance;

great fun, to plunge along and never look . . . and in no time at all, it seemed (though we had walked seven or eight miles), we were tramping into Stalden; feeling like shouting to everybody we met: "*Don't* ride down from Zermatt! Wait till it's downhill and then walk!"

The shrines in the village were heaped with flowers this morning—for the Fête de Dieu, our host told us; and three ruddy and sunburnt little girls, almost startlingly dark-faced in their white dresses and veils—with wreaths on their little heads and bouquets in their hands, were standing bashfully beside the largest shrine, waiting to be taken somewhere. They looked very shyly at us. . . .

Good little Stalden; with a look back at its belfry, we were down beside the rock-caverns of the enlarged and rocketing Visp, then out in the Rhone Valley, with the Rhone young and dusty-colored and unexciting; we remembered it at Avignon and other places, a great, green, rolling thing.

"Gorgeous clouds above the valley," say my notes . . . we turned up it. Ah, *this* was what we had wanted to do for so long. Eighty miles of it and its long magnificence before we should reach Lake Geneva; there would be no April primroses, such as we had seen from the train, but the Dents du Midi would be there, and the clouds of our dark morning—now tearing apart into a fine day; also the towering cliffs.

Our road was dusty but not bad, with pleasantly few motors; what there were, were flying at top speed. The sun was out again, and every village decorated for the fête; Sion was particularly gay, with hosts of little girls in white carrying flowers; we went slowly there, to watch them. . . . But the sun was hotter every minute, and with all the peaks above us we simply couldn't have the top up—so we tore along instead: much relieved at last, on coming to a bend in the river, to see before us the shadow of a tall forest, and feel a dampness. Delicious! The road darkened with spray; behind the forest was a beautiful great leaping fall, the Sallenche, sending its dew far out over the trees, and us.

We halted to see the leaves sparkle. High and *very* roaring.

the Sallenche—we felt surprised not to have heard of it from somebody. Its river "drains the glaciers of the Dents du Midi," then leaps, conspicuously enough, its 200 feet into the rocky reception of this forest—making a spot at which to stop and "take something" at the forest's very cordial little restaurant: in this case, nothing more exciting than two lemonades. (The waiter, who had come out expectantly, gave us rather a horrid smile as he set them down.)

And then we wandered a little in the forest. A bicyclist went by, out in the hot sun, with a stuffed rucksack on his back; glanced superiorly in at us, wasting time in the lovely shadow, and pedaled on. O pleasant Sallenche, we said; he doesn't know what he is missing! . . . Or perhaps he did. We passed him further on and were sorry to sift dust over him; for he was a nice-looking boy, extremely burned, evidently traveling by himself on that bicycle of his, and taking it rather hard. . . . We were convinced, too, that he didn't need half that mound of belongings—unless he was camping out and had to carry blankets.

Vineyards increased, after this, and so did the Dents du Midi. The valley widened uninterestingly, the Rhone left us, flinging off to bury its gray moraine-waters in the blue of the lake—after it emerges, it is never gray again; then we came to an inlet with tall trees, and everything grew interesting.

Fishing-boats lay in it with their great red sails half-furled; the lake was beyond, and the snow-clad mountains; after the inlet came a charming quai with grass and flower-beds, tables under the thick shade of pollarded trees, and a white hotel opposite.

Well, said we, driving up, this isn't Montreux; but let's lunch here.

It was Ville Neuve as a matter of fact: a place of perpetual meals. Late as it was, waiters were running back and forth across the road with loaded trays; we settled at a table by the water and were greatly entertained. Steamers came and went, tourists drove up; we even had the Castle of Chillon to look at, across the water into which its towers descend—a fact which somehow adds to any castle's romance—and well out toward the mountains was a tiny island, Île de la Paix, "laid out and planted with three elms by a lady a century ago." Our book added that the sight of it "recalls Byron's lines":

> And then there was a little isle,
> Which in my very face did smile,
> The only one in view.

What Wordsworthian lines, for Byron. . . . But the poet might have been sitting in our chairs when he conceived them, if they needed so tense and profound a thing as conception; for the islet, and the elms, smiled in our faces too. Was the lady who planted those elms a Byron addict? We tried to remember our Maurois. . . . Let's see, when did Byron live?

Out in the water two gray swans were swimming about, and a baby swan. Sometimes the baby scrabbled on its mother's back and rode there between her wings, with only its downy head visible; we tried for some time to get a picture of it in that comfortable spot—riding about, with the Dents du Midi to look at; would they not have an effect even on the mind of an infant swan? But Mother, apparently disliking publicity for her offspring, either swung the wrong way or bobbed too hard in a wake, or else the baby ducked entirely into her deep feathers; we gave it up and took a mere snapshot of swans.

We liked this place, however; why not stay here instead of at Montreux, which we could see across the rounding end of the lake, looking far too big?

"Suits me!" said Babs, putting the camera away; and we went across the road. A big, airy corner room was vacant; the view of the inlet and the fishing sails was marvelous from there —as was the pure snow of the Dents du Midi. From this height, too, the disturbance that steamer-paddles made in the crystal water was a thing to watch; the boats turned here, so their great wakes trailed away under the mountains, circles of silver and topaz in the intense blue. . . . The boats each had an immense Swiss flag drooping astern—both flags and boats, on Geneva, were bigger than any we had seen, and Geneva itself unfalteringly blue all over; Baddy is quite solemn about it. "This blue tint is ascribed by Sir Humphrey Davy (who lived some years at Geneva, and died there in 1828) to the presence of iodine; a view that the Swiss scientific men do not accept."

I should think not. Iodine, indeed; what sordidness! It was just their own lake being a forget-me-not, of course—with a streak of gentian here and there. Smiling, we went out to see the forget-me-not and its green edges—in a now cooled and rested Nicolette; and as we were starting who should come along but our young bicyclist, pedaling wearily and making for the curb. He let his pack down upon it with a relieved thump—his shirt was soaking, beneath it; we were glad to see him stroll to the tables, drop into a shady seat and seize a large cool glass of something that a waiter hastened to bring him.

As we came back from our drive, the towers of Chillon were dark against the beginnings of the sunset. From this road above the castle, the mountains are unspeakable, and soon the sunset clouds were all gloriously flaming. The Dents du Midi, *massifs* of pure snow above purple and blue, went rose-color, then were tipped with flame; purples, flaming peaks and all, reflecting in the glassy water.

Those fiery clouds, we thought, would surely bring a fine day tomorrow. . . .

"Rain," says the diary; "slept late, climbed up back of Montreux." One mountain field of narcissus, with a consummate view, had to be enough for us; we were a long time finding it, and I think took the wrong road; but their scent had come misleadingly down a hill to meet us. A lovely field; with a fragrance sharp, brazen, delicious—like cymbals being clashed by angels.

"Steep hill!" said Nicolette; and took us plungingly down.

Montreux, like Mentone, was full of tea and English spinsters; a neat, *soigné* town, winding luxuriantly, blooming luxuriantly. Reposing on one of its hilltops, we spied something that looked familiar. A little old car with a London license, positively senile, built high off the ground, but in an amusing state of efficiency still—enough so, to get its owners to Switzerland, at any rate: "A Lizzie from England, having tea!" said Babs, smiling.

"With one wheel on the sidewalk! Lizzie, I'm ashamed of you."

For the little vehicle, its "G.B." plate looking strange on a Model T, was parked at a drunken angle against the garden of the tea-place. We drove on, feeling we had seen a friend; took tea ourselves "somewhere up the shore in exotic plants," my notes say—Montreux exists in a sort of haze of castor-beans—adored another sunset, drove up the shore to Vevey and Lausanne, returned, and lingered long at dinner. Byron's little isle swam in color, the Dents were going dim and lavender; no one makes any noise about Ville Neuve, but we didn't see why. And there was a pleasantness about its spirit; our waiter, rather a burly creature, was so much nicer than he looked . . . seemed to like to have us linger and stare forever at snows—even vouchsafed himself a few murmurings as to their beauty, and that, from a waiter, always makes the world seem a cheerful place.

Blondined ladies occasionally drove up, with their noisy escorts—but then one sees them anywhere; and there were plenty of nice honest families touring with children, sometimes very swanky families touring with nurses and children—and dogs—who halted under the tree for a meal and afterwards sent the dogs into the lake after sticks. At such moments—with the air alive with yelps, and dog-wakes scooting disturbingly about—the baby swan scrabbled onto its mother's back and was carried farther out from shore, Mother stretching out her long swan-neck and hissing beautifully if any dog came near. (I noticed they turned obediently back.)

"Left Ville Neuve early," says the diary. "Charming morning, swans active. Boat with yellow sails beating out against the wind . . ." while my notes begin, "Early start! Montreux getting ready for the Fête des Fleurs . . ." both of us apparently impressed with the journey we were going to take that day.

"To Vevey, Châtel St. Denis, Charmey, tea by Spieg; Interlaken and Grindelwald. Jaun pass," continues the diary.

Now you can't get above Vevey without seeing a preternatural view, and this morning there was mist stringing romantically across the mountains; a fat roll of white cloud, not far above the water, so that blue-green mountainsides and snowy heads peeped out above it.

And when we gained the upland, apple trees and lilacs bloomed in the chalet gardens. So long since we had seen them . . . we feasted on their dear simplicity; this was a country for lilacs. Châtel St. Denis, a charmingly pretty town, was trimmed with evergreens from the fête of yesterday; yellow flowers were strewn in its street and before the farmhouses—immense chalets, these were, with neat stables under the same roof; fine rich fields accompanied them. . . . "Narcissus, competing with other weeds! A roadman smiled at us as he walked along; he had a narcissus-blossom in his lips. All the roadmen looked nice. And Switzerland had a steam-roller; no unrolled rocks here!"

This was a grand upland. Tips of snow-mountains appeared ahead of us; sheets of narcissus by an evergreen wood . . . and cows in the road. . . . (This is the region of Gruyère cheese.) Gruyère is a high little village three thousand feet up, and on its peak is "an old castle of the Counts of Gruyère, who became extinct in the 16th cent; flanked with massive towers and walls, and supposed to date from the 5th cent. . . . The natives speak a Romanic dialect."

Well, well; age and Romanic dialects in Switzerland; we should have liked to detour to Gruyère, whose heights and castle we could see from our now violently descending road, but were uncertain as to how much (and what) lay before us that day.

Broc, as a matter of fact, came next—a charming little hill-town also decorated with yesterday's flowers; then we continued downhill, all in spruces, to a roaring stream and its bridge. A mule was standing there, objecting to his load; his young driver was kind, and tried all the blandishments, but the mule was at the state where he would only kick and dance. It *was* a great load of wood.

"Green wood, too!" muttered Babs; and went over to help. Nothing availed; the lad started taking off some of the load and Babs fell to cleaning spark-plugs. Nicolette had been badly over-lubricated that morning, letting out a stream of blue smoke behind herself; she was still very perky, but we were beginning to know what over-lubricating meant in a day's progress.

A peasant came across the bridge, as this was going on, and took off his hat to us.

"Aren't they sweet," said Babs contentedly; "they never stare. You can clean all the spark-plugs you want to."

We reflected, with smiles, what the sight of a young woman working over an engine would have been in France, or even Italy, and were glad to be in calm incurious Switzerland for a change; then the mule started on, and so did we.

At Charmey, another neat pretty town so hilly that it seemed to shoot upward to the sky and then fall delightfully down again, we bought lunch from a voluble Swiss shop-keeper (I remember hurrying, because Nicolette was standing on such a violent slant) and dropped into the Jaun Valley below. On the map it looked like a nice valley; every inch of it was a lunch-place. We chose spruces and a brown brook.

The brook here crossed the road on its way from one pasture to another; cattle were feeding on the lower slopes of the mountains. Later they would climb among the spruces, and the peasants would follow them; dairying would go on in the little huts we saw far up. . . . Maybe the cheese we were eating had been made there; an idea that made the next bite of it all the more wonderful. Fresh, this Gruyère, bought so near its source—fresh as oranges devoured in their own grove; one could smell the whiteness of the clover that the herd had cropped making the lovely pallor of the cheese. And how the insides of the holes shone! those holes are somehow half the charm of Gruyère: deeper in color than the body of the cheese itself, a virginal and charming primrose, but with a bold buttercup shining. Was it this keen air that made them glisten so? or Alpine sunshine glinting on brook-water. . . .

I think, as we sat there with little pasture flowers thick about us, and the faint, lovely, outdoor *dong* of cow-bells on the air, we ate the idea of all this as much as anything. . . . Brook-music freshened our solid bread, white violets were in our pot of jam; we watched the sunlight on the pastures. They ran in peaks up among the fir-woods, snows were peeping above; had it not been for their high etherealness, our surroundings might have been (a very rich) Vermont.

But we were getting toward the Bernese Oberland.

Cows here seemed to be eating what *should* be hay-crop; yet one bows to Swiss methods. Grass would grow again, once the grazers were off it—grow fast in this moist richness and a hot Swiss sun; up the brown dots would go, in thinner air, among the enviable spruces; happy peasants, to spend months there. . . . Lovely, solitary Switzerland—troubled, no doubt, with tourists later on; visit its valleys in the spring, and you and the flowers and the cattle have them.

And everything that can be snowy, is. Ex-wintrily snowy; even our Matterhorn, a silver rapier now, would show its rock-scars in July.

On and on wound the valley. The village of Jaun ends it; a tiny thing at the foot of grandeurs. It had the tiniest chapel, with a belfry and a bright wood cornice, above the road on a shelf of its own; facing the valley view. . . . The road forked; we took the fork that went up. Ha! the Jaun pass—with no preliminaries. That is the way for a pass to begin; you get somewhere quickly. Right away there was a red *d* on the map; Nicolette, in all the gaiety of clean spark-plugs, did it with a whirl, and Babs gave her a gleeful pat. *Would* she have done the Simplon? Well, rather.

Up and up, with marvelous peaks across a gorge; serrated peaks of peculiar structure, the Hochmatt, the Dent de Ruth,

"OO! HERE'S THE PLACE WITH THE YUNGFRAU—THE WHOLE RANGE!"

Taken from the train, coming down from Mürren

toothy, pale mauve and lovely, with snowy tips; soon, the top of the pass. We paused to let Nicolette boil, get water, and take pictures. Babs sat on the precipice wall looking dreamily off to snowy distances—muffled in coats, but very much Babs; I took one of her on that sightly wall. The mountains were dreamy, too; beautifully lost and found, in a soft surge of clouds on deep sultry blue.

Were there storms coming up?

Babs came off the wall and we picked flowers under the spruces; an Alpine daisy, pale in that shadow, but with such a furry pink stem, also three cowslips. We had not seen *them* since weeks ago, above Portofino. . . . Marsh-marigolds grew in moist spots among the firs, with Alpine gentian and the mauve primroses that we call Chinese; a nice mingling.

An old roadman saluted us; doffed his black felt hat and almost smiled. A grim-looking creature he was, with harsh features and a sort of boiled complexion, just right to work on passes; and he was doing something very momentous in the roadside gutter with pick and shovel. Gutters *are* momentous on mountains; we felt pleased to have thawed his grimness. . . . But his half-smile was for Nicolette too, I felt.

Round a corner of big spruces we now came on a chalet, flower-trimmed and most unexpected: the Hotel Pension Alpine Rose! The rosy-cheeked, blue-frocked landlady in her white apron leaned out, duster in hand, over a box of pink petunias, to stare at us; she evidently thought we ought to stop. I glanced up at her thinking, "Someday we will!" for I suppose not many travelers had come this way yet.

And here was a sign, SOMMET DU COL. We thought we had already seen the view from this pass; twisted through more of the immense spruces—and stopped. "*Such* white ones," say the notes. "Them! The Seats of the Mighty!"

I remember that we looked at each other with tears in our eyes. . . . The purest, the most magnificent . . . whether these were the Niederhorn, Triesthorn and Megisserhorn, quite near us, or the backs of the great Monch, Jungfrau, and

Bretthorn farther away (and twice their height) we did not know; but here was whiteness diving to depths, whiteness shining upward upon blue, and if we had found the blue and white of Della Robbias affecting in a city square, what about a *world* of forget-me-not blue and white, sun-smitten, with rosy flowers warm in the grass, and the fragrance of spruce everywhere?

We slid toward a deep valley. "Spruce-velvet, to snow; peaks lavender," say my notes. The valley wound far away, great white clouds reared and Nicolette, on that immenseness, looked pathetically small. I got out, partly to pick a flower, partly to take her picture: the burberrys very rumpled, and Babs looking back at me. . . . I don't know why the burberrys were in such a mess that afternoon; we usually had them very flattened and neat.

Böltigen was in the valley; a well-to-do place with a merry stream running through it, gardens on terraces, and wonderful big chalets all poetry and "God bless our house" carved on their beams in script . . . also apple and pear trees espaliered on balconies and stairways. Böltigen was the most hand-wrought village we were to see. "Handsome houses," says Baedeker; house is no word for these embroidered structures, so set off by blossoming trees and rosettes of perfect lettuce. If one weed appeared in these little gardens, or a speck of anything that was not perfect, I believe the inhabitants would faint. Vigilance is in every leaf of Böltigen; everything grows just so much, the brook babbles just so loud, its very mountains rear and roll among clouds carefully planned, one is sure, to make them look higher than they are.

"English car; nice man and girl; raised hat to our G.B." It was good to see those pleasant English faces. . . . We passed a coat lying in the road; that might be a serious matter for somebody. Great hootings and wavings; a peasant-boy went to see about it; and then we drove down and down Böltigen's enchanting narrow valley—"a rollicking glacier stream always beside you," the notes say.

And why does no one except the Swiss seem to inhabit

Swiss villages? People take houses in other countries; a chalet would be charming. Mere living would have its picturesqueness; even milk, that mildest of bartered commodities, would come down a mountain path to you—as we just then saw some coming. A muscular youth was leaping down rocks and striding blithely; crossing the brook with a flat can strapped to his back, from which came the sound of milk splashing. Well-exercised milk. And blossoming may and a cascade, behind the young peasant and his blue blouse, did not detract from the picture.

Backgrounds have a way of backing-up foregrounds, here.

And we had café-crême at the village inn in Latterback; a high, dark chalet with an extra supply of balconies, and great scarlet begonias on the lower one. Good Frau Beer, our hostess, sat us at a marble-topped table by the begonias; Nicolette stood below, on one edge of the little snow-white road, looking most content. She liked this well-cared-for country.

"Noble pitcher of milk, great coffee-pot. Generous, in Suisse!" say the notes.

A peasant lad and girl met in the road; he leaped from his bicycle and gave her a bag of wild strawberries—at which she peeped, in delight. His face was powdered with glacier-cream; probably he worked on one of the passes and, this being Saturday, had come down for the week-end. They talked for a minute, then she rushed off; with bread and salad in her basket, and such an anticipating face. (*He* was coming to supper!)

"I think they're—I don't know what you call it here—but I think they're 'walking out' together," said Babs, with a quaint expression.

Haymaking came next, along the lovely road to Wimmis: a row of great shady lindens beside a field stretching away to woods and a stream, and a dazzling snow mountain—so near that it filled all the sky. An old woman in dark-blue, having put down her scythe under the trees, was pouring tea out of a thermos bottle into a huge pink-and-white cup. Beyond her haymaking was going on, with carts and haycocks and men;

but she and the pink-and-white cup were having a minute to themselves. . . .

We had never seen haying with a snow peak so close, lending its spiritual beauty; could one be as hot, making hay under that sublime supervision? On Como there were snow peaks, but across the lake; and there was so much to distract one, fishing, and reflections. Here it was just haying—and snow.

In fact, it was Switzerland. We tooled blithely along an upland with a huge view into a valley, a wall of mountains beyond, and the sky a garden of clouds; behold, a small open car approaching, full of dark figures; it stopped, and one of the figures leaped out. . . .

"Halt!" he cried; and when Babs did not absolutely stand Nicolette on her nose, his hand flew to his hip. (Idiot! couldn't he see we were stopping?) Another gendarme leaped out, and they both assailed us: Bum rsht bla! in very thick German. Very stern and tall they were, in black uniforms with scarcely a touch of gold; and what they wanted of us we did not know. . . . All at once they began talking French—queer, thick French, but I understood. The Permise de Circulation, they demanded to see, and while Babs unlocked the tin pocket, I in my turn assailed the chief officer, sitting opposite me. In olive-green, he was, with orange trimmings; very agreeable and smart, and with a smiling blue eye. I asked him (in *my* queer French) why we were held up like this, on a mere road.

He explained smilingly that so many people drove through Switzerland without licenses, that they felt obliged to ask for every one's papers. He was sorry to cause us this trouble; he hoped Mademoiselle and myself were enjoying la Suisse, etc., etc.; his blue eyes were full of a really charming response, and by the time Babs and the tall black gendarmes were through with each other, everything was on a most social basis.

"Au revoir, mesdames!" cried the pleasant one, smiling over his decorated collar at my child—who, still rather stern and not to be cajoled so easily, was haughtily locking up the portfolio.

"They'd *better* be nice!" she muttered, starting Nicolette again.

"Well," I said, "I suppose they do have to be careful—passes and everything, you know . . . and people probably try to slide through them."

"Expect they do!" said she, more cheerfully. "After all, A.B.—these hills!"

For we were going down one. Not our first, but Swiss hills always surprise you. This one evidently planned to plunge us all the way down to the Lac de Thoune; and it did. We slid into Spiez, enraptured at coming to blue water again; such a late-afternoon blue—and late sun on the wall of mountains across Thoune; the lofty, delicately patterned wall (pale violet at the moment, tipped with golden-white) that makes deep-colored Thoune a thing of wonder.

That drive along it was a joy. Villages were full of Swiss charm; beds of orange lilies inside little picket-fences, and little inns with gardens by the water. One could have stopped anywhere. Leissigen, Darligen; then a point with rich dark woods and fields beyond it—good-by, Thoune! For across its meadows, Interlaken was beginning.

We knew it, and its larger spic-and-spanness, but in this light it was transfigured; and when we came to the spot where the trees of the park divide and the dazzling Youngfrau fills the gap, we stopped. Pink snow, on that blue!

We simply whirled into the road that leads to Grindelwald. It twisted among little fields and cottages and gardens, all radiant in the last sunlight; heavens, what dandelions . . . and what chalets, in the narrow valley we turned into. Their first stories were of whitewashed rock; strong, they are, and snowy clean; brilliant their geraniums as the muslins in their windows, which, again, were as white as the pear-blossoms in their fields. Beyond Zwei-Lütschinnen, this was, where the two streams come together, one dark-gray and one clear: up the left-hand valley we were going, with the dashing glacier stream beside us, and bright small meadows and whitewashed apple trees . . . and the Wetterhorn at its head. Great snowy thing, white and fair above the little farms, fabulously white above a white apple tree in bloom ("crab-apple!" said Babs): it led us on, presiding over our last miles . . . we, blissful though weary, Nicolette strangely laboring.

"Expect it's those spark-plugs again," said Babs. I didn't think so; but as we crossed a bridge under towering spruces and began on a climb, she ceased laboring—without even a sigh.

"*Must* be spark-plugs!" said my child; and climbed determinedly out.

"But you cleaned them, darling!" I protested.

"Oh yes," said she coolly, opening the bonnet. "Thought so . . . they're filthy." And she sought among the tools.

"Filthy!" she repeated, holding one of them to the light; "I wish garages wouldn't do that for you!" and she blew with special fervor.

For the gorge was darkening. High overhead a rich golden sky was coming; I looked down the valley, with its mauve cliffs and its wildness, and took a picture of Babs laboring there, with her tired face, in all that mountain beauty. . . . Dim, it would be, but I must have it. A bird gave a note here and there, the stream was rushing as if to cheer her—but I couldn't get those sounds of evening in.

Our road did a hair-pin, and up the hill was a small roof nearly hidden in trees.

"Shall I go up there, lamb," I said, "and see if they'll help us? In case she *won't* go?"

Babs straightened up a minute. "All right, if you want to, A.B.! Want to wait up there and I'll come along? *I* think she's going to go, you know!"

And we smiled at each other.

The little house had box-hedges beside its path; by them sat a grumpy old grandsire who assured me, in slow grunts, that he and his son might be able to help us. They had horses, yes . . . but just then a sound came through the spruces and round the turn bobbed Nicolette, roaring powerfully.

"Don't stop!" I cried, dashing toward them.

"Oh, she's all right!" called Babs—whirling prudently by however. "I'll stop just up here. . . ."

"Splendid!" I gasped, climbing in. "Why, she's wonderful, again—" for we were steaming up a fresh bit of hill.

The little railway was keeping us company now, and soon lights were before us; Grindelwald. Lights were scattered in its bowl of a valley, its mountains towering up; Grindelwald's three. The Eiger nearest—great black thing, all webbed with white streaks; the Monch, with its sharp peak; and round its shoulder, the "bridal" Jungfrau peeping. Nicolette fled with us up a long, gradual grade—and here was a chalet looking at them too. A big one, with plenty of balconies; an inn. Of course! This was where we had stayed before, only we had come upon it the other way . . . Nicolette stopped before its path, up which I hastened, and across the porch; the same landlady—merely courteous at first, then beaming with recognition.

"Oui, madame—mais oui!" and she opened the door very wide; she didn't say she had a *"belle chambre,"* but I knew she had.

It was the very room we had had before; up two flights, clean and wooden; with patchwork quilts on the beds, an enormous view from the windows, tree-leaves waving, and a small, white-painted tin wash-stand.

"Bien, madame!" and we hastened downstairs; Nicolette dashed off to her garage, and—yes! we could have dinner on the porch.

Chilly washing, upstairs—we had always been a little cold in that room; but we grinned for joy as we went about, laying out a thing or two, flannel shirts, a brush and comb, our simplest possessions, bumping into each other from mere unnecessary swiftness and good-will; bustling happily around. How good it was to have so little to bustle about, especially as the air made one feel slashingly executive; in short, how good it was to be here again. How heartening, even the simple wooden creak of the chalet's stairs as we ran perilously down them, positively at the risk of our necks—arm in arm to the last step, here, and who should say us nay?

Other guests had retired inside to the stove; we had the wide porch to ourselves. Also a bunch of very optimistic pansies, with a lot of yellow in their purple. (There was a bed of them, outside.) Food arrived at once, as food should; well and decorously served, if this *was* a chalet. . . . But we had come a long way, we felt, in manners, customs, and everything, since our half-Italian meal at Ville Neuve that morning; this place was more like a little hotel at home. Rumpsteak and fried potatoes—a New England meal, and a very rural one at that, though hot and excellent: we took our time about it. The potatoes instantly got cold (as they always do), but we looked at mountains and didn't mind. . . .

Very dusky now, the valley, but with somewhere in it a steady roaring; our Schwartz Lütschine discoursing—with spring fervor, and night clearness. High and low on that unmodeled darkness, which still held (as Alpine valleys do at nightfall) a sense of greenness and depth and occupation, many small lights were now dotted; small, separated, and golden, each one in a peasant's hut. Cowbells sounded, soft with distance; in the morning we should see those cows, fair spots upon the green. "The pastures of the valley," said the guidebook, "support 6,000 head of cattle."

It doesn't look it; but there are ramifications one doesn't see; folded mountain meadows, and bits poked up into the woods. . . . A Swiss landscape is quite made of folds, each one with its localized name.

But by what name does one call a second afterglow? For the hitherto pallid dusk above the Eiger, Monch, and Jungfrau, was strangely lighting. Gone an hour ago was the gold that had brightened our spruce-filled gorge, the sky, though clear, seemed just to be waiting for evening; yet here was unmistakable afterglow coming behind the summits, a faint rose, deeper in the hollows, sweet with snow. It grew brighter, more sure of itself; shaping itself upon a cumulus cloud, like a big pink snapdragon up beyond the peaks.

THE OLD BLACK STATUE OF JEAN D'ARC BY THE DOOR OF HER CHURCH AT DOMRÉMY

We walked out across the road to a seat the chalet had, under a great elm. No porch-roof here; everything opened before you to its widest. The air was soft, like the glow, yet markedly snowy; we sat close together and watched the enormousness of the sky. It seemed to me I had never seen so much of it, or of such heart-searching magnificence, as from that humble bench in Grindelwald, where peasants with their cans of milk or their long pipes, sit down to rest. . . .

For this chalet of ours was like a little inn in England with a "pub" attached; a path led by the pansy-bed, under tall elms and past shrubbery to a side door that swung, in the evening, with some frequency—and whence, if they did not come freshly tugging up the hill, arrived the milk-cans and the orderly long pipes. For it was all very orderly; and this evening we had the bench to ourselves. A trifle chill, for the pipes.

There were intimations of stars, now; the Three were darkening, though plainly visible—Alps always seem to be visible except when heartlessly buried in clouds. The Yungfrau, who had been unearthly up to now, looked closer as her snows grew pinker; pink being a "local" color. . . . Think of having the Jungfrau local.

A vision she was, peeping daintily down at us: lights in the dusky valley, even the cow-bells, seemed to exist merely for her, so much did she glorify the world beneath. Her rough neighbor the Eiger had a light too, half-way up its dark side; a tiny one, looking lost in all that desolation. Babs saw it; and then after some search I found it. . . . Why, that must be the climbers' hut! I had been told there was one; and tonight there was some one in it, warming by its fire. Incredibly romantic it seemed, up there in ice and rock; this one spark, so small you had to look to find it—a bit of brave human warmth, glowing a little (as you could see if you looked *very* hard) on the snow and black, broken rock about it.

It gave us creeps in the hair to think of anybody being up there. . . .

The Jungfrau was dimly glowing even now; we rose reluctantly, but going upstairs we had to clutch the banisters, we were so rocking with sleep.

Great stars shone in the branches of the elm tree; we took one look and staggered away, dropping our clothes anywhere, abandonedly bumping off our boots; then sank in feathers. . . . Feather-beds, woodenness, tin washstands, all belong in the Alps; we wouldn't, for anything that could be offered us, have had it different.

What bright stars! What air, straight from snow on the mountains, coming in our windows; and the Lütschine, below, roaring wonderfully.

CHAPTER XXX

GRINDELWALD, ALSACE, AND LONDON

SUN., 1st after Trinity. Rather lovely day; a good deal of rain. Afternoon, took 8 mi. walk up Upper Glacier, etc. Very tired."

We were not used to tramps that included a lot of climbing, but we loved walks in woods in a gentle rain, and there was a path "direct from Grindelwald to the Upper Glacier; very interesting . . . but not to be attempted without a guide."

We attempted it; wouldn't have had a guide for a fortune. Went up one way and down another; very rough going, very beautiful cliffs and boulders, blue ice, ferns and mosses. There was a torrent, of course; we found our way along, exulting in the nearness, the actualness of everything. . . . One could sit, without preface or pre-decision, on these boulders; put our noses in their moss, if we wished, pick a flower or a small fern, without deciding whether it was "worth our while" to do so; climb an extra crag—do so many things we couldn't in Nicolette. Oh, a walk was a fearful luxury after motoring. Cool, cool, the woods, after a hot sun—and the sun of a glacial neighborhood can be most burning hot when it comes out only in sultry flashes, as it did today; and if the mountains were under cloud that sad fact nevertheless gave us, on our return, the magnificence of a clouded sunset above the roarings of the Schwartz Lütschine.

And we felt we had really done something on a rainy Sunday; always an agreeable feeling. Clouds were still down next day, but we waited. We ought not to wait over, but we would. Must have a clear day for Murren!

Also, we were lame in every bone and did not feel like

more tramping, so we took some films to Interlaken and started for a picnic up the Grimmialp; that name was irresistible. Its valley was parallel to the one we had come down, two days before, and (we thought) must resemble it in charms; not at all. Not much view, steady climbing, a very slimy road. But we had afternoon coffee at Latterbach again, hot milk and begonias as before, and went slipping easily down past the lake; surprised, on reaching home, to find ourselves much rested.

But then Nicolette always did that for us. A drive was a *great* luxury after tramping!

In the morning the Jungfrau was even more obstinately obscured, but our consciences by this time were non-est. Wait? Naturally. We drove gaily off for Brienz.

The road goes along its sunny shore—for the sun, oddly enough, was out, and colors optimistic. We lunched in a little lakeside garden, and were enchanted. Bright flowers were about us, the bright water beside us, mountains across it richly wooded; and just for a little action, a fisherman in yellow oilskins going by in a blue-green boat with an outboard-motor. It made us think of the old haymaking woman with the thermos; science, in Suisse! And the fisherman (a nice, middle-aged soul with a brown beard) seemed aware of it. Two large yellow fishpoles were on duty, sticking far out over the water; he sat in the stern, a picture of complacence, watching them do the work; glancing pleasantly in at us as he passed, then beaming at the fishpoles again.

Perhaps he was the only fisherman on the lake that had a motor. His wake, of a quite trifling order as wakes go, came swashing comfortably along the lake's edge; a simple, splashy sort of music, but one that could stir the grasses, and set the whole shore murmuring to itself. It was pleasant to see the murmuring being done. Switzerland *is* a nice, obvious place, I thought, with blue sky for its *summum bonum;* a place as restful to us as had been the cats and sunny corners of Venice during our unintended holiday there. Italy on the whole had been a serious meal; Switzerland was dessert! One revels in a sense of scenic irresponsibility. These landscapes are not "by" anybody with a difficult name, or of any "period"; they are of all time. . . . Any greatness is restful, from Michelangelo in the chapel of San Lorenzo, on; our Angelos of mountains were now hidden, but we had a lovely sense of them up there among those vaporous clouds; almost reflected in the lake. Its colors, surely, had hints of their ethereal snows?

BITTE LANGSAM! was everywhere along this road; please slowly. Did this reflect a national mood—a sort of locomotive horror? For the native cars simply crawled. *Bitte, langsam!* No one was to go faster than they; yet though they drove with maddening slowness, they also drove very badly—all over the road. Babs, usually so uncomplaining, lost all patience with them, and muttered direful things under her breath whenever we approached a rear with a "C.H." on it.

"C.H."—that had been one of our puzzles in Italy; so many cars bearing those letters. Ireland, we knew, was S.E.—also incomprehensible, till you found it was Gaelic; and C.H. turned out to be Canton Helvetia. . . . Switzerland's official name, and we had never heard of it. It makes a nice riddle. "What country is C.H.?" And nobody knows.

But there were wonderful pinks and pansies along this road; red roses and orange lilies. Chalet-fronts looked with kind eyes at the lake; they all had geranium window-boxes and fresh white muslin curtains. "No lace, in Switzerland," my notes gratefully observe. The range opposite was streaky with snow, the Giessbach fell out of spruces; an old village with a belfry was on a point, and on the water were two reflections —with a shape of light between, and ruffled edges. The dark reflection had spots of pale green in it because of the hill-pastures; we liked to see those spots of farming upside down, their seriousness flitted-at by a breeze.

"Villages simple and unspoiled; the children all blond and pretty, with such happy faces . . ." my notes say. "Life must be pleasant, on Brienz! Potatoes very large!" (I love to copy bits like that.)

We drove, in mere exuberance, nearly to Brünig, where

the pass begins. We were going over it tomorrow, but what of that? "Ho!" said Nicolette; "doesn't look much to *me!*" and turned neatly round in the little mountain road. Two imposing waterfalls faced us—the whole valley, with the Aare winding in it. We were satisfied with this (we thought) and aimed for home, but at Zweilütschinnen, reflecting that after all this was our last day, we switched abruptly up the other valley to Lauterbrünnen, and its meadows of buttercups; in fact to a hamlet with a terrific name beyond, where the valley ends, and cliffs begin, and ladies who can't climb used to take a *chaise à porteur.* I remember my mother's being put in one of those chaises—while we children started off on horseback, feeling very sorry for her—and wanted to drive up now and see what the cliffs looked like.

They looked very real, as well as very beautiful, towering above us with their violet chasms; and as we drove the short distance back to Lauterbrünnen, the clouds rolled up! Just like that. They simply peeled off the mountains . . . and there was all we had waited for—looking down at us; with blue sky around it. We could hardly believe our eyes. What a valley—with the Jungfrau in full glory above it. It is a route, though it doesn't look it; everybody winds round those curves, and is crushed by the glittering creature up above. To this valley she gives audience . . . and we, worshippers, drew very slowly near; could hardly drive for staring at her. Sometimes she withdrew herself behind a cliff, or spruces; a swing of the little road, and there she was again. . . . The Matterhorn? Yes—while one is in Zermatt; here, it is the Jungfrau. It seems there can be no other snow so beautiful; lifted so beautifully aloft. She is *all* snow; glitters as if she were ice in the sun. Perhaps she *is* ice, up there; but the guide-book thought not.

"The Jungfrau (13,671′) with her dazzling shroud of eternal snow . . . now appears in all her majesty. The proportions of the mountain are so gigantic, that the eye in vain attempts to estimate them; and distance seems annihilated by their vastness."

Thus Baddy; gasping a little. It takes something to make

our staid chaperon labor this way, but it seems that The Editor (as he is always referred to) did a good deal of climbing in order to write his book. "Since 1811," he says, "when the summit of the Jungfrau was reached for the first time . . . the ascent has been frequently accomplished, even by ladies. The expedition is extremely fatiguing. . . . The Silberhorn, once deemed inaccessible, was ascended for the first time, on August 4, 1863, by Ed. von Fellenberg and the Editor, pioneered by the guides P. Michel, H. Bauman, and P. Inabit of Grindelwald. The party started at 4 A. M., traversed the Eiger and Guggi glaciers, ascended the Schneehorn to the right, and crossing the N. slope of the Jungfrau, attained the summit of the Silberhorn at 4:30 P. M. [A lot in that little word, *attained.*] The next night was passed on the precipitous E. icy slope of the Schneehorn, not one of the party venturing to close an eye."

Hurray, Editor; that is the way to find out about things; and when he tells you about avalanches, "those terrible and magnificent phenomena," you feel he is right; that he probably listened to them that dreadful night on the Schneehorn, when nobody ventured to close an eye. (Though avalanches chiefly occur—do they not?—under a hot sun. . . .)

Down here, the "dazzling shroud of eternal snow" was just peacefulness. We had no desires in that direction; we preferred to look. The Staubbach was now near us; "dust-brook," the name means. Dust when I was twelve; dust always, I suppose. It falls, or rather films and hangs, for nearly a thousand feet . . . and should be seen in the morning, Baddy says. (Alas, this was not morning.) "The best point of view is in the meadow immediately in front of the fall, to the *left* of a seat indicated by a flag." Perdition! we sat in Nicolette.

Yet the dust-brook seemed sufficiently beautiful. We parked Nicolette by a tea-garden and ran for the *funiculaire* (Mürren, Mürren, before it was any later!); were soon creeping upward into light, wildflowers, and spruces. (We had done this before, but who could resist crawling up it again?) Mürren is the highest (inhabited) village in the Alps; from nowhere else, unless you climb somebody's "extremely fatiguing" summit, are the snows so universal. Also, pictures can be taken from the train window, with summits posing for you again and again; or great tails of glaciers making their slow way downward.

The village, when you get there, has sweet walks up pastures with crocuses like Zermatt, pink ragged-robin, and clumps of white birches growing on a green hump,—though with Tremendousness just across the gorge, almost as convenient as the ragged-robin. . . . For a rest, you can stare at grass for a while, or the path under your feet; when you lift your eyes again, there is the *massif* waiting for you. Always the *massif*. Billows, hurricanes, of sunny white; the blue of shadows, falling a mile or two, one does not often see equalled. And how that ridge went curling along like a breaking wave of pure snow, for miles, it seemed; a wave hundreds of feet high.

We took a frightened snap-shot of that; picked a flower or two, and fled. Beyond Mürren's little station, where the horse and mule path starts down, is a spot where you can sit and meditate if you wish; a modest hut with a porch and tables, and more view than anywhere. Everything enormous is just opposite; climbers with alpenstocks, also peasants with mules, stop there for beer. Having time before the last train went, we stopped on that porch for coffee and rolls and honey; oh, the very best. Of course we were starving, two steps in the pastures of Mürren accomplishes that; and the nice, healthy, rosy-cheeked woman brought us what she had. She even suggested eggs—"a poached egg to your tea," as they say so cheerfully in England; there, a revolting idea, here, we simply fell on those eggs. The source of them went clucking and stepping about the little chalet; a dozen or so very healthy hens, all nodding, darting cordially about after treasures. What a nice, unperturbed place for them to live; and fancy the Monch, Eiger, Jungfrau, Schneehorn, and Silberhorn looking down on hens! How heartening, to the hungry climber with a spy-glass. . . . Or would it be maddening?

And the chalet had bee-hives, too, with honey being made

every moment, to judge by the way the bees flew back and forth from the field. Everywhere in the Alps one sees these cheerful-looking hives painted in bright, primary colors to attract the bees; for if the creatures, in this vast region, wanted to swarm, where might they not fly? Over the other side of the Jungfrau, maybe; and lose their queen, and lose each other, and get where there was nothing to swarm on. . . .

But it was delightful to eat where things came from, instead of in the civilized remoteness of a dining-room; our porch in Grindelwald gave us that feeling. There one heard the bees, saw the vegetables—ten feet away in rows; beheld the milk coming up the road—smelt it in the cowy air of evening. It and the sunset came together. Sometimes the afterglow caught it too, though by that time, along with bees and the sun-soaked flowers, cows had usually gone to bed and a smell of snow and rock set in; Grindelwald's evening scent. . . . We were sorry to leave that chalet. It was a trifle beery, extremely peasantish, and utterly wooden; but wouldn't it be grand to stay here, in the woodenness? Play it was a hut on inaccessible mountains? It was hut enough, for us; and one would probably exist on *eien*. . . .

For I had had to speak German to that rosy-cheeked woman, great goodness; and German eggs are such funny things. (No funnier than French ones, though, when one hears them called *oofs*. . . .)

We trotted up to the train—which slid unemotionally off with us. Cog-wheels always do that, just when you've been in something stupendous, and stupendousness continued, out of the window. It was impossible to sit still. Beside ourselves, there were only three passengers,—one of those an engineer in a greasy cap, who kept his head steadily out of a front window; so we darted about here and there, with the camera ready for action. Sometimes one of us had it, sometimes the other; an agitated half-hour.

"Oh, look at that!"

"Quick . . . get it? Fine."

"*What* a spruce!"

"Here's that brook, dashing—"

"Boulders! No, couldn't get that; we went across too fast."

We did indeed. The cog-wheel must have been hurrying. That brook was a roar and a whiteness, and no more; and torrents can't repeat themselves, the way summits do.

"But here's that place with the Jungfrau— Oo! the whole range. . . . I don't see why these shouldn't turn out well—do you?" I said rather helplessly; for I had taken that last one.

"No," said Babs, "I don't *think* they'll be over-exposed, this late in the day. That's usually the trouble, you know."

"Yes. Snow. So fearfully bright . . ." and we lapsed into seats, exhausted.

Last love to the Jungfrau, now with a tinge of gold on her whiteness; and down the roof-steepness of the dive into the valley, with the engineer's greasy cap still reassuringly out of the window. . . . A restful valley it seemed, as we drove down it; turning often to stare up, watching the Yungfrau finally vanish behind spruces, then swinging beside our Schwartz Lütschine again, straight at the reward of the Wetterhorn. Almost as snowy as that beauty in the other valley; and soft, now, with gold; a glorious creature. The little apple tree was there too; cool blue, in valley shadow. A fabulous neighborhood; and Nicolette charging along undaunted. . . .

Sunset more golden, shadows filling in; the noise of the torrent—beside which Babs had labored; up and up, to our valley, and the light in the climbers' hut. It was like our first evening; rose and gold were on the Three, then dusk and star glitterings; but tonight we wandered up to Grindelwald's little street. Empty it was, but brightly lighted; which was nice, because we had important purchases to make. Grindelwald's shops are all wood-carving, mostly bears or cuckoo-clocks; enter a shop, in fact, and the world *turns* to bears. Millions of bears, of every size, in dark-brown wood.

What *we* wanted was salt-spoons; tiny shovels, made of bone. (Bear's bone?) We found some, buried in a welter of other things, and bought a jam spoon too. We had never had a jam spoon, and a white one seemed a good idea. Jam would slip off it so easily.

Nothing more! Babs dragged me away, and we looked at starlit mountains. . . . I somehow do like bears.

But the street was interesting, in a mountain-village way. It had a gorge behind it, the Lütschine roaring and tumbling with great violence below, and the Eiger, very rocky and frowning, going straight up. In the darkness, with its snow-streaks lighted from the village glow, it was really grand. . . . But *they* can't see what *we* can see! we almost sang, as we went downhill with great strides; for there was nothing to compare with the front of our chalet for view.

Breakfast there was our last, and therefore memorial. We packed Nicolette rather badly, standing in the road with an eye on everything else; and slid off for the Brünig pass and Lüzern. Interlaken first, however, for a literary interview, arranged by letter; so in a hotel garden, with a walled stream rushing by, I sat in an iron chair and was interviewed.

Foreign interviewing is very different from ours; at once more and less formal. Babs had politely excused herself on a plea of getting films, and near me was a large and commanding woman, sitting straight and a trifle stony in her yellow-painted iron chair. I was surprised at this, for our correspondence had been very friendly; but perhaps it is the thing in this country to have ice formally broken—that is, to have ice first, and then break it; for very soon the good woman became natural, beamed, haw-hawed, asked a hundred questions (there, the interview began to seem natural), let herself go in true Continental style. She told me how many articles she had been doing for magazines; and how she would love to go to America, yes, yes! She hoped that someday . . . but farming was now so very bad. (She had a large "place," and looked after it very personally.) It was hard to get workers, she said; she herself had just been out in the fields for days, to see to the loading and shipping of the turnips.

"Turnips?" I asked; somehow not expecting them.

Ach, yes! Tons of turnips. It was a great crop with them.

Then we turned from turnips to books, and my plans for future writing; the sun shone cordially on the gravel, the stream rushed busily—and so did the interview. In fact, our new friend soon became reluctant to part with us, and said—addressing Babs, who had returned from her expedition—that she had a bit of free time now, and would like to travel with us a little way! I suppose we looked a trifle stupefied at this, for she repeated it. Travel with us, in the car—yes. She would love to!

"But—I'm awfully sorry—but she is a *very* small car," I said, still a little bewildered. "She has only two seats. She's all filled with luggage, you see!"

For there at the gate Nicolette stood; obviously overladen. Our friend—evidently unacquainted with motoring—looked at her an instant; a light and carefree glance.

"Oh, I would sit on the bonnet," she said smiling, then laughing heartily. "I would indeed, dear lady! I would do anything, to come with you!"

But it was more than time to go; Babs had been doing eyebrows at me. Talking about everything under heaven, mountain passes, the weather, Nicolette's difficulties in carrying her load, we made our way to the gate. Farewells, smiles and wavings, were exchanged as we turned round in the little street,—good heavens, should we have to back many more times? yet the last thing I heard, thinning pathetically with distance, was:

"Goot-by! I would go with you, if—"

But we had crossed the stream.

And there were so many things to say, as we drove quietly along Interlaken's neat street, that we said very little. Chiefly, I felt sorry to have had to refuse our friend's ardently made request; I hate refusing people, and we should have enjoyed her cheerful company, but when it comes to a mere question of cubic inches . . .

Fuming slightly, we reached Lake Brienz; and relaxed.

Soothing, its blue-green beauty; its flowers and cottages and content.

"Let's look at the prints," said Babs; but at the first glance, rage seized us. The Como pictures were clear—that was the maddening part of it, for there were white spots all over them. . . . Yes, there were dark spots on the films. Bad developing. That shop! . . . And it had looked so big and fine and glittering. Bellagio had done such a beautiful job for us, we thought an accurate Interlaken would do even better—and now look at this.

Well, one or two were good for something; the one of the little church with the fresco—and we were so fond of that church; but we'd never trust a big, glittering-looking shop again. Never!

And the lake had another job of soothing to do. We stared about; and by the time the pass was before us, felt ourselves again. . . . Ah, this was nice; a damp pass, with moss on its rocks. Woods kept on, and hair-pins; spruces hung delightfully over us; but this Brünig was a very mild pass, we assured each other. At home we'd just think it a hill! Rather long, of course, and near the summit there were fine, far-away prospects; but to think we had ever wondered if Nicolette would go over it! Forgive us, darling; you could do ten passes like this.

"Gorgeous day," says the diary. It was. We sailed and sailed downwards, past the Lac de Sarnen; had tea in an inferior garden and sailed on, down and down, to the splendid deep green of Lüzern itself and its winding arms. A charming lake, but in a way the most sophisticated of them all; even Como is more buried in its mountains. Though when you walk on Lüzern's park-like quai, and look out from under the pollarded trees (and across all sorts of bright boat-doings), at the panorama of snow peaks across that miraculous water, it is very lovely.

We had to take Nicolette round a few corners, and past the church with the twin steeples, to see the Lion again, reflected solemnly in his pond beneath the cliff. He hushes one, that Lion, lying there with a faithful expression.

The whole place is lovely; grasses in the pond, a water-lily in bloom, trees shadowing it. There is so much more that could be done to it; and they haven't done it, and one is so glad. . . .

Lüzern's outlet newly enchanted us—rushing smoothly under the old, Swiss-looking tower on a catty-cornered wooden foot bridge (very Swiss, to have it wooden); a fine air blowing down from the lake, snow mountains in sight, and booths selling plants and flower-seeds on the sunny quai-wall; a most cheerful spot in this very cheerful town. We bought a "mixed packet" of seeds (whose odd, and very Swiss, results have been a pleasure ever since) and went off to find a bank. . . . It was just around a corner, very shiny and Swiss; as our letter of credit was now very low, we negotiated a cheque. . . . But how it had held out, that letter of credit! One hundred pounds, minus the few notes we still held, had brought us this far—all the way from London; eleven weeks—and we had stopped in such *nice* places. . . . The Continent had been very good to two wanderers.

We walked again on the quai; slept well, somewhere back of the outlet—and that was really all we asked of Lüzern; for in the morning we were off and away.

Off, a little soberly, for we felt we were leaving Europe, now. Also we had spent the evening before drawing a line across the map of France, and found that the battle-fields were in our way and we should have to go through them; but first there would be Basel and the Swiss customs.

The snow mountains were long in saying good-by, as we climbed from the lake; Pilatus, his generous bulk streaked with snow, superintended things, and continued to superintend them for miles. Rich farming, he looked at. One big barn had cows visible inside, and two cats sitting happily at the door, waiting for milking to be done. Dog-teams, carrying milk, were thick upon the road; we met dozens of them hastening in to town with their loads. Big dogs, short, furry, curly dogs, all wagging their tails and helping master the best they could. "Master in shafts; dog, in harness, pulling beside him. Dogs always happy!" The last word of my Swiss notes.

SOMBER AND MASSIVE, THE PORTE-CHAUSSÉE, ABOVE THE JADE-GREEN RIVER
Verdun

Basel, which we remembered merely as a station where you run a long way to get your breakfast, was unexpectedly nice; hilly, with big trees, and rambling old houses on the Rhine. Babs had never seen that stream before; we had lunch in a balcony with geraniums, looking down on it. It was nice and green. We drove off, very contented with Basel; and Swiss customs were absolutely nothing to get through.

"Do you realize that this is the fourth Customs we've been through," said Babs, "and they haven't opened our bags yet?"

On we coursed. The minute Switzerland stopped and Alsace began, wild carrot stopped too; Alsace evidently did not approve of it. The land was beautiful, just over the border, green and gold with buttercups; but no canopy of lace was over the meadows. We quite missed it. In fact Alsace to us seemed a queer, foreign place; we couldn't see why France had been so obsessed over getting it back. In its villages, great half-timbered houses of no type on earth shouldered each other along dirty, crooking streets; though between towns the fields would be exquisitely kept. Alsace's passion is not its towns.

And Alsatian drivers would *not* get out of the way; as a rule we climbed a gravel-heap and got round them.

Bread, casks of wine, and logs of wood seem to have to be carried on the roads of Alsace. We met quantities of the little bread-carts, being pushed by hand . . . and more and more we were astonished at the forests of Alsace. Miles of them, half-grown, but dense and uninterrupted; perhaps these were what France wanted when she so desired its return! The sun shone delightfully through their greenery; our only difficulty that afternoon was that Nicolette seemed to need water all the time, and the forests had no brooks. Coming out into fields at last, we stopped at a peasant's house; the old woman let us have some from a half-filled wooden tub, but she had so little herself and evidently treasured the contents of that tub so much, that we took only a little and paid her a good deal.

She nodded her wrinkled head many times, beaming at us

as she grasped the coins. All alone she was in her cottage, but she had trained a vine over one end of it, and her little garden was very neat.

Our next stop was at a canal. I remember Babs's leaning agilely down and down, and my fearing at first that she couldn't reach the water. Alsace seemed to be having a drought; doubly unfortunate, because Nicolette was really leaking now; Babs had investigated, and—yes—it was our radiator letting down drops.

"Dash!" said she. "Can't we get back to England first? I don't want to stop and have this mended!"

We drove on through the pleasant, waving country—it looked a little more like France; and that evening as afterglow faded, found, quite by chance, the Pomme d'Or. Lights were lighted in the one street of Luxeuil-les-Bains—this region was full of *bains*—and we saw a sign. POMME D'OR, REPAS, 3.9.9, said Michelin—how wonderful it was to have him again, to guide us; we had been basking in the idea of him as we drove. Ah, here was France again—we were in Haute Saône, now; hand-made linen curtains, a dining-room with palms and flowers—and *the* most hot, deliciously cooked dinner; yellow satin quilts, and the sweetest maid to bring us breakfast.

It seemed odd (and rather slothful) to have it in bed, we had grown so used to the tonic Swiss fashion of giving it to you outdoors; and the pretty maid could *not* understand about *confiture*.

"Pain et beurre," she repeated in sweet bewilderment; *"pas de croissants . . . pain et beurre*—et *de la confiture, madame?"*

I assured her that was the idea. The very best sort, when it came—and everything else to match. Such rich hot milk, as good as Switzerland's; and we never expected that.

But the Pomme d'Or is now no more. There is luxury around the corner, by Luxeuil's park and spring . . . but not the Pomme d'Or, or the warm smiles of little madame and monsieur. . . . Babs and I had those; and drove away, happy and rested, into the rain.

The diary for that day is mostly names. "St. Loup, Bains-les-Bains, Contrexéville, Neufehatel, Domrémy, St. Mihiel, Verdun. Rain all the time." For the *bains* towns continued, even to the climax of a small village called Bains-les-Bains; and we wanted to go scudding across the map but it wasn't easy driving in the rain. Slimy clay roads, through more of the beautiful beech forests; we had a bad skid in a village, lunched in a long thin town all empty hotels and bath-places, and my first French notes begin, "Rain in Domrémy."

Not that it hadn't been rain everywhere, but rain seemed to go with Domrémy. Outside, the horses stood by the bars, looking miserable; the cows lay down, their fat backs at the storm, looking defiant. They *would* have their noonday nap. Our road, shadowed with poplars, gave a twist into the open at Domrémy's beautiful old bridge; the Meuse goes into a wide pool below the bridge with big-leaved water-plants at its edge.

"The low hills brush back from Domrémy. . . ." Did Boutet de Monvel come here one day and draw it? We were sure we had seen somewhere a water-color of this. Such a little old village, under its great trees; and Jean d'Arc's little church, with a funny old black statue of her in front of it, is just across a bend of road from the bridge. . . . Jean must have loved the ducks in the river, I thought; perhaps she had washed her clothes on its edge. Between showers, we saw a woman in a lavender dress going down among the water-plants to bend over the washing-stones; and Jean was a great girl before ever the call came to her—fit for any toil; though it scarcely looked like toil, there by the waving water-flowers, the clear brown of the pool.

Domrémy's old houses are very small, and buff and white, with flowers in their tiny gardens; the whole village is Jean. Inside the church is another statue of her (in color), life-sized, erect, and very Romanized; in the nice old black one outside she is humbly kneeling, with uplifted hand and arm; an honest, awkward, peasant-like pose, much more like the girl she was. . . . Dégas, who knew his country, has her in an orchard as she was—a peasant, thick-wristed and strong, gazing with awestruck eyes, but all a peasant's believing soul, as the vision appears to her. . . . For everybody seems to believe Jean d'Arc had a vision. Nobody objects to the idea at all! Is it because the results were so actual and military? Strange, how reluctant we are to be spiritual, in this life.

Country beyond Domrémy was misty and dreamy in the rain. (It had come on again.) Bands of crops curved away over vast swales, dark strips of woods were on their crests. We gazed at it, wondering whether to make our way to Rheims by way of Bar-le-Duc, or by Verdun. Bar-le-Duc was a heap of ruins, we heard—no more currant jam—and we really wanted to see Verdun. So we let the road fork when it wanted to, and kept on to the north. . . . No fences or hedgerows here; peasants took their places. A soaking herdsman stood motionless in his long blue cape, with its hood up over his head; a poor old woman under an umbrella was not so fortunate, and seemed to be shivering wet. Beyond that field were significant gaps in a row of cherry trees, and a church had had a close call; the house beside it was shattered to bits.

"Vaucouleurs got it badly on the outskirts," say my notes, "but nice simple cottages that looked French, and would someday take age pleasantly, had been built beyond the demolished section. . . . To Commercy, a gray-blue road with a yellow edge pleating along, perfectly straight and up-and-down; Nicolette smelt as hot as a hot biscuit on some of the folds. But she flew over them victoriously; was not this her native land, and didn't she do nearly everything in it on high? Her tail was very frisky, however; another bad skid on a corner."

"It took all my nerve to keep her in the road," Babs afterwards confided.

We took the shortest way to Verdun.

In St. Mihiel, in the most pouring rain we had had all day,

Babs found she needed matches. We crept along, peering out into the driving wetness, looking at this clay-colored ruin and that, and thinking what a horrible time St. Mihiel must have had—and there, at last, was an *épicerie.* I undid my curtain and bolted in. A cosy place, the little shop—it smelled dry and nice, of cheese and coffee and bread; the *allumettes* were quickly handed me, with a kind and friendly smile, by the stout, red-faced *patron,* and I darted out again, quite unstiffened. One did get stiff, sitting and sitting in a sort of spray; it was a cold spray, and St. Mihiel, as we went on, seemed all mud-color to us . . . doubtless because of the muddy streets and roads at which we had had to stare so much.

All day, we had been staring at them!

And the Meuse should have been beside us, but I don't in the least remember it. Mud again, I suppose. . . .

Verdun! One thought of ruins and tragedy, but here was a beautiful old bridge, gray and heavy-arched, with a towered gate over the deep, jade-green river; quiet within its walls. Ivy massed itself beside and upon the towers; we rejoiced that they had been spared.

Somber and massive, that Porte-Chaussée; solid, low, and old, lies Verdun along its river. We took tea in a strangely light-minded little bakery, however, and sampled the *dragées;* for Verdun—at whose name a sort of knell sounds in one's heart—specializes on the gayest sort of little decorated cakes.

And we went on in the morning for what proved to be a harrowing drive. We had not meant to cross France through the battle-fields, but our route took us there willy-nilly; here we were, being harrowed. We even bought an emotional little book, *Guide to the War Zone,* and took a loop of our own, looking at things; forts with weeds grown over them, and flies still buzzing in their tunnels.

"After all these *years,*" said Babs, biting her lip. "Come along, A.B.!"

And a painter friend used to talk to us about Fleury; the charming little village it was to paint in. Fleury is a stone door-step, a broken mile-post, piles of weeds. In some places the desperate peasants have reclaimed the land; but that afternoon, across wide, desolate, uninhabited country, with rain coming down terribly upon a little yellow road all potholes, we saw what barbed wire and *chevaux de frises* really are. And the front lines so appallingly near each other. We couldn't believe it. . . .

Here the armies lay, and watched each other. And the rain fell like this. . . . (Everything in this region has been left as it was; is to be left so, forever.)

Nicolette went bumping and splashing in and out of the potholes, we looking with horror at the ploughed-up, whitened ground of the approach trenches—scarcely noticing the bumps, or even Nicolette . . . so much so that when we started down toward the basin of Suain, Babs exclaimed, putting on the brake violently.

"Why, Nicolette's lost her water-cap!"

She had indeed. Gone was the bright circlet we had grown to have such an affection for, as it led us over hill and dale. We jumped out.

"No telling where she lost it, of course," said Babs, staring disconsolately about; and we both ruffled in the wet bushes.

"Expect it was back in those potholes," I said. The bushes were too thick, the grape-vine wonderfully tangled; we could never find it, here.

"Strange it could come unscrewed, though," murmured Babs; "I always put it on—tight, you know. . . . And she's leaking enough, without having water jumping out of that hole all the time. . . . It will, you know."

" 'Suppose so!" I said. "And towns aren't very promising just around here—to shop in; are they?"

"They aren't," said Babs; and we gripped hands, sorrowfully.

We went on into Suain, on its mild hill, gazing with rage at the beautiful stone tracery left in the rose-window of a church, with only one wall standing; and had a most cheerful stay in Châlons-sur-Marne.

Red velvet, I think we had red velvet in our room; a lovely shade of pale old red; and the glory of the Marne, it seems, is still upon Châlons. Blithe looks met us, and gay faces; shop-windows were well filled; and the wine here (Châlon's specialty) was pale red, like the velvet, and admirably sweet—if you like sweet wine; we were unprofessional enough to like no other sort. . . .

The sky lightened, and we dashed off with expectations to Rheims.

It loomed interestingly on the horizon with its twin spires, then amazed us with its noise; but we lost our hearts to an exquisite Madonna in a row of sculptured saints on the cathedral. (For here was its crippled beauty, looking down on us.) Of the twelfth century, she is; her stone scarf clings lightly to the fine shape of her head. What lovely ladies must have lived then; for there is self-forgetfulness in that face.

She is worth a hundred Jeans, bright and splendid though the Maid is, in the square below; only she could not, like Jean and her horse, be taken off and hidden. . . . How miraculously had this cathedral escaped!

The street-cries were terrific on our way back.

One ragged old man went along, on his rickety cart, howling steadily; no one stopped him or interrupted his cries. It must be dreadful to go along splitting your throat, and no one paying any attention. . . .

"Po—ra-poo! Po—ra-ga-ba—pooo!"

And then a young woman in bed-slippers, selling newspapers, set up a wonderful howl. Contralto, this was, and finely melodious. We halted to listen to it. It seemed worthy to celebrate something that went deeper than newspapers, only we couldn't think what. . . . Couldn't they change her into the cathedral? Soften her down a bit, and take off her bed-slippers? She might do requiems, then. A requiem would be beautiful, in that voice.

Other cries came along, all very loud and unceasing: "Rheims, persistent place," say my notes.

Flattish country followed, prosperous and fair, with but few battle-traces. We were out of the worst of the devastation. Pine woods had been set out, and many were the nurseries of young trees. . . . Poor France, trying so hard to recover; and the brunt of it came on the peasants. They were at it now, delving and straining. Yesterday was the day for remembering one's soul and forgetting the earth; today they were at it with fresh energy, recreating with their labor the underlying structure of the life of France. Not everywhere, as here, did the peasant's mattock ring on buried iron, the toe of his sabot catch on hidden barbs and shell-cases; in the easier south, or on the mountainsides, we had seen him just as industrious. We revived all our feeling about him. Someday the peasants will redeem even Fleury. *"Belle et bonne France, on ne te connait pas!"* says George Sand.

We survived Soissons and its ruins, slept at St. Quentin, lunched at Cambrai—dear old Cambrai, whose *spécialité* is beans—we had some for lunch, and they were nice though not highly peculiar beans; and had the radiator mended in Arras.

Not another mile would we go, so bothered about water-supply; there wasn't much to see, we could have stopped, earlier, in far richer places; but we liked Arras very much. I don't know exactly why we liked it, as we tramped about, but we were in a ludicrous state of happiness that evening; couldn't be very depressed, so near England.

"This little pig went to market, this little pig stayed at home!" I was even reciting (in what connection I cannot imagine) as we went down an empty street, saying how charmed babies always were with this ditty, and with their toes, when my narrative had unexpected effect.

"Poor fools!" cried Babs, bursting into a great laugh; and we shouted, relieved by this nonsense, all the way down Arras' brick sidewalk to the inn.

"St. Pol, Hôtel de France," says the diary (a special place for lunch); then, "Dévres, via very small roads; Boulogne, Hôtel du Nord, one shower, the rest sunlight."

The rest sunlight; that was its last entry.

And this afternoon of flying through France was delightful. What towns we met were sweet old ones, then our road plunged through woods and began to ripple—deep, sharp ripples, great fun because you couldn't see what was going to come up and meet you. You surmounted one, gingerly, then went flying down the other side; up again, then down—over and over. Sunlight was on the tops of the woods, we had no worry about radiators; vastly jolly, this rushing up and down, with blue sky overhead and great snowy white clouds, such as we hadn't seen since Switzerland. . . . Yes, France was going to be sweet to the last; and from the grassy sea-front, Boulogne, that evening, gave us a flaming sunset. Dear channel, lapping harmlessly on seaweedy stones; we paced the cliff, sniffed the salt, and could hardly wait for tomorrow.

In fact, so much had fancy preceded us, we already felt as if we were on the other side; we were glad, in the morning, the skies were half-bright, but did it really matter? Even Nicolette's loading seemed parenthetical; and then we watched for the cliffs of England. . . .

Were there ever such sponge-cakes (tuppence, to be sure, when they used to be a penny) as those on the wharf in Dover? And then we were on a high railway-bridge, over the tracks —and why was that van coming straight at us?

"Huh!" said my child; and switched across.

We had been driving on the right! Three months of habit; should we ever remember, now? An ivied country-side, villages thickening, London long of approach, but very much London when we reached it: Westminster Bridge, and Big Ben across it; Parliament Square, the Abbey—how beautiful and pearl-gray; the momentous island at the mouth of Great Smith Street—we went the wrong side of it once; it all looked wonderful to us, as did an English twilight, with lights coming out.

"Well, we've made our loop, A.B.," said Babs, steering carefully past the little windows where the choir-boys practice—we always meet a push-cart there; and I nodded. That was what we used to say on rides, when we came back to our own road up to the farm again: Well, we've made a loop! whether it was five miles or forty; and this had been a dear little loop . . . about four thousand miles. Nicolette ground as calmly against her curbstone as if she had never left it; and down Marsham Street that night, we were sure, slept the sleep of one who after long and fearsome wandering, returns to her own.

For London was so pretty! We had left her still wintry, and here she was, shaking greenery at us from all her open spaces —one forgets how many of them there are; blue sky and fluffy clouds overhead, and all Mayfair with flower-boxes at its windows. It was wonderful to have this weather to go about in.

Good-by, leafy London; something more than leafiness is calling us . . . a spot where our roots are far down, like the bushes and trees along our old walls. I thought of Babs' poem.

My thoughts are far across
The unbroken seas,
To where the soft rain
Is spreading a lavender mist
Over the new green
Of those hills
That are the houses of my heart.

And she and I went to the bow of the boat as it plunged across the north of Ireland, to feel the spray in our faces. We felt as if we might get home faster, that way.

INDEX

(1)